LANDS *of* PROMISE *and* DESPAIR

A California Legacy Book

Santa Clara University and Heyday Books are pleased to publish the California Legacy series, vibrant and relevant writings drawn from California's past and present.

Santa Clara University—founded in 1851 on the site of the eighth of California's original 21 missions—is the oldest institution of higher learning in the state. A Jesuit institution, it is particularly aware of its contribution to California's cultural heritage and its responsibility to preserve and celebrate that heritage.

Heyday Books, founded in 1974, specializes in critically acclaimed books on California literature, history, natural history, and ethnic studies.

Books in the California Legacy series appear as anthologies, single author collections, reprints of important books, and original works. Taken together, these volumes bring readers a new perspective on California's cultural life, a perspective that honors diversity and finds great pleasure in the eloquence of human expression.

Series editor: Terry Beers
Publisher: Malcolm Margolin
Advisory committee: Stephen Becker, William Deverell, Peter Facione, Charles Faulhaber, David Fine, Steven Gilbar, Dana Gioia, Ron Hansen, Gerald Haslam, Robert Hass, Jack Hicks, Timothy Hodson, James Houston, Jeanne Wakatsuki Houston, Maxine Hong Kingston, Frank LaPena, Ursula K. Le Guin, Jeff Lustig, Tillie Olsen, Ishmael Reed, Alan Rosenus, Robert Senkewicz, Gary Snyder, Kevin Starr, Richard Walker, Alice Waters, Jennifer Watts, Al Young.

Thanks to the English Department at Santa Clara University and to Regis McKenna for their support of the California Legacy series.

LANDS *of* PROMISE *and* DESPAIR

Chronicles of Early California, 1535–1846

EDITED BY ROSE MARIE BEEBE
AND ROBERT M. SENKEWICZ

SANTA CLARA UNIVERSITY, SANTA CLARA, CA

HEYDAY BOOKS, BERKELEY, CA

Library of Congress Cataloging-in-Publication Data
Lands of promise and despair : chronicles of early California, 1535–1846
/ edited by Rose Marie Beebe and Robert M. Senkewicz.
   p. cm. — (A California legacy book)
Includes bibliographical references and index.
 ISBN 1-890771-48-1
 1. California—History—To 1846—Sources. 2. Frontier and pioneer
life—California—Sources. 3. Spaniards-—California—History—Sources.
4. Indians of North America—California—History—Sources. I. Beebe,
Rose Marie. II. Senkewicz, Robert M., 1947- III. Series.
 F864 .L26 2001
 979.4—dc21
                              2001005460

Cover Art: "A California Indian woman carrying green seed pulp, and a California majordomo like those who came from Spain." Fr. Ignacio Tirsch, S.J. Courtesy of the National Library of the Czech Republic.
Cover/Interior Design: Rebecca LeGates
Printing and Binding: McNaughton & Gunn, Saline, MI

Orders, inquiries, and correspondence should be addressed to:
   Heyday Books
   P. O. Box 9145, Berkeley, CA 94709
   (510) 549-3564, Fax (510) 549-1889
   www.heydaybooks.com

Printed in the United States of America

10 9 8 7 6 5 4 3

To the memory of Antonio María Osio, the Californio, *whose* History of Alta California *opened up so many wonderful possibilities for us*

Contents

LIST OF MAPS

Acknowledgments

It is a pleasure to acknowledge the many people who have assisted us in the preparation of this work. Malcolm Margolin, publisher of Heyday Books, has supported and challenged us constantly. The fact that this volume is much different from and—we happily admit—superior to the proposal we gave him two years ago is due to his probing questions, fertile imagination, and insightful suggestions.

At Santa Clara University, we have received timely and consistent assistance. Grants from Peter Facione, dean of the College of Arts and Sciences, and Dennis Gordon, director of International Programs, made a research trip to Spain possible. Support from Don Dodson, associate provost, assisted in the final stages of the project. Ellwood Mills of the Media Services Department proved to be a most generous and skilled wizard in preparing many of the graphics and illustrations. At Orradre Library, we have benefited time and again from the excellent care of Alice Whistler and the reference staff with the Orradre California Collection, as well as Cindy Bradley, Carolee Bird, and the interlibrary loan staff, and Anne McMahon, the university archivist.

Many students and scholars of California history have shared their knowledge and research with us, directing us to paths we would not have found otherwise. Marie Duggan of Keene State College generously made available her own research on the Silberio and Rosa case. Peter Uhrowczik did the same with his own work on Bouchard. John Johnson and Linda Agren of the Santa Barbara Museum of Natural History suggested the Chumash artifacts reproduced in this volume. Fr. Virgilio Biasiol, O.F.M., and Cresencia and Dale Olmstead of the Santa Barbara Mission Archive Library cheerfully helped us navigate through the treasures of that repository and have always made our visits there a real pleasure. W. Michael Mathes shared his deep knowledge of all phases of the development of the Californias. Carmen Boone de Aguilar of Mexico City steered us toward Baja California sources and helped us try to unravel the intricacies of the peninsula's colonial history. Harry Crosby and Doyce Nunis helped us track down the drawings of Fr. Ignacio Tirsch. Glenn Farris offered helpful suggestions about the Russian presence in California. We are deeply grateful to all of these good friends, fellow students, and generous scholars. We, of course, are solely responsible for the contents of this volume.

We were extremely fortunate to interact with a tremendously helpful group of individuals and institutions while we were seeking the textual and illustrative materials for this book. María Luisa Martín-Merás, directora of the Museo Naval, and María Luisa Ferrer Garcés, directora of the Museo de América, graciously allowed us to spend as much time as we needed examining the wonderful collections of their institutions. David S. Reher of the Universidad Complutense de Madrid kindly and generously assisted us in dealing with a number of other repositories in Spain. Miroslava Hejnova, head of the Manuscripts and Early Printed Books Department of the National Library of the Czech Republic, arranged for us to receive the Tirsch drawings, skillfully juggling our request with the schedule of the public exhibition of the drawings. Charles Faulhaber, director of The Bancroft Library, and the library staff always offered us their customary excellent and knowledgeable service with both texts and illustrations.

We also benefited from the generous assistance of the following individuals and institutions: John F. Schwaller and the American Academy of Franciscan History, Marlene Smith-Baranzini and the California Historical Society, Jennifer Redmond and Sunbelt Publications, Harry Knill and Bellerophon Press, Russell Skowronek, Msgr. Francis J. Weber, Richard A. Pierce, Dawson's Book Shop, Ballena Press, The Book Club of California, the California State Library, the Jay I. Kislak Foundation, the Historical Society of Southern California, the San Diego Historical Society, the City of Monterey and Colton Hall Museum, the Instituto Panamericano de Geografía e Historia (Mexico City), the Southwestern Mission Research Center, the University of California Press, the University of Wisconsin Press, the University of Oklahoma Press, the Arthur H. Clark Company, Beacon Press, Penguin Books, the Center for Medieval and Early Renaissance Studies, the Biblioteca Nacional (Madrid), the Museo del Prado, the Archivo General de Indias (Seville), Art Resources and the Musée du Louvre, the Braun Research Library at the Southwest Museum, the Honnold-Mudd Library at Claremont Colleges, the American Museum of Natural History, the Huntington Library, the Peabody Museum, the Seaver Center for Western History Research, and the International Marine Publishing Company.

At Heyday, we were truly fortunate to work with Jeannine Gendar, whose editing consistently improved our work, and Rebecca LeGates, whose design and layout have greatly enhanced what we gave her. Working with both of them was a truly collaborative effort. We appreciate their professionalism and their friendship.

Many thanks to Chrisanne Beebe, who sacrificed a good portion of her summer vacation typing many of the selections for this book. Her critical eye, objectivity, and sense of humor helped us determine which pieces would appeal to readers. Finally, our faithful friend Oliver provided support and constant supervision throughout the entire preparation of this book. He is pleased to know that he can go "off duty" for a while, but only until the next project begins.

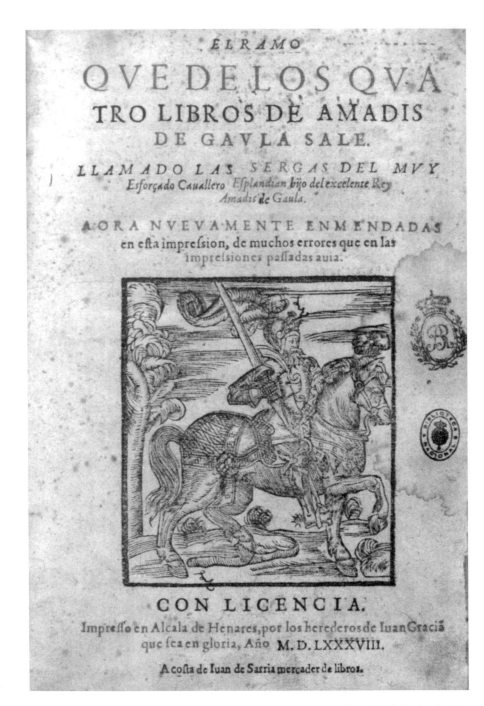

ELRAMO
QVE DE LOS QVA
TRO LIBROS DE AMADIS
DE GAVLA SALE.

LLAMADO LAS SERGAS DEL MVY
Esforçado Cauallero Esplandian hijo del excelente Rey
Amadis de Gaula.

AORA NVEVAMENTE ENMENDADAS
en esta impression, de muchos errores que en las
impressiones passadas auia.

CON LICENCIA.

Impresso en Alcala de Henares, por los herederos de Iuan Graciã
que sea en gloria, Año M.D.LXXXVIII.

A costa de Iuan de Sarria mercader de libros.

Title page of the 1588 edition of The Labors of the Very Brave Knight Esplandián, *the chivalric novel in which "California" first appeared as an island on "the right-hand side of the Indies." Courtesy of the Biblioteca Nacional, Madrid.*

Introduction

The past few years have witnessed a number of California sesquicentennials, as the state has commemorated the 1848 discovery of gold, the 1849 gold rush and state constitutional convention, and the 1850 admission of the state of California to the Union. A number of scholarly and popular conferences were held and important additions to the literature of California history were published. The history of the American state of California received critical and perceptive attention. But what about the long history of European presence in this region before the gold rush? What did those forty-niners and American immigrants find when they arrived? We offer here a series of letters, reports, reminiscences, and other documents that tell the story of California from the time the Spanish first set foot on its soil in the 1530s until the end of California's experience as a territory in the Mexican republic in the 1840s.

A number of excellent works dealing with this period are already in print. This book, however, examines this epoch from angles rarely seen in works in the broad field of "California history." First, the picture of California offered here is drawn from the point of view of its residents. When we see Mexican California authoritatively described by Richard Henry Dana in *Two Years Before the Mast* or the writings of such early explorers as Jedediah Smith or John C. Frémont, we tend to forget that they did not live here for very long. We likewise tend to forget that many of the descriptions we have of California missions and *ranchos*** were composed by foreign visitors—the Englishmen George Vancouver and Frederick William Beechey and the Frenchmen Jean François de Galaup, Comte de la Pérouse, and Auguste Bernard Duhaut-Cilly, for instance. They were all simply passing through. The problem is not that these writings are wrong or invalid. Quite the contrary. Many of the observations made by the seven authors we have just mentioned are acute and penetrating and deepen our understanding of California. The question is rather one of perspective. While an outside perspective is essential for a full understanding

---

* Spanish words are defined in the Glossary, beginning on page 485.

of a place, it needs to complement an inside perspective. Americans would never say that the accounts of foreign travelers to these shores, even such perceptive ones as Alexis de Tocqueville *(Democracy in America)* or Frances Milton Trollope *(Domestic Manners of the Americans),* could reveal all there is to know about Jacksonian America. We would say that these accounts, while excellent, lack the feel of America and the intimacy that membership in the American community provides. But, sometimes without realizing it, we give foreign authors the last word about Spanish and Mexican California.

But how do we get at the insider's view of early California? No great literature in the familiar forms of drama, poetry, or fiction was produced in California before 1846, and there were few men or women of letters. This is not surprising, for California was then a frontier area. But while literature in the formal sense did not exist, traditions did, especially those of the people who were already living here when the Spanish arrived. Do not be misled, as you read Miguel del Barco's description of an Indian child grabbing his mother by her "uncombed and dirty hair" or Fermín Francisco de Lasuén's statement that the native way of life "differs little from that of the lower animals," into thinking that California lacked culture, technology, or grace before the arrival of Europeans. Among some three hundred thousand people, more than a hundred distinct languages were spoken, and it was not unusual for one person to be fluent in several of them. No wonder Vicente de Santa María was astonished by the facility with which the Indians of the San Francisco Bay region learned to pronounce Spanish. When Lasuén, describing native food-gathering practices, said that "they satiate themselves today and give little thought to tomorrow," he had entirely failed to recognize a practical and sustainable way of life developed after centuries of acquaintance with and exquisite observation of the natural environment. Perhaps blinded by imperialist zeal and religious fervor, Europeans perceived the transience of California's native material culture, the lack of European-style agriculture, and especially the lack of a written language as evidence of a savage, incoherent, hand-to-mouth existence.

Fortunately, many of the indigenous traditions of California, especially those which are rooted in the pre-contact period, have been preserved and retold—a virtue of oral traditions is their longevity. Many of those which recount the creation of the world or tell the stories of the origins of a particular group have now been published and astutely presented by the modern descendants of the first Californians. These fall before the time period we are discussing in this volume, but other indigenous traditions appear in what the Indian peoples told the soldiers and missionaries they met, in how they reacted to them, and in how they treated them. Each account of the first contact between an indigenous group of people and an exploring party or a military excursion contains within it, sometimes deeply buried, the vibrant traditions of California's native peoples.

Another inside view of early California comes from the first European explorers and settlers—early travel literature. These accounts were usually written by Spaniards or Mexicans but also by Russians and by Anglo-Americans who came to California relatively early and attempted to adjust and accommodate themselves to a different culture.

Another set of sources are available to us because colonial California was part of the far-flung Spanish empire. For better and worse, one of the things that the Spanish empire bequeathed to subsequent European ventures was the institution of the imperial bureaucracy. Spanish colonists were required to be tireless record keepers; the sheer volume of records they produced is so overwhelming that one occasionally wonders how they had time to do anything else. Besides a host of laws, the colonial archives are stuffed with regulations interpreting the laws—and with secondary regulations interpreting the primary ones. There are military service records, land titles, court records, and a multitude of other official documents. Then there is correspondence. Soldiers were always writing back to headquarters; missionaries were constantly composing reports for their superiors; and settlers were always ready to take pen in hand to complain about problems with their cattle or lands or hired hands. All this material, especially the official documents, can seem dry and obscure at first reading. But, if approached patiently, they can open unique windows into the complex texture of daily life.

Finally, there are *testimonios,* or reminiscences. Many of these were recorded by interviewers hired by Hubert Howe Bancroft in the 1870s to collect oral accounts as raw material for their employer's projected history of California. When this work was finally published in the 1880s, it stretched into seven hefty volumes. Bancroft's staff sometimes tried to direct the interviews into areas of their own choosing and to put words into their interviewees' mouths. In addition, the interviews were often conducted some forty or fifty years after the events they relate. As a result of this, the *testimonio* material has to be used with caution. But this is not a unique problem in historiography. African-American slave narratives, for instance, were often composed decades after the events they describe;

yet, used carefully and creatively, they have been demonstrated to throw considerable light on the periods they chronicle. Used carefully, the Bancroft *testimonios* can do the same.

In short, the problem with California is not one of insufficient sources, but rather of choosing from the extensive number that are available. We hope that the selections we have made in this volume will enable readers to get a genuine experience of Spanish and Mexican California from the inside.

There is one more way in which California is viewed differently here than in most histories; in this case, the difference is not so much about point of view as it is about the amount of space encompassed. We have tried to be faithful to the way most people living here used the word "California" from the 1530s to the 1840s. In those days, California was the first place one came to, sailing up the western coast of Mexico; it began at a tip of land about two hundred miles west of Mazatlán. From that tip, Cabo San Lucas, it headed north and west for an undetermined distance. Later, it would be divided into a lower part (Baja California) and an upper part (Alta California), but for most of the period we examine here, these were simply two inseparable parts of the place called "the Californias."

For a good amount of time after Alta California was founded in 1769, the Californias were governed as a single unit, with one governor. The Kumeyaay people lived on both sides of the border that was superimposed on their land, and the San Diego *presidio* was responsible for the safety and protection of areas of California that extended well into Baja California. The two regions always shared the same institutional structure of *presidios, missions, ranchos,* and *pueblos.*

Most importantly, Spanish Alta California developed out of Baja California. The issues and problems with which the residents of Alta California had to struggle during the period we examine had all been confronted earlier by the residents of Baja California. Alta California's leaders, especially its religious and military leaders, consistently developed their own policies in the light of what they took to be the lessons of Baja California's history. Some of them, such as Junípero Serra and his great adversary, Governor Felipe de Neve, worked in Baja California before they headed north.

The development of the United States is generally envisioned as a movement from the east coast to the west, but for an accurate conception of California, we need to expand our view. The first mission to be founded in California was in Loreto, in the Mexican state of Baja California Sur. Above the doorway of the restored mission church is the inscription *"Madre y cabeza de las Californias,"* mother and head of the Californias. This is the historical reality, and we have attempted to be faithful to that reality in choosing the texts and documents for this volume.

Exploration

Exploration

The long and complex Spanish experience with California began when Spaniards first set foot on California in 1533, over half a century before the British attempted to colonize Virginia in 1585, and almost three-quarters of a century before the founding of the Jamestown colony. But California as an imaginative concept existed even before 1533. The word "California" was invented in a popular novel published in Spain in 1510, and that novel was influenced by the already developing history of Spain in the Caribbean. In the world of the imagination, "California" was tightly bound to the Spanish project of national expansion.

The thrust into California was part of the second stage of Spanish expansion in North America. The first stage had begun in the Caribbean, with Columbus's first voyage, in 1492. For the next quarter century, Spain's activity in the New World was basically limited to these islands and the surrounding coastal areas of the South and North American mainlands, where Spain had originally hoped to establish a series of trading bases with the rich lands of the East. But instead of the expected, though exotic, Asian peoples, Spain found itself faced with new lands and new peoples. In formulating policies for this unexpected reality, Spain fell back on what it knew, which was its own conquests of the Moors.

The second phase of Spanish expansion began in 1519, and it was directed into the Mexican mainland. This phase brought Spain face to face with an advanced and prosperous civilization that was, in its own fashion, an empire. Spain's encounter with this civilization and its ability to overcome it by force of arms brought issues of conquest and military force much more directly into the consciousness of its rulers: how to conquer these new lands and how to overcome the resistance of these new peoples; how to extract and exploit whatever wealth the land and its peoples possessed; how to treat the conquered peoples, how to convert them into Hispanics, and how to make them Catholics; how to consolidate the conquest; how to integrate this part of Spain's possessions with the fabulous expanse of empire which the nation was assembling in Europe, the Americas, and Asia; and how to keep the empire expanding.

California began to figure in these questions from a very early date; the Spanish arrived there less than forty years after the first voyage of Columbus and only a dozen years after the conquest of Mexico.

While California was not formally colonized by Spain until the end of the seventeenth century, it had an important role in Spain's geopolitical calculations well before then. As a mysterious place to the north, it was regarded as a potential path to the mythical "Strait of Anián," the hoped-for maritime path through the North American continent. Later, as Spain developed an active trade with Asia, California became a refuge for vessels arriving after the hazardous crossing of the northern Pacific Ocean. In the broad sweep of Spain's concerns in America, California was hardly central, but it was an integral part of the imperial designs that propelled Spain during its Golden Age.

1492
The First Meeting

CHRISTOPHER COLUMBUS

The first Europeans to come permanently to the New World were a people flushed with victory in a war of religious conquest. On January 2, 1492, Boabdil, the last Moslem ruler of Granada, surrendered to the armies of Fernando of Aragón and Isabela of Castilla. Spain congratulated itself for a successful reconquest *(reconquista)* of its land from the adherents of Islam, who, because they had entered the peninsula centuries earlier from Mauritania (Morocco), were called Moors. While the actual history of the long struggle between the various Moorish and Spanish rulers and factions was quite complicated, a popular version took hold among the peoples who created early modern Spain: heroic Spanish Christians, assisted by no less than the apostle St. James (Santiago), who was believed to be buried in the northern town of Compostela, defeated the followers of Mohammed in a seven-hundred-year crusade. This became an essential element of the Spanish self-concept, inevitably coloring the way the Spanish would conceptualize their encounter with another group of non-Christians across the Atlantic Ocean.

Spain had already ventured into the Atlantic in the 1470s and 1480s, as Castilian forces subdued the native peoples of the Canary Islands. At the same time, Portuguese vessels were establishing a series of military and trading outposts farther and farther down the African coast. Portuguese ships reached the tip of that continent in 1488 and Portugal seemed to be advancing inexorably toward the Indies and their wealth. The successful conquest of Granada and the knowledge gained in the Canary Islands campaigns encouraged the Spanish monarchy to attempt to outflank the Portuguese by gambling on a possible Atlantic route to the riches of the East.

Isabela came to an agreement with the Italian navigator Christopher Columbus a few months after the victory at Granada, and Columbus undertook the first of his four attempts to reach the East by sailing west that summer. When he met the Taíno people on the island he called San Salvador, his reaction to them set the tone for the manner in which Europeans from many nations would regard the indigenous peoples they met. Among the things he found remarkable were their way of dressing, so different from that of the Europeans, and their gestures of hospitality, which led him to speculate that they might easily be made to serve Spanish masters. The two excerpts which follow are from his log entries describing that first contact.

FROM THE *Log of Christopher Columbus*

At dawn we saw naked people, and I went ashore in the ship's boat, armed, followed by Martín Alonso Pinzón, Captain of the *Pinta,* and his brother Vicente Yáñez Pinzón, Captain of the *Niña.* I unfurled the royal banner and the Captains brought the flags which displayed a large green cross with the letters *F* and *Y* at the left and right side of the cross. Over each letter was the appropriate crown of that Sovereign. These flags were carried as standard on all of the ships. After a prayer of thanksgiving I ordered the Captains of the *Pinta* and the *Niña,* together with Rodrigo de Escobedo (Secretary of the fleet) and Rodrigo Sánchez of Segovia (Comptroller of the fleet) to bear faith and witness that I was taking possession of this island for the King and Queen. I made all the necessary declarations and had these testimonies carefully written down by the Secretary. In addition to those named above, the entire company of the fleet bore witness to this act. To this island I gave the name San Salvador, in honor of our Blessed Lord.

No sooner had we concluded the formalities of taking possession of the island than people began coming to the beach, all as naked as their mothers bore them, and women also, although I did not see more than one very young girl. All those that I saw were young people, none of whom was over thirty years old. They are very well-built people, with handsome bodies and very fine faces, though their appearance is marred somewhat by very broad heads and foreheads, more so than I have ever seen in any other race. Their eyes are large and very pretty, and their skin is the color of Canary Islanders or of sunburned persons, not at all black as would be expected because we are on an east-west line with Hierro in the Canaries. These are tall people and their legs, with no exceptions, are quite straight, and none of

An illustration from the title page of the volume in which a letter by Columbus announcing his discovery was first published, In Praise of the Most Serene Fernando, King of Spain. *The fact that the letter was included in the book, an account of King Fernando's capture of Granada in 1492, indicates the close connection that existed in the Spanish mind between the reconquest of the Iberian peninsula from the Moors and the encounter with the non-Christian peoples across the Atlantic. Courtesy of the Jay I. Kislak Foundation.*

them has a paunch. They are, in fact, well proportioned. Their hair is not kinky, but straight and coarse like horsehair. They wear it short over the eyebrows but they have a long hank in the back that they never cut. Many of the natives paint their faces. Others paint their whole bodies, some only the eyes or nose. Some are painted black, some white, some red; others are of different colors.

The people here call this island *Guanahani* in their language, and their speech is very fluent, although I do not understand any of it. They are friendly and well-dispositioned people who bear no arms except for small spears, and they have no iron. I showed one my sword, and through ignorance he grabbed it by the blade and cut himself. Their spears are made of wood, to which they attach a fish tooth at one end or some other sharp thing.

I want the natives to develop a friendly attitude toward us because I know they are a people who can be made free and converted to our Holy Faith more by love than by force. I therefore gave red caps to some and glass beads to others. They hung the beads around their necks, along with some other things of slight value which I gave them. And they took great pleasure in this and became so friendly that it was a marvel. They traded and gave everything they had with good will, but it seems to me they have very little and are poor in everything. I wanted my men to take nothing from the people without giving something in exchange. They brought us parrots, balls of cotton thread, spears, and many other things, including a kind of dry leaf that they hold in great esteem. For these items we swapped them little glass beads and hawks' bells.

Many of the men I have seen have scars on their bodies, and when I made signs to them to find out how this happened, they indicated to me that people from other nearby islands come to San Salvador to capture them; they defend themselves as best they can. I believe that people from the mainland come here to take them as slaves. They ought to make good and skilled servants, for they repeat very quickly whatever we say to them. I think they can easily be made Christians, for they seem to have no religion. If it pleases Our Lord, I will take six of them to Your Highnesses when I depart, in order that they may learn our language.

1510
The Invention of "California"

Garci Rodríguez de Montalvo

The name "California" first appeared in a work published in Seville in 1510 by Garci Rodríguez de Montalvo entitled *The Labors of the Very Brave Knight Esplandián*. Rodríguez de Montalvo was born in the middle of the fifteenth century. He participated in the final phases of the *reconquista* and was knighted for his service at Alhama de Granada in 1482. By the 1490s, he was hard at work on his five-volume set, *Amadís de Gaula,* one of the first of many published books of fiction on the themes of chivalry and courtly love which so captivated the Spanish reading public during the age of exploration and conquest. The first four volumes represented Rodríguez de Montalvo's reworking of oral legends that were centuries old. The fifth volume, whose composition was begun in the 1490s and which was partly influenced by the tales brought back to Spain by Columbus and the early explorers, was Rodríguez de Montalvo's own creation. It concerned the adventures of Esplandián, the son of Amadís. The passage reproduced below is taken from chapter 157 of the book.

At this point in the novel, the "pagans" (i.e. Moslems) are attacking the Christian city of Constantinople. Word of this reaches even to the fictional island of California in the Indies. It is inhabited only by women and ruled by a queen named Calafia. She convinces her women to join the pagan alliance and they sail to Constantinople. Their fabled griffins, creatures with the heads and wings of eagles but the bodies of lions, prove to be especially formidable fighters and capture and kill many Christian defenders of the city. But the griffins are unable to distinguish between Christian and pagan males, and soon take to killing Calafia's allies as well. Accordingly, she has to remove them from the battle. Instead, she and a male warrior, Radiaro, challenge Amadís and his son Esplandián, who is called "the Knight of the Great Serpent," to combat. When she visits Constantinople to confirm the challenge, she sees Esplandián and is smitten with love for him. During the combat Esplandián defeats Radiaro, and Amadís bests Calafia, who is taken prisoner. During the final battle for the city she sends a message to her women not to participate in the battle, and the pagans are routed. Esplandián marries the daughter of the emperor, who then abdicates so that Esplandián and his new wife can rule. Calafia becomes a Christian and marries Esplandián's cousin, Talanque. The two of them return to California, where Rodríguez de Montalvo says "they underwent many amazing adventures, including very large challenges, many battles and victories over great seigniories, but we decline to say more about what became of them because, if we wished to do so, it would be a never ending story."

The names Calafia and California were rooted in the Arabic word *khalifa,* which enters English as "caliph." The use of the word is clearly meant to call to mind the *reconquista.* In the novel, California is consistently associated with gold and wealth. Queen Calafia and her women left the sea to enter the battle "wearing their golden armor that was studded all over with very precious stones which were found on California Island as abundantly as rocks in a field." In her challenge to Amadís and Esplandián, Calafia identified herself as "the very courageous ruler of California Island, where an amazing abundance of gold and precious stones are found." When Calafia went to meet Esplandián to formalize the challenge, her robes "were made entirely of gold and many precious stones." Also, she wore a "finely designed headdress with a huge volume of twists and turns, and when she finally put it on her head it was like a capeline: it was made completely of gold and studded with gems of great value." In this work of fiction, "California" is associated with wealth, conquest, indigenous people who are willing to convert to Christianity, and indigenous women willing to give themselves to European men.

Esplandián was a very popular work, a quintessential chivalric novel. After its publication in 1510 it went through at least ten more Spanish editions and was translated into French, Italian, German, and English in the sixteenth century. Hernán Cortés is known to have read it. Towards the beginning of Cervantes's *Don Quixote* (1605), two of Quixote's neighbors, a priest and a barber, become convinced that Quixote's eccentric behavior stems from his having read too many of these sorts of novels, so they go through his library, determined to burn the offending works. The first book they select for their bonfire is none other than *Esplandián.* But by that time, "California" had evolved from an imagined to a real place.

FROM *The Labors of the Very Brave Knight Esplandián*

I tell you that on the right-hand side of the Indies there was an island called California, which was very close to the region of the Earthly Paradise. This island was inhabited by black women, and there were no males among them at all, for their way of life was similar to that of the Amazons. The island was made up of the wildest cliffs and the sharpest precipices found anywhere in the world. These women had energetic bodies and courageous, ardent hearts, and they were very strong. Their armor was made entirely out of gold—which was the only metal found on the island—as were the trappings of the fierce beasts that they rode once they were tamed. They lived in very well-designed caves. They had many ships, which they used to sally forth on their raiding expeditions and in which they carried away the men they seized, whom they killed in a way that you will soon hear. On occasion, they kept the peace with their male opponents, and the females and the males mixed with each other in complete safety, and they had carnal relations, from which unions it follows that many of the women became pregnant. If they bore a female, they kept her, but if they bore a male, he was immediately killed. The reason for this, inasmuch as it is known, is that, according to their thinking, they were set on reducing the number of males to so small a group that the Amazons could easily rule over them and all their lands; therefore they kept only those few men whom they realized they needed so that their race would not die out.

On this island called California there were many griffins, because these beasts were suited to the ruggedness of the terrain, which was a perfect habitat for the infinite number of wild animals that lived there and that were not found in any other part of the world. When these griffins had offspring, the women ingeniously covered themselves in coarse hides in order to capture the young; then they took them back to their caves, where they raised them. When their plumage was even, they fed them so often and so cleverly with the captured men and the boys they bore that the griffins became well acquainted to the women and never harmed them in any way. Therefore, every man who ventured onto the island was immediately killed and devoured by the griffins; and even though they had eaten their fill, they never for that reason stopped seizing the men, carrying them aloft as they flew through the air and, when they tired of carrying them, dropping them to their certain deaths.

1513
Conflict in the Caribbean

Bartolomé de las Casas

Despite initial setbacks, Columbus placed a permanent settlement on the place he named the Spanish Island *(La Isla Española,* or Hispaniola) in 1496. By the time of his death in 1506, Spanish explorers had traversed the Caribbean, struggling to reconcile the new indigenous peoples they were meeting with the Asian nations they had expected to encounter. The impossibility of this reconciliation slowly made them realize that this was indeed a New World. The traces of gold they did find whetted their appetites, and their treatment of the Caribbean Indians, pressed into virtual slavery to explore for gold or to work on landed estates, became increasingly brutal. Some participants in the colonization project, especially members of the clergy, began to object. As early as 1511, Dominican friar Antonio de Montesinos caused a controversy when he denounced the treatment of indigenous peoples during a sermon from the pulpit of the cathedral at Santo Domingo. "By what right and justice do you hold those Indians in such a cruel and horrible servitude?" he thundered. "Are they not human?"

The greatest Spanish voice raised on behalf of the indigenous peoples of the Caribbean was that of Bartolomé de las Casas. Born in Seville in 1484, he came to the New World to seek his fortune in 1502. He was ordained a secular priest in 1512, the first priest to be ordained in the New World. He served as chaplain on a number of expeditions against the Indians in Cuba, and he received both land and Indians as recompense for his services. But a conversion which he experienced over the course of a few years led him to become a vocal critic of the Spanish treatment of the natives of the Caribbean. He entered the Dominican order in 1522 and continued his crusade against cruelty against the Indians. At one point he suggested that black slaves be brought from Africa to perform the extreme labors that were being forced upon the Indians. He soon recanted this idea, and he had some success in persuading Carlos V to decree better treatment for the Indians. However, as bishop of Chiapas in the 1540s, he was less successful when he tried to force the landholders of that region to moderate their treatment of their subjects. He then returned to Spain and authored a number of works on the treatment of the Indians. The following excerpt, taken from *A Brief Account of the Devastation of the Indies* (published in 1552), describes a massacre at Caonao in Cuba in 1513.

FROM *A Brief Account of the Devastation of the Indies*

In the year one thousand five hundred and eleven, the Spaniards passed over to the island of Cuba, which, as I have said, is the same distance from Hispaniola as the distance between Valladolid and Rome, and which was a well-populated province. They began and ended in Cuba the same as they had done elsewhere, but with much greater acts of cruelty.

Among the noteworthy outrages they committed was the one they perpetrated against a *cacique,* a very important noble, by name Hatuey, who had come to Cuba from Hispaniola with many of his people to flee the calamities and inhuman acts of the Christians. When he was told by certain Indians that the Christians were now coming to Cuba, he assembled as many of his followers as he could and said to them, "Now, you must know that they are saying that the Christians are coming here, and you know by experience how they have put So and So and So and So and other nobles to an end. And now they are coming from Haiti (which is Hispaniola) to do the same here. Do you know why they do this?" The Indians replied, "We do not know. But it may be that they are by nature wicked and cruel." And he told them, "No, they do not act only because of that, but because they have a god they greatly worship, and they want us to worship that god, and that is why they struggle with us and subject us and kill us."

He had a basket full of gold and jewels and he said, "You see their god here, the god of the Christians. If you agree to it, let us dance for this god. Who knows, it may please the god of the Christians and they will do us no harm." And his followers said, all together, "Yes, that is good, that is good!" And they danced around the basket of gold until they fell down exhausted Then their chief, the *cacique* Hatuey, said to them, "See here, if we keep this basket of gold, they will take it from us and end up killing us. So let us cast

A depiction by the Flemish engraver Theodor de Bry of the episode recounted in this selection, included in the 1614 edition of Las Casas's A Brief Account of the Destruction of the Indies. *Some European governments, especially Protestant ones, were eager to popularize the atrocities of Catholic Spain in the New World. This "black legend"—that Spanish behavior against the peoples of the Americas was uniquely savage—enabled these governments to gloss over their own barbaric treatment of Native Americans. Courtesy of The Bancroft Library, University of California, Berkeley.*

away the basket into the river." They all agreed to do this, and they flung the basket of gold into the river that was nearby.

This *cacique,* Hatuey, was constantly fleeing before the Christians from the time they arrived on the island of Cuba, since he knew them and what they were capable of. Now and then they encountered him and he defended himself, but they finally killed him. And they did this for the sole reason that he fled from those cruel and wicked Christians and had defended himself against them. And when they had captured him and as many of his followers as they could, they burned them all at the stake.

When tied to the stake, the *cacique* Hatuey was told by a Franciscan friar who was present, an artless rascal, something about the God of the Christians and the articles of the Faith. And he was told what he could do in the brief time that remained to him, in order to be saved and go to Heaven. The *cacique,* who had never heard any of this before, and was told he would go to Hell, where, if he did not adopt the Christian Faith, he would suffer eternal torment, asked the Franciscan friar if Christians all went to Heaven. When told that they did, he said he would prefer to go to Hell. Such is the fame and honor that God and our Faith have earned through the Christians who have gone out to the Indies.

On one occasion, when we went to claim ten leagues of a big settlement, along with food and maintenance, we were welcomed with a bounteous quantity of fish and bread and cooked victuals. The Indians generously gave us all they could. Then suddenly, without cause and without warning, and in my presence, the devil inhabited the Christians and spurred them to attack the Indians—men, women, and children—who were sitting there before us. In the massacre that followed the Spaniards put to the sword more than three thousand souls. I saw such terrible cruelties done there as I had never seen before nor thought to see.

1514
The Task of Conversion

When the cruelty toward the peoples of the Caribbean became known in Spain, there were some who advocated regularizing the treatment of the Indians and specifying the conditions under which force could legitimately be employed against them. In 1514, the court ordered the preparation of a document that was supposed to be carried by all the *conquistadores* and read (in Spanish) to any Indians they encountered. The document was known as the *Requerimiento* (requirement, or requisition), for its use was mandated by the crown. Before any hostilities were commenced, the Indians were supposed to be given the chance to agree to its terms.

The document, relying on Christian notions of what constituted a just war as well as some Moorish ideas on the conditions necessary for a holy war which had made their way into the Spanish worldview, gave its audiences a series of selective lessons in biblical history and let them know that Pope Alexander VI, a Spaniard, had recognized Spanish claims across the ocean. It is safe to say that this document, in the practical order, did not have a major impact on the way the natives of the Americas were treated.

The document was widely derided from practically the moment it was issued. Las Casas, for instance, remarked that when he read it he did not know whether to laugh or cry. But, as ridiculous as it was, it does demonstrate that an ethical concern about the treatment of indigenous peoples reached into the center of the Spanish government very soon after Spain became a colonial power. The same cannot be said for many other European countries. An excerpt from the document follows.

THE *Requerimiento*

On the part of the King, Don Fernando, and of Doña Juana, his daughter, Queen of Castile and León, subduers of the barbarian nations, we their servants notify and make known to you, as best we can, that the Lord our God, living and eternal, created the heaven and the earth, and one man and one woman, of whom you and I, and all men of the world, were and are descendants, and all those who come after us. But, on account of the multitude which has sprung from this man and woman in the five thousand years since the world was created, it was necessary that some men should go one way and some another, and that they should be divided into many kingdoms and provinces, for in one alone they could not be sustained.

Of all these nations, God our Lord gave charge to one man, called St. Peter, that he should be Lord and Superior of all the men in the world, that they should obey him, and that he should be head of the whole human race, wherever men should live, and under whatever law, sect, or belief they should be; and he gave him the world for his kingdom and jurisdiction.

And he commanded him to place his seat in Rome, as the spot most fitting to rule the world from; but he also permitted him to have his seat in any other part of the world, and to judge and govern all Christians, Moors, Jews, Gentiles, and all other sects. This man was called the Pope, as if to say Admirable Great Father and Governor of Men. The men who lived in that time obeyed that St. Peter, and took him for Lord, King, and Superior of the universe; so also have they regarded the others who after him have been elected to the Pontificate, and so it has been continued even until now, and will continue until the end of the world.

One of these Pontiffs, who succeeded St. Peter as Lord of the world in the dignity and seat which I have before mentioned made donation of these isles and terra firma to the aforesaid King and Queen and to their successors, or Lords, with all that there are in these territories, as is contained in certain writings which passed upon the subject aforesaid, which you can see if you wish.

So their Highnesses are Kings and Lords of these islands and land of terra firma by virtue of this donation; and some islands, and indeed almost all those to whom this has been notified, have received and served their Highnesses, as Lords and Kings, in the way that subjects ought to do, with good will, without any resistance, immediately, without delay, when they were

17

informed of the aforesaid facts. And they also received and obeyed the priests whom their Highnesses sent to preach to them and to teach them our Holy Faith; and all these, of their own free will, without any reward and condition, have become Christians, and are so, and their Highnesses have joyfully and benignantly received them, and have also commanded them to be treated as their subjects and vassals; and you too are held and obliged to do the same. Therefore, as best we can, we ask and require you that you consider what we have said to you, and that you take the time that shall be necessary to understand and deliberate upon it, and that you acknowledge the Church as the Ruler and Superior of the whole world and the high priest called Pope, and in his name the King and Queen Doña Juana our Lords, in his place, as Superiors and Lords and Kings of these islands and this terra firma by virtue of the said donation, and that you consent and give place that these religious fathers should declare and preach to you the aforesaid.

If you do so, you will do well, and that you are obliged to do to their Highnesses, and we in their name shall receive you in all love and charity, and shall leave you your wives, and your children, and your lands, free without servitude, that you may do with them and with yourselves freely that which you like and think best, and they shall not compel you to turn Christians, unless you yourselves, when informed of the truth, should wish to be converted to our Holy Catholic Faith, as almost all the inhabitants of the rest of the islands have done. And besides this, their Highnesses award you many privileges and exceptions and will grant you many benefits.

But if you do not do this, and wickedly and intentionally delay to do so, I certify to you that, with the help of God, we shall forcibly enter into your country and shall make war against you in all ways and manners that we can, and shall subject you to the yoke and obedience of the Church and of their Highnesses; we shall take you and your wives and your children, and shall make slaves of them, and as such shall sell and dispose of them as their Highnesses may command; and we shall take away your goods, and shall do all the harm and damage that we can, as to vassals who do not obey, and refuse to receive their lord, and resist and contradict him; and we shall protest that the deaths and losses which shall accrue from this are your fault, and not that of their Highnesses, or ours, nor of these cavaliers who come with us. And that we have said this to you and made this Requisition, we request the Notary here present to give us his testimony in writing, and we ask the rest who are here present that they should be witnesses of this Requisition.

1519
The Market in Tenochtitlán

Bernal Díaz del Castillo

By 1518 the Spanish had outposts on most of the larger Caribbean islands. Reports of gold on what is now the Mexican mainland led the governor of Cuba, Diego de Velásquez, to send an expedition under Hernán Cortés to investigate. On the coast near Tabasco, Cortés read the *Requerimiento* and engaged in some skirmishes with the local population. He was then given twenty indigenous women. One of them possessed the language skills that enabled him to communicate with the peoples of the region. Cortés called this woman Doña Marina and eventually had a child with her. Doña Marina, also called La Malinche, confirmed what Cortés had heard, that many of the tributary groups in Mexico were extremely dissatisfied with Aztec rule. With fewer than five hundred Spanish soldiers, Cortés began a long march through the mountains to the Valley of Mexico. He was joined by thousands of Indian allies. On November 8, 1519, at the fabulous Aztec capital of Tenochtitlán—a huge city in a lake, connected to the mainland by three narrow causeways—he met the emperor Moctezuma II. One of Cortés's soldiers, Bernal Díaz del Castillo, later wrote an account of the expedition in his work *The Conquest of New Spain*.

For generations of adventurers all across Europe, the possibility of exploiting wealth like that of Mexico sparked hopes of personal and national enrichment that drove them across the ocean. The excerpt below describes the Spanish wonder at encountering the great Aztec market at Tlatelolco in Tenochtitlán.

FROM *The Conquest of New Spain*

On reaching the great marketplace, escorted by the many *caciques* whom Moctezuma had assigned to us, we were astounded at the great number of people and the quantities of merchandise, and at the orderliness and good arrangements that prevailed, for we had never seen such a thing before. The chieftains who accompanied us pointed out everything. Every kind of merchandise was kept separate and had its fixed place marked for it.

Let us begin with the dealers in gold, silver, and precious stones, feathers, cloaks, and embroidered goods, and male and female slaves, who are also sold there. They bring as many slaves to be sold in that market as the Portuguese bring blacks from Guinea. Some are brought there attached to long poles by means of collars around their necks to prevent them from escaping, but others are left loose. Next there were those who sold coarser cloth and cotton goods and fabrics made of twisted thread, and there were chocolate merchants with their chocolate. In this way you could see every kind of merchandise to be found anywhere in New Spain, laid out in the same way as goods are laid out in my own district in Medina del Campo, a center of fairs, where each line of stalls has its own particular sort. So it was in this great market. There were those who sold sisal cloth and ropes and the sandals they wear on their feet, which are made from the same plant. All these were kept in one part of the market, in the place assigned to them, and in another part were skins of tigers [jaguars] and lions, otters, jackals, and deer, badgers, mountain cats, and other wild animals, some tanned and some untanned, and other classes of merchandise.

There were sellers of kidney beans and sage and other vegetables and herbs in another place, and in yet another they were selling fowl, and birds with great wattles [turkeys], also rabbits, hares, deer, young ducks, little dogs, and other such creatures. Then there were the fruiterers, and the women who sold cooked food, flour and honey cake, and tripe had their part of the market. Then came pottery of all kinds, from big water jars to little jugs, displayed in its own place; also honey, honey-paste, and other sweets, like nougat. Elsewhere they sold timber too, and boards, cradles, beams, blocks, and benches, all in a quarter of their own.

Then there were the sellers of pitch pine for torches, and other things of that kind, and I must also mention, with all apologies, that they sold many canoe-loads of human excrement, which they kept in the creeks near the market. This was for the manufacture of salt and the curing of skins, which they say cannot be done without it. I know that many gentlemen will laugh at this, but I assure them it is true. I may add that on all the roads they have shelters made of reeds or straw or grass so that they can retire when they wish to do so and purge their bowels unseen by passersby, and also in order that their excrement shall not be lost.

But why waste so many words on the goods in their great market? If I describe everything in detail I shall never be done. Paper, which in Mexico they call *amatl*, and some reeds that smell of liquid amber and are full of tobacco, and yellow ointments and other such things are sold in a separate part. Much cochineal is for sale too, under the arcades of that market, and there are many sellers of herbs and other such things. They have a building there also in which three judges sit, and there are officials like constables who examine the merchandise. I am forgetting the sellers of salt and the makers of flint knives, and how they split them off the stone itself, and the fisherwomen and the men who sell small cakes made from a sort of weed which they get out of the great lake [Texcoco], which curdles and forms a kind of bread that tastes rather like cheese. They sell axes too, made of bronze and copper and tin, and gourds and brightly painted wooden jars.

The first meeting of Cortés and Moctezuma, with La Malinche between them. From the Lienzo de Tlaxcala, *an indigenous account of the conquest composed in the 1550s at the behest of the viceroy. Courtesy of the Department of Library Services, American Museum of Natural History (Neg. No. 330881. Photo. Rota).*

We went on to the great *cue* [temple], and as we approached its wide courts before leaving the marketplace itself, we saw many more merchants who, so I was told, brought gold to sell in grains, just as they extract it from the mines. This gold is placed in the thin quills of the large geese of that country, which are so white as to be transparent. They used to reckon their accounts with one another by the length and thickness of these little quills, how much so many cloaks or so many gourds of chocolate or so many slaves were worth, or anything else they were bartering.

Now let us leave the market, having given it a final glance and come to the courts and enclosures in which their great temple stood. Before reaching it, you pass through a series of large courts, bigger I think than the Plaza at Salamanca....

Before we mounted the steps of the great temple, Moctezuma, who was sacrificing on the top to his idols, sent six priests and two of his principal officers to conduct Cortés up the steps. There were 114 steps to the summit....Indeed, this infernal temple, from its great height, commanded a view of the whole surrounding neighborhood. From this place we could likewise see the three causeways which led into Mexico....We also observed the aqueduct which ran from Chapultepec and provided the whole town with sweet water. We could also distinctly see the bridges across the openings by which these causeways were intersected, and through which the waters of the lake ebbed and flowed. The lake itself was crowded with canoes that were bringing provisions, manufacturers, and merchandise to the city. From here we also discovered that the only communication to the houses in this city, and of all the other towns built in the lake, was by means of drawbridges or canoes. In all these towns the beautiful white plastered temples rose above the smaller ones like so many towers and castles in our Spanish towns, and this, it may be imagined, was a splendid sight....

Having examined and considered all that we had seen, we turned back to the great market and the swarm of people buying and selling. The mere murmur of their voices talking was loud enough to be heard more than three miles away. Some of our soldiers who had been in many parts of the world, in Constantinople, in Rome, and all over Italy, said that they had never seen a market so well laid out, so large, so orderly, and so full of people.

1521
The Conquest of Mexico

When Cortés and his soldiers and allies entered Tenochtitlán, they quickly managed to make Moctezuma a virtual prisoner within his own city. The Spanish became in effect his palace guard, and they kept him isolated from his own nobles and his own people. Moctezuma was allowed to issue commands and give the appearance of ruling, but he was in their power.

Moctezuma was paralyzed by a combination of factors. The most powerful of these was probably the new military presence he had to confront: not so much the military presence of the *conquistadores* as the presence of the six thousand Indian allies of Cortés. The emperor was quite aware that the arrival of the Spanish and their ability to mobilize such a strong indigenous force had changed the political balance of power, and he did not know what to do. Prophecies which had predicted the long-awaited return of the god Queztalcóatl at a time close to the time when Cortés had first appeared off the coast, and a series of omens presaging disaster also confused him.

Once ensconced in the city, the Spaniards began to loot it and melt down religious artifacts. This increased the frustration of the nobility against Moctezuma. At this time, Cortés learned that an expedition from Cuba, under Pánfilo de Narváez, had arrived at Veracruz to relieve him of command and take over the conquest. Leaving about half his men in Tenochtitlán under the command of Pedro de Alvarado, he quickly headed for the coast. His men displayed their newly acquired gold to Narváez's soldiers, and they abandoned their commander for Cortés. He returned to Tenochtitlán with them after an absence of thirty-five days.

In the city, Alvarado's brutality had sparked a rebellion led by Moctezuma's nephew Cuauhtémoc, and the Spaniards were pinned down. When Cortés arrived, the Aztecs allowed him back into what he did not realize was a trap. On July 20, 1520, the "sad night" *(noche triste),* the Spanish

The final battle for Tenochtitlán, from the Lienzo de Tlaxcala. *Courtesy of the Department of Library Services, American Museum of Natural History (Neg. No. 329245. Photo. Logan).*

fought their way out of the city, but only after suffering a great loss of life. Before leaving, they murdered Moctezuma.

Once outside, Cortés and his men reorganized themselves and in the following spring, with their Indians allies, they began a siege of the city. The defenders were seriously weakened by smallpox, which the Spanish had brought into the city. There was tremendous suffering and death as a result of the siege and the plague. According to a surviving account, "There was no fresh water to drink, only stagnant water and the brine of the lake, and many people died of dysentery. The only food was lizards, swallows, corncobs, and the salt grasses of the lake." The city fell on August 13, 1512, after the Spanish captured Cuauhtémoc. Great destruction and cruelty followed.

The following laments were composed by Aztec survivors.

AZTEC POEMS

Broken spears lie in the roads;
we have torn our hair in our grief.
The houses are roofless now, and their walls
are red with blood.

Worms are swarming in the streets and plazas,
and the walls are splattered with gore.
The water has turned red, as if it were dyed,
and when we drink it,
it has the taste of brine.

We have pounded our hands in despair
against the adobe walls,
for our inheritance, our city, is lost and dead.
The shields of our warriors were its defense,
but they could not save it.

We have chewed dry twigs and salt grasses;
we have filled our mouths with dust and bits of adobe;
we have eaten lizards, rats, and worms...

    ***

Our cries of grief rise up
and our tears rain down,
for Tlatelolco is lost.
The Aztecs are fleeing across the lake;
they are running away like women.

How can we save our homes, my people?
The Aztecs are deserting the city:
the city is in flames, and all
is darkness and destruction...

Weep, my people:
know that with these disasters
we have lost the Mexican nation.

The water has turned bitter,
our food is bitter!
These are the acts of the Giver of Life...

***

Nothing but flowers and songs of sorrow
are left in Mexico and Tlatelolco,
where once we saw warriors and wise men.

We know it is true
that we must perish,
for we are mortal men.
You, the Giver of Life,
have ordained it.

We wander here and there
in our desolate poverty.
We are mortal men.
We have seen bloodshed and pain
where once we saw beauty and valor.

We are crushed to the ground;
we lie in ruins.
There is nothing but grief and suffering
in Mexico and Tlatelolco,
where once we saw beauty and valor.

Have you grown weary of your servants?
Are you angry with your servants,
O Giver of Life?

1535
Taking Possession of California

HERNÁN CORTÉS

After the conquest of Tenochtitlán, Cortés established such institutions of Spanish rule as municipalities and laws throughout central and southern Mexico. Spanish forces reached the Pacific Ocean in 1522 and founded the city of Zacatula on the Michoacán coast. The precious metals of the Aztec empire became Spanish possessions, and the gold of the New World financed Spain's rise to European preeminence in the sixteenth century. But Cortés's power excited the envy of other *conquistadores,* and it also came into conflict with the desire of the Spanish government to exercise its own authority in this new region. In 1527 the crown established an *audiencia,* or royal court, in Mexico City with various governmental powers. Cortés thus found his authority circumscribed. He returned to Spain to argue his case in 1530, but he was not able to recover all of his former powers. However, he was given the title of Marqués del Valle de Oaxaca and a commission to explore in the Southern Sea, as the Pacific Ocean was then known.

Cortés hoped to find a wealthy civilization similar either to that of the Aztecs, whom he had conquered, or the Incas, whose wealth was beginning to be known in Mexico. Failing that, he hoped to find a northern waterway through America that would reduce the length of the sea journey west from Spain to Asia. Eventually this fabled waterway would be called the Strait of Anián. Over the next two centuries the French and the British, starting from the eastern end of the North American continent, would expend considerable effort looking for this same route. They called it the Northwest Passage.

The first journey Cortés outfitted was led by Diego Hurtado de Mendoza. It sailed north but did not reach Baja California. Cortés entrusted the second expedition to a distant relative, Diego de Becerra, who was

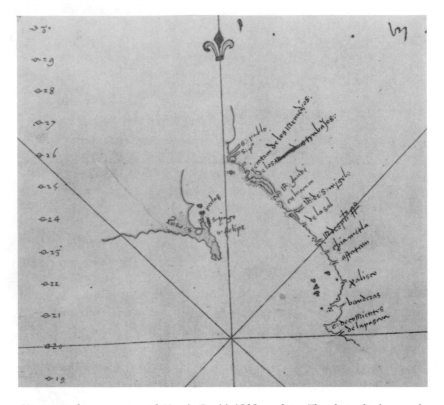

Map prepared in connection with Hernán Cortés's 1535 expedition. The relationship between the newly discovered region and the mainland is left unclear. A number of voyages were undertaken over the next decade to ascertain what this relationship actually was. The last letters of Cortés's name for the place where he landed, "Santa Cruz," are visible on the map, to the left of the newly found location. The inscription at the bottom, in the water, reads "San Felipe," which was the name Cortés gave to the hills he reconnoitered. Above it is "Santiago," the name he gave to the island just south of the bay (now Isla Cerralvo). The last inscription, referring to the two islands at the entrance of the bay, reads "perlas" (pearls) and reflects what the conquistador had begun to learn about the surrounding area and what he hoped the sources of his riches would be. Courtesy of the Honnold-Mudd Library Special Collections, Claremont, California.

killed in a mutiny led by the ship's pilot, Fortún Jiménez, shortly after they left port in 1533. Under Jiménez's direction, the vessel reached a bay on what was thought to be an island. It was the Baja California peninsula, which at the time contained roughly seventy thousand inhabitants. Jiménez and twenty crewmen were killed when they attempted to land. The survivors barely made it back to the mainland. They told Cortés that the natives they had seen had large collections of pearls. This news renewed

Cortés's zeal, and he himself led another expedition to the bay at which Jiménez had landed.

Cortés reached his destination with three ships on May 5, 1535. He established an incipient colony there, which he named Santa Cruz. It was located near present-day La Paz, on the gulf coast of Baja California. The colony was an ill-fated venture. The hostility of the indigenous peoples and the harshness of the terrain made survival difficult, and the colony was abandoned the next year. A permanent Spanish settlement in California would not be established for another hundred and fifty years. The following excerpt is from a legal document stating that Cortés had formally taken possession of California. It was subsequently composed and filed by the royal scribe Martín de Castro, who had landed in California with Cortés. Such ceremonies of "taking possession" were an important part of the way in which the Spanish arrived in a new land.

FROM THE EYEWITNESS TESTIMONY OF THE ROYAL SCRIBE MARTÍN DE CASTRO

Then the Marqués...stated that he takes and holds, in the name of His Majesty, the control and possession of the said land, newly discovered, where we are, and of all the others that extend from it and fall within those regions and demarcations, as a basis for continuing the discoveries, conquest, and settlement of those lands in the name of His Majesty. As a symbol and act of said possession, the said Marqués gave as a name to the said part of the bay the Port and Bay of Santa Cruz, and he walked back and forth across the said land from one part to the other and with his sword struck certain trees which were there and ordered the men who were there that they accept him as Governor for His Majesty of those said lands, and he made other acts of possession....All this took place peacefully and without any contradiction by any person that was or appeared to be in opposition.

1542
Ensenada and San Diego

Juan Rodríguez Cabrillo

The failure of the Santa Cruz establishment did not lessen interest in exploring the Pacific. Cortés himself sent out another expedition under the command of Francisco de Ulloa in 1539. Ulloa sailed along the west coast of the mainland, up the Gulf of California to the Colorado River, and then down the eastern coast of Baja California. He turned into the Pacific at the tip of the peninsula and headed more than halfway up the Baja California coast to the Isla de Cedros or slightly beyond.

In 1540 another sea expedition to the gulf took place, a maritime complement to Francisco Vásquez de Coronado's epic land exploration of northern Mexico and the southwestern United States. This expedition, headed by Hernando de Alarcón, entered the Colorado River.

It is not clear exactly when the peninsula off the western coast of the Mexican mainland actually began to be called California. Most likely, it occurred sometime in the late 1530s or early 1540s as a sardonic acknowledgment that the legends of rich islands to the west with which some indigenous people along the Pacific coast tantalized the Spaniards had little basis in fact.

When the Coronado expedition returned without finding any golden cities or other riches on their overland trek, which stretched into western Kansas, Viceroy Antonio de Mendoza decided to refocus his resources on a maritime effort toward developing the Asia trade. He entered into a partnership with Pedro de Alvarado, the brutal veteran of Cortés's conquest of Mexico who had sparked Cuauhtémoc's rebellion, to organize a naval exploration to the north and west. After Alvarado was killed during the Mixton War in 1541, Mendoza decided to send the bulk of the fleet across the Pacific to the Philippines under the command of one of his relatives, Ruy López de Villalobos. Three vessels were assigned to the northern expedition: the 200-ton galleon *San Salvador,* the 100-ton *Victoria,* and a launch named the *San Miguel.* Command fell to one of Alvarado's lieutenants, Juan Rodríguez Cabrillo, who was also the owner of the *San Salvador.*

A native of Seville, Rodríguez Cabrillo traveled to the New World at an early age and participated in the conquest of Cuba. He may, in fact, have been present at the massacre at Caonao that Las Casas described. He was in the expedition that the Cuban governor sent from Cuba to Mexico to re-call Cortés in 1520 and was one of the many soldiers who joined Cortés's army instead. He subsequently served in the army of Pedro de Alvarado that attacked and conquered the Quiché and Tzutuhil peoples of Guatemala and was rewarded for his service with Indian slaves and land. He became involved in trade with Peru, and this led him into shipbuilding. Eventually he was placed in charge of Alvarado's proposed fleet. It was in this capacity that he was appointed to command the expedition north in 1542.

The aims of the expedition were to seek rich cities or kingdoms and to discover any information which might help the trade with Asia, either by happening upon the Strait of Anián or by discovering if the Pacific coast of California itself might trend toward the west and the Spice Islands. The only record that we have of this voyage is a summary of a report prepared in 1543 by Juan León, a notary of the *audiencia* in Mexico City. León apparently had access to some written accounts of the voyage and he also took testimony from the survivors of the expedition after they had returned. León's actual report has not survived. The summary was most likely prepared in 1559 by Andrés de Urdaneta, an Augustinian friar who was himself a pilot. Virtually everything that we know of Rodríguez Cabrillo's expedition comes from this one source.

The expedition left the port of Navidad on June 27, 1542, and reached the California coast on July 3. They sailed along the western coast of Baja California for the next month. The Guaycura and Cochimí peoples, who had experienced the Spanish presence during the explorations of Ulloa in 1539, refused to meet with them. Although they saw signs of habitation at various points on the coast where they landed, they encountered none of the inhabitants, who were doubtless keeping them under close watch from the land. When the Spaniards surprised four Cochimí north of the Isla de Cedros, the Indians quickly fled.

The expedition continued north. On August 22 they landed at the modern site of San Quintín, where they formally took possession of the land in the name of the king. They named the place La Posesión. Continuing north they reached the large Bay of Ensenada and then arrived at a sheltered bay they called San Miguel (San Diego). After about a week there, Rodríguez Cabrillo headed north once more and passed two islands, which they named after their two ships. These two Channel Islands are now known as San Clemente and Santa Catalina. They entered San Pedro Bay, which they called the Bay of Smoke *(Bahía de los Fumos)* because of the burning chaparral. They spent a night anchored in Santa Monica Bay. Continuing northward they entered Chumash country and reported seeing an "Indian village close to the sea, with large houses like those of New Spain." The Chumash had so many canoes in evidence that they named one village Canoe Town *(Pueblo de las Canoas)*. Continuing through the Santa Barbara Channel, they reached Point Conception. Unable to turn the point because of very brisk north winds, they returned to the Santa Barbara Channel. Eventually they made their way north to the vicinity of San Francisco Bay, but the weather prevented them from sighting it. They did enter Monterey Bay and were so impressed by the snow on the coastal mountains that they named the range the Snowy Mountains *(Sierras Nevadas)*.* By this time it was late November, and the stormy and windy weather forced them to return again to the Channel Islands. On San Miguel Island, Rodríguez Cabrillo broke his leg, which soon became gangrenous. He handed over command of the expedition to his chief pilot, Bartolomé Ferrer, and died on January 3, 1543. Ferrer resumed the journey on January 19 and eventually reached a spot somewhat to the north of Point Arena, perhaps close to the present California-Oregon border. On February 28, with the ships buffeted by a severe storm, the sailors vowed to make a pilgrimage to Our Lady of Guadalupe if they survived. The wind did shift and they were able to head south. The ships limped back to Navidad on April 14, 1543.

The excerpt which follows from the expedition's diary begins on Friday, August 25, 1542, when the expedition was at La Posesión, about 175 miles south of San Diego. It continues with their stays among the Kumeyaay people at San Mateo (Ensenada) and San Miguel (San Diego). This excerpt therefore records the first Spanish exploration on both sides of the current border between Baja California and Alta California.

---

* This refers to the coastal mountain range between the San Francisco peninsula and Monterey Bay.

FROM THE OFFICIAL ACCOUNT OF THE RODRÍGUEZ CABRILLO EXPEDITION

The following Friday they went in search of water and came upon some Indians at the watering place. The Indians, who were very quiet, showed them a pool of water and a salt marsh. Using gestures, they indicated that they did not live there, but inland, and that there were many of them. That afternoon, five Indians came to the beach and they were taken back to the ships. The Indians appeared to be intelligent. As they boarded the ship the Indians motioned to the Spaniards and began counting the number of Spaniards there. The Indians indicated with gestures that they had seen men like the Spaniards before, men who had beards. The Spaniards had brought dogs with them as well as crossbows and swords. The Indians had smeared their bodies, thighs, and arms with a white pitch which had been applied to look like slashes from a knife. They resembled half-dressed men in slashed breeches and doublets.

They motioned that there were Spaniards in the vicinity, a five-day journey away. They also indicated that there were many Indians in the area and that they had much corn and many parrots. The Indians covered their bodies with deerskins, some of which were tanned in the way Mexicans tan the hides used for their sandals. They are large and healthy people. They carry their bows and arrows like the people of New Spain do, using flint arrowheads. They had said that the Spaniards had traveled inland, so the Captain gave them a letter to take back to the Spaniards.

They left the port of La Posesión on Sunday, August 27, and sailed on course until they discovered an uninhabited island two leagues from the mainland. They named the island San Agustín. It is probably two leagues in circumference and there is a good port there. They continued sailing windward along the coast with favorable light winds. The following Wednesday, August 30, they encountered strong northwest winds, which forced them to seek shelter on the island of San Agustín. They found signs of people on this island as well as two cow horns and very large trees the sea had tossed ashore. The trees looked like cypresses and were more than sixty feet long. They were so thick that two men could not reach around one of them. Some of the trees were cedars and there was a large amount of this timber. There is nothing else of value on this island, but it is a good port. They remained on the island until the following Sunday.

They left the island of San Agustín on Sunday, September 3, and sailed on course. The following Monday they anchored at the shore, seven leagues windward along a coast running north and south. They continued on course, sailing with fair weather and light winds along a coast running north and south until Thursday, September 7, when they anchored in a small bay formed by the land. Here the coast ceases to run in a north-south direction and turns to the northwest. There is a large valley at this small bay and the land is level at the coast. Inland there are high mountains and uneven terrain that appears to be good. The entire coast is rocky. The bottom of the ocean is level and not very deep, for at half a league from shore they cast anchor at ten fathoms. There is an abundance of plant life on top of the water here.

On Friday, September 8, they sailed windward with light winds and encountered crosscurrents here. They anchored at a point that forms a cape and affords good shelter from the west-northwest winds. They named it Cabo de San Martín.* It forms a tip from one end and the other. Some high mountains that come from behind end here, and other, smaller mountains begin. There is one large valley, yet there appear to be many others. The land is good. The port, located at 32½ degrees, north of the island of San Agustín, is unobstructed and shallow enough to take depth measurements.

While at Cabo de San Martín they went ashore for water. They found a small, freshwater lake and replenished their supply of water. Forty large, naked Indians came to the watering place with their bows and arrows and roasted maguey and fish to eat. They could not communicate with the Indians. They took possession of this place and remained at the cape until the following Monday.

On Monday, September 11, they left Cabo de San Martín and sailed about four leagues along the coast in a north-northeast to south-southwest direction. From there the coast turns to the northwest. The land is high and bare. The next day they sailed about six leagues along the coast in a northwest-southeast direction. The entire coast is rocky and clear. The following day, even though the weather was dreadful, they sailed about four leagues along the coast from northwest to southeast. The mountains are high and jagged. The following Thursday they sailed ahead about three leagues and cast anchor at a point that extends into the ocean and forms a cape on both sides. It is called Cabo de la Cruz and is located at 33 degrees. There is no water or wood and they did not find any sign of Indians.

---

* Now called Cape Colonet—about seventy miles south of Ensenada.

Cave painting of a pronghorn antelope, roughly ninety miles north of San Ignacio, composed by those who lived in California well before the arrival of Spanish explorers. From The Cave Paintings of Baja California *by Harry W. Crosby, courtesy of Sunbelt Publications and Harry W. Crosby.*

They left Cabo de la Cruz, but because the weather was miserable along the coast from north-northwest to south-southeast, the following Saturday they found themselves only two leagues from the cape. Along the shore they saw Indians in very small canoes. The land is very high, bare, and dry. All the land from California to this spot is sandy ground along the shore, but another type of land begins here. The soil is reddish in color and appears to be better.

On Sunday, September 17, they continued on their voyage. About six leagues from Cabo de la Cruz they found a good, protected port. In order to reach it they passed by a small island that is near the mainland. At this port they replenished their supply of water from a small rainwater lake. There are groves of trees similar to the silk-cotton tree, except the wood is hard. They found large, thick timbers tossed ashore by the sea. This port is called San Mateo and is located at 33⅓ degrees. They took possession of the port and remained there until the following Saturday. The land appears to be good, the terrain is even and high. There are large savannahs and the grass is like that in Spain. They saw herds of animals similar to cattle, which wandered in droves of one hundred or more. From their appearance, gait,

Two Pericú women, from southern Baja California, from Shelvocke's Voyage Round the World. *One is clothed in a type of birdskin, while the other wears deerskin. Courtesy of The Bancroft Library, University of California, Berkeley.*

and long wool the animals resembled Peruvian sheep. They have small horns about the length of a *jeme* and the thickness of a thumb. Their tail is broad and round and about a palm's length.

On Saturday, September 23, they left the port of San Mateo and sailed about eighteen leagues along the coast until the following Monday. They saw very beautiful valleys, groves of trees, and terrain that was both level and uneven. They did not see any Indians, however.

The following Tuesday and Wednesday they sailed about eight leagues along the coast and passed by three uninhabited islands located at 34 degrees, three leagues from the mainland, which they named Islas Desiertas.* One of the islands, about two leagues in circumference, is larger than the others, and provides shelter from the west winds. On this day they saw

* The Coronado Islands, about ten miles off the coast just south of the present international border.

what appeared to be smoke signals on land.* There are large valleys and the land appears to be good. In the interior there are high mountains.

The following Thursday they traveled about six leagues along a coast that ran in a north-northwest direction. They discovered a very good, protected port located at 34⅓ degrees which they named San Miguel. After casting anchor they went ashore and encountered some Indians. Three of them waited, but the others fled. They gave gifts to the three Indians, who gestured that people like the Spaniards had headed inland. The Indians appeared to be very scared. That night the Spaniards left the ships on a small rowboat and went ashore to fish. Some Indians were on shore and began to shoot arrows at them, wounding three men.

On another day, in the morning, they sailed further into the large port with the small boat. They had brought two boys with them who did not understand their attempts to communicate with gestures. They gave each boy a shirt and then sent them away.

The next morning three large Indian men came to the ship. With gestures they indicated that bearded men who were clothed liked us and armed like the men on the ships were wandering about the interior. They called the Christians *"Guacamal."* They gestured that the men were carrying crossbows and swords. They ran around as if on horseback and motioned with their right arm that the men were throwing lances. They indicated that they were afraid because the Spaniards were killing many Indians in the region. These people are large and healthy and they cover themselves with animal skins. While they were at this port, a violent storm came from the west-southwest and south-southwest directions, but because this was a good port they did not suffer at all. This was the first storm they had experienced. They remained at this port until the following Tuesday.

---

* They may have been witnessing a controlled burn, a widespread tool for land management among the native peoples of California. Burning increased the yield of acorns and seeds and enabled animals to forage for food more easily.

1602–1603
Monterey Bay

Sebastián Vizcaíno

Rodríguez Cabrillo and Ferrer found no cities of gold, no inland waterway, and no dramatic westward tilt to the land of California. Therefore,
attention gradually shifted to Asia, where the majority of ships from Alvarado's fleet had headed. López de Villalobos had in fact reached the
Philippine Islands and claimed them for Spain. This had little practical effect, since he died in Java and his crew returned to Europe as captives
aboard a Portuguese ship. However, Felipe II, casting about for additional
sources of revenue and tempted by the islands' possibilities as a coastal
staging area for the China trade, sent Miguel López de Legaspi to conquer
the islands. López de Legaspi brought them under Spanish rule in 1565.
By the early 1570s, the seat of government had been moved to Manila Bay,
which boasted one of the best harbors in Asia and was well situated to receive spices from the islands in the south of Asia and silk from China.
These items were heavily in demand in both New Spain and Europe, and a
flourishing trade across the Pacific quickly developed.

In 1566, Esteban Rodríguez and Andrés de Urdaneta established that
the best sea route from Manila to New Spain was through the northern
Pacific Ocean to California and then down the coast to Acapulco. With the
development of the trans-Pacific trade from Manila, California assumed
greater importance, as the first land to be reached after the long ocean
crossing. A ship was lost off Guam as early as 1568, another suffered the
same fate ten years later, and all through the period a number of other
ships were forced to return to Manila because of storms. The necessity of
finding a port somewhere in California where Manila ships could put in
for repairs and provisions after the hazardous Pacific crossing was a frequent subject of discussions in New Spain and Madrid.

These discussions became somewhat more intense after 1579, when the English captain Francis Drake appeared in the Pacific and attacked Spanish settlements and shipping. Drake's voyage intensified Spanish concern with protecting the Manila trade route.

Interest in the possibilities of California increased again in 1584 when Francisco Gali, returning from Asia, encountered a strong northerly current that he speculated could be caused by waters from the Strait of Anián entering the ocean. This report caused a stir, and Pedro de Unamuno was ordered to reconnoiter the California coast on his return voyage from Manila in 1587. He spent a few days at Morro Bay, but fog prevented his putting in anywhere else along the California coast and he sailed to Acapulco. Two days after he arrived there, the English pirate Thomas Cavendish captured the galleon *Santa Ana* off the coast of Cabo San Lucas. Cavendish looted the richly laden ship, ordered the passengers and crew off, and set the vessel afire. After he left, the crew was able to extinguish the blaze and sail the boat's charred skeleton to Acapulco. This episode added still more urgency to Spain's need to find out more about California.

In 1594 the Portuguese Sebastián Rodríguez Cermeño, who had been pilot on the *Santa Ana* and who had refused Cavendish's invitation to become his own pilot, was given command of a Manila-bound vessel and instructed to explore the California coast on the return voyage the following year. He anchored at a bay he named San Francisco (now called Drake's Bay), interacted with the Miwok people of the area, and explored the vicinity in the galleon's launch. When a storm destroyed the galleon and all of its cargo, Cermeño outfitted the launch and headed down the coast. He put in for food and water wherever he could and was fed by friendly residents of the coast. He thought he heard one group of Indians somewhat south of Monterey say "México, México" as they brought him some acorns to eat. He noted the entrances to Monterey and Santa Monica Bays and reached the Mexican mainland after a harrowing thirty-two-day voyage. The loss of the Manila cargo had made the voyage a financial failure. This led Viceroy Gaspar de Zúñiga y Acevedo, Conde de Monterrey, to suggest that the next voyage should originate in New Spain, with the sole purpose of charting the California coast.

Sebastián Vizcaíno was a logical choice to head the expedition. He was born in Extremadura, Spain, in 1548. In 1583, after serving in the Spanish invasion of Portugal in 1580, he came to New Spain. Three years later he went to Manila, where he established himself as a merchant. He returned

Exploration Voyages of
Rodríguez Cabrillo, Cermeño, and Vizcaíno

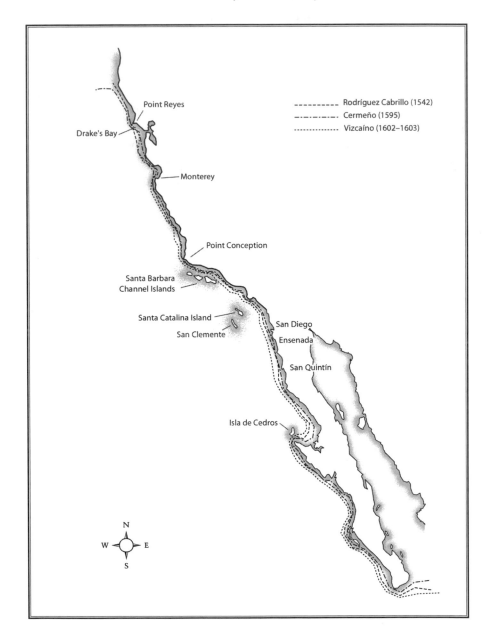

Point Reyes

Drake's Bay

Monterey

Point Conception

Santa Barbara
Channel Islands

Santa Catalina Island

San Clemente

San Diego

Ensenada

San Quintín

Isla de Cedros

Rodríguez Cabrillo (1542)
Cermeño (1595)
Vizcaíno (1602–1603)

N
W E
S

to Mexico in 1589 and began to seek licenses to engage in pearl fishing and mining in California. He traveled to California in 1596 and on September 3, near Cabo San Lucas, he established an outpost which he rather grandly named *Nueva Andalucía*. He then headed north to the place where Cortés had established the short-lived settlement of Santa Cruz in 1535. Because of the friendly reception he received from the Guaycura people, Vizcaíno named this site the Bay of Peace *(Bahía de la Paz)*. Such amity was not general, and Vizcaíno was attacked north of La Paz in the beginning of October. A series of storms inhibited further exploration and the colony was abandoned in November. Vizcaíno petitioned for permission to return to California. Instead, he was given command of the voyage to the north.

Viceroy Zúñiga's formal instructions to Vizcaíno charged him to proceed directly to Cabo San Lucas. Staying as close to the land as possible, he was to try to enter as many bays and rivers between there and Cape Mendocino as he could. He was also instructed not to go too far inland and to avoid antagonizing the Indians. Finally, he was told to mark the entry of the ports and to give them all saints' names. Although he was cautioned not to change established names, in fact he renamed a considerable number of places that had been visited before. Some historians argue that he simply disregarded his instructions; others state that he was not given accurate charts of previous voyages and that it was therefore almost impossible for him to recognize where he was in relation to earlier travelers.

Vizcaíno's expedition consisted of three large vessels and two hundred men. They left Acapulco on May 5, 1602, and headed north, reaching Cabo San Lucas on June 11. They spent time reconnoitering up the Pacific coast of Baja California until they arrived at San Diego on November 10. They reported that the port "must be the best to be found in all the South Sea... protected on all sides and having good anchorage." They landed on the 12th, and after Mass "a hundred Indians appeared on a hill with bows and arrows and with many feathers on their heads, yelling noisily at us." A delegation of two men and two women approached, and they accepted some gifts from the Spaniards. A few days later Vizcaíno and several others visited the Kumeyaay village close to where they had landed.

They left on November 20 and continued north. On Santa Catalina Island, Vizcaíno was shown a carved figure that he took to be an idol: "It resembled a demon, having two horns, no head, a dog at its feet, and many children painted all around it." The Indians seemed to be telling him not to approach it, but he disregarded those wishes and "made a cross, and placed the name of Jesus on the head of the demon, telling the Indians that this was good and from heaven but that the idol was the devil." How much the residents understood or agreed with this theological discourse is not clear. Then the ships passed through the Santa Barbara Channel. As had been the case with Rodríguez Cabrillo sixty years earlier, they found themselves being escorted by Chumash in canoes, "rowing so swiftly that they seemed to fly."

Continuing up the coast they arrived on December 16 at a harbor which appeared to them to offer shelter. Vizcaíno named the bay after the viceroy, whose title was Count of Monterrey. From Monterey, Vizcaíno decided to send one of the boats back to New Spain with the sick. That vessel departed on December 29 and Vizcaíno continued northward. He bestowed the name Point Reyes *(Punta de los Reyes)* on the promontory that bounded the body of water Cermeño had named San Francisco Bay, but they did not stop there to look for the *San Agustín,* for fear of losing a favorable wind. They reached Cape Mendocino on January 12 and there, with his orders fulfilled and many of his crew sick, Vizcaíno turned back. He arrived back at Acapulco on March 21, 1603. He later traveled to Japan, in 1611, as part of an attempt to open commercial relations between that land and Spain. He spent the rest of his life in New Spain and died toward the end of the 1620s.

The first excerpt below is from the journal of the expedition. The author is not specifically named, but it is usually referred to as Vizcaíno's diary. The second excerpt is from a letter he wrote to King Felipe III on May 23, 1603, in which he describes Monterey Bay in greater detail.

FROM THE DIARY OF THE VIZCAÍNO EXPEDITION

We arrived at the port of Monterey on December 16 [1602] at seven in the evening. The next day the General ordered *Alférez* Alarcón to go ashore with the necessary materials to build a shelter where Mass could be celebrated, to see if there was any water, and determine what the land was like. He found freshwater, and near the shore he found a large live-oak tree, where he built the protective shelter to celebrate Mass. Then the General, *Comisario,* Admiral, Captains, *Alférez,* and the rest of the men went ashore. After Mass was celebrated and the skies had lifted, for it had been very foggy, we found ourselves in the best port that one could hope for. Besides being sheltered from all winds, it has many pine trees suitable for masts and lateen yards and many live oaks and white oaks. There is an abundance of water and everything is near the shore. The land is fertile and the climate and soil are like that of Castile. There are many game animals, such as stags that look like young bulls, deer, bison, very large bears, rabbits, hares, and many others. There are also many birds, such as geese, partridges, quail, cranes, ducks, vultures, and many other species of birds that I will not mention so as not to be burdensome.

The land is very populated. An endless number of Indians appeared at different times and many of them came to our camp. They seem to be gentle and peaceful people. Using gestures, they said there are many settlements inland. Besides fish and shellfish, the foods these Indians eat on a daily basis are acorns and another nut that is thicker than a chestnut. This is what we were able to understand from them...

The weather was extremely cold and the men worked very hard gathering wood and storing water for our voyage to Cape Mendocino. The cold was so intense that when dawn broke on Wednesday, New Year's Day, 1603, all the mountains were covered with snow. They looked like the volcano in Mexico. The well from which we had been taking water was frozen to the thickness of a palm's width. The earthen jugs filled with water had been left outside during the night, and they were so frozen that even if they rolled them around not a drop leaked out. Seeing that we were in a difficult situation, everyone pulled together to help, including the General, who helped carry the jugs and also did other tasks. Even though he was ill, Captain Peguero came to our aid with the help of *Alférez* Alarcón and the pilots, who worked without stopping to rest. On Friday night, January 3, we were ready.

On this day, the General, accompanied by the *Comisario* and ten archers, headed inland in a southeast direction. They had heard there was a large river that emptied into the ocean, as well as another fine port. They also wanted to get a closer look at the terrain, the animals, and the people.

The General had traveled about three leagues when he discovered another fine port, into which emptied a large river. This river flowed from a range of high, snow-covered mountains with large pine trees, black and white poplars, and willows. There was a large riverbank, along which could be found livestock as large as cows, even though they looked like stags. However, their hide was different, it was wooly and dragged on the ground. Each horn was more than three yards long. They tried to kill one but did not wait long enough. They did not find any people, because they

Manila Bay, the hub of Spain's commerce in Asia, as sketched by Fernando Brambila at the end of the eighteenth century. Courtesy of the Museo Naval, Madrid (MS 1724-6).

were living in the interior on account of the cold. The General sent *Alférez* Juan Francisco and four soldiers to a *ranchería* to see what was there. They found that it was deserted and returned. As soon as the General and the rest of the men returned to the Admiral's ship at nightfall, we raised the anchor and set sail at midnight, aided by a land breeze.

A LETTER FROM VIZCAÍNO TO KING FELIPE III OF SPAIN

Mexico, May 23, 1603

Among the most important ports that I discovered was one located at 37 degrees latitude, which I named Monterey. I wrote to Your Majesty from there on September 28 of this year, stating that this port is all that one could hope for. It is a convenient stopping place along the coast for ships that are coming from the Philippines. The port is sheltered from all winds, and along the shore there are many pine trees that could be used for ship masts of any size desired. There are also live oaks and white oaks, rosemary, vines, and roses of Alexandria. There are many rabbits, hares, partridges, and other genera and species found in Spain, especially in the Sierra Morena, as well as different types of birds. It is a pleasant place. The area is very populated by people whom I considered to be meek, gentle, quiet, and quite amenable to conversion to Catholicism and to becoming subjects of Your Majesty. The Indians have strong bodies and white faces. The women are somewhat smaller and have nice features.

Their clothing is made from sealskins. They tan and dress the hides better than how it is done in Castile. Seals are found in abundance. They have a large amount of flax and hemp, from which they make fishing lines and nets for catching rabbits and hares. Their boats are made of pine and are very well constructed. They go out into the ocean with fourteen oarsmen and they can sail with ease even during a strong storm.

I traveled more than eight hundred leagues along the coast and kept a record of all the people I encountered. The coast is populated by an endless number of Indians, who said there were large settlements in the interior. They invited me to go there with them. They were very friendly to us, and when I showed them the image of Our Lady they were drawn to it and wanted to join us. They were very attentive during the sacrifice of the Mass. They make use of various idols, as I already have reported to the Viceroy. They are very knowledgeable about silver and gold and said that these metals can be found in the interior.

1620
The First Plan for Missions in California

Antonio de Ascención

Antonio de Ascención, a native of Salamanca, studied mathematics and navigation at the university there and at the College for Pilots in Seville as well. He was ordained a Carmelite priest in 1590 and came to New Spain seven years later. A group of reformed Carmelites had arrived in Mexico City in 1585, establishing religious houses there and in other urban centers of New Spain. A group of Carmelites then petitioned to go as missionaries to the Philippines, which led to three of them being sent on the Vizcaíno voyage, though its object was to travel not to the Philippines, but the California coast. Ascención's nautical education earned him a place on the expedition. Because these three Carmelites were on the voyage, the bay directly below Monterey was named Carmel.

After his return from the expedition, Ascención become a purveyor of what one historian has called "early California propaganda." He argued in the face of official disinterest that California ought to be colonized and settled because of its potential wealth and strategic location. He urged that the colonization effort begin at the tip of the peninsula, at San Bernabé, the area now known as Cabo San Lucas. The institution which Ascención urged as the core of the colonization effort was the mission, then coming into prominence in the northern frontier of New Spain. He urged that men from his own religious community be put in charge of the California missions, thus demonstrating the eagerness of the religious orders to engage in this sort of missionary activity. Ascención made many such recommendations after his return from the Vizcaíno expedition. The excerpt below is taken from a report he penned in 1620.

Ascención's proposal, the first for the establishment of missions in California, identified a number of issues that would become crucial when missions were created in Baja California in 1697 and Alta California in 1769. He clearly recognized that establishing a mission was a process involving military as well as religious actors. He insisted that the process would work only if the military personnel were themselves deeply religious. He further insisted that the final determination regarding treatment of the native peoples ought to rest with the religious personnel. Both of these desires were unlikely to be realized among the rough, hardened, and part-time troops of the frontier. Ascención also believed that even if military force were necessary to establish a foothold among the native peoples, they would then spontaneously see the superiority of the Spanish way of life—especially its agriculture—and voluntarily Hispanicize themselves. Such results were to remain out of reach for most California missionaries.

FROM A REPORT BY ANTONIO DE ASCENCIÓN

The entire realm of the Californias can be pacified and settled. Its natives can be brought into the union of the faithful of Our Holy Mother the Roman Catholic Church and converted to our Holy Catholic Faith through the preaching of the Holy Gospel. However, for this to be accomplished at a moderate expense to His Majesty, what should be sent, ordered, and provided are as follows.

Two small ships of two hundred tons should be made ready and equipped at the port of Acapulco, as well as a frigate with boats and skiffs that can be of service to the ships. They should be abundantly furnished with stores and munitions for war, supplies, rigging, sails, and anything else that may be necessary to settle in the lands of infidels and gentiles [unconverted Indians]. While these things are being provided and made ready, as many as two hundred soldiers who are also good sailors should be recruited in Mexico. Bear in mind that they should be veteran soldiers skilled in arms and seamanship. This will permit anyone to be called upon at any time to perform whatever task is necessary. Make sure that they are good and honorable men, so that there will be peace, unity, and camaraderie on the journey by sea and land. A sufficient number of men with these qualities can be found very easily in Mexico if His Majesty raises their pay to compensate them for the two roles they will be called upon to perform. They should receive their pay and provisions promptly and in a timely fashion.

The duty of recruiting these people should be assigned to one or two Captains who are good Christians and God-fearing men as well as persons of merit who have served His Majesty faithfully on other occasions, such as at war on land or sea. It should be their responsibility to appoint the officers of their company. They must be satisfied that these men will perform their duties in a careful, Christian manner. They also should be experienced men who know how to fulfill the responsibilities entrusted to them, because the order and good discipline of the soldiers depends on these men. This expedition should be entrusted to a courageous and talented person who has had previous experience with similar duties and is accustomed to them. He thus will know how to command with love and authority and will treat each person as an individual. And, be certain that this is a God-fearing person, one who keeps his own counsel, and someone who is not only zealous in his service to His Majesty but also in matters relating to the conversion of souls. A person with these qualities can be appointed General of the armada. Everyone, from Captains to soldiers, will be under his command and will obey him at all times and follow his orders.

The General, Captains, soldiers, and all others who go on this expedition must be given express orders to hold themselves in strict obedience to and comply with the religious who are accompanying them. Without their orders, counsel, or recommendations, no act of war or any other grievance shall be committed against the heathen Indians, even though they might provoke it. In this way, everything can proceed in a peaceful, Christian manner with love and tranquility, which is the method to be used in pacifying this realm and preaching the Holy Gospel. The preparations and expenses are intended for this purpose. If it is not done in this manner, all efforts will fail, and time and money will be wasted. In New Spain, experience has shown many times that in conquests and attempts to settle new lands, the Lord our God has more often been offended than He has been served.

The religious who should go on this expedition are the Discalced Carmelites. They are the ones to whom His Majesty has entrusted the conversion, religious instruction, and teaching of the Indians in this realm of the Californias. On this first expedition there will be a total of six religious, namely, four priests and two lay friars. In the name of His Majesty, the Superiors of this religious order will be asked to identify and appoint

LANGUAGE GROUPS OF BAJA CALIFORNIA

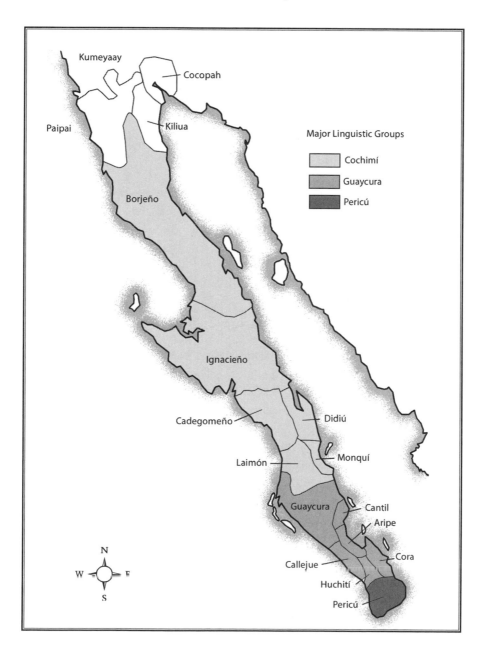

Kumeyaay

Cocopah

Paipai

Kiliua

Major Linguistic Groups

Cochimí
Guaycura
Pericú

Borjeño

Ignacieño

Cadegomeño

Didiú

Laimón

Monquí

N

W   E

S

Guaycura

Cantil

Aripe

Callejue

Cora

Huchití

Pericú

people for this voyage. These people must meet the requirements of the enterprise, that is, be holy, loving, learned, and congenial men who not only know how to advise, guide, and direct souls, but can also resolve, with sound Catholic doctrine, any problems that might arise.

By observing the indults and benefits granted by the Supreme Pontiffs in favor of the new conversions in order to increase their numbers, these holy men, with their piety, modesty, simplicity, and religious graciousness, will succeed in winning the affection and hearts of the General, Captains, and all the other soldiers. In this manner they can lead them along the holy path of virtue. They can persuade and admonish them in a loving manner to confess their sins and receive the Holy Sacrament of the Eucharist with all possible devotion and resolution and to offer their body and soul in service to His Divine Majesty, asking that He grant them safe passage on their journey. By focusing on this matter with the proper spirit and devotion, these religious will win the hearts and spirit of everyone and they will be able to maintain control to ensure that there is peace, love, and unity among everyone. If by chance there should be some conflict among the men, they could reconcile them with discretion. In this way the grudges, annoyances, and hostilities, as well as mutinies, revolts, and insubordination which usually occur in similar enterprises can be avoided.

The religious will be provided with everything necessary for their journey, such as materials necessary for celebrating Mass and administering the Sacraments, books, vestments, and other items that can be given as gifts to anyone who might be sick. Also, at His Majesty's expense, a number of small items should be placed on board. These items could include Flemish trinkets such as colored glass beads, imitation garnets, small bells, small looking glasses, knives, inexpensive scissors, Parisian Jew's harps, and some articles of clothing. These items should be divided among the religious and the soldiers so that, wherever they land or choose to settle, they can distribute these pleasing gifts to the infidels they meet. With signs of love and good will, in the name of His Majesty, the gentile Indians will eventually feel love and affection for the Christians. They will also recognize that the Christians have come to their lands not to take away what the Indians have, but to give them what they have brought, and to save their souls. This is a matter of great importance, for it will enable the Indians to become calm, humane, and peaceful. Then they will obey the Spaniards without opposition or repugnance and receive willingly those who have come to preach the Holy Gospel and the mysteries of our Holy Catholic

Faith. Moreover, the Indians will be grateful, and as recompense or payment for what they have been given, they will assist us by sharing what they consider to be of value from their land, namely food, as has happened to us.

With this preparation, the soldiers and religious can set sail on the ships once they have been made ready. However, absolutely no women may board ship or travel with the men, to avoid offending God and to prevent quarrels among them. Even if there are no favorable winds, the ocean currents that head in the direction of the tip of California will enable the ship to land within a month's time, at most, at the Bay of San Bernabé, which is at the Cape of San Lucas, at the tip of California. This is the most suitable place for the first settlement.

After landing at the Bay of San Bernabé, try at once to set up camp at the most suitable position and place. It should be designed so that the houses protect one another. The first thing to build is a church, so that the priests can celebrate Mass there each day. If the General, Captains, and soldiers go to confession and receive the Sacrament when they arrive in this realm, this will be a very good and sacred way to properly initiate the enterprise. With the help and grace of Our Redeemer Jesus Christ, they will succeed in their endeavors to pacify the realm and convert its inhabitants to our Holy Catholic Faith.

The stronghold that will serve as a castle, watchtower, and defense against adverse situations should be built at a strong, commanding spot at a high elevation. From this place, one can be assured of safe passage to the sea. This would be a very advantageous way of sending for and receiving reinforcements by sea, in case the need should arise. The Portuguese have commonly done this where they have established themselves in India. This strategy or precautionary measure has proven to be very beneficial to them. This castle stronghold should be stocked with artillery that will be brought for this purpose, together with other defenses that usually are constructed at similar fortifications. Weapons and supplies will be kept there. There should be a watchtower above the castle from which a guard can monitor all comings and goings at the camp, because in the land of the infidels, even though the Indians may appear to be friendly and men of peace, one must not trust them too much. First, one must live among the Indians with great circumspection, vigilance, precaution, and astuteness, but also with a kind and loving watchfulness. They should be treated with love and affection and rewarded with gifts that were brought at His Majesty's expense to attract and win them over. A trading house should be built so that the Indians can gather there to trade and barter with the Spaniards and among themselves. This will greatly facilitate the communication between the Indians and our people, and love and friendship will develop.

From this place they can send the ships, frigate, and other boats to the Christian settlement of Culiacán, to the islands of Mazatlán, or to the *pueblo* of La Navidad to bring back everything that is needed for settling the land, as well as food, cows, sheep, goats, mares, and hogs. The animals can be transported alive from one point to the other in two to four days at the most, because the sea is about fifty leagues wide and the waters are safe and calm. These animals can be raised on this land because it is fertile and suitable for this purpose. They will multiply easily. Wheat and corn can be grown and vineyards and orchards can be planted so that food does not have to be transported from afar. The Indians can be taught how to grow the food and will want to learn when they see how they will benefit.

In addition to what has been said above, the Spaniards will be able to establish fisheries for pearls and other fish because there is an abundance of both here. The pearls and fish can be sent to New Spain so they can be sold in Mexico. Very fine salt works can be established and salt can be extracted from nearby mines. Once these operations have been put into place, with peace, love, and the goodwill of the natives, the religious can focus their attention on their ministry and begin the conversion of these Indians in the manner that seems most appropriate to them. With great prudence and gentleness they will be able to sow the seeds of the new Christian Church that will be planted there. It would be wise to bring Indian musicians from New Spain. With their trumpets and other instruments the divine services can be celebrated with devotion and ceremony. They also can teach the Indians to sing and play the instruments. It would be wise to select some of the brightest Indians. Then, from among this group, the most docile, clever, and talented young men and boys can be chosen. They should be taught the Christian doctrine and how to read from the Spanish primers. By knowing how to read they will also learn the Spanish language. They should also learn how to write, sing, and play all types of musical instruments. A strong building is built on a firm foundation. If care is taken at the very beginning, the end results will be positive.

It is very easy for the children to learn our language in this manner. When they are older they can teach the people they know, their children, and their families. Thus, in a few years everyone will know the Spanish language. This will be of great benefit because then there will be no lack of ministers to teach and guide the Indians along the path to heaven and salvation. They then can proceed to establish other Christian settlements and convert the Indians who are scattered in the mountains, drawing them out with love, kindness, and gentleness. Care should be taken not to send the Christian soldiers out in too many directions, so as not to decrease the number of soldiers at the garrison and thus weaken it. For, if the Indians are instigated by the devil to revolt or rebel against the Spaniards, someone must be there to fight them off and keep them at bay. If their actions warrant it, they should be punished for their boldness.

California as an Island

California's location along the Manila trade route heightened Spain's desire to try to keep information about the harbors, coves, rivers, and currents of this remote but potentially important region under tight control—for California might also be a tempting location for pirates and privateers planning to attack the Manila galleons. The result was that much basic information about California remained unknown to the world at large from the fifteenth to the seventeenth centuries. Was California connected to the mainland, or was it actually an island, as Rodríguez de Montalvo had presented it? This question puzzled cartographers in Europe and elsewhere for quite some time.

1540s

The early confusion over the geography of California is nicely illustrated in this map from the 1540s for Alonso de Santa Cruz's *Islario de Todas las Islas del Mundo (Atlas of the World's Islands)*. California is shown both as a peninsula and as an island. The inscription below the island reads *"isla que descubrió el Marqués del Valle"* (island that Cortés discovered). The top inscription reads *"la sept cibdad"* (the seventh city), a reference to the legendary cities sought during the northern expeditions of Francisco Vásquez de Coronado. Further reference to this expedition is contained in the middle inscription, *"Tierra que envió a descubrir don Antonio de Mendoza"* (land which Antonio de Mendoza sent people out to discover). Mendoza was the viceroy who dispatched both Vásquez de Coronado and Rodríguez Cabrillo.

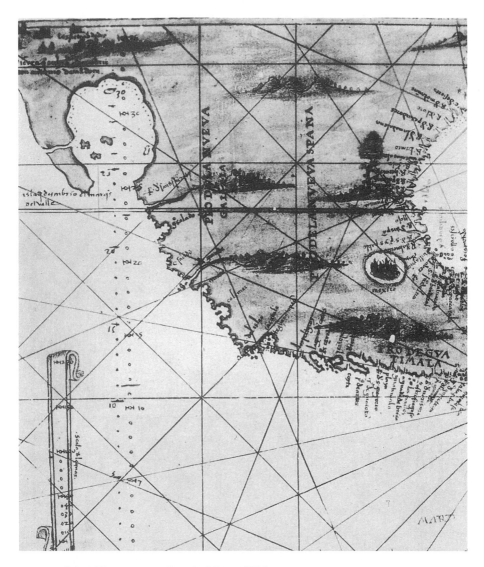

Courtesy of the Biblioteca Nacional, Madrid (BMN 2791).

1541

This map is dated 1541, although it was not published until 1770, in Francisco Antonio Lorenzana's *Historia de Nueva España*. It was the work of Domingo del Castillo, a pilot in the 1540 expedition of Hernando de Alarcón. The map makes use of the discoveries of Ulloa as well as those of Alarcón, and it clearly shows what the Alarcón voyage demonstrated: that the land off the western coast of the mainland was a peninsula. Some authorities doubt that the word "California," which appears on the southern part of the peninsula, was actually on the 1541 map.

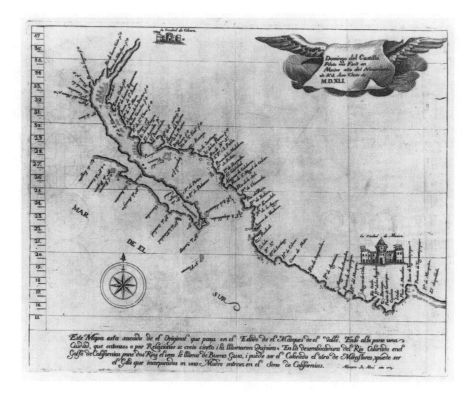

Courtesy of The Bancroft Library, University of California, Berkeley.

1587

This 1587 map from the atlas of Abraham Ortelius sums up the consensus about California at the end of the sixteenth century, that it was a peninsula connected to the mainland. Somewhere to the north, past some snow-covered mountains, was the legendary region of Quivira. Even farther north was the region of Anián, and perhaps even farther north, the Strait of Anián offered a water route through North America. The tip of California is called "Cabo California" (Cape California)

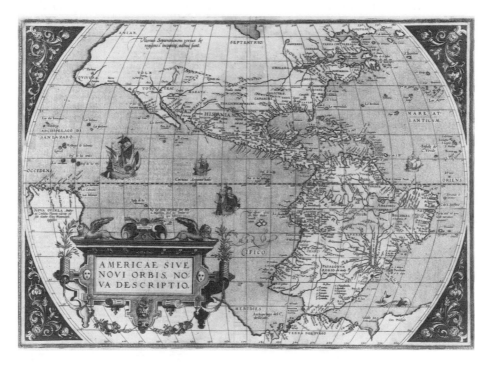

Courtesy of The Bancroft Library, University of California, Berkeley.

1625

The consensus that California was a peninsula connected to the North American mainland unraveled in the seventeenth century, largely because of the writings of Fr. Antonio de la Ascención, one of the three priests on the Vizcaíno expedition. A trained cosmographer, Ascención came to the conclusion that California was an island. Ascención's views were widely publicized when Juan de Torquemada included large excerpts from his 1610 report on the voyage in his monumental work *Monarquía Indiana*. This view, from someone who was a member of one of the most sustained explorations of the Pacific coast of North America made up to that time, had a great impact.

This map, published in England in 1625, is a good example of Ascención's influence: California is drawn as an island off the coast. The names shown on the map are fairly faithful to those given by Vizcaíno, from Cabo San Lucas in the south to Cabo Mendocino in the north. The Puerto de Señor Francisco Draco (Port of Sir Francis Drake) is fit in between Point Reyes and Cape Mendocino.

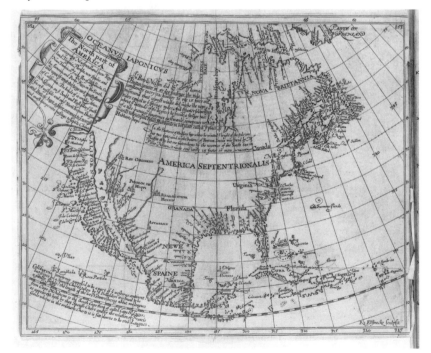

Courtesy of The Bancroft Library, University of California, Berkeley.

1638

Published in Amsterdam in 1638, this map demonstrates the confusion about California that persisted after Ascención's theory was publicized: here it seems that California is separated from the mainland, yet also connected to it.

Courtesy of Museo Naval, Madrid.

1656

This French map was published in 1656. The picture of California depicted here, a bean-shaped island off the coast of North America, remained the established view of European mapmakers for another forty years.

Courtesy of The Bancroft Library, University of California, Berkeley.

1701

In 1683 a group of Spaniards led by Admiral Isidro de Atondo y Antillón, including Jesuit missionary Eusebio Kino, landed on the coast of Baja California to establish a permanent settlement there. The effort failed and was abandoned in 1685. Kino returned to Sonora but remained interested in opening a missionary field in California. Since the sea effort had failed, he decided to investigate the possibility of opening a land route to California. To that end, he undertook a series of travels to the north. His desire for a land route grew even greater after a permanent Jesuit mission was established in Loreto in 1697. When he reached the Gila River and then the Colorado River, he knew for certain that California was not separate from the mainland. The map he drew in 1701, *"Passo por Tierra a la California"* (Land Passage to California), eventually settled the question of California's geographic nature.

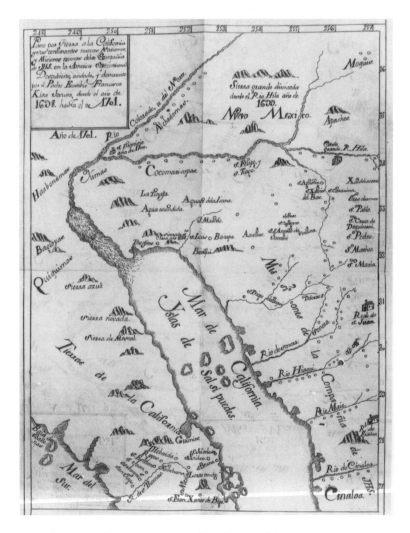

Courtesy of The Bancroft Library, University of California, Berkeley.

1726

This map, which appeared in Shelvocke's *Voyage Round the World,* was published in 1726 but held to the "traditional" view that California was an island. This notion did not entirely disappear until late in the eighteenth century.

Courtesy of The Bancroft Library, University of California, Berkeley.

1767

But the irony was that California was, in many respects, an island, and it remained one throughout the Spanish and Mexican periods. The Jesuit missions on the peninsula were generally supplied not by the land route Kino had discovered, but by sea, across the Gulf of California. This map, prepared by José Antonio de Alzate y Ramírez in 1767, offers a graphic illustration of California's isolation. As one gets closer to the mouth of the Colorado River, the number of Spanish settlements declines dramatically, and large sections of the map are simply filled with Indian names like "Land of the Pimas" or "Yumas." Around the compass in the extreme upper left is written "The nations which live in this part of California are unknown." The map clearly illustrates the fashion in which the Sonoran desert and its inhabitants blocked Spanish expansion.

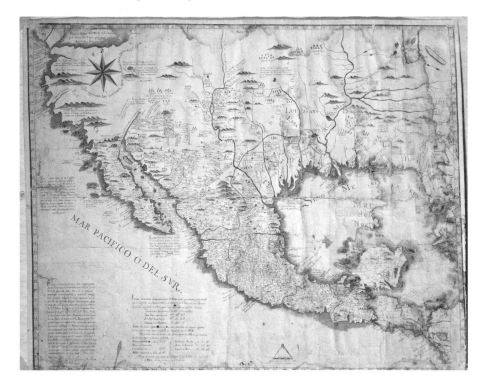

Courtesy of the Museo Naval, Madrid (7-A-9).

When the California frontier was pushed north a scant two years after the Alzate map was created, the same pattern continued. Despite periodic attempts to open a land route from the mainland of New Spain and Mexico to Alta California, the province continued to be supplied from the sea. This was especially the case after the Quechán rebellion in 1781 made the Colorado River area unsafe for Spanish and Mexican travelers. Supplies and mail continued to arrive by sea, when they arrived at all. In the 1790s, foreigners began arriving in California with their stores of assorted goods. They all came by sea, whether from England, the United States, South America, or Russia. The products that California exported—sea otter skins, cattle hides, tallow—all left by sea. And when invaders came to plunder the country in 1818 or to take possession of it in the 1840s, they arrived in warships. In many ways, eighteenth and nineteenth-century California under Spain and Mexico, might as well have been the island depicted off the shore of the mainland in the drawings of the seventeenth-century geographers.

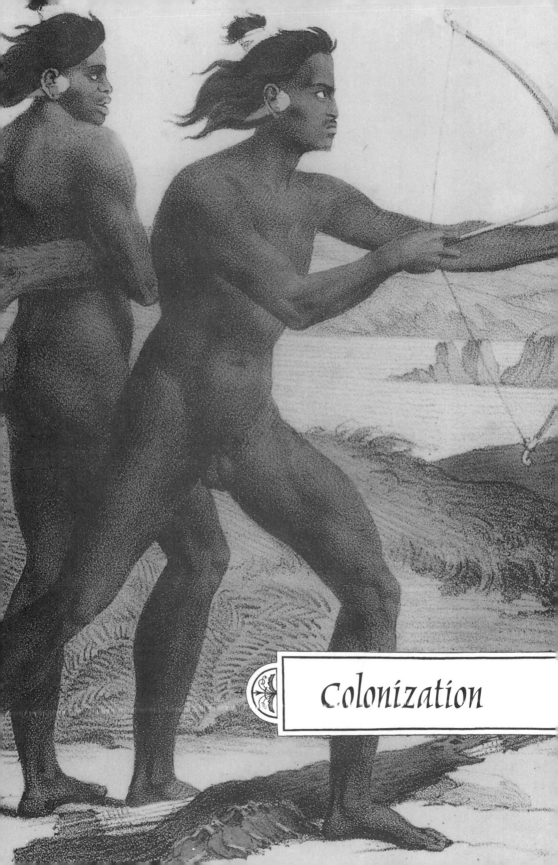

Colonization

Colonization

The Spanish expansion in the New World lasted over three centuries and involved millions of people. It also involved the transfer and adaptation of any number of cultural expressions and institutions in such diverse areas as language, art, religion, and government. Three such interrelated institutions—the town *(pueblo),* the *presidio,* and the mission—played important roles in the development of California, with the sometimes conflicting goals of townspeople, soldiers, and missionaries framing the settlement of New Spain.

First, the town. The Iberian municipal tradition stretched back to the days of the Roman empire and was strengthened during the *reconquista.* The *conquistadores* brought this strong urban tradition with them across the sea. By 1575 the Spanish had established over two hundred distinct municipalities in the Americas. As much as possible, they were laid out around a central plaza with land for houses *(solares)* distributed in a fashion that was meant to be more or less symmetrical and orderly. Plots of arable land for agriculture *(suertes)* outside the urban area were also distributed.

Cities and towns were founded in New Spain from the beginning of the conquest. As the frontier went north, towns were often in the vanguard. Guadalajara was established in 1532, Zacatecas in 1546, Durango in 1563, and Santa Fe in 1610. By the time Spanish development of the Californias was well under way in the eighteenth century, towns were a normal part of frontier life, and settlements existed as far north and west as present-day Arizona, at Tucson, Tubac, and Yuma. Although a considerable number of Spaniards also lived in and around the *presidios,* the towns were a crucial component of frontier life.

These *pueblos* were, above all, frontier towns. The northwest of Mexico, then as now, could be a harsh and difficult land. A number of these towns had originated as mining camps, but minerals did not exist either in abundance or in locations that made them easily extractable. And the Sonora desert was not the most hospitable place to grow crops or raise cattle. Composed of former soldiers, miners, colonists, Indians, and their families, the frontier towns were more often gritty and dusty pockets than the stable and secure foundations of Spanish prosperity they were intended to be. But they still pointed to the ultimate aim of colonization, which was to transform the land and its people into productive parts of the Spanish empire; for all their imperfection, they were nonetheless symbols of the society into which New Spain was designed to evolve.

Second, the *presidio*. The word, meaning a garrison or a fortified establishment, entered the Spanish language from Latin in the sixteenth century, and it referred to Spain's forts in Morocco. Both the word and the institution it described were quickly put to use in northern New Spain. After silver was discovered in the late 1540s in Zacatecas, three hundred miles northwest of Mexico City, a rush of miners descended on the region. The indigenous Chichimecs were much less sedentary than the more urban and clustered people around Tenochtitlán had been, and they quickly learned to raid the convoys that carried supplies north and silver south. The government established a series of *presidios* along the caravan routes to guard the miners and settlers and also to serve as bases for mobile expeditions against the Indians. During the Chichimec War, which lasted until the end of the century, over thirty *presidios* were founded. They continued to be placed in strategic locations during the seventeenth century as well. A series of Indian revolts along the frontier, sparked by the great Pueblo Revolt of 1680, resulted in another round of *presidio* building, and by 1700 a series of fortifications dotted the map all the way to El Paso and Santa Fe in the far north.

As some *presidios* were founded, others withered, and coordination among them left much to be desired. An inspection tour by Pedro de Rivera of twenty-three of the existing twenty-four *presidios* in the 1720s (Loreto in California was the only one he did not visit) led to the promulgation of a report in 1729. Four *presidios* were suppressed as a cost-saving measure, and the others were reorganized in an attempt to make them function more efficiently. The regulations had little effect. Over the next few decades, additional *presidios* were founded to support the expansion into Texas and to combat the revolts of the Seri people and others in Sonora. At the same time, other *presidios* were allowed to languish and die. The Marqués de Rubí undertook another inspection tour of the *presidios* in 1766, and his recommendations were embodied in a new set of regulations issued in 1772.

None of the *presidios* were grandly constructed. Mostly made of adobe, they consisted of enclosed quadrangles sometimes complemented with towers at one or more of the corners. Equipment was often in short supply, and most of the *presidios* were manned at less than full strength for much of the colonial period: soldiers were often part-time soldiers and part-time colonists, while the commanders tended to be ranchers or merchants who sought to use their positions to further their commercial endeavors. Many *presidios* later became the nuclei of extensive civilian settlements.

Finally, the mission. The origins of what would become the mission system in California stretch back to the very beginnings of the Spanish presence in the New World. In the 1490s, the Spanish adapted the Castilian institution of the *encomienda* to define their relationships with the peoples of the islands they were claiming as their own. In *reconquista* Spain, Christian warriors were given jurisdiction over the people who lived in the areas they had taken from the Moors. In return for protection, the people were "entrusted" (the Spanish word is *encomendar*) to the knight and had to give over a certain amount of their labor to him. In the Caribbean, the Indians were forced to labor for the *conquistador*. The labor—often searching for gold—was generally extremely brutal. As we have seen, criticism of this system was soon voiced, and the critiques made their way to the court. In 1512, Spain promulgated the Laws of Burgos, which attempted to rein in the worst abuses of the *encomienda* system, but the system survived and took root in Mexico after the conquest by Cortés. Protests against it continued. In 1542, Spain promulgated the New Laws, which abolished Indian slavery, prohibited the holding of *encomiendas* by public institutions and by the clergy, forbade new *encomiendas,* and provided that already existing *encomiendas* could not be passed from one generation to the next. This last provision would have destroyed the system in one generation if it had gone into effect, but massive resistance on the part of the *encomenderos* in America prevented that. The crown drastically weakened the New Laws and allowed the *encomienda* arrangements to continue. The institution was gradually modified and lost its central place in the continuing Spanish conquest, but it was not formally abolished until the eighteenth century.

As a reaction to the brutality and persistence of the *encomienda,* Las Casas and other religious advocated establishing separate areas for the Indians in which they could be protected from the worst abuses of the system. In 1516, Las Casas pushed through the court a proposal which would have abolished the *encomiendas* and set up autonomous Indian villages, each governed by an indigenous *cacique* assisted by a priest and a secular administrator. This proposal was never implemented, but the idea of gathering the Indians into their own villages and separating them from the Spanish population persisted. In the Caribbean, in fact, "congregating" the Indians into towns *(congregaciones)* or "reducing" them into compact population centers *(reducciones)* also appealed to the secular authorities, since the catastrophic population decline was making it more difficult to organize the scattered survivors into work parties. Clustering the Indians into tight settlements was also consistent with Iberian municipal tradition, so the move appealed to royal authorities who were charged with Hispanicizing the indigenous peoples.

In central Mexico, many of the Indians already lived in more or less compact communities. As each locality was brought under Spanish control, a church was constructed, sometimes on an earlier indigenous ceremonial site. These sixteenth-century churches combined European elements with spaces for outdoor ceremonies that also accommodated indigenous religious traditions.

A tug of war for control often ensued among the clergy, especially the members of the religious orders, such as the Franciscans, Dominicans, and Augustinians, and the *conquistadores.* As the conquest expanded, religious authorities took more of the lead, trying to congregate the more scattered Indians on their own and create a religious space separate from the area of the *encomienda* and *repartimiento.* The Mexican bishops called for such steps in 1537, and as the effort took hold to create such *congregaciones* or *reducciones,* they became essential to Spanish expansion in New Spain.

These efforts became even more important as the frontier moved northward, where subduing the indigenous peoples proved to be no easy task. As early as 1541, widespread resistance, the Mixton War, broke out near Guadalajara. North of Zacatecas, the situation was even more unsettled, as the mobile Chichimecs proved adept at avoiding stationary Spanish positions and inflicting considerable damage on both the military and the silver trade. By the 1580s, it was clear that a new strategy had to be adopted. At the same time, the religious orders were anxious to evangelize the northern Indians. Thus the government adopted the policy of establishing new *reducciones,* which along the northen frontier were more frequently termed missions, in order to bring the semi-nomadic Indians of the north under Spanish sway and introduce them into the Spanish way of life. The Franciscans and the newly arrived Jesuits were both quite active in the north. The Franciscans evangelized extensively as far north as New Mexico, while the Jesuits worked in the northwest.

The large atrium that was a characteristic feature of the monastery churches of central Mexico gradually expanded as the missions moved farther north, until the atrium was turned into a mission cloister, which sometimes entirely enclosed and embraced a large complex of shops, storehouses, dormitories, and offices, as well as a church. The missions also controlled extensive lands, where the Indians were supposed to be taught agriculture and ranching. As the mission system spread, however, the religious authorities found themselves mirroring, to some extent, the secular *encomenderos* whose excesses had partially led to the establishment of the missions in the first place: the missions relied of necessity on force or the threat of force. The indigenous laborers at the missions were generally treated much less brutally than indigenous laborers in *encomiendas, haciendas,* and mining enterprises elsewhere in New Spain. Their labor, however, was still coerced.

There never was one unified and standard mission system in the Americas. Missions evolved over time, and regional variations abounded. In some cases large numbers of Indians lived at the mission site, but in other instances it proved impossible or unfeasible to gather large numbers into a stable community near the church complex. In some localities, like seventeenth-century New Mexico, Indians whose lifestyle was already sedentary were congregated at the missions, but it proved much more difficult to entice nomadic groups in the same region to settle there.

The colonial government that established the missions intended for them to be temporary institutions. The Indians were to learn the Spanish religion, language, and way of life, and then after a period of ten years or so, the church was to be turned into a regular parish (a process known as "secularization"). The mission lands were to be divided among the Indians, who would then take their places in society as Spanish and Catholic farmers and ranchers.

As Enlightenment ideas gradually spread from Europe and Bourbon Spain into eighteenth-century New Spain, the missions began to be viewed with a more critical eye. Their frank paternalism did not sit well with new ideas about liberty and equality. The slow pace of secularization led to criticism that the missionaries were keeping the Indians too separated from the Spanish settlers and in a kind of perpetual servitude in order to preserve their own privileges, riches, and land. By the mid-eighteenth century, the mission system in the north was already on the defensive in significant parts of New Spain. Some missions were beginning to accommodate themselves to the rising criticism by allowing greater contact between the mission Indians and the settlers.

The colonization of the Californias was heir to most of these developments and trends. Since colonization proceeded from the south, the first area to experience a permanent Spanish presence was the Baja California peninsula. Understanding the Spanish experience in Baja California is crucial to understanding the colonial history of Alta California; the history of the southern peninsula presaged in quite significant ways the history of its northern extension. In Baja California the interplay between the military and religious leaders, and between the *presidios* and the missions, set much of the tone in the early years. The founding expedition was a joint military and religious enterprise, as were explorations of the frontier. And serious tensions arose between these two groups over issues of control of the territory's development, and especially over control of the Indians. The same sorts of issues would mark the development of Alta California from the very first years of its founding.

1697

A Permanent Spanish Presence in California

Juan María de Salvatierra

Plans to develop Monterey as a haven for the Manila galleons never materialized. The very year Vizcaíno returned from his voyage, the Conde de Monterrey was transferred from his post as viceroy of New Spain and made viceroy of Peru. His successor, Juan de Mendoza y Luna, Marqués de Montesclaros, opposed the development of a new port in California. Mendoza argued that what the Manila fleet needed was not a haven on the California coast, which they reached near the end of their journeys, but a port in the middle of the Pacific Ocean. He suggested that Spain develop such a port in two as yet undiscovered islands, Rica de Oro and Rica de Plata, that were thought to exist in the northern Pacific. His argument carried the day, and the plans for Monterey were shelved. As it turned out, the Manila trade flourished without a California port.

In the seventeenth century, vessels would simply change course to the south when they were approaching Cape Mendocino and continue on to Mexico. After such a long voyage, few captains were in the mood to linger and explore along the coast. In addition, Manila ships usually arrived along the California coast in November or December, when the weather was likely to be unsettled, and this too discouraged delay. Hence, knowledge about this part of the coast did not appreciably increase after Vizcaíno's journey. For most of the seventeenth century, in fact, California was treated as an island, off the beaten track. If it were going to be developed, it would have to be developed in a different sort of way than had been the case on the mainland. After the voyage of Vizcaíno, the viceroys tried to spark the development of California by encouraging private enterprise. Pearls were the only form of wealth known to exist there, so the viceroys attempted to encourage colonization by granting licenses to develop pearl fisheries. Nicolás de Cardona, the nephew of a Spanish entrepreneur, made the first voyage for this purpose in 1615, but he was unsuccessful in establishing a Spanish presence on the gulf coast. Another attempt was made by Francisco de Ortega in 1632, but his vessel was wrecked near La Paz and he was forced to abandon the attempt. Unsuccessful attempts were made through the 1640s and 1660s.

As it turned out, California was not colonized until it began to receive attention as a potential mission territory in the northern frontier. By the late 1670s the Jesuits had established missions in Sinaloa and were moving northwest into Sonora. They had received a generous gift for their northern missions in 1671, and that started them thinking about moving across the gulf into California. In the late 1670s the governor of Sinaloa, Isidro de Atondo y Antillón, decided that a joint commercial-missionary expedition might succeed in establishing a presence in California. He found willing partners in the Jesuits. Eusebio Francisco Kino, a recently arrived Italian Jesuit, was assigned to accompany the expedition.

Kino was born in the Tirol in 1645. His interests in science and mathematics led him to consider service in China, where Jesuits with such expertise had gained considerable influence in court circles. But he eventually was sent to New Spain, where he arrived in 1681. He soon turned his energy to writing a book about a comet that had appeared the year before, and then he was chosen by his superiors to be one of three men to accompany Atondo y Antillón.

The expedition landed at La Paz in 1683. They quickly became embroiled in a controversy between the Pericúes and Guaycuras and were forced to leave. So they sailed north to San Bruno, where they established a mission. But problems with supplies and crops forced them to abandon it in 1685. During the brief existence of the San Bruno outpost, Kino was sent to Sonora to beg for provisions from the Jesuit missions among the Yaqui people there. This experience convinced him that a network of prosperous Sonora missions could support the California enterprise. He also believed that some of Atondo y Antillón's bellicose acts, such as firing a cannon into a group of Indians at La Paz, had hindered the missionary effort. Kino therefore asked to be assigned to the Sonora missions, where he commenced establishing new missions among the Pima people.

Kino found an ally in another Italian Jesuit, Juan María de Salvatierra. He had spent thirteen years working in the missions among the Tarahumara people. In the early 1690s, the Jesuit superior of New Spain ordered Salvatierra to undertake an inspection of the northwest, and in the course of this assignment he spent many days with Kino, who converted him to the California cause. Salvatierra spent the next few years in administrative positions at the Jesuit colleges at Guadalajara and Tepotzotlán, just outside of Mexico City. From there he lobbied for the California project and it received official approval in 1697. The arrangement stipulated that no public funds were to be used for the project; it was to be financed entirely by the Jesuits. They raised money to start an endowment, called the "Pious Fund," to support the California missions. In return they received an extraordinary amount of power over the peninsula and over the soldiers who were to accompany them. The Jesuits paid the soldiers' salaries, and they were granted the power to choose and dismiss military officers and civil authorities.

Since Kino was deemed too valuable in Sonora to be allowed to go to California himself, another Italian Jesuit with experience in the Tarahumara missions, Francisco María Piccolo, was assigned to accompany Salvatierra. The advance party consisted of Salvatierra, nine men, and a collection of nonnative livestock, whose introduction would tremendously alter the ecology of California. They landed on October 19, 1697, about one hundred and fifty miles north of where Cortés had attempted to establish himself almost two centuries earlier. They were the only Europeans in a land that contained at least fifty thousand inhabitants. They quickly moved to establish a rudimentary fort and church. They referred to the site for the first few years as simply a "fortified place" *(real)*. The inhabitants called the location Conchó, and the Spanish named it Loreto, after a city in Italy where devotion to the Virgin Mary flourished.

The excerpt below is from a letter written by Juan María de Salvatierra soon after the establishment of the compound at Loreto. This part of the letter strikes many notes that would be sounded again and again in the development of both Californias, especially the wariness with which the Spanish and the indigenous peoples approached each other as they negotiated along the whole spectrum between amity and force.

FROM A LETTER BY JUAN MARÍA DE SALVATIERRA

The next day, early in the morning of Friday, October 18, we reached the bay shaped like a half-moon. As we viewed the area from the ship, it all appeared green. The bay must be about four or five miles across. I went ashore with the Captain.... Quite a few Indians with their wives and little children came to receive us. They knelt down to kiss the crucifix and the Virgin. Their settlement was situated about half a harquebus shot from the sea. We went with the natives to see the water holes. We discovered them in a small valley flanked on the south side by a *mesa* (all flat and more than a *pica* in height); a high plateau on the west extends for the distance of a harquebus shot to the sea.

The site seemed ideal to me, since we could easily entrench ourselves. The north side is protected by a high hill. The lowland of the valley where we were forms a small lake of somewhat brackish water but suitable for the animals. Beyond the valley, on the other side, it spreads out into an extensive area covered by reeds, from which arrows shot at us would lose their force before reaching us, whereas our firearms are effective for that distance. We can also graze our herds within sight.

At the time of our coming, the entire mesa was covered with mesquites, furnishing us with good shade. While resting under their shade at siesta time, Captain Romero, Ensign Tortolero, and I measured the trunk of one and found that it was more than three *varas* across. This amazed the Captain, inasmuch as he had made a certified statement in Acapulco informing the Treasurer, Don Pedro Gil de la Sierpe, that he had seen no wood in California, and now he beheld these mesquites extending for miles! Since it was already late and time to eat and take possession of the land, I returned to the ship, most satisfied with what I had seen....

On Saturday, October 19, I went ashore with Captain Juan Antonio Romero and took official possession of the land. We worked until we had cleared part of the mesa where the first settlement was to be established. All the animals were unloaded. Since it was all so new to the Indians, many of them—women mingled with men—gathered at the beach.

An amusing incident occurred which made all the Indians laugh and us also. The men are stark naked; the women wear a skirt from the waist to below the knees. This dress is tightly woven from reeds and other grasses, a material which makes a rustling sound much like that of maize kernels when shaken. Inasmuch as the natives had never seen pigs before, they were

Juan María de Salvatierra posed for this portrait about a year before he left for California. Courtesy of The Bancroft Library, University of California, Berkeley.

very curious about them, especially on finding them so tame that they could come right up to them without being harmed. When the women also came up close to see the pigs, the animals, on hearing the rustling of the skirts which sounded like corn grains being rattled, ran after the women, grunting the whole time. The faster the women ran, the louder was the rustling of their skirts, as though calling the pigs with greater insistence. The amusing incident lasted until real corn was brought to quiet the animals.

We were kept busy the next four days unloading clothing, maize, and flour. The natives gave us a hand in all our tasks; and there were three or four Indians who carried the third of a mule pack from the beach to the *Real de Nuestra Señora de Loreto.* We gave a bit a maize to all who carried anything from the beach, which is about two harquebus shots away and can be clearly seen from the settlement. But as the beach extends along part of the reedy area which is on the other side of the canyon where the clothes were unloaded and is not at the exit of the canyon itself, quite likely some of the carriers pilfered objects as they made their way through the reeds.

Nearly all the natives, however, were very honest....Inasmuch as the Indians have a ravenous appetite for maize, the devil tempted them on that score. On seeing us so few, they thought that out of fear we would give them all the maize they wanted. Ever since landing, I have been boiling a pot about an *almud* at a time and distributing it cooked to them. Those who do anything at all for us receive a handful of maize before getting their *pozole;* the rest get a few handfuls of the grain.

I go about with the notebooks of Father Juan Bautista Copart* and discuss with the natives some part of our Holy Faith. All the good is to be attributed to that missionary, who worked out such an excellent catechism. The natives are amazed, and I am happy to see that the word of God sinks into their soul as the rain does into the earth.

Realizing the danger we were in because the Indians coveted the supply of maize, and seeing how they inched closer to the grain sacks, we piled up some thorny mesquite branches all along the surrounding trench. So fierce was their angry reaction that we feared they would begin their attack on us at once. It was to no avail that we assured them that they were good people and that only one or another was a thief.

On seeing the imminent danger we were in, I asked Captain Romero to leave us for our defense one of the two mortars he had brought on the galliot.

---

* A Jesuit who had been on the Atondo y Antillón expedition.

It was immediately unloaded, the Captain and the sailors genuinely helping us. We chopped off a thick mesquite tree and placed it four paces from the trench. Holes were chiseled into the log and the mortar was firmly fixed to it. The mortar can easily be swung around to every side, dominating the entire *real,* all the vale, the entire mesa, and even all the seashore that can be seen from the settlement. The few of us here spent the entire night ever on the alert....The enemy did not immediately carry out the initial threat. That night, October 23, a downpour drenched us who were so sure it never rains in California....

The galliot set out on Sunday, October 26. Many of the Indians, seeing us so few and alone with the maize supply, were tempted to force us to give them all they wanted and demanded. They wished to stay all day with us, eating the whole time without helping us at all. They were so reluctant to withdraw from the *real* at nightfall that it was special grace of the Blessed Virgin that they did not immediately attack us. They refused to obey us and retire when night came on. In the midst of this almost daily danger of their beginning hostilities against us, especially during the first few days when we were alone, it was fortunate for us that some of the natives dared to come forward in our defense and to check the audacity of the rest....

We had another downpour, which soaked all the ground so that the water began flowing in abundance. Inasmuch as we are without shelter, we were hard put to keep our things dry and the trench intact. And since each of us tried to find some bit of protection in the midst of these downpours, we would repeat laughingly these words, "It never rains in California; it never rains in California."

1716
A Foray into the Wilderness

Francisco María Piccolo

After establishing the mission and *presidio* at Loreto, the Jesuits founded a number of other missions in the general vicinity, either along the gulf coast (San Juan Bautista de Ligüí and Santa Rosalía de Mulegé, both in 1705) or in the mountains to the west (San Francisco Javier Viggé Biaundó in 1699 and San José de Comondú in 1708). The general direction of their efforts was to the north and west of Loreto. This led them to organize further expeditions to the north in search of additional sites.

One such expedition was undertaken in 1716. It was led by Francisco María Piccolo. A native of Palermo in Sicily, he had arrived in Baja California shortly after Salvatierra and founded Mission San Francisco Javier Viggé Biaundó. He was serving at Santa Rosalía de Mulegé when he undertook this journey among the Cochimí people. This joint religious-military expedition started from Mulegé and ended up at a place later called San Ignacio, about sixty-five miles to the northwest, where a mission would be founded in 1725. Piccolo's account reveals the close observation and keen assessment of evangelical possibilities which often characterized the missionary travel accounts, not only in Baja California but in the New World as a whole.

From a Report by Francisco María Piccolo

We set out on the evening of November 13 from Santa Rosalía de Mulegé with six mules heavily laden, two of my servant boys, and three soldiers—José Altamirano, Juan de Villalobos, and Sebastián Martínez. That day we advanced only a few leagues.

On November 19 we set out, accompanied by these settlements and many other Indians who were constantly joining us. They kept giving us the

Baja California Missions

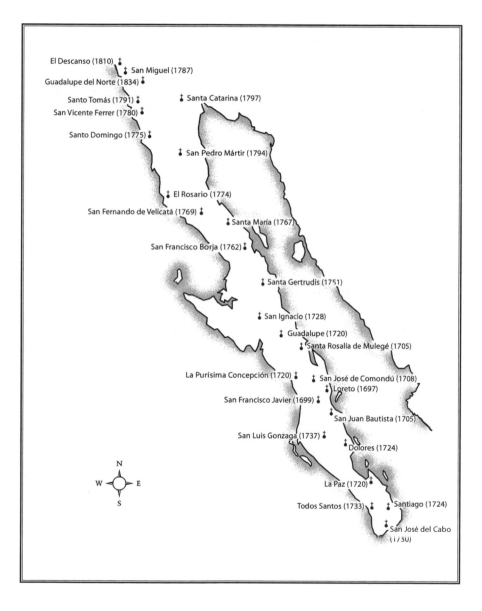

El Descanso (1810)
San Miguel (1787)
Guadalupe del Norte (1834)
Santo Tomás (1791)
San Vicente Ferrer (1780)
Santa Catarina (1797)
Santo Domingo (1775)
San Pedro Mártir (1794)
El Rosario (1774)
San Fernando de Velicatá (1769)
Santa María (1767)
San Francisco Borja (1762)
Santa Gertrudis (1751)
San Ignacio (1728)
Guadalupe (1720)
Santa Rosalía de Mulegé (1705)
La Purísima Concepción (1720)
San José de Comondú (1708)
Loreto (1697)
San Francisco Javier (1699)
San Juan Bautista (1705)
San Luis Gonzaga (1737)
Dolores (1724)

N
W — E
S

La Paz (1720)
Todos Santos (1733)
Santiago (1724)
San José del Cabo (1730)

pitahayas they plucked along the trail. They moved the branches, stones, and thorns blocking our path so that we could advance more easily. These expressions of friendship increased our assurance. The optimism of all was great. In fact, God had to check it, as will be seen.

As we entered the valley, where the river takes its rise, and the animals saw all that lush green, they rushed headlong into those extensive reed-lands, driven not so much by thirst as by the Demon of the North, who, it would seem, had permission from the Lord to hurl three of the animals into the lake. In all truth they [demons] would gladly have cast all of them into it. Two of them were horses which were loose, and the other was an untamed stallion carrying a chest of hardtack for our journey and other provisions: sugar, chocolate, and all my effects for the trip. What I felt most deeply was the damage done to the image of Our Lady pierced by arrows.

I stayed alone on the banks to watch over the other restless animals. All the Indians plunged into the lake without knowing what to do. But as they were unacquainted with such animals—they had never seen mules or horses—confusion reigned supreme.

The animals were stuck too deep in the mud in the lake to get out. One of the soldiers, Sebastián Martínez, in order to save the life of the stallion

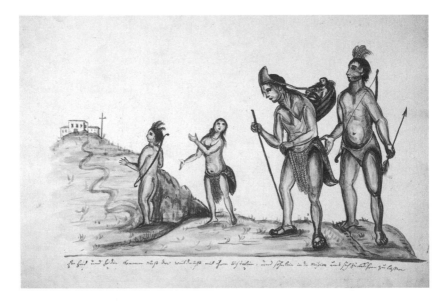

"Out of the wilderness a heathen and his wife are coming with their daughters and son to the mission to be converted," by Fr. Ignacio Tirsch, S.J. Courtesy of the National Library of the Czech Republic.

which had sunk with the chests to the bottom of the lake three times, dove in fully dressed. With a knife he cut the rope holding the chests and also the packsaddle's cinch. Lightened in this way, the poor stallion, half-dead, was hauled to the shore. My other horse, thrashing about vigorously and valiantly, tired out and, not finding any way to get out, died before they got around to rescuing it.

On opening the chests, we found all was hopelessly drenched. Only the chocolate, because the water was so cold, could be dried and eaten. The image of Our Lady was not badly damaged. I love Her dearly; She has accompanied me from Spain. She helped out much in the Tarahumara expeditions. But nowhere did She suffer as much as in California: arrow wounds and shipwrecks.

The Indians were saddened. The women were deeply moved at seeing in what condition the things taken out of the chests were found. Nonetheless, they did not hesitate to devour the dead horse, inasmuch as the San Marcos Indians with me knew that horse meat is very good.

Thus far Lucifer had his way. But his joy was quickly changed to profound disappointment when he saw that we were stopping at the very spot where these wretched Indians were wont to meet for their diabolic and deceitful races, wizardry, and all their evil actions. He realized that in the hills crossed by the trails (called *hidalgur* in their language) of their infernal priests, people from everywhere came, not for their dances and evil deeds, but to adore Jesus Christ and revere His Holy Cross.

After all the excitement of the disaster abated, the captain of Nabademil sent messengers to summon those Indians who did not know about our arrival. Here was the reason: although word had spread that I was to come, they did not believe it. The poor naked natives from eighteen settlements, despite the intense cold and with the *pitahayas* in season, immediately obeyed the summons and reached the place on the second day. They marveled in amazement at the chapel, or rather leafy arbor, built in honor of the Lord, where they were wont to erect such in honor of Satan.

In my first talks I explained to them why I had come. As I finished speaking in the chapel, the Indian chieftains arrived to inform me that they did not bring their wives because they simply could not believe what they saw, nor were told why they were being summoned, but that they were satisfied and delighted. I conferred the canes of captains on the most important men of the settlements and gave each a blanket and a loincloth.

Three settlements along the river consecrated to San Vicente Ferrer came with some of their women, who brought me their little children to be baptized. Among them were twelve, age three, four, and five years old, who, without ever having seen me before, hugged me. They moved me even more deeply when, after baptism, they were the first to come to Mass, which they attended so devoutly that they seemed to be Christians of long standing. Fifty infants were baptized on this occasion. Of the three sick children baptized in August by my servant José, when the natives took him to see the river, two had died immediately. When I asked about the third, they told me that he too had died. Thus these three are already in heaven praying for their parents.

On the feast of the Presentation of Our Lady in the Temple, Mass was sung here with all the solemnity possible in an arbor. We also began a Novena to Our Lady, chanting Her Litanies daily, a devotion most pleasing to these natives. After the singing of the Mass and Litanies, an old man, a great shaman as I was informed, exclaimed aloud in utter amazement, "All this is very good!"

In the midst of all my happiness, I was tortured by no small concern: I had so little corn for so many people. We had no more mules to carry it. We had brought only four sacks of corn and a *fanega* of wheat to plant. Two pots of *pozole* were regularly prepared for the noon meal; and for the evening meal, two of *atole*. For two settlements this was a small daily ration. And because the purpose of my journey was to see the river and the lands watered by it, tasks not to be accomplished in one day, I gave out all I had brought with me.

These multitudes of Indians stayed with me for four days; after that, they began to leave, both because of the intense cold and the *pitahayas* that attracted them. I think that the main motive was their hunger.

I asked them for the names of all their settlements. And, as they saw that I was jotting them down, they insisted that I also record the others from which no natives had come here, but nonetheless belong to this jurisdiction. Noticing that I was amazed at the large number of settlements—fifty in all—they told me that further to the north the sum total of natives was much greater.

1734
Indian Rebellion

Sigismundo Taraval

By 1734, the Jesuits had founded thirteen missions in Baja California. Most of them were to the north of Loreto among the Guaycura and Cochimí peoples. However, starting in 1720, they had begun to spread into the south as well. This brought them into their first contact with the southern Guaycuras and the Pericúes. One of the Jesuits' aims was to establish bases in localities that might serve the Manila galleons on their way home. By 1734, they had placed five establishments in the southern region: at La Paz (1720), Dolores (1721), Santiago (1724), San José del Cabo (1730), and Todos Santos (1733).

This rapid expansion occasioned resistance among the residents of the south, and in 1734 open rebellion broke out. Among the Pericúes, chiefs and shamans were accustomed to having more than one wife. The Jesuits, in an attempt to break the power of these groups, vigorously attacked the institution of polygamy. In response, the indigenous leadership organized a fierce resistance. In September the Indians attacked La Paz and killed the one soldier who was there to guard the mission. In early October, two priests were killed at the missions of San José del Cabo and Santiago. Sigismundo Taraval, a priest at Todos Santos, was forced by his soldiers to leave the mission before the Indians attacked and he took refuge on an island off La Paz. All the southern missions except Dolores were destroyed.

Taraval made his way to Mission Dolores, where the captain of the Loreto *presidio,* Esteban Rodríguez, arrived to organize a military response. Rodríguez, with about twenty soldiers and a hundred Indian allies from the northern missions, journeyed by water to La Paz, where they took up positions in the ruined mission. During November the mission was twice attacked by the rebellious Indians.

What follows is Fr. Taraval's account of the defense of La Paz. His story involves not only the military defense of the ruined mission but also the Spanish effort to determine the loyalties of the various native peoples. Without the active assistance of a large number of Indian allies, the Spanish military action would not have succeeded. The Spanish were especially concerned about the Callejues, a Guaycura group whom Taraval believed to be generally friendly but about whom the military leadership had considerable doubts. Besides the Pericúes, the Spanish were also concerned about the Aripes, Coras, and Huchitíes, all parts of the larger Guaycura group. Reading the intentions of native groups always involved considerable uncertainty among both missionaries and soldiers. The Pericúes in the following selection, who feigned peace as they approached La Paz to attack it, were playing on this uncertainty.

FROM *Indian Uprising in Lower California*

A
t La Paz we found the gates, house, and church all burned down and in ruins. We found a room of a house in better condition, although roofless and extremely filthy....

After the Captain indicated the place these men were to occupy and guard, inasmuch as there was now adequate protection at camp, he decided to put forth every effort to find the Callejues. As a result, the next day he sent all the archers he had over to Cerralvo, a place opposite the island that bears this same name and whose mountains were frequently the haunt of the Callejues, furnishing them with what supplies they required for the journey. After having been gone three days and having searched diligently, they returned. What information they brought back with them was distinctly favorable: they had met the natives, who were all peaceful; they had scoured the mountains and had found no rebels; had searched the neighboring country and found none; but after they had started toward La Paz and had nearly arrived, four of them had been captured and taken to the captain [headman] of the *ranchería* of the Huchitíes and his two sons. At this point it is essential to supply some information about this *ranchería,* its activities, and its captain, in order to explain what follows.

If the mission of La Paz proved the thorn in the sides of the missionary fathers, the *ranchería* of the Huchitíes was undoubtedly the crucible. This had always been the refuge of culprits, the annoyance of the missions, and the terror of all the Indians. Within past years they had killed off half of the *ranchería* of the Pericú nation, had annihilated nearly the entire *ranchería* of the *pueblo* of Todos Santos during the early days of its foundation, and in short, they did what they pleased, relying on their numbers and bravery and the fact that all feared them. These Indians would come one day and say that they wished to become Christians; on the next they would remark that they did not care to do so. Again they would come, even if out of self-interest to have their children baptized. Then weeks, months, and even a year would elapse before they would reappear. At another time they would come and make various promises but leave after dark without fulfilling them....

On the thirteenth, the Callejues arrived in a body. It was well that they avoided the main road, for had they been traveling on it, they would have met the rebels. The latter, however, came before dawn on the following day to launch an attack. By the time the sentinels were aware of them, they were already close at hand; for in this region, because of its crevices, *arroyos,* and mountains, it is impossible to see for more than a short distance. While our guards were shouting "To arms, to arms!" and while every one of us was arming, the enemy had time enough to occupy the ravines and ditches, which had not been fortified, inasmuch as this would have required the labor of many months. From this point they began to send over a shower of arrows, receiving in reply heavy firing. Yet as they were all under cover, they suffered only slight injury. From here the enemy continued for a time to discharge arrow after arrow; then, realizing that little or no damage was being inflicted, they approached, intending to surround the camp; however, the heavy fire that greeted them prevented this plan from materializing. Then all withdrew to cover, continuing all this time to discharge arrows. Under cover of this shelter they hurled taunts and threats at the soldiers, daring them to leave the stockade, saying they would leave there at dawn, which was just breaking, and that they were expecting a large number of reinforcements, who would wipe us out. Nonetheless, since we did not cease firing, they did not dare launch an assault, especially when they saw one of their men who ventured forth hit by an arrow shot by one of our Indian allies, and by several shots from our garrison. Knowing that day was about to break, that the ones they were expecting had failed to arrive, and that during daylight it would not be so easy to escape the bullets as they had the arrows, they fled. Our men would have followed them had they not feared to fall into an ambush or encounter in the mountains with the reinforcements expected by the enemy. As a result of the fight, seven of our men were found to have been slightly wounded, among them our Captain, who had been hit in two places. This was a small number, considering the many arrows falling....

Those who had previously suspected the Callejues were not appeased even after they had every reason, proof, and cause to be so. Now that the natives were within the fortifications, they were even more restive. Nor was this the worst misfortune; for they went around instilling in their comrades this same suspicion, doing this so frequently and talking so constantly that there was scarcely a man who was not on his guard. For three days this continued, and during this time apprehension caused more misery than had previously been aroused by actual danger. On the fourth day two soldiers were sent, or rather came, to talk to me early in the morning; they were men who had not been distrustful before the last uprising, nor should have been, since they had experienced, as had I, the natives' loyalty. Notwithstanding, they arrived, considerably frightened, to warn me of what might happen. "Father," they cried, "we are lost! The Callejues are deserting; they are plotting with the Aripes, Coras, and Pericúes; they have already sent out a call to arms to the Huchitíes; and they are now trying to win over to their ranks the Indian allies of Mission Dolores. When the rebels approach they will no doubt give their war cry and kill everyone inside the fortifications. They are fully aware that our force inside the fort is small and that when our men are killed it will be the end of all this, and then, Father, good-bye to the Californias for many years to come. All the soldiers are aware of this; this is what all the Indians are saying; this is also confirmed by Luis Gonzaga, interpreter and captain of the Indians at Mission Dolores." Never have I been more deeply stirred than I was by these eloquent words! I replied that I fully realized the gravity of the warning, that I was acquainted with everything, and would speak instantly to the Captain.

Without delay, I asked the Captain what the news was. He replied that he had been advised of what I have just referred to; but that, after searching diligently, he had been unable to find on what it was based. The soldiers, however, could not be so persuaded, and all or nearly all, convinced that some lurking danger threatened, assembled and urged the Captain to withdraw. They explained how this could be accomplished, stressing, in order to convince him, the many hidden perils to which he was exposing his men. The Captain needed every ounce of his courage, valor, and willpower to stand firm and not yield, for not only did he have to face what the rebels might perpetrate, but also the slight support he might expect from his own

Depictions of the deaths of Fr. Nicolás Tamaral at San José del Cabo and Fr. Lorenzo Carranco at Santiago in 1734. Drawn in Madrid to illustrate the narration of these events, these appeared in the first written history of California, Miguel Venegas's Noticias de California, *published in Madrid in 1757. Courtesy of the Bancroft Library, University of California, Berkeley.*

troops. I did everything in my power to quiet them, as well as to uncover any untruths, but to no purpose....

Then, on the morning of the twenty-ninth, many natives were seen to be approaching; many of them appeared on each side of our camp. They were divided into two groups. All made signs to indicate that they did not wish to fight. As soon as the guard cried "To arms!" and the Callejues saw them, they rushed eagerly for their weapons, since they had long anticipated this event, and attacked them like a whirlwind, breaking down the gate and storming the trenches in their eagerness to attack them. The Indian allies from Mission Dolores also joined in the fray. When the rebels saw that their treachery had been discovered, they became as fainthearted as our men were courageous. Thus the battle began. The Captain, being aware of the numerical superiority of the enemy, gave the order to retire; to this, however, his men, although inferior in strength, turned a deaf ear. And when they saw that the enemy was already beginning to fall back and weaken, they pressed on more and more. Then the rebels, realizing the size of their forces and the smallness of ours, somewhat recovered their courage and attempted to force our men back. But in so doing, several of them were wounded. Enraged, they again attacked their opponents. When the enemy returned to the contest, the Captain turned and gave the order to retreat, not only because of the danger but also to see if they could lure them within range of our guns. But our allies, deaf to his orders, turned to meet the rebels. This caused the Captain to fear that the enemy might overcome them, and that it might be necessary for them to receive aid from the soldiers, for these men had been left behind to watch the camp in case of attack by the rebels, to guard us, and to prevent us from being surrounded, since the enemy was capable of any treachery. When the Captain, however, saw that it was impossible to make the allies retire and that the superior forces of the enemy might, moreover, inflict considerable damage, he sent two or three soldiers to encourage, direct, and guide them. This act inspired our men with fresh energy, while the urge to kill a soldier revived the spirits of our opponents. And so the combat was waged as before, first one side advancing and then another, although our allies gained ground steadily. The soldiers had to be replaced, however, since they were heavily loaded and were afoot, whereas they were accustomed to use horses. Without these mounts, and with the incessant advancing and retreating, they were soon exhausted. As ground was gained through the aid of these reinforcements, after each assault the rebels finally fell back until they no longer dared attack. This gave our side so great an advantage that the enemy was soon put to flight. The fight had lasted four hours. Of our forces, sixteen men had been wounded, some seriously, one being badly injured in the stomach, another in the throat, and another by an arrow that had gone through his mouth and come out behind his ear. None died, however, and all made a miraculously quick recovery.

1744
Tensions between Missionaries and Soldiers

Juan Antonio Balthasar

The southern rebellion was put down with the assistance of troops from the mainland, led by Bernal de Huidobro, the governor of Sinaloa. Huidobro's astute diplomacy with the Indians, offering gifts and various concessions in exchange for their peace, was also successful.

In 1737, a *presidio* was established at San José del Cabo. Huidobro appointed Pedro Antonio Alvarez de Acevedo as captain. The Jesuits did not approve of this appointment, partly because Alvarez de Acevedo had clashed with Jesuit missionaries on the mainland, but mostly because he, unlike the commander at Loreto, was independent of their control. The Jesuits resisted his authority the whole time he was in California. By the mid-1840s, however, some of them realized that the control they had traditionally exercised in Baja California would be impossible to sustain in the long run, so they acquiesced in a series of steps to weaken it. These included giving up their right, in 1744, to appoint the Loreto captain. A few years later, they gave up their right to appoint the *presidio* soldiers.

These moves were not welcomed by all the Jesuits. A 1744 report by Juan Antonio Balthasar, a Swiss Jesuit who had worked in the Sinaloa missions in the 1730s and was on an official visit to California, gives the reasons why many California Jesuits resisted the change. The report highlights the divergent interests of the missionaries and the military and voices the missionaries' belief that only the Church prevented the exploitation of Indian labor by other Spaniards. Such tensions had long been a staple of life along the missionary frontier of New Spain. They would appear yet again when a military and missionary expedition extended Spanish power into Alta California.

FROM A REPORT BY JUAN ANTONIO BALTHASAR

If the soldiers have control, they will want lands to sow, pastures for their horses—in fact, all that is best in the country, under the pretext that the King's service demands it, that they are working for the King, that the King is to be preferred to all. They will strip the missions of their few miserable possessions, acquired at such great effort but altogether insufficient to maintain them.

And, if the missions oppose their efforts of usurpation, there will follow numerous lawsuits, disagreements, quarrels, complaints, slights, appeals to Guadalajara and Mexico City; judges will come here and factions will be created. So that things will not come to this pass, repeating what has happened in Sonora and Sinaloa, we would almost prefer not to have any missions here.

The commanders and soldiers will want the Indians to work for them, sow the fields and help them. Obviously, great harm will result if we cannot instruct them nor raise their children while they become steeped in vice. We already know that when the missionaries oppose the orders given by the military, they counter with the claim that we are trying to enslave the Indians and reserve them for our profit. They make every effort to remove the natives from our guidance and have them serve only the military. Hence, they goad the Indians not to obey us and then not to pay any attention to us. On seeing how mistreated and insulted they are by the insatiable avarice of the Spaniards, the natives either rebel or live the life of savages. All the advice and pleas of the missionaries fail to get them back on the right road; nor is punishment of any avail. That is because they are backed by the soldiers, who look after their own interest and have no regard for the souls of the natives, which are thus lost.

Heretofore, because of their dependence on us, the California soldiers have been able to pay little attention to diving for pearls, and much less were they allowed to busy the Indians of our missions in such activity, inasmuch as forcing the natives to such work proved in years past an obstacle to the conversion of the peninsula and resulted in the deaths of several greedy divers. But, if the commanders and soldiers are free, pearl diving will become their main occupation. And, on the pretext of securing the royal tax (as happened in the mines, although this is their least concern, their main one being their own advantage), they will attempt to force the Indians to help them and to work. And what work! The cause of death for many; the frequent cause of illness. They are mistreated and only learn mischief.

1744
Life in the Missions

Sebastián de Sistiaga

After the stabilization of the situation in the south, the Jesuits continued to found missions in Baja California. Much of their effort went into continuing to push back the frontier in the north. This 1744 report by Sebastián de Sistiaga gives a flavor of life in the mission of San Ignacio. The report indicates the reliance of the missionaries on native catechists—young men trained by the missionaries to direct the religious life of the native settlements.

The report also demonstrates that in Baja California the Indians were not gathered into compact settlements close to the missions, as would generally be the case in Alta California. The climate and topography were such that the land could not support large numbers of people gathered into one settlement. Rather, the Indians lived in nine different settlements at some distance from the mission, and even then they often left these settlements to go out in search of food farther away. The report thus highlights the wide variety of living arrangements that could coexist even in the same general vicinity. Missions were flexible and adaptable institutions.

The report also indicates that California missionaries, like Christian missionaries throughout the Americas, placed great emphasis on the sacrament of Penance (confession). In this ritual, Indian penitents accused themselves before a priest of failure to observe various Christian mandates, often concerning sexual behavior. In this way it was hoped that baptized Indians would gradually internalize Spanish Christian values and norms.

The Baja California environment generally proved hostile to the kind of settled agriculture the Jesuits wished to introduce. Despite bountiful years in some places, the mission system as a whole never became self-sufficient. It continued to rely on imports of food and supplies from the Jesuit missions on the mainland.

From a Report by Sebastián de Sistiaga

From the year of its [Mission San Ignacio's] foundation (1728) until the present one of 1744, the baptisms in it add up to 2,746. Most of the deaths have been due to the numerous epidemics that have afflicted the natives. The present total population, including every state and age, comes to 1,196.

These natives—the most numerous of all the groups who have been discovered and converted—are like all the others were, while they were still pagans: undisciplined and haughty, and scattered through the woods and rugged mountains. The unproductive lands force them to wander about in search of herbs and roots, and especially water, so extremely scarce in the region. It is only with great effort and ceaseless exertion that they can support themselves. In order to overcome their hunger, they must be continually on the move, forced to traverse vast distances to gather from their sterile lands the bit of fruit some of the trees produce, and even then not always reliable.

In the summer and autumn their hunger is stilled with less effort because, during these two seasons, provided it has previously rained, they gather from some thorny bushes a fruit called by the natives of the opposite shore *pitahayas,* the softest and sweetest of all. In the hills there are wild prickly pears. But when spring has been dry—a frequent occurrence—there is little or no fruit to be had, inasmuch as in Lower California it usually rains very little except in the southern tip, where regular rain falls. When it fails to rain, there is little to eat.

This scarcity explains why a settlement, even when small, must roam over an extensive territory for sustenance. If the people stay in one place they cannot support themselves. This doubles the effort and exertion needed to search for and find them in order to preach to them and convert them to our Holy Faith.

Thus did the sons of St. Ignatius have to search about for them until God, through Father Luyando, inspired and illumined them with the light of faith and religious knowledge. For several years they remained scattered in remote areas from which, with gentle urging, they were encouraged to emerge and join, as far as the land would permit, the main center. Here they could be fed better; not as great an effort had to be expended to instruct them, nor did the missionary have to visit them during their distant peregrinations.

The scattered natives have formed nine towns. Even fewer would have been established had the relatively small territory surrounding them been able to support them. The names of the nine towns are as follows: San Ignacio, the main center; San Francisco de Borja; San Joaquín; San Sabas; San Atanasio; Santa Mónica; Santa Marta; Santa Ninfa; Santa Lucía. The natives do not live permanently in these towns because they are forced to leave them in search of food. But, thanks be to God, nothing is lacking in the organization of a real town, since in their peregrinations and wanderings they observe everything proper to town life.

They do not fail to assist at Mass on days of obligation. Daily, on arising, which is quite early, they direct their thoughts to Jesus Christ and His Most Blessed Mother by singing the *Alabado* that the Spaniards recite. After these prayers and the recitation of the catechism by way of questions and answers, one of the catechists in every town gives them a doctrinal talk in which he explains to them the mysteries of our Holy Faith and all the motives for never-ending hope, accompanied by an exhortation to be contrite for their sins. He also points out to them the supernatural motives for such contrition and, where appropriate, those of faith and hope.

After explaining the articles of faith, he asks them whether they believe and the motives he has expounded for doing so. After the same has been done for hope and contrition, all answer "yes." By the repetition of these acts the Indians—even the recently baptized—form habitual states of these supernatural virtues.

After such instruction and practice, the catechist asks some few chosen ones to repeat what has been said. This is done every day until all in each town have been called on. This continuous cycle in the teaching of the catechism does away with the danger of forgetting or ignoring what is so necessary in knowing and understanding the essentials for eternal salvation.

The Rosary of the Most Blessed Virgin Mary is recited by alternating groups on their knees. The Litany, which is sung, concludes this pious exercise. The natives then set out to search for food in the hills. They spend most of the day in this effort. What remains of each day is used in gathering wood to prepare their food or burn in winter to keep warm while they sleep.

Before retiring they again recite the Rosary on their own initiative and devotion, and they make an act of contrition.

What is most amazing is that, alone and far away from the missionary, they observe this same schedule in their towns, and even away from them. Were the missionary always with them, it would still be surprising for people so recently converted to attend to such devotions and exercises, when we recall that among civilized nations, even after centuries of conversion, it is hard to get people to devote half an hour of devotion, not every day of the week, but only a single time. Undoubtedly, these souls are profoundly affected at the time of baptism, when they are bathed in the light of faith.

One of the principal benefits conferred by this pious exercise is that it helps them to understand the Holy Sacrament of Penance. Annually, and always when seriously ill, those who have reached the age of reason make certain to call the missionary to hear their confession. No one goes to confession without first being adequately instructed that Jesus Christ is the author of this Sacrament, why He instituted it, and knowing its essential parts and all else that is required to render it valid and fruitful, and the defects which destroy its good effects.

1760s
The Natural and Social World
of California

Miguel del Barco

The cataloguing and classification of the natural as well as the social world of the Americas was a major effort of European science in the seventeenth and eighteenth centuries. While the taxonomy seems, at times, to have been designed to bolster the European belief that their own natural and social worlds were superior to those of the Americas (and of Africa and Asia), there is nevertheless much information contained in such accounts that is not available anywhere else.

Much of the most useful material comes from missionaries. Even if they believed that the cultures they were encountering were at best inferior to Christianity and at worst the handiwork of the devil, they knew that their work of conversion would be facilitated by close study. An outstanding example of this is the *Jesuit Relations* of New France, an amazingly rich collection of material on the Native Americans of eastern Canada and the northeastern United States. In Baja California, the missionary who reported most systematically was Miguel del Barco, a Spaniard who worked in California from 1737 to 1768. After the Jesuits were expelled from New Spain, he lived in Bologna until his death in 1790. The renowned Mexican Jesuit Francisco Clavigero, author of the important volume *The Ancient History of Mexico* as well as a work on the history of Baja California, was a fellow exile in Bologna. The two of them often consulted each other as they composed their scholarly works, a collaboration that benefited both authors.

Del Barco composed his work with the purpose of correcting what he took to be significant errors in the first work published in Europe about California: *Noticias de California* (translated into English as *The Natural and*

Civil History of California) by Miguel Venegas, a Jesuit who had composed the work in Mexico City from reports written by California missionaries. Neither Venegas nor the Spanish Jesuit who substantially edited the volume before its publication in Madrid had ever been in California.

FROM THE WRITINGS OF MIGUEL DEL BARCO

Wild Sheep

In California are found all the usual kinds of domestic animals that serve the common use in Spain and in Mexico. Although the missionaries did not find them there (they were transported later from the coast of New Spain) they have adapted very well. There are horses, mules, donkeys, oxen, sheep, goats, swine, and lastly, dogs and cats.

In California there are two kinds of wild beasts unknown in Old or New Spain. The first kind is what is called *tayé* by the natives in the Monqui language. This is an animal about the size of a year-old calf, very much like the calf in appearance, though its head resembles that of a deer. The horns are extremely stout and like those of a ram, although more twisted and less open than the latter's. The feet are large, round, and cleft like those of oxen, the skin like a deer's, except of shorter hair and somewhat spotted. It has a small tail and good-tasting meat and is a real delicacy.

This animal is always in the mountains and it is told of him that, when he is pursued by Indian hunters and finds himself in a tight spot, he approaches the edge of a precipice and jumps off, taking care to land squarely on his head so that his thick horns can absorb the impact of the fall. Once down, he gets up and runs away, having frustrated the hunters, who look at him from the heights without venturing themselves to attempt a similar trick. In truth, the horns are so strong and so well made that it appears that Nature's Author gave them to the beasts so that they would elude their pursuers in the aforementioned manner. It is also reasonable to assume that He gave their entire head such a constitution that they should suffer no ill effects from such a hard blow....

Leopardos (cougars)

There are also many *leopardos* (cougars), the type that are commonly called *leones* in the kingdom of Mexico. The California natives call them *chimbiká*

These two drawings of San José del Cabo were done by Alexander-Jean Noël, a member of a Spanish-French scientific expedition that observed the transit of Venus from just outside the town in 1769. The first [top] is a sketch of the village. The second [bottom] records the funeral of the expedition's leader, Abbé Chappe d'Auteroche, who perished in a typhus epidemic. Courtesy of Réunion des Musées Nationaux / Art Resource, New York.

Fr. Ignacio Tirsch, a native of Bohemia, served as the priest at Mission Santiago from 1763 to 1768. While there, he created a series of at least forty-six drawings and watercolors of life in California. His subjects included Indians, Spaniards, plants, and animals. When the Jesuits were expelled from California, he took his artwork back to Europe with him. His creations provide a singular glimpse of eighteenth-century California. All drawings by Fr. Ignacio Tirsch, S.J. Courtesy of the National Library of the Czech Republic.

Next page, top (clockwise from top left):
"A Peruvina tree or wild pepper tree."
"A sweet-scented herb."
"A red Brazil tree."
"Vergonzosa, a little tree called oregano which, when touched, shrinks as if it is wilting."
"Palo de Tabardillo, very good against a high fever."
"Birdfoot."
"Nopal."
"Choya."
"Carambullo."
"Cardón."
"Pitahaya agria."
"Cakalosuchil Colorado."
"Juca."
"Conguistle."
"Cakalosuchil Blanco."
"Biznaga."

Next page, bottom (clockwise from top left):
"A starfish which moves when taken out of the water. It is without doubt a living being."
"A large seashell which is used as a drinking utensil by the Indians."
"A little mussel called barquillo *(little ship), which is driven by the wind on the ocean as if it were a little boat."*
"Concha Nacar from California. This mussel (abalone) also has a beautiful vivid color, even more shiny and more beautiful than seen in the picture."
"A white mussel appears as if it were engraved by the most artistic hands."
"Concha azul, or the blue mussel (abalone) from California, which is not found in other oceans. Inside it is covered with a high vivid blue; the most beautiful enamel process cannot be that elegant. The ornament is done so well that it is like a beautiful flower."

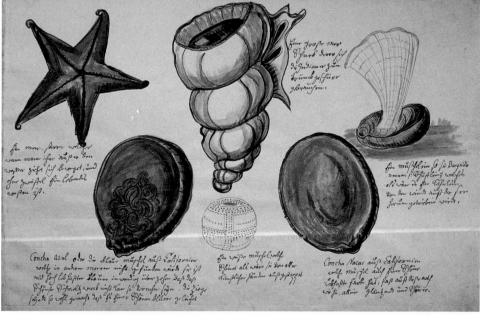

"Chupa mirtos *(flower sucker), cardinal, California sparrow, bluebird.*"

"A spotted raven from California [and] a useful bird that eats all kinds of dirty stuff and carcasses called Zopilote and Aura. But the bird does not grow larger."

"A wild male sheep and leopard."

"How two Californi Indians killed a deer with arrows, how they skinned it in the field and prepared it for roasting."

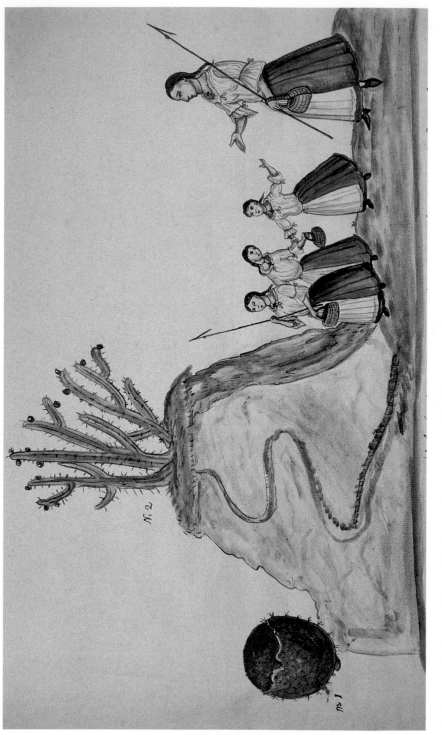

Tirsh's caption for this image: "Picture of the dresses which are worn by all females, young as well as old, in the mission of California, which they get from the Father. Here you see the young girls with their teacher. They go into the forests and on top of the hills in order to gather the very precious fruit called pitahaya. Inside it is beautiful red, on the outside it has a prickly green shell."

in the Cochimí language, which means "large wild cat." They inflict great damage on cattle, but mainly on the young of horses, of which they kill many. These foals may be a year or a year and a half old and still they do not escape these cats' terrible claws. They also will venture to attack and scratch grown horses of both sexes, though this occurs only rarely. It is for this principal reason that the missions do not raise young horses, other than those horses and mules necessary for the needs of the mission itself. Were it not for this, they would be able to sell to the garrison as many as needed for the soldiers without the necessity of having them brought over by boat from the coast of the Yaqui and Mayo, as has always been done. At times, even the missions have bought horses from these shipments, although they had no shortage of mares. Their issue was that limited.

These *leones* or *leopardos* also attack people, and stories of several cases are well known. We will only mention two of them here in order to bring to light the boldness of these vicious animals. These incidents happened in these latter years.

An Indian of Mission San José de Comondú was walking alone and was attacked by a *león*. The Indian was carrying a long, pointed knife and he used it to defend himself by wounding his enemy. Even so, the *león* would not desist but continued to maul him with his claws. Finally the man fell dead, and the *león* went away badly wounded. Quite by accident, the dead man's body was discovered in the field later. He was swollen and disfigured already. Many Indians went there, saw the body, and by conjecture they identified him. They saw the bloody knife, and by the tracks of the *león* and other marks on the ground, they realized that there had been a fight and that they had knocked each other down. They followed the *león's* bloody tracks in order to kill him. But this was not necessary, because, after a long stretch, they found him dead of his wounds. This happened in the 1760s.

When this wild beast has killed some quarry, be it either a deer or a foal, he sucks the blood right away and eats as much of the flesh as he wishes, mainly around the neck (that is usually the place he chooses to kill his prey). He drags the rest some distance away and tries to hide it by covering it with branches or whatever he can find. His object is to return to have another meal the following day if he should not kill something else. (If he has succeeded in getting new game, he never returns to the previous day's kill.)

Buzzards

Buzzards, with their extremely sensitive smell, are soon aware that something is dead, and many of them gather around, flying in circles high above the cadaver that they intend to devour. Indians use this signal sometimes to locate a deer killed by some *león* and so to claim the meat. The *león,* however, has oftimes given painful showings of his resentment, as happened in the case just mentioned. This is so because the day before the fight, very near the same place, the above-mentioned Indian, being en route to the mission, had discovered the *león's* kill (it was a deer), and he took the meat with him. Later that evening he had informed his relatives of this. The following day the *león* came to look for what he had stored and, not finding it, he was so mad that he attacked the man as he was returning home, as we have already said....

Hummingbirds

Finally there is frequently found in California what they call in New Spain *chupamirtos* (hummingbirds), and *colibrí* in other places. This is such a small bird that it can easily be mistaken for some type of large fly. Moreover, although on account of its size it is the smallest of the known birds, because of its fine green and gold coloring it must be counted among the most beautiful. It is superior to all the rest even in its detachment from earthly things, as much as this is possible to a sensitive living being. It seems that it disdains setting foot on the ground, or even on trees, in order to repose as do the rest of the birds. I have never seen them in this manner of rest, nor have many others who are knowledgeable on this subject and whom I have asked. They stop exercising their wings only when they are in their nests, sitting on their eggs or rearing their young ones. It must be presumed that at night they also retire to their nests. They eat the finest and most delicate food, the nectar of flowers. In order to get this food, the bird does no more than approach the flower in flight, introduce its thin beak (which is long in relation to its body), and suck the substance. In the meantime it is holding its feet in the air and moving its little body in a position suitable to eat. If, at this time or when it is in its nest, by chance a person comes near, it suddenly makes such a noise with its wings as to scare the person who frightened it.

It is no less remarkable in the construction of its nests. I saw one of these made below a grapevine. The whole body of the little nest was in the air, and only on the upper part did it hang from a type of dry and hard strap made from the fibers of the *mezcal* plant, which the people there use to tie the stakes on top of which the arms and shoots of the vines are propped up. Some pieces or ends of these ties or straps (which become hard soon after they are first used) end up hanging down. The nest was therefore fastened on its upper part to one of these straps, and all the rest of it was totally in the air. From this it can be inferred that the hummingbird, guided by different rules of architecture contrary to the common ones, begins its construction on the upper part of its building, and it places the foundations on this part. Placed against the little stick or strap from which the nest is to hang, it attaches and entwines some of its materials. To these it joins and ties others, and in this manner it is necessary that it continues working downward, at least on one side of the nest, until the bottom of the nest is reached. Once this has been accomplished all around, it must then proceed upward, forming circles until it finishes this job. Or, if it is not made in that manner, then it is necessary for it to commence making complete circles at the top, and from there, it must proceed downward with the complete little construction until it closes it at the bottom. This would be more difficult. The hollow, or capacity, of this nest is almost that of a half-shell of an ordinary hen's egg, except it is a little narrower and somewhat deeper than such a shell.

Mezquites (Mesquite)

Mezquites are found frequently in California. The tree is large and has many branches whose wood is very strong and heavy. Carpenters refuse to make windows and doors out of this wood for this reason. The trunk does not ordinarily grow straight, but instead, a short distance from the ground, it divides itself into twisted branches. There are very few of these trees that would have two or three *varas* of straight trunk. They almost always grow on flat, low land such as is often found on the little plains on both sides of *arroyos,* and not on top of hills, even though plains may occur there also, nor even on the slopes of hills. And if in some places (they are few) they can be found on the slopes, they do not grow very large, but appear as thickets or little more. When *mezquites* are near watering places where travelers often stop for the necessary rest at night or at midday, the shade of these trees is very useful. The mounts make use of both the shade and the limbs. One uses a small machete to cut the most tender of these for the mounts to eat, as there is not usually any grass in such places. Mules eat it readily, not just the leaves, which are very small, but also the young shoots, which are not yet too thick or too hard.

Cardón

Cardones* [are] trees which, because of their great size, are giants among all the fleshy types of which we have been speaking. About four or six hands-breadth from the ground, or higher perhaps, it divides itself into several arms or boughs which, forming an elbow at the beginning large enough to allow each other growing space, then grow straight upward to a height of twelve and even fifteen varas. These boughs are heavy as beams, all equally thick. Furthermore, they do not become thinner as they grow taller, as happens with other trees, but rather they keep the same thickness on their highest parts as they had in the beginning. Only the trunk, before it divides itself into branches, is proportionately thicker than they are. It bears its fruit on the highest parts of its branches and the fruit, as it is on the point of ripening, properly resembles (when seen from below) turned tops of the type that boys use at play, stuck into the tree by their tips. They are not even lacking the little crown that such tops often have. This crown, however, is nothing but the dried and shriveled-up flower, which they keep until they are fully ripe; seen from below, it represents perfectly the little crown of a top. This fruit resembles these tops in its color as well as its shape, because the outside has a color of wood, tending somewhat to yellow or, better, to buff, even though the color of the tree is a perfect green. When this fruit ripens to perfection it opens up like a pomegranate and displays inside a pretty red color. Almost all of it is made up of seeds surrounded by viscous humor and this only in a small quantity. For this reason the Indians can get nothing to eat from it other than these seeds, which are coarser than the coarsest of gunpowders. These seeds are very black and they have a high luster. With the help of fire and sun, the Indians clean the fibers that the seeds have and toast them to keep them from spoiling, and so preserve them for the winter, when there is greater lack of food. These seeds of the cardón are very much esteemed by the Indians.

---

* Pachycereus pringlei, a huge columnar cactus.

Although this tree is thorny, it is not so much nor in the manner of the sweet *pitahaya*. The *cardón* exceeds this latter greatly in size, and it likewise exceeds it proportionately in the coarseness of its striations and also in its color, the *cardón* being a more perfect green. The striated beams I mentioned before are the branches. All of them, in the same manner as the *pitahaya* tree, are made up of a mass or fleshy part full of humidity and, for their stability, of a light wooden framework such that, when dry, it resembles more what they call there *corcho* (coral tree) than wood of any strength, such is its lightness and porosity. Therefore one finds that, if he should cut a branch or arm of a *cardón,* the first thing he would find (after the skin, which is thin and tender like that of an apple) would be pulp for a space of perhaps four fingers. Next is the framework, which, resembling a large tube, is thin, round, and hollow. Within this framework there is another one similar to the first one, but more delicate, and it is the heart of the tree, through which it nourishes itself and grows....

The framework, or large tube, of the *cardón* has frequent holes, some of them so big that a hand can fit through, which would seem to weaken it even more than its very porous nature has already determined. It is surprising, therefore, that such a weak framework of such little solidity can support a beam so high and so heavy because it is full of fleshy pulp and moisture. Furthermore, it is surprising that such a weak framework supports it with such strength that not even the violence of the winds can knock or chop it down. One will sooner find a whole *cardón* laid on the ground uprooted by the fury of a hurricane, as they are very often encountered, than one of their branches knocked off by a similar wind, even though its generous striations are suited to a more violent impression by the wind.

If a small piece is cut from one of these arms, say two or more handsbreadth, and the pulp (which is most of it) is mashed down and later it is wrung out, a liquor is obtained in great abundance. When this liquor is boiled and the foam is skimmed away, it becomes like a balsam, and it is surprisingly good to cure wounds and sores.

Even though this tree is so entirely permeated with moisture, it grows only in arid land, whether it be plains or hillsides, as long as there is no humidity, as the *cardón,* no less than the *pitahaya,* is an enemy of moist places. Whence come that moisture and that liquor of which it is so full? Not from the rains, as these are very scarce in California, and it is for this reason that, unless there is a permanent water source and of sufficient size that watering can be done with adequate frequency, nothing can be sown or planted trusting only to rainwater, as it will dry up in a short time. The *cardón,* even though years may pass without rain, does not show any feeling on account of this, but perseveres with the same serenity, with the same green and fresh color, and with the same moisture as always. Neither can it be due to dews, as these are not common, but rather they are rare. If rains and dews are not sufficient to support the life of an introduced tree, such as an olive tree, a grapevine, or a fig tree, they should much less be able to support a *cardón,* which has so much juice inside that there is no European tree that can equal it in this respect, and even perhaps in America itself there is no tree which surpasses it in this property.

Jojoba

Jojoba [is] found in all California, although in some places it is more abundant than in others. It grows on the dry slopes of hills and mountains. It does not bear fruit every year, but only when it has rained well in winter for several days; then the jojobas are loaded with plenty of fruit. They grow in small bushes, about four or five handsbreadth high. The adult plants have leaves similar to one of the divisions of the leaves of a rosebush, a little smaller, but smooth, somewhat thick, and without any tip, unless it is at the juncture with the branches, so that they form a little shovel like those of the mangrove, though the green color of this latter is very bright and showy, and the color of the jojoba is a green tending to gray. Its fruit, which is what they call jojoba proper, is the size of the meat of a hazelnut or somewhat larger but a lot longer, so that one jojoba might be equal to two hazelnuts. Its color is white inside and brown outside, but brighter, tending perhaps to a dark blond color. I will write down its virtues here, copied word for word from a prescription, printed in Mexico, year 1749, with permission of the Royal Tribunal of Physicians.

Virtues of Jojoba

1. First, they are extraordinarily effective against urinary disorders and the retention of urine due to an abundance of phlegm. The manner of using them is to take five or six, diluted in wine, broth, or hot water.
2. Against flatulence, indigestion, and obstructions, taking them in the form prescribed above, or eating them by themselves.

3. Against any wound, applied in the form of a plaster on the same wound, and repeating this until the wound closes.

4. They are extremely effective to stop a cancer which is beginning, and to cure one which has already introduced itself. The manner of using them in these cases is to extract oil from them the same way it is extracted from almonds, and to rub with it the ulcerated part, continuing this until the cancer has been extinguished. Marvelous results have been experienced in this regard.

5. To facilitate childbirth for women, giving five or six of them in broth or wine when the urgency of childbirth approaches.

6. Against any kind of fever, particularly tertian, taken before the beginning of the paroxysm of the fever in the manner already indicated.

7. For those who suffer abdominal cramps or difficulties in regularity.

8. To end fiery hangovers, which they call heartburn. To end the type of pain they call intestinal, and to end qualms of nausea in those who are wont to suffer them when they want to eat or drink. They should be taken for several days either by themselves or diluted in wine or broth.

All these virtues have been experienced with good results, particularly insofar as concerns the urinary disorders, the easing of childbirth, arresting cancer, and curing flatulence.

Conchas Azules (Abalone)

On the exterior coast there are found some shells, proper to it, which are perhaps the most beautiful in the world. This is because their luster usually is greater and finer than that of the finest mother-of-pearl. These shells are darkened and covered with a pleasant and extremely vivid blue of the appearance of light, swiftly moving clouds, and it is as fine as that of lapis lazuli, that is, as if there was an extremely fine membrane of an overlaid transparent varnish through which the silvery bottom shines. It is said of these that, if they were common in Europe, they would outshine mother-of-pearl. Even on this exterior coast these shells are not found everywhere, because they do not exist from Cabo San Lucas up to 26 or 27 degrees of latitude. From there upward they are found, though not in all parts. At 31 degrees, on the coast that is west of the new Mission Santa María, there are not any. We do not know if that is beyond their limit, or if they continue to exist farther north. These shells are somewhat deeper than ordinary, and on one side only they have five or six round holes that look as if they had been made with a thin drill. They are single, without having another shell to cover them, in contrast to the common way of other shells, even those where pearls grow, which are double, one functioning as the bottom and the other as the top....

Indian Women of Cabo San Lucas

These Indian women of Cabo San Lucas wear their hair long, loose, and hanging on the back. They make some very graceful necklaces from figures cut out of mother-of-pearl and mixed with berries, little reeds, snail shells, and pearls. The front of these neck adornments hangs down to the waist. They also make bracelets similarly and of the same material. Even these barbarians living in that remote corner of the world are inspired to create these inventions, in order to fulfill their wish to present a good appearance. The color of the people of all this Pericú nation is generally less dark and even notably fairer than that of the rest of the Californians.

The dress of the Cochimí women of the north is different and poorer, as it begins at the waist and ends at the knees in some territories, a little lower in others. In front they wear a sort of skirt formed by the small joints of very small reeds which they cut close to the nodes, both above and below. They throw away the reeds themselves, as they are no good for their purpose, and keep only the joints. They bore a hole through these and they string them up in strings or thin cords which they get out of the agave plants, the same way one would string up a rosary. These closely packed strings are then tied by one end to other little cords which are tied to the waist and are hanging loose on the opposite end. They reach down at least to the knees, although in some territories they wear them longer, almost halfway down the leg. In this manner, all together, they constitute a little curtain which protects their modesty, even if not their bodies against inclement weather. They cover the opposite part with a deerskin, or with that of some other animal which the husbands might have killed. From Mission San Borja, at 30 degrees of latitude, northward, the Indians have the custom of covering their bodies with small cloaks made of the pelt of sea otter or hare, rabbits, or some other animals....

The manner in which women of Christian California (and even farther north) carry their children is the following. They put the child in a small net which does not close up as a purse, but remains open on the upper part. They line the bottom of the net with dry plants, particularly using the soft pelts of rabbits, hares, or other animals. This keeps the net open at the top and at the same time it cushions the child from the discomfort of strings and knots. After they became Christians and had some clothes, they added to some of these a piece of cloth to better protect the child. On both sides of these nets there are long cords from which they form a long handle. They hang the net with the child from anywhere using this handle. When they are moving from one place to another, they carry their children on their backs, the strings of the net being held in a bundle from the mother's forehead. When the child is a little older, they do not usually carry it in the net, but in their arms. And when they are about two or three years old, they have them sit on their mother's shoulders, as if riding horseback, and so that their feet come to the front, resting on the breast of the mother, who will then take one foot of her child in one hand and the other foot with the other hand so that he does not fall down. At the same time, the little boy secures his position by grabbing tightly with his little hands the uncombed and dirty hair of his mother. When the child has learned to hold on tight while sitting this way, one woman alone can carry two children, one sitting on her shoulders and the other one, only a few months old, at her breast or inside the net on her back. Sometimes they may even carry three: two of them as I have just described, and the third one, about four years old, led by the hand as he walks beside his mother. All this does not prevent the woman from taking along with her all her belongings....

1768
The Decision to Move Farther North

JOSÉ DE GÁLVEZ

The Jesuit era in Baja California came to a sudden and unexpected end in 1767 for reasons that had virtually nothing to do with California. In Europe, the growing influence of the Jesuits, especially in education, and their tight loyalty to the papacy made them increasingly suspect in the eyes of the continent's monarchs, notably the Bourbons. The order was expelled from Portugal in 1759 and from France five years later. In Spain a food riot in 1766 gave Carlos III the opportunity to move against them. Casting them as the scapegoats for the disorder, he ordered their expulsion from Spain and its empire in 1767.

With the Jesuits on the way out, the viceroy appointed career soldier Gaspar de Portolá as the first governor of California. Portolá had served in the Spanish army in campaigns in Italy and Portugal and was assigned to New Spain in 1764. He arrived at Loreto and promulgated the order for the Jesuits to be expelled on December 26, 1767. On February 5, 1768, all sixteen Jesuits in California departed from Loreto. The viceroy arranged for Franciscans from the Apostolic College of San Fernando in Mexico City to replace them. The first group arrived in California on April 1. They were led by a veteran missionary, Junípero Serra. A native of Majorca, he had been an eminent philosophy professor in Palma before he volunteered for the American missions and joined the College of San Fernando. He served in the college's missions in the Sierra Gorda from 1750 to 1758 and was mission president there from 1751 to 1754. After 1758, he was based in Mexico City. He held some administrative positions in the college and undertook preaching journeys to various regions of Mexico. As soon as he arrived in California, Serra began assigning his men to staff the former Jesuit missions.

Left: José de Gálvez. Courtesy of The Bancroft Library, University of California, Berkeley. Right: Carlos III in hunting garb, painted by Francisco Goya. Courtesy of the Museo del Prado, Madrid.

In May a meeting about California was convened by José de Gálvez. A native of Málaga, Gálvez was serving as a judge in Madrid when Carlos III appointed him as visitor-general of New Spain in 1765. The triumph of England in the Seven Years War had removed Bourbon France from North America and had expanded the British empire all the way west to the Mississippi River, where it touched the northeastern border of New Spain. Spain had received the Louisiana Territory as a result of the war, and this meant that it now possessed a very long North American frontier with England. At the same time, Russian moves across Siberia to Alaska posed a similar threat to the northwestern frontier. In this context, Gálvez's task was to strengthen the viceroyalty by reorganizing its defenses and finances. He was given very broad authority to accomplish these aims. He organized campaigns against the Seri and Pima Indians in Sonora in 1767 and he moved to San Blas in 1768. Because Spain had received word from its ambassador in Moscow that Russia was intensifying its activities along the North American coast, Gálvez decided that occupation of the fabled port of Monterey would be the best way to try to thwart the Russian moves.

The following document is the record of that May meeting. Besides Gálvez, those present included a naval commander, Miguel Ribero Cordero, an engineer, Miguel Costansó, and two ship pilots, Vicente Vila and Antonio Fabeau y Quesada. The participants agreed that the expedition should be a combined land and sea effort and that both parts should rendezvous at Vizcaíno's port of Monterey.

From the Record of a Meeting at San Blas, Mexico

In the harbor and new settlement of San Blas on the coast of the South Sea on the sixteenth day of May of the year 1768, the Most Illustrious Señor Don José de Gálvez, of His Majesty's Supreme Council of the Indies, Quartermaster General of the Army, Visitor-General of the Tribunals and of the Royal Treasury of these Kingdoms, empowered with fullest authority by the Most Excellent Señor Marqués de Croix, Viceroy, Governor, and Captain General of this New Spain, summoned to his quarters in the government buildings the Engineer Don Miguel Costansó; the Commander of the Navy and this harbor, Don Manuel Ribero Cordero; Don Antonio Fabeau de Quesada, Professor of Mathematics and experienced in the Navigation of these Seas and those of the Philippine Islands; and Don Vicente Vila, Pilot of the Royal Armada of His Majesty on the Atlantic Ocean and designated as Chief Pilot of the vessels that ply this Pacific Ocean.

A Royal Order of His Majesty sent by His Excellency the Marqués de Grimaldi of the Council and First Secretary of State, under date of the twenty-third of January of this year, to the Most Excellent Señor, Marqués de Croix, Viceroy of this Kingdom, having been read to them, imparting definite knowledge of the attempts which the Russians have made to facilitate their communication with this America, warned His Excellency to dispatch instructions and orders to the Governor of California to observe from there the designs of that nation and to frustrate them as far as possible; and the *Junta* was also informed of the official letter and order of His Majesty, a copy of which His Excellency the Viceroy had passed on to the Señor Visitor-General so that, being fully acquainted with it and putting into practice the former plans of occupancy with a *Presidio* at Puerto de Monterey, situated on the Great Ocean, on the west coast of California, he might adopt those measures he deems most expedient in order to explore by land and by sea so important a harbor, sending an engineer so that, having taken exact observations and having made a map of the harbor, the useful project of establishing ourselves at that place may be accomplished....

At the same time it was also agreed that it would be most important to undertake an entry or search by land, at the proper seasons, from the missions to the north of California, so that both expeditions might unite at the same harbor of Monterey, and by means of the observations made by one and the other they might acquire once and for all complete knowledge and in this way aid greatly the founding of a *presidio* and settlement at that place which is truly the most advantageous for protecting the entire west coast of California and the other coasts of the southern part of this continent against any attempts by the Russians or any northern nation.

In consequence of all this, the Illustrious Señor Don José de Gálvez, with the approval of all, agreed and resolved that there be made ready at once all the necessary supplies of provision, rigging, sails, and whatever else is thought useful and indispensable to be put aboard the two aforementioned new brigantines which are to undertake the voyage to the harbor of Monterey by leaving the coast and the chain of islands behind and undertaking the voyage on the high seas, thus to reach the proper latitude as far as the winds of the season will permit so as not to experience the delays, misfortunes, and sicknesses which were suffered by the expeditions of Don Sebastián Vizcaíno and others made during the last two centuries....for it should not be difficult to take possession of some advantageous site there, granting that the natives of that place show themselves as peaceful and friendly as they have on other occasions.

Finally, there is left to the care and resolution of the Illustrious Señor Don José de Gálvez the examination and decision on his arrival in California whether it be possible to send at the proper time persons satisfactory to him with the corresponding party and detachment which are to make the entry or journey by land to the aforementioned Puerto de Monterey, for it will always be most prudent and advantageous to bring together the two expeditions at that place.

1769
A Beachhead at San Diego

MIGUEL COSTANSÓ

After the San Blas conference, Gálvez proceeded to California to take personal charge of organizing the expedition. When he arrived in July, he symbolically set up his headquarters at Santa Ana, a mining settlement that had always been outside of Jesuit control. Gálvez had great plans for Baja California: new mining enterprises, improved methods of ranching and agriculture, profitable pearl fishing and trade, and towns and villages for Indians as well as settlers. He foresaw a large fair at Loreto twice a year that would attract merchants from Guadalajara and beyond. Soon, he thought, Alta California might develop into something similar—a strong, stable, and prosperous collection of Spanish urban settlements which would establish for once and for all Spain's presence on the northern Pacific coast.

By the time Gálvez first met Serra at Santa Ana in October, he had come to realize that the San Blas plan for the occupation of Monterey could not be carried out without additional resources; California possessed neither the mineral wealth nor the manpower to fund the expedition, and Gálvez knew that he would need the assistance of the Church to put his plans into effect. He found in Serra a more than willing collaborator. Serra almost immediately began to round up volunteers among the Franciscans and to calculate what mission goods, livestock, possessions, and indigenous converts could be put into the service of the journey to the north.

José de Gálvez was genuinely a man of the Enlightenment, a philosophical movement that emphasized the possibilities of human reason and was skeptical of the traditional claims of religion to offer the only guide to proper human thought and action. There is considerable irony in the fact that José de Gálvez, who represented Carlos III, the preeminent enlightened Spanish monarch in the eighteenth century, was forced to rely on the mission—an institution firmly rooted in the past—to attempt to establish the future of

Route of the Portolá Expedition (1769)

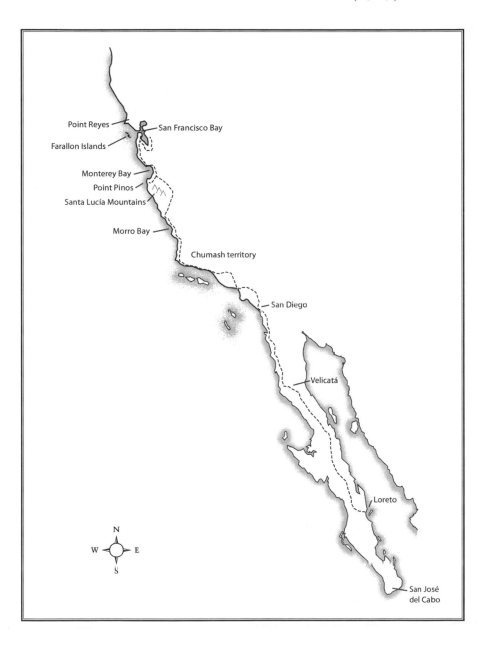

which he dreamed. And the Franciscan missionaries of the College of San Fernando, with whom Gálvez was forced to work, were men who were especially unaffected by the intellectual changes wrought by the Enlightenment. In parts of New Spain like New Santander and sections of Sonora, officials and some missionaries were beginning to rethink the traditional notion of the mission as an isolated and protective enclave, deliberately out of touch with the rest of frontier society. They were beginning to suggest experimentation with other models based on greater contact between Indians and the Hispanic settlers of the region. But the College of San Fernando was not part of this movement. Its missionaries in the Sierra Gorda, including Serra, had consistently kept converted Indians isolated and had often quarreled with the civilian and military authorities. The college had argued in the 1760s that secularization of the Sierra Gorda could only be contemplated in the distant future and it was not until 1769 that secularization became acceptable, in order to free up some men for the California fields. The ends that Gálvez desired—an open, urban, and prosperous California—and the means he was forced to use to try to obtain them—the traditional mission system—were at severe cross purposes.

As it was finally arranged, the expedition consisted of five parts under the overall command of Portolá. Two parties were to travel by land, two by sea, and an additional supply ship was to follow. The first vessel to depart was the *San Carlos,* which left La Paz on January 9, 1769. It was commanded by Vicente Vila, who had participated in the San Blas conference. After a stay at Cabo San Lucas, the *San Carlos* rounded the tip of California in February and headed out. It was driven far out to sea by a storm. Wracked by scurvy, the survivors of its crew and the contingent of soldiers on board did not arrive at San Diego until April 29. The second vessel, the *San Antonio,* under the command of old Manila hand Juan Pérez, left Cabo San Lucas on February 15 and arrived first in San Diego, on April 11.

The first land expedition was headed by Baja California veteran soldier Fernando de Rivera y Moncada, who had served in the California military since 1742 and had commanded the *presidio* at Loreto for twenty-five years. The expedition consisted of twenty-five soldiers, three muleteers, and forty-four Baja California Indians, whose task was to tend the horses and other animals the expedition requisitioned from the missions along the way as it headed north. Rivera and his party left Loreto on September 30. At Velicatá, located slightly above the most northerly mission of Santa María, they were joined by Fr. Juan Crespí. He had been a student of Junípero Serra in Majorca and served with him in missions in the Sierra Gorda in Mexico before being sent to Baja California in 1767. The Franciscans appointed him record keeper of the entire expedition. The group left Velicatá on March 24. Blazing the trail, the expedition arrived in San Diego on May 14. On the way, thirty of the forty-four Baja California Indians deserted the party. The other land expedition included both Portolá and Serra, along with an additional forty-two Baja California Indians, thirty of whom opted to desert along the way. This group left Velicatá on May 15, after Serra had established a new mission there. Following the route Rivera had established, they arrived in San Diego on July 1. There they discovered many weakened and sick members of the three expeditions that had arrived before them. Portolá assigned as many healthy crew members as he could to the *San Antonio* and sent it to San Blas on the mainland to try to procure additional supplies. The third vessel, the *San José,* left Loreto for San Diego on June 16, but it was lost at sea with all hands.

The men quickly set up a basic camp and a primitive church. The missionaries decided to dedicate the church on the feast of the Triumph of the Holy Cross to commemorate a Spanish victory over the Moors on that feast in the year 1212. Then, with San Diego at least minimally occupied, Portolá decided to push on for Monterey, over the objections of Rivera, who thought that the group ought to consolidate itself at San Diego and await the return of the *San Antonio* or the arrival of the *San José* with supplies. With one boat gone and Vila unwilling to risk the other with an inexperienced crew, the trip to Monterey would have to be undertaken by land. Portolá himself took command of it and ordered Rivera to bring twenty-seven of his soldiers along. Pedro Fages, a soldier who had arrived from Spain with a group of Catalán volunteers, was also part of the group, along with six or seven of his soldiers. The expedition's engineer, Miguel Costansó, seven muleteers, two servants (one each for Portolá and Rivera), and fifteen Indians from Baja California were also ordered to be part of the group. Rounding out the party were two priests, Frs. Juan Crespí and Francisco Gómez. That left only Serra and two priests, eight soldiers, eleven Baja California Indians, a blacksmith, a carpenter, and Serra's personal servants at the military and religious compound in San Diego. Vila and a few sailors stayed aboard the *San Carlos* in the bay.

The following excerpt from Costansó's diary describes how the expedition set out from San Diego.

From the Diary of Miguel Costansó

The departure of the expedition from San Diego took place on June 14, 1769. The two divisions of the land expedition marched together, the Commander making this disposition on account of the great number of animals and packs. For of provisions and supplies alone were carried one hundred [packs], which he believed necessary to supply the whole company during six months, and to provide for the case of delay of the packets, although it was thought impossible that in the meantime the one or the other of them should fail to reach Monterey.

The following order was observed on the marches: at the head rode the Commander with the officers, the six men of the Catalán volunteers, who had joined the expedition at San Diego, and some friendly Indians with spades, pick-axes, crowbars, axes, and other implements used by sappers to cut the brush and to open a passage wherever necessary. Next followed the pack train, which was separated into four divisions, each one with its muleteers and an adequate number of soldiers of the garrison as an escort. In the rear guard came Captain Fernando de Rivera, with the rest of the soldiers and friendly Indians convoying the spare horses and mules.

The soldiers of the *presidio* in California, of whom justice and fairness oblige us to say that they worked incessantly on this expedition, use two sorts of arms—offensive and defensive. The defensive arms are the leather jacket and the shield. The first, whose shape is that of a coat without sleeves, is made of six or seven plies of white tanned deerskin, proof against the arrows of the Indians except at very short range. The shield is made of two plies of raw bull's hide; it is carried on the left arm and with it they turn aside spears and arrows, the rider not only defending himself, but also his horse. In addition to the above they use a sort of leather apron, called *armas* or *defensas,* which, fastened to the pommel of the saddle, hangs down on both sides, covering their thighs and legs that they may not hurt themselves when riding through the woods. Their offensive arms are the lance—which they handle adroitly on horseback—the broadsword, and a short musket which they carry securely fastened in its case. They are men of great fortitude and patience in fatigue; obedient, resolute, and active, and we do not hesitate to say that they are the best horsemen in the world, and among those soldiers who best earn their bread for the August Monarch whom they serve.

It must be borne in mind that the marches of this body with so great a train and [so many] obstacles through unknown lands and on unused paths could not be long, not to mention such other reasons that made it necessary to halt and camp early as the necessity of reconnoitering the country from day to day in order to regulate the marches according to the distance between the watering places and consequently to take the proper precautions. Sometimes they resumed their journey in the afternoon immediately after watering the animals, upon the reliable information that on the next stage there was little or no water, or a scarcity of pasture.

Stops were made, as the necessity demanded, at intervals of four days, more or less, according to the extraordinary hardships occasioned by the greater roughness of the road, the labor of the sappers, and the straying of the animals—which happened less frequently with the horses—that had to be sought by their tracks. At other times, stops were made because it was necessary to accommodate the sick when there were any—and in course of time there were many whose strength gave way under the continuous fatigue and the excessive heat and intense cold.

But the pack animals themselves constitute the greatest danger on these journeys and are the most dreaded enemy—though without them nothing could be accomplished. At night, and in a country they do not know, these animals are very easily frightened. The sight of a coyote or fox is sufficient to stampede them, as they say in this country. A bird flying past or dust raised by the wind is likely to frighten them and to make them run many leagues, throwing themselves over precipices and cliffs, defying human effort to restrain them. And it afterwards costs infinite pains to recover them, nor is this always possible; and those that were not killed by falling over a precipice or lamed in their headlong race are of no service for a long time. This expedition, however, suffered no serious detriment on this account, owing to the care and watchfulness which were always observed; and although on some occasions the animals were stampeded, no accident or injury whatever followed, because the stampede was of short duration.

In the order and manner described, the Spaniards made their marches over vast territories that became more fertile and more pleasant the farther they penetrated to the north. In general, the whole country is inhabited by a large number of Indians, who came forth to receive the Spaniards, and some accompanied them from one place to another. They are very docile and tractable, especially from San Diego onward.

1769
The Santa Barbara Channel

JUAN CRESPÍ

The Portolá group headed north and reached what is now Orange County on July 22. Within a week they were at the Santa Ana River, camping on its bank opposite an Indian village on July 28. Two days later the party entered the San Gabriel Valley and arrived near what is now the center of Los Angeles on August 2. Following Sepúlveda Canyon, they entered the San Fernando Valley and stayed on August 7 near what would become Mission San Fernando. From there they headed north through the Santa Clara Valley. The excerpt below from Crespí's diary, heavily edited by Francisco Palóu, begins on August 11, when the group had left its camp near the Chumash settlement of Kamulus, near the present Los Angeles/Ventura County line.

FROM THE DIARY OF JUAN CRESPÍ

Friday, August 11: In the afternoon seven chiefs came to visit us. They were accompanied by a large number of Indians carrying bows and arrows. The strings of the bows were loose, which is a sign of peace. They brought us a gift, an abundant amount of seeds, acorns, walnuts, and pine nuts which spread out in front of us. The chiefs, who had learned who was in charge, offered the Commander, the officers, and us several necklaces of small white, black, and red stones. The texture and composition of the stones was similar to coral. There must have been more than five hundred gentiles present.* The Governor gave them some beads.

---

* The missionaries divided Indians into "neophytes" and "gentiles." "Neophyte," an early Christian term, described those who had recently been baptized, and was applied to Christian Indians. Gentile, originally a non-Jew, was used in the Acts of the Apostles to describe those who were the primary objects of the missionary activity of St. Paul, and hence was later applied to Indians the missionaries hoped to convert.

Since the valley continues on, the place was named Santa Clara. The site is very suitable for a mission because it has everything there that is required. It is six leagues from Santa Rosa and ten leagues from Santa Catalina de Bononia. I calculated the latitude and it came out to 34 degrees 30 minutes. The gentiles gave us sage and a large load of it was placed on a mule. The rest was divided among everyone.

Saturday, August 12: We left Santa Clara at three in the afternoon on this day, which happened to be the feast of Santa Clara. We continued traveling in the same valley in a west-southwest direction. Creeks and gullies formed by the floodwaters that flow from the mountains during the rainy season made the road rough and uneven. We stopped at the bank of one of the creeks that had plenty of water. After traveling about three leagues from camp, we came upon a *ranchería* of gentiles. They were as friendly as the others. As soon as we arrived they came with their baskets of *pinole* and pine nuts. We gave them beads in return. We named this *ranchería* San Pedro Amoliano, with the hope that this saint will look after these poor people and lead them to accept baptism.

Sunday, August 13: After the two of us had said Mass, which was attended by everyone, we left this place at about eight in the morning, traveling through the same valley, which continues to the southwest and begins to widen. We traveled two hours, during which time we must have gone two leagues. We stopped near a *ranchería* of gentiles which was a short distance from a creek. Since this creek is very wide and has a great deal of water running through it, undoubtedly formed by the many creeks of the Santa Clara Valley, we decided that this creek was a river. The *ranchería* consists of twenty houses made of grass. They are shaped in a spherical form like a half orange, with a vent at the top through which light enters and smoke goes out.

I went with the other Father to see the river, which is not very far from the *ranchería*. It seemed to us that the riverbed must have a width of fifty *varas* of sand and about eighteen *varas* of flowing water. The water was very shallow and level with the land. The great plain we saw extended far to the south. It seemed to us that the level land reached as far as the shore. The gentiles gave us their baskets of seeds as gifts. We reciprocated by giving them beads, which made them very happy. We named this river and this place The Holy Martyrs Hipólito and Casiano. In the afternoon two earthquakes were felt.

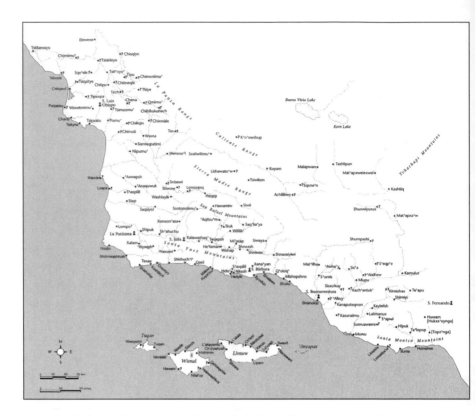

As Fr. Crespí's diary indicates, the area through which the Portolá expedition traveled was heavily populated. This map, which relies on painstaking research carried out by John Johnson of the Santa Barbara Museum of Natural History, reconstructs Chumash settlements as they existed at the time of Crespí's visits.

The expedition camped near Kamulus, northwest of the future site of Mission San Fernando, on the night of August 10. From there they headed in a general westerly and southwesterly direction. They camped in the general vicinities of Fillmore, Santa Paula, and Saticoy on August 11, 12, and 13. On August 14 they arrived at the coastal village of Shisholop, which Crespí dubbed La Asunción in honor of the feast of the Assumption of the Virgin Mary the next day. This was the settlement Rodríguez Cabrillo had dubbed "pueblo de las canoas." From there they followed the shoreline and passed through a number of Chumash settlements. They were at Misopshno (Carpintería) on August 17 and arrived at Syuxtun (now Santa Barbara) on August 18. They traveled very little on August 19. On August 20 they were in the vicinity of what is now Goleta, in the area of the towns of Helo', S'axpilil, 'Alkash, and Heliyik. Courtesy of the Santa Barbara Museum of Natural History and the Archaeology and Ethnography Program of the National Park Service.

Monday, August 14: At seven in the morning we left the camp accompanied by three gentiles who came to show us the watering place. We traveled along the plain in a west-northwest direction. After traveling for about two and a half hours we arrived at the shore, where we saw an acceptable town, the most populous and best laid out of any we had seen on the journey up to the present time. It is situated on a point of land that juts out from the same beach. The town stands out from the beach and appears to look out over the waters. We counted about thirty large, comfortable, and well-constructed houses. They are shaped like spheres with roofs of grass. According to the people we saw and who came down to the camp, there were close to four hundred souls there. They are a large and healthy people, quick, industrious, and clever. Their skill and ability stand out particularly in the construction of their canoes. They are made from good pine planks which are joined together well to form an elegantly shaped canoe with two bows. They maneuver the canoes as skillfully as they construct them. Three or four men go out to sea in the canoes to fish. The canoes can hold as many as ten men. They use long oars with two blades and row with an indescribable ability and speed.

Everything they make is meticulously constructed and well finished. What is most amazing is that the only tools they have for working with wood and stone are tools made of flint. They have no knowledge of the use of iron and steel. Nevertheless, we saw that some of them had pieces of knives and sword blades which they use for carving meat and cutting open the fish they take from the sea. The soldiers traded with the gentiles and gave them beads in exchange for baskets, pebbles, and wooden plates. The plates were of different sizes and shapes and could not have been more elegant if they had been made on a potter's wheel. They gave us a lot of fish, especially bonito, which was very delicious. Judging by the great abundance of fish and the ease with which it was caught, this must be the season for it.

We set up camp a short distance from the town near a riverbank. The river water comes from a deep bed within the mountains and flows out to the sea. Along the north side the river runs through a valley which has fertile land. They make good use of this because there is an abundance of water. In the afternoon some chiefs came from the mountains so they could see us. Some islanders from the Santa Bárbara Channel who happened to be in this town also came to see us. They told us that twelve canoes had gone to the islands to bring back the people who wanted to see us. I named this town La Asunción de Nuestra Señora. I hope that through the intercession of this great lady, such a fine site, which lacks nothing, will become a good mission. I calculated the latitude and for me it came out to 34 degrees 36 minutes, but for Señor Costansó it came out to 34 degrees 13 minutes.

Tuesday, August 15: The two of us said Mass, which was heard by everybody. At two in the afternoon we set out and headed in a westerly direction along the edge of the sea. Right at the beginning we crossed the river, which was somewhat difficult because of the rocks and the large amount of water that flowed over them. We traveled about two leagues along the sandy beach. The distance between the sea and the rugged, bare mountains to our right is wide in some parts and narrow in others; so narrow that there is no room to pass without difficulty. After traveling two hours we stopped near a small *ranchería* that had a few small grass houses. Their only source of water is a small pool. Some people were fishing in a canoe that was probably seven *varas* long. The people of the *ranchería* immediately called out to them and they returned to shore with very many large fish. The chief and his entire village came to the camp with the fish and many seeds which he gave to the Governor, who reciprocated with his gift of beads. They were very happy. They gave us more food than everyone could eat. During the night they annoyed us by keeping us awake, playing some doleful pipes or whistles all night long. This made our sentinels more watchful. I named this *ranchería* Santa Conefundis.

Wednesday, August 16: At about half-past six we headed out, following the same westerly route which runs from here to the beach. After traveling two leagues we arrived at another town that was larger than Asunción. We counted sixty well-built houses constructed in the same manner as those of the first town. It has a fine creek with good running water that flows to the sea. Before reaching the sea, the creek runs into a small rise in the land. The current slows and the water backs up, creating an estuary.

There is only enough land at the seashore near the *ranchería* to build the town. The hills in the immediate area have fertile soil and are covered with good grass. I do not know if in the valleys between the hills there is a creek or level ground. It is necessary to explore the region, because if it has water and level ground, it would be a fine place for a mission. The Indians are very tranquil and good-natured. We noticed that they had seven canoes and they were fishing from them in the ocean.

Top, left to right: Olivella shell bead-making kit, Santa Rosa Island; Serpentine bowl inlaid with olivella shell beads, unprovenienced Santa Barbara County, Phelan Collection. Bottom, left to right: Chumash basket collected by navigator on whaling ship Equator, *about 1819; Abalone and bone fishhooks from Santa Cruz Island. All photographs by George H. Huey. Courtesy of the Santa Barbara Museum of Natural History.*

As soon as we arrived everyone came to see us. They brought a huge supply of smoked or roasted fish for us to eat until the canoes could bring back fresh fish. Soon after, the canoes landed on the beach and they brought us plenty of bonito and perch. They gave us so much fish that we could have loaded down all the pack animals if we had a way to prepare and salt the fish. In addition to what they had already given us, they gave us dried fish, which was prepared without salt. They do not use salt in their food. We took the fish with us in case we needed it on the journey and we did make good use of it. One of this town's chiefs was in the town of Asumpta when we passed by. He was the one who lavished the most attention on us. He is a man of strong build and normal features. He is a wonderful dancer and that is why the soldiers named this place the Town of the Dancer (*Pueblo de El Bailarín*). I, however, named it Santa Clara de Monte Talco. I calculated the latitude and it came out to 34 degrees 40 minutes. There are groves of willow, cottonwood, alder, and live-oak trees along the creekbed of this town.

Thursday, August 17: We set out from this place at half-past seven and continued traveling in a westerly direction. We climbed some steep hills covered with grass. The grass land ends abruptly at a cliff overlooking the beach. Between the hills and the beach there is a passage along the sand dunes. We probably had traveled about half a league when we arrived at a point of land which forms a small bay with the previously mentioned town on the opposite side of the beach. We found a very large town at this point. We counted thirty-eight houses like the ones already described. Some of them were so large that they could house many families. At the edge of town all the inhabitants were waiting for us. There were as many people there as at Asumpta. We went to the *ranchería* to greet them. The Commander gave the chief some beads as a gift. We set up camp in a clearing not very far from the *ranchería.* From north to south the area spanned about a league. The soil was good and dark and densely covered with grass. From east to west it spans four leagues. There are many willow, cottonwood, alder, and live-oak trees in the area. There is also an abundance of firewood. The very high mountains to the north are wooded in some parts but not in other.

Friday, August 18: At seven in the morning we left this place and traveled across the clearing in a westerly direction because the beach was nearby. We were accompanied by the chief from the *ranchería* that we had just visited. The chief from the other town, the one who had come last night with many Indians who wanted to follow his example, also came. These Indians were very happy and in a festive mood. After traveling one league we came upon the ruins of a *ranchería*. The gentiles told us that about three months ago Indians from the mountains had come down and killed all the people. Two and a half leagues from where we started we came upon the ruins of another *ranchería* that had suffered the same fate. There are springs at these places and this is where the *rancherías* obtained their water. We saw bear tracks on this march, which lasted four hours.

After traveling four leagues we arrived at a large *ranchería,* much larger than the other ones. It was near a long peninsula that jutted into the sea. With some difficulty we crossed a large estuary that extends far inland. We passed by the *ranchería* and then set up camp at a distance of two gunshots from the *ranchería*. Shortly after we arrived, all the people came, bearing a generous gift of fish, which they carried in seven very large bundles. We reciprocated by giving them beads. They left quite pleased. A while later, the canoes that were out fishing returned. Everyone then came back, young and old, with a gift of fresh fish amounting to four loads. More than five hundred people, males and females of all ages, came to the camp with this gift. They spent practically the whole day with us.

Near the *ranchería* there is a spring of good water. Near the camp we found a large lagoon that does not seem to be seasonal, for there is a spring in the middle of the lagoon. There are many large live-oak trees in the open spaces. We named this town Laguna de la Concepción. The latitude could not be calculated because it was a cloudy day. The islands can be seen from here.

Saturday, August 19: We set out today simply to get away from so many people. Heading west over the mesas, we went down to a dry creek lined with alder and live-oak trees. From that point on, there is a plain with good, black soil. We stopped there after having traveled no more than half a league. We moved away from the beach, which was steep and bordered by high hills. We stopped in a valley where the running water is absorbed by the sand. Not far from the water's source the valley is covered with live-oak and alder trees. On the summit there are pine trees.

People from a *ranchería* came to visit us. They undoubtedly live nearby. The soldiers who went out to explore this morning came back in the afternoon. They reported that they had found large settlements inhabited by many people who received them warmly. That night ten unarmed gentiles came to our camp. A guard was placed on duty to keep them company and entertain them until morning.

Sunday, August 20: At eight in the morning, after Mass, we set out, following the plain in a westerly direction. We traveled on level ground between the mountains and some hills which extend along the coast. The land is good. There is much grass and fully grown live-oak, alder, and willow trees. There also are Castilian roses. After traveling about three leagues, a long bare point of land came into view. From the west a large estuary enters by way of two different mouths one-half league from each other. The estuary is bordered on the north by a good piece of land of moderate length. It is completely isolated. The island is very green and covered with trees. We saw a large town there with more than a hundred houses. The estuary extends out to the west, forming many marshes and lagoons. There are other towns along their banks. We could not determine exactly how many towns were there, but some of our soldiers said there were four. Those four added to the town on the island added up to five towns altogether. The town on the island appears to be the largest. We passed through the middle of one of these towns on our way to the watering place. We had set up camp near there.

Shortly after, the gentiles from the towns arrived with roasted and fresh fish, seeds, acorns, *atole,* and other kinds of food. They urged us to eat. By their facial expressions they seemed pleased that we had come and were staying in their land. The Governor gave them gifts of beads and ribbons. They were very pleased. The soldiers traded with them and obtained various objects such as baskets, feather headdresses, and pelts.

The entire area along the route, as well as that which can be seen from the camp, is extremely beautiful. Pasture land abounds and the area is covered with live-oak, willow, and other trees. The land appears to be very fertile, capable of producing anything one might want to plant. These gentiles seem to have excellent provisions, especially all types of fish. In fact they brought so much fish to camp that it was necessary to tell them not to bring any more because it would eventually spoil. They were not satisfied with only giving us their food, they also wanted to entertain us. It was clear that there was a rivalry between the towns. They were competing with one another to see who could give the best presents and feasts in order to win our favor. In the afternoon the leaders from each town came, one after the other. They were adorned, painted, and decorated with feathers. They carried hollow reeds in their hands. The movement and noise of these reeds

helped them keep such good time to the music and such unison to the ca-
dence of the dance that they produced real harmony. These dances lasted all
afternoon and it was very difficult for us to get rid of these people. They
were sent away and with gestures were told emphatically not to come during the night and disturb us. However, it was all in vain. As soon as night fell
they returned, playing some pipes. The noise grated on our ears. It was
feared that the noise might frighten the horses, so the Commander went
over to see the Indians with his officers and some soldiers. They gave the Indians some beads and begged them to leave. They told them that if they
came back and interrupted our sleep they would not be warmly welcomed
as friends. This was enough to make them go away and leave us in peace for
the rest of the night.

1769
Searching for Monterey

GASPAR DE PORTOLÁ

After leaving the Santa Barbara area, the Portolá group continued along the coast. They reached Morro Bay on September 8. The rugged coastline to the north soon made it necessary to turn inland, and they did so on September 15. After crossing a series of difficult mountain passes, they followed the Salinas River toward the sea and on October 1 camped on the bank of a river just a few miles from its mouth. Knowing that they were near the latitude at which they expected to find Monterey Bay, they spent about a week exploring the vicinity. They came upon Carmel Bay and the Carmel River, but nothing looked like what the Vizcaíno expedition had described. They decided to press on and broke camp on October 6.

The failure of the Portolá group to recognize Monterey Bay when it was literally at their feet has often been accounted for by the claim that Vizcaíno's descriptions were exaggerated. Yet, as the excerpts from Vizcaíno's writings included earlier in this volume indicate, his descriptions, while praising Monterey, were generally sober and clear.

The reasons for this expedition's failure to realize where they were probably stemmed from the fact that they were approaching by land. The main source they had with them was a navigation guide published in 1734 by José González Cabrera Bueno, a pilot on the Manila route. The California section of Cabrera Bueno's guide was based on the account of Fr. Antonio Ascención, who, as we have seen, had been with Vizcaíno. Cabrera Bueno thus described entering Monterey Bay from the south, at Point Pinos and following the coast until the port itself was reached. In fact, when Vicente Vila and Junípero Serra entered the harbor by sea the next year, they immediately recognized the place from what they had read about it. But the Portolá party was following the Salinas River, which they incorrectly thought was the Carmel River. Since they thought that Point

Pinos was probably north of the Carmel River, they were confused when
they saw it to the south, and they were never completely able to reconcile
what they were seeing with the geography they expected to encounter.
When they did catch sight of the Carmel River in their explorations of the
area, they saw its water level low, as it would be at the end of the dry season.
Therefore, they did not make the connection between what they thought
was a nameless creek and the river close by Point Pinos. Second, they came
to the bay at the mouth of the Salinas River. Most people who stand there
today or climb any hill in the same vicinity would not think of the body of
water in front of them as a bay. Most of the time, one simply cannot see all
the way up to Santa Cruz, let alone beyond it to Point Año Nuevo.

The Portolá group, however, knew none of this. They only knew that
they had been sent to find a bay. The only thing that looked to them like a
bay was Carmel Bay, and that obviously was not Vizcaíno's port. So they
pressed on. Not realizing that they were walking on the shores of what
they were seeking, they crossed the Pájaro River, saw redwood trees for
the first time, and on October 17 reached the San Lorenzo River, which
empties into the northern part of Monterey Bay. They passed Point Año
Nuevo on October 23 and reached Half Moon Bay a few days later. From
there, Portolá sent Sergeant José Francisco Ortega into the mountains.
When the men of his party climbed into the hills they quickly recognized
Point Reyes, the landmark of Cermeño's San Francisco Bay (Drake's Bay),
some forty miles to the north, and they made further explorations. From
Sweeney Ridge (outside of Pacifica) they spied a great inland body of
water, San Francisco Bay. The entire expedition then crossed the ridge and
explored parts of the San Francisco peninsula for the next few days. Ortega led a small party around the southern end of this new bay and up its
eastern shore, but he soon returned, reporting that hostile Indians and another "estuary" had blocked his progress. Confused, increasingly irritable,
and running low on supplies, the expedition decided to return south.
They reached the area around Point Pinos in early December. Portolá
then sent Rivera into the hills in a last-ditch effort to catch a glimpse of
the elusive port of Monterey. When Rivera's party returned and reported
failure, Portolá convened a staff conference. What follows is the record of
that meeting. Beneath the legalisms and the pieties designed for consumption in Mexico City, it is easy to discern the frustration of men who were
unable to find what they were looking for, after they had traveled fifteen
hundred miles to find it. Also, the frustrations of Rivera y Moncada are

palpable. Part of Rivera's critique of Portolá for having launched the expedition without sufficient supplies stemmed from the fact that Rivera, born in New Spain and the member of the expedition most familiar with California, resented having to take orders from a Spaniard like Portolá, who had only recently arrived in the New World.

After the meeting's conclusion the party abandoned the search for Monterey. They turned south and arrived in San Diego on January 24, 1770.

FROM THE RECORD OF THE MEETING AT POINT PINOS

Dear Sirs:

On November 11, the members of the expedition, finding ourselves at 37½ degrees, according to calculations by Don Miguel Costansó, the *Alférez* of Engineers, met to decide how to proceed. He added that the *farallones* that could be seen were signs of the port of San Francisco. A vote was taken and everyone agreed that the expedition should return to Point Pinos to set up camp. Once there, we could consider carefully and in detail how far we had traveled and, in particular, determine how to proceed in terms of the mountains that obstructed our path. And this is exactly what we did. After we arrived at Point Pinos, Captain Don Fernando de Rivera set out to explore the aforementioned mountains. He soon realized that the port of Monterey, as he understood it to look, was not to be found near those mountains. These are my reasons for again requesting that all the officers be brought together for a meeting, imploring that the Reverend Fathers lend their assistance so that we can come to a unanimous decision as to what is in the best interest of our service to both Majesties. In addition, we find ourselves in a deplorable state with regard to provisions, for we only have sixteen sacks of flour left.

May God Our Lord keep Your Lordship many years

Point Pinos
December 5, 1769
Your most loving and faithful servant kisses the hand
of Your Excellency.
Gaspar de Portolá

Portrait of Gaspar de Portolá from municipal building, Lérida, Spain.

Declaration of the Engineer Don Miguel Costansó

This officer recognizes that the lofty goals that guide this expedition are of profound interest to the glory of God, the King, and the superiors who have placed their trust in him to contribute his part to the success of the enterprise. And, without acting rashly, which would weigh on his conscience, his honor and credibility are ultimately hanging in the balance until he reaches the end of what may be an impossible goal.

He, as well as everyone else, knows that two ships have been sent to rescue this expedition.* It is very possible that one of the ships will appear along the coast, most likely at the spot that was designated where we would wait for them. Moreover, he is certain that this expedition, with the sixteen sacks of flour and the rest of the provisions it has at the camp, can extend its stay at this place a bit longer if they carefully conserve what they have and distribute it judiciously. In order to avoid jealousy among the men, all of the provisions should be shown to them, without exception. The provisions should be doled out equally to the soldiers and the officers, without favoring one group over the other. The officers are in the position to set the example by coming to the aid of the soldiers, who are in dire need. After everything has been consumed and if there is no ship in sight or the possibility of some other type of aid, the entire expedition should go back to San Diego. From there they can inform His Excellency the Viceroy and the Illustrious Señor Visitor-General of the state of the expedition and wait for word from these superiors. Or, if they are unable to wait for a response, they can continue retreating.

Rendered at the bay of Point Pinos on December 7, 1769

Miguel Costansó

Declaration of Lieutenant Don Pedro Fages

This officer explains that, in order to attain the goal of this expedition without hindering its success or putting the men in jeopardy, the expedition should be divided into two groups. The first group should be under the command of an officer who should remain at Point Pinos to wait for relief from the ships that are expected to arrive. This port appears to be the most satisfactory one according to all who know it. It was determined that the mountains that are within view are the Santa Lucía Mountains, according

---

* The *San Antonio,* which had gone to San Blas, and the *San José,* which, unknown to them, had sunk.

to Captain Don Fernando de Rivera y Moncada, who recognized them from descriptions made by the pilot Cabrera. They are high, white cliffs six leagues from Point Pinos. They extend along the coast and are near a medium-sized, horn-shaped estuary that looks like a *farallón* that has been divided by the same coast. The observations of the Engineer Don Miguel Costansó verify that these are the Santa Lucía Mountains and so does the precise survey of the coast up to 37 degrees 40 minutes.

The second party or group could return to the Cañada de los Osos,* where they could take as much time as they needed to kill these animals and prepare and dry the meat. In this way they could come to the aid of the first group in the event they found it necessary to turn back. All the provisions at the base camp and the sixteen sacks of flour should be consolidated with any provisions that some individuals may have kept for themselves. No exceptions should be made for anybody.

After all the provisions have been accurately accounted for, they should be divided among the two groups. Once the first group has eaten everything, they should join the second group at the Cañada de los Osos so that aid can be brought to them. Together they can retreat to San Diego, assuming that no ship has appeared yet and there is no longer any hope of being able to survive at Point Pinos. From San Diego they can inform their superiors.

Ensenada de Pinos, December 8, 1769

Pedro Fages

Declaration of Captain Don Fernando de Rivera y Moncada

This is the third time that I have been called to a meeting or council to give my opinion. It should be evident to Your Excellencies that I have already documented my views and I believe that I should have been excused from doing this again. In my last account, which I gave at the port from which we have returned, I concluded by saying that we would be here for as long as the *Señor Comandante* deemed necessary. Truthfully, it is up to the *Señor Comandante* to make the logical and fair decision to free these servants of the King from the threat of total ruin due to the lack of provisions, for they have served him faithfully for so long. We have gone hungry for days for lack of food, and this is why it happened. It was not necessary to have a meeting when we left San Diego traveling toward the channel of Santa Bárbara. By means of an official communication I tried to inform the

---

* Cañada de los Osos (ravine of the bears) is near San Luis Obispo.

Commander of the danger in which we found ourselves. His response to me in San Diego was that he and the soldiers would eat what they had and if there was no food for the soldiers, he would not eat either. Later, at the channel, I even went a step further and suggested to him publicly that the trip had been made against the better judgement of the Illustrious Señor Visitor-General. Before ordering us to leave, two ships were dispatched, yet we found ourselves without one. When I had the opportunity, I brought up the subject of what had happened to the first Spaniards who entered into Florida so he would remember.

Now then, I have given my report in this fashion and I have repeated the same thing during the entire trip, which is evident to all the members of the expedition. However, it remains for me to inform the *Señor Comandante* of the unrest among the soldiers. This should be feared if we completely run out of provisions. First, it is not beyond the realm of possibility that they will desert. For example, nine days ago two mule drivers disappeared. When I went to look for them I saw their tracks heading south. After four days of searching I returned in the evening. Second, the soldiers will begin to steal and commit other bold acts. Third, they will be insubordinate. Imagine all the problems that could result from this. The person who is responsible for this expedition should consider these points very carefully, for it seems to me that many very serious problems can arise.

In some fashion we have achieved the goal of our trip with ships and provisions. Beyond 37½ degrees we saw a port, good land, abundant water from a river, and a creek that was flowing, as well as timber and dry wood that can be used for building. And, even if we did not reach our destination, that is, the port of Monterey, we did search for it right and left and round and round.

In my opinion, the land, water, and many Indians are worthy of consideration. With the arrival of a ship or supplies, we could venture forth under the command of our own leader, set up camp at that port, and report everything we see.

Finally, I conclude that it is my opinion that the *Señor Comandante* should make the decision. If his decision is to stay here longer to wait for the ships or some other relief, I beg the Señor to be kind enough to allow me to return with the twenty men that the Illustrious Señor Visitor-General assigned to me for this undertaking. I then can report on what was discovered as well as the situation at hand. In that way, appropriate measures can be taken and orders given, which I could take back with the help of God if his Illustrious Lordship wished to continue to avail himself of my services.

So that what I have stated will be on record wherever, however, and whenever it is needed, I hereby sign and date this document at the inlet of Point Pinos on December 7, 1769.

Fernando de Rivera y Moncada

Declaration of the Commander of the Expedition

With the utmost honor and sense of duty, I believe that all the members of this expedition can testify to the efforts that were made to find the port of Monterey, venturing up to a position of 37½ degrees according to the observation made by the *Alférez* of Engineers, Don Miguel Costansó. After we had gone beyond 38 degrees it was decided that there should be a meeting, which took place on the eleventh of this past November. Fearful that we might be stranded at the port after having traveled so far, the decision was made to turn back. That is exactly what we did and we were fortunate that God granted us clear skies all this time. There was no doubt in anybody's mind that this was the right thing to do. The expedition had always traveled along the coast. On the remaining part of our journey through the mountains, which everyone believed to be the Santa Lucía Mountains, we were forced to go around them because they were impenetrable. Our only consolation was that we did end up at the spot where the port was supposed to be located and we were able to explore the area along the way in great detail.

With this goal in mind, Captain Don Fernando de Rivera set out to carefully explore the area. Upon his return he reported that he saw nothing more than a high mountain range that was difficult to traverse on horseback and on foot. The Captain said that he saw a high, white mountaintop. Below, at the edge of the sea, he saw a low hill, but no port. For this reason I vote to have the expedition turn back, since they did not find the so-called port of Monterey. One can assume that one hundred and sixty years later these ports may have been hidden by the weather. At Point Pinos, where we are located now, an iron basket from the main mast of a ship was found.

With great sorrow, this expedition must turn back because it did not find the port. However, the Reverend Fathers, the officers, and I would be willing to suffer the greatest of deprivations and wait to see if relief would arrive on the ship.

Point of Pines, December 7, 1769

Gaspar de Portolá

Summary of the votes to decide how to proceed

Engineer Don Miguel Costansó: He understands that the retreat will be necessary, since no ship has appeared to come to the aid of this expedition. He leaves it up to the *Señor Comandante* to initiate the retreat now or after all of the provisions have been consumed.

Lieutenant Don Pedro Fages: I agree that the expedition should retreat, as long as it is done as I have outlined in the declaration I have already given.

Captain Don Fernando de Rivera y Moncada: He says that the retreat should be as he has outlined in his declaration.

Commander of the Expedition: In light of the burden placed on this expedition because of the lack of provisions and the fact that all hope has been lost of finding the port of Monterey as it was described by the pilot Cabrera, I vote to have the expedition turn back. The Most Excellent Señor the Viceroy and the Illustrious Señor Visitor-General should be informed of all the effort that was expended.

Considering the unfortunate circumstances which beset this expedition and the fact that it was unable to find the port of Monterey after traveling up to the location of 37 degrees 40 minutes, the decision of the council seems prudent to us. So that it will be on record, we hereby sign this document at Point Pinos, December 7, 1769.

Fr. Juan Crespí
Fr. Francisco Gómez

1770
A Beachhead at Monterey

Junípero Serra

When the Portolá expedition returned to San Diego, it found the garrison in desperate condition. The Kumeyaay had attacked the compound on August 15 and killed Fr. Serra's personal assistant, José María Vergerano. The missionaries were frustrated by their inability to entice any of the Kumeyaay to accept their faith. The failure of the Portolá expedition to find Monterey depressed everyone even further. "You have come from Rome without having seen the Pope," Serra dourly remarked to the commander.

Now there were a total of seventy-four mouths to feed, and neither of the two ships they were awaiting, the *San José* or the *San Antonio,* was anywhere in sight. Portolá finally decreed that the site would be abandoned on March 19, the feast of St. Joseph, if assistance did not arrive by that date. Serra prayed and prayed, and when the sail of the *San Antonio* appeared on the horizon on the very last day, he felt that his prayers had been answered. But the vessel sailed right past San Diego. Juan Pérez was bound for Monterey, where he expected that an outpost had been established. He stopped near Santa Barbara to make repairs and there found out from the local Chumash that all the Spaniards had returned from their trip north. Then he turned around and headed for San Diego, arriving on March 23.

A joint sea and land expedition was then planned. The land party again was commanded by Portolá. They left on April 17 and arrived at Point Pinos on May 24. This time they recognized the place. When the *San Antonio* sailed in on June 1, there was no doubt that this was indeed Vizcaíno's harbor. An outpost similar to that of San Diego was established with a simple base camp and a make-do church built close to each other. To mark the enterprise they located a tree that looked like it might be the one under which Mass had been celebrated in 1602 by the Carmelites. They decided to hold the opening ceremonies there. Serra described the scene in a letter to the Guardian (Superior) of the College of San Fernando.

Retrato del Rev. Padre Fray Junípero Serra. Apostol de la Alta California, tomado del original que se conserva en su Convento de la Santa Cruz de Querétaro.

Por J. Mosqueda, pinxit.

No evidence exists that Junípero Serra ever sat for a portrait. This depiction, done in the early twentieth century by a Mexican priest, Fr. José Mosqueda, is the most familiar one. He said that he based it on an older painting which had long hung in the city of Querétaro and was apparently lost during the Mexican revolution of the 1910s. Courtesy of the Santa Barbara Mission Archive Library.

FROM A LETTER BY JUNÍPERO SERRA

Carmel, June 12, 1770
Hail Jesus, Mary, Joseph!
Very Reverend Father Guardian Fray Juan Andrés
Venerable Father and my dear Sir:

In accordance with what I have mentioned in my former letters to Your Reverence, having now completed a full eight months as minister of San Diego Mission, I have appointed in my place the Father Preacher Fray Francisco Gómez, who, with Father Preacher Fernando Parrón, will stay behind and look after the place. And so on April 14, Saturday of Holy Week, in the same port, I went aboard the packet boat *San Antonio,* also called *El Príncipe,* to sail for Monterey, leaving Father Preacher Fray Juan Crespí to accompany for a second time the land expedition. This was to start as soon as they saw our boat set sail.

We left the said port on the sixteenth of the same month, since neither God nor the wind allowed us to start on Easter Day. He obliged us to sanctify that great feast day, and because of that fact I rejoiced greatly.

The voyage was somewhat trying, and for many days, far from getting nearer to Monterey, we were getting farther and farther away from the goal of our desires. The result of it all was that the voyage lasted a full month and a half; and on May 31, we entered and dropped anchor in the port—the object of so many controversies. We now recognized it without any questions as being, both as to its underlying reality and its superficial landmarks, the same and unchanged spot where our ancestors the Spaniards landed in the year 1603. It is plain justice that we should definitely put out of our minds all thought, or any lingering fancy, of the port's having disappeared, or being no longer in existence. These false notions have been circulated by reports emanating from the recent land expedition.

On the very night of our arrival we learned that the land expedition had already arrived eight days before and was encamped two leagues away, near the Carmel River. The next day Father Crespí came to meet us with the officers of the expedition. Our rejoicings were great on both sides. On meeting, I issued an invitation to all, for the day after tomorrow—a Sunday and the feast of Pentecost—to participate in the celebration of the first Mass and the erection of the standard of the Most Holy Cross in that country. We all agreed to it.

The day came. A little chapel and altar were erected in that little valley, and under the same live oak, close to the beach, where it is said Mass was celebrated at the beginning of the last century. Two processions from different directions converged at the same time on the spot, one from the sea and one from the land expedition; we singing the Divine Praises in the launch, and the men on land, in their hearts.

Our arrival was greeted by the joyful sound of the bells suspended from the branches of the oak tree. Everything being in readiness, and having put on alb and stole, and kneeling down with all the men before the altar, I intoned the hymn *Veni, Creator Spiritus,* at the conclusion of which, and after invoking the help of the Holy Spirit on everything we were about to perform, I blessed the salt and the water. Then we all made our way to a gigantic cross which was all in readiness and lying on the ground. With everyone lending a hand, we set it in an upright position. I sang the prayers for its blessing. We set it in the ground and then, with all the tenderness of our hearts, we venerated it. I sprinkled with holy water all the fields around. And thus, after raising aloft the standard of the King of Heaven, we unfurled the flag of our Catholic Monarch likewise. As we raised each one of them, we shouted at the top of our voices, "Long live the Faith! Long live the King!" All the time the bells were ringing, and our rifles were being fired, and from the boat came the thunder of the big guns. Then we buried at the foot of the cross a dead sailor, a calker, the only one to die during this second expedition.

With that ceremony over, I began the high Mass with a sermon after the Gospel; and as long as the Mass lasted, it was accompanied with many salvos of cannon. After taking off my chasuble after Mass, all together we sang in Spanish the *Salve Regina,* in harmony, in front of the wonderful painting of Our Lady, which was on the altar. The Most Illustrious Inspector General had given us the picture for this celebration, but with the obligation of returning it to him afterwards, as I will do when the boat sails.

As a conclusion to the liturgical celebration, standing up I intoned the *Te Deum Laudamus;* we sang it slowly, and solemnly, right to the end, with the responses and prayers to the Most Holy Trinity, to Our Lady, to the Most Holy Saint Joseph, patron of the expedition, to San Carlos, patron of this port, *presidio,* and mission, and finally the prayer of thanksgiving.

May God be thanked for all things! Meantime, having put off my vestments, and while I was making my thanksgiving after the Mass of the day, the officers proceeded to the act of taking formal possession of that country in the name of His Catholic Majesty, unfurling and waving once more the royal flag, pulling grass, moving stones, and other formalities according to law—all accompanied with cheers, ringing of bells, cannonades, etc. In

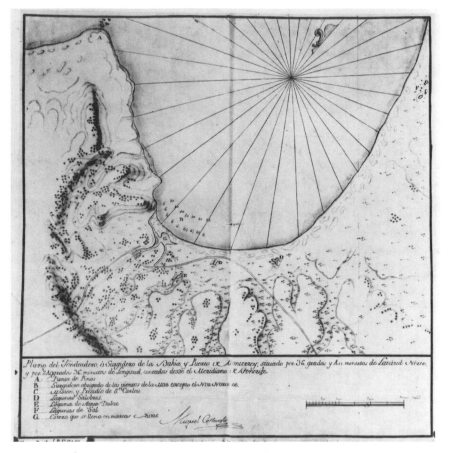

Map of Monterey prepared by the engineer Miguel Costansó in 1770. The numbers in the water are depth soundings. The letters are: A, Point of Pines; B, anchorage protected from sea winds except those from the north-northwest; C, mission and presidio of San Carlos; D, brackish lake; E, lake of sweet water; F, salt lakes; G, estuary affected by the tides. Courtesy of The Bancroft Library, University of California, Berkeley.

addition there was a banquet served afterwards to all of us gathered together on the beach; later a walk at sunset along the ocean concluded the celebration, when the men of the land expedition returned to their Carmel, and we to the boat.

A few days later the expedition moved to a pretty plain about a rifle shot from the beach, and there established the *presidio* and the mission to it. Thus our dear College may now count this new mission as one more on the list. It is called "San Carlos de Monterey."

1771
Encounter at San Gabriel

FRANCISCO PALÓU

After fulfilling his orders to establish San Diego and Monterey, Portolá left California and returned to Mexico. He later served as governor of Puebla and eventually returned to his hometown of Lérida in Spain, where he died in 1786. Portolá appointed Pedro Fages, a Spaniard who had been on the expedition, as commander of Monterey. Fages, as senior military officer, became the chief official in Alta California. Portolá's successors as governor of the Californias, Matías de Armona and Felipe de Barri, resided in Loreto.

The military concentrated on constructing more permanent fortifications at the two *presidios,* while the missionaries began the process of founding additional missions. San Antonio was founded south of Monterey in July 1771. San Gabriel was established in September of that same year, in a location which had served as a camping area for the 1769 Portolá expedition.

The founding of San Gabriel was the occasion for an important element in the missionary narrative of Alta California, which is presented here. In this account, which comes from Fr. Francisco Palóu's biography of Junípero Serra, a number of themes that permeated the missionary self-understanding were clustered together. The Indians were presented as being, at first, either indifferent or hostile. They were soon won over by the richness of the Christian tradition, especially by representations of the Virgin Mary. The soldiers, by mistreating and raping Indian women, were the most serious obstacles to the spread of Christianity in California.

Francisco Palóu published his biography of Serra in Mexico City in 1787. Palóu was a longtime friend of the founder of the missions. As a student of Serra's in Majorca, he accompanied his teacher to America. They served together in the Sierra Gorda and then in Baja California. When

Serra left for Alta California, he appointed Palóu as superior of the Baja California missions. Palóu himself came to Alta California in 1773 and served as superior there while Serra was visiting Mexico City. He founded Mission San Francisco in 1776 and remained there for most of the time until he returned to Mexico in 1785. He began writing his biography of Serra while he was in California and finished it in Mexico City. He also composed another historical work, entitled *New California,* and served as Guardian of the College of San Fernando. He died in 1789.

FROM *The Life of Junípero Serra* BY FRANCISCO PALÓU

On the aforementioned day, August 6, Fathers Fray Pedro Cambón and Fray Angel Somera, with a guard of ten soldiers and muleteers with the pack train of provisions, set out from San Diego. They traveled in a northerly direction, following the route of the [Portolá] expedition. After traveling about forty leagues, they arrived at the *Río de los Temblores,** which had been so named since the days of the first expedition. When the group was deciding on the choice of a site, a numerous band of pagans, led by two chiefs and armed, made its appearance. Amid fearful war cries, they attempted to impede the mission's founding. One of the fathers, fearing that a battle was imminent and that casualties would result, brought forth a canvas painting which depicted Our Lady of Sorrows and held it up for those barbarians to see. No sooner was this done than they were conquered by that beautiful image. They threw down their bows and arrows, and the two chiefs rushed forward to place at the feet of the Sovereign Queen the beads they wore around their necks as gifts of their great esteem. Thereby they showed they wanted to be at peace with us. They called together the Indians of the nearby villages, whence an ever growing number of men, women, and children came to see the Most Holy Virgin. They came bearing various seeds, which they placed at the feet of the Most Blessed Lady, thinking she would consume them as other humans did.

Similar actions were performed by the pagan women at the port of San Diego after its inhabitants had been pacified. When they were shown another painting of the Virgin Mary, Our Lady, with the Infant Jesus in her arms, and the news was spread to nearby villages, the natives came in to

---

* The Portolá expedition had experienced earthquakes *(temblores)* in this vicinity in 1769.

Language Groups of Alta California

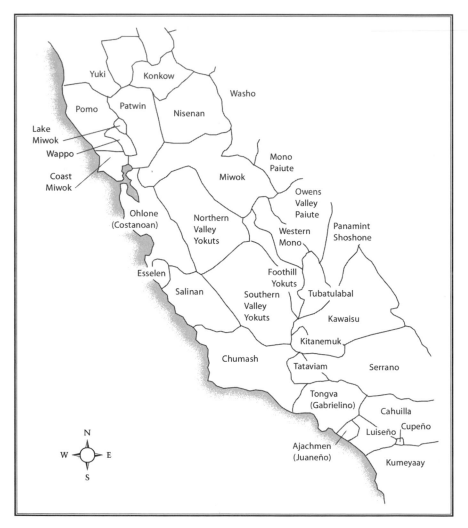

Shown here are the tribes of Alta California affected by the Spanish missionaries. The last Alta California mission was San Francisco Solano, in Sonoma.

see it. And since they could not come into the enclosure because of the stockade, they called the Fathers and they stuck their breasts in between the posts of the enclosure, meanwhile signifying in a vivid manner that they came to give milk to that tender and beautiful Child in possession of the Fathers.

After the pagans of Mission San Gabriel had seen the painting of Our Lady, they changed so much that they came time and again to visit the friars. Nor could they find sufficient means to show their happiness that the Fathers had come to live among them. The friars tried to reciprocate with endearing expressions and with gifts.

They continued to survey that great plain and began the mission at a place they judged well suited, performing the same ceremonies used in the founding of the other missions. The first Mass was celebrated under a shelter on the feast of the Nativity of Our Lady, September 8. The next day, they started to construct a chapel to serve as a temporary church, and a dwelling place for the Fathers, and barracks for the soldiers, all of palings and surrounded by a stockade for defense in any emergency. The pagans themselves cut and carried the greater part of the lumber for the constructions; they helped in building the small houses. For this reason, the Fathers were hopeful for happy results, that the pagans would not delay in embracing the sweet yoke of the law of the Gospel.

When those natives were most happy, one of the soldiers blighted their goodwill by offending one of the leading chiefs of those villages, and (what is even worse) by offending our Lord God. Because both he and his wife were outraged, the chief desired to take revenge. He gathered together the inhabitants of the nearby villages and invited the able-bodied men to take up arms. These warriors came upon the two soldiers who, at a distance from the mission, were guarding and grazing the horses. One of the soldiers happened to be the evildoer. When these soldiers saw so many warriors approaching, they put on their leather jackets to protect themselves against arrows and held their arms in readiness. They had no opportunity to notify the *presidio* guard, who was ignorant of the soldier's crime. When the pagans came within musket-shot distance, they let loose a volley of arrows, all directed at the soldier who had been the culprit. He aimed his musket at the Indian he considered the boldest, whom he presumed to be the chief and, firing, killed him. As soon as the rest saw the havoc and realized the power of our men in weapons, which they had never before experienced, and that their arrows inflicted no harm, they fled hastily, leaving dead the unfortunate chief, who had first suffered insult and now death. As a result, the Indians were cowed.

A few days after this incident, the Commandant arrived with the Fathers and the supplies for Mission San Buenaventura. Fearing that the pagans would attempt to avenge the death of their chief, he determined to increase the guard of Mission San Gabriel to the number of sixteen. For this reason, and because of the little trust he had in the other soldiers in view of repeated desertions, the founding of Mission San Buenaventura had to be suspended in order to await the outcome of events at San Gabriel. There the two missionaries destined for San Buenaventura, together with all the supplies for the same mission, remained for further orders. The Commandant went up to Monterey with the other soldiers, together with the one who had killed the pagan, in order to withdraw him from the sight of the other Indians, although the scandalous deed he had perpetrated was unknown to the Commandant and the Fathers.

1772
The Division between Alta and Baja California

Rafael Verger, Juan Pedro de Iriarte, and Francisco Palóu

When the Franciscans from San Fernando realized that the Alta California missions were going to succeed and expand, they knew that they did not have the capacity to staff the missions of both Baja and Alta California. At the same time, the Dominican order was also looking for a missionary field, and the two orders agreed to divide the old and new missions. The Franciscans would work from San Diego north, while the Dominicans would take over the older missions and construct new ones from Velicatá north.

The first excerpt below is the agreement between the officials of the two orders, dated April 7, 1772. The second excerpt, written by Palóu, describes his journey north the next year. He placed a marker on the boundary on August 19, 1773, the very first boundary between Baja and Alta California. It was located about thirty miles south of the present international boundary between Mexico and the United States.

From *Historical Memoirs of New California*

Concordat

Most Excellent Sir:

Fray Rafael Verger, present Guardian of the College of San Fernando in Mexico, and Fray Juan Pedro de Iriarte, Minister of the Holy Order of Preachers and Commissary of the Mission which, by order of his Majesty (God save him) he conducted to this Kingdom for the Peninsula of California.

We have agreed upon the following division: the Dominican fathers shall take in their charge the old missions which this College has in California and the above-mentioned frontier of San Fernando Velicatá, extending their new conversions in this direction until they reach the confines of the mission of San Diego on the harbor of that name; and, placing their last mission on the *arroyo* of San Juan Bautista, this mission shall terminate five leagues farther on, at a point which projects from the Sierra Madre and ends before reaching the beach. Once arrived there, they can turn to the east, slightly to the northeast, and in this way they ought to come out at the head of the Gulf of California and the Colorado River, following afterwards the direction pointed out to them by your Excellency in the royal council. And if in the country between the Colorado and San Diego a suitable road to the north or northeast should appear, they can also take it without prejudice to the other Order. It is agreed that the Fathers of the College of San Fernando shall retain the missions that they now have, from the port of San Diego, following the road which they have opened to Monterey, the port of San Francsico, and farther on.

Palóu's Description of the Boundary Between Baja and Alta California

On the nineteenth of August we came to the place which had been designated in the agreement, approved by the royal council, and confirmed by his Excellency for the limit of the missions of the reverend Dominican Fathers and the beginning of those of San Fernando. We came provided with a cross made the preceding day from a large alder at the *arroyo* of San Juan Bautista and bearing this inscription:

DIVIDING LINE BETWEEN THE MISSIONS OF OUR FATHER SANTO
DOMINGO AND THOSE OF OUR FATHER SAN FRANCISCO 1773

We planted it on a high rock which is in the rock itself, just as though it had been made for the purpose of serving as a pedestal for the cross. As soon as we had set it up and venerated it, we sang with extraordinary joy the *Te Deum Laudamus,* giving thanks to God our Lord for our arrival in the land of our destination. The Holy Cross was not put on the very point of the

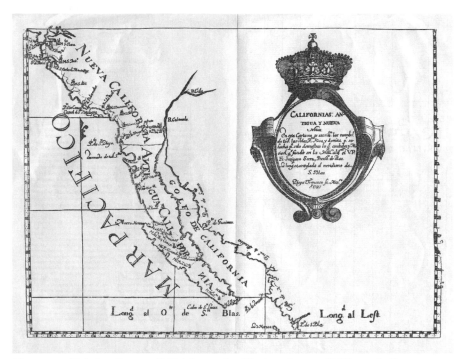

This map, published in Francisco Palóu's biography of Junípero Serra in 1787, was the first to show any sort of boundary between the two Californias. The line divided the mission territory of the Franciscans from that of the Dominicans. Courtesy of The Bancroft Library, University of California, Berkeley.

Sierra Madre, which terminates before reaching the beach, as is stated in the agreement, because that point is more than three leagues from the highway, but at the conclusion of that range, which was judged by us friars and by the soldiers and sergeant who were well acquainted with the road to be in line with the point. It is five leagues distant from the *arroyo* of San Juan Bautista and about fifteen from the port of San Diego, so that where the cross marks the division one begins to descend a very steep slope until one is about to enter the place named Los Meganos, where we halted on the twentieth. Continuing our journey, delaying just long enough to examine the pack train, we reached San Diego on the morning of the thirtieth.

Settlements

Settlements

The reactions of California's native peoples to the Spanish ranged all along the spectrum from assimilation to resistance, but there was a common thread joining them. California's indigenous peoples, throughout Alta and Baja California and during both the Spanish and Mexican periods, consistently aimed to retain their autonomy and carve out an advantage for themselves.

Those who entered a mission generally did so because it seemed to be the best way to attain a specific goal: food in times of drought or in the face of a landscape so changed that it could not produce the traditional resources; the promise of health when unknown diseases were ravaging traditional communities; the hope of security that might come from alignment with the obviously well-armed soldiers; or the help of a powerful deity in times of distress and confusion. Once at the missions, the Indians often grafted a Christian surface onto their ancient ways and created their own forms of syncretistic Christianity, as indigenous peoples had been doing for centuries throughout the Americas. They proved adept at playing the missionaries and the soldiers off against each other, using the priests as protection from the more brutal soldiers but knowing at the same time that the military offered a market for their goods and labor that might exceed what the missionaries would allow.

Those who remained beyond the reach of the missions sometimes traded with the Spanish, sometimes acted as guides for military or ecclesiastical journeys into the interior, sometimes stole horses and cattle from the mission and *presidio ranchos,* and sometimes fought fiercely against the newcomers. In circumstances that bore scant resemblance to anything their ancestors had ever faced, the indigenous peoples sought to survive on their own terms in a land that was becoming someone else's.

The tensions that existed between the military and the missionaries also helped frame the Spanish settlement of Alta California. We have seen this in Baja California, but three matters combined to make these tensions more toxic in Alta California. First, the Franciscans did not begin their missionary activity with the kind of authority over the military that the

Jesuits had enjoyed. The Franciscans and the military both knew the extent of the power that the Jesuits had exercised, and Baja California served as a powerful symbol for both groups: as a powerful attraction for the missionaries, and as a threatening model for the military. Second, the military, especially the professional officer corps from which California's governors often came, was increasingly influenced by Enlightenment ideas about equality and liberty, which made them genuinely opposed to the paternalism which the mission system imposed on the indigenous peoples. Third, the land was more productive in Alta California than in Baja California, and therefore the missions' perceived monopoly was a greater affront to others in Alta California than it had been in Baja California.

In Alta California, the missionaries proved themselves a powerful force. Their potential was revealed early, when Serra traveled to Mexico City and was able to persuade the authorities there to remove the Monterey commander from his post in 1773. The military reacted to this triumph by harassing the mission system wherever possible, by attempting to strengthen the *presidios,* and by attempting to create other centers of population and power (the *pueblos)* as a counterweight to the missions. An important part of this strategy was the military's attempt to encourage the immigration of more settlers into Alta California.

Instability in New Spain after 1810 as the independence movement struggled for home rule complicated the military's efforts. The resources of colonial officials were focused on this conflict, and they were unable to send to Alta California the supplies and provisions that the military would need if they, their *presidios,* and their *pueblos* were to challenge the missions. By the end of Spanish rule, the missions were in most respects the centers of population and economic affairs of Alta California.

1772
Soldiers and Indians

LUIS JAYME

The tensions between the missionaries and soldiers that we have seen in Baja California quickly appeared in Alta California. The missionaries consistently complained that the soldiers' brutal treatment of the Indians, especially their abuse of women, turned the native Californians against the Spanish and therefore against the missionaries. One of the earliest extant complaints along these lines comes from the first mission, San Diego. It was penned in 1772 by Fr. Luis Jayme, only three years after the establishment of the Spanish presence there. Jayme's letter accuses the *presidio* garrison of systematic abuse of native women.

The specifics of Jayme's charges cannot be conclusively demonstrated to have occurred precisely as he said. He had been in California for less than a year and a half, and as he admitted in the letter, his own grasp of the Kumeyaay language was far from perfect. He also seems to have been unaware of the possibility that rivalries between Christian and non-Christian native people, or between those from Baja California and those from the San Diego area influenced what he was told by the few indigenous people with whom he was able to communicate directly. In the larger context, however, it is absolutely clear that the abuse and rape of Indian women were all too common in the frontier regions of New Spain, including Alta California. There is no reason to suppose that San Diego was not also the site of such atrocities.

Luis Jayme, like 16 of the 142 missionaries who worked in California, was a native of Majorca. He was born there in 1740 and arrived in San Diego in 1771. He worked there until his death in 1775. The excerpt that follows is from a letter he wrote on October 17, 1772, to Fr. Rafael Verger, the guardian of the College of San Fernando. The letter had a specific political purpose: Jayme gave it to Junípero Serra, who was leaving that day for Mexico, where he was going to try to visit the viceroy to complain about the way in which the Spanish officials in Alta California, notably Pedro Fages, were treating the missionaries and the Indians. Jayme's letter supported the ideas that Serra intended to argue before the viceroy.

From a Letter by Luis Jayme

With reference to the Indians, I wish to say that great progress would be made if there were anything to eat and the soldiers would set a good example. We cannot give them anything to eat because what Don Pedro [Fages] has given is not enough to last half a year for the Indians from the Californias [Baja California] who are here. Thus little progress will be made under present conditions. As for the example to be set by the soldiers, no doubt some of them are good exemplars and deserve to be treated accordingly, but very many of them deserve to be hanged on account of the continuous outrages which they are committing in seizing and raping the women. There is not a single mission where all the gentiles have not been scandalized, and even on the roads, so I have been told. Surely, as the gentiles themselves state, they are committing a thousand evils, particularly those of a sexual nature. The Fathers have petitioned Don Pedro concerning these points, but he has paid very little attention to them. He has punished some, but as soon as they promised him that they would work at the *presidio,* he turned them loose. That is what he did last year, but now he does not even punish them or say anything to them on this point. I suppose that some ministers will write you, each concerning his own mission, and therefore I shall not tell you about the cases which have occurred at other missions. I shall speak only of Mission San Diego.

At one of these Indian villages near this mission of San Diego, which said village is very large, and which is on the road that goes to Monterey, the gentiles therein many times have been on the point of coming here to kill us all, and the reason for this is that some soldiers went there and raped their women, and other soldiers who were carrying the mail to Monterey turned their animals into their fields and they ate up their crops. Three other Indian villages about a league or a league and a half from here have reported the same thing to me several times. For this reason, on several occasions when Father Francisco Dumetz or I have gone to see these Indian villages, as soon as they saw us they fled from their villages to the woods or other remote places, and the only ones who remained in the village were some men and some very old women. The Christians here have told me that many of the gentiles of the aforesaid villages leave their huts and the crops which they gather from the lands around their villages and go to the woods and experience hunger. They do this so that the soldiers will not rape their women, as they have already done so many times in the past.

No wonder the Indians here were bad when the mission was first founded. To begin with, they did not know why they [the Spaniards] had come, unless they intended to take their lands away from them. Now they all want to be Christians, because they know that there is a God who created the heavens and earth and all things, that there is a hell, and glory, that they have souls, etc., but when the mission was first founded they did not know all these things; instead, they thought they were like animals, and when the vessels came at first, they saw that most of the crews died; they were very loath to pray, and they did not want to be Christians at all; instead, they said that it was bad to become a Christian because they would die immediately.

No wonder they said so, when they saw how most of the sailors and California Indians died, but now, thanks be to the Lord, God has converted

A Spanish cavalry soldier equipped for duty along the northern frontier of New Spain at the beginning of the nineteenth century. The numbered elements of his equipment include (1) the leather jacket; (2) saddle tree; (3) musket; (4) saddlebags; (5) lance; (6) pistols; (7) shield; (8) boots and spurs; (9) wooden stirrups; and (10) cartridge belt. Courtesy of the Ministerio de Educación, Cultura y Deporte. Archivo General de Indias (MP. Uniformes 81. Soldado de Cuera).

them from Sauls to Pauls. They all know the natural law, which, so I am informed, they have observed as well or better than many Christians elsewhere. They do not have any idols; they do not go on drinking sprees; they do not marry relatives; and they have but one wife. The married men sleep with their wives only. The bachelors sleep together, and apart from the women and married couples. If a man plays with any woman who is not his wife, he is scolded and punished by his captains. Concerning those from the Californias I have heard it said that they are given to sexual vices, but among those here I have not been able to discover a single fault of that nature. Some of the first adults we baptized, when we pointed out to them that it was wrong to have sexual intercourse with a woman to whom they were not married, told me that they already knew that, and that among them it was considered to be very bad, and so they did not do so at all. "The soldiers," they told me, "are Christians, and although they know that God will punish them in hell, they do so, having sexual intercourse with our wives." They said, "Although we did not know that God would punish us for that in hell, we considered it to be very bad, and we did not do it, and even less now that we know that God will punish us if we do so." When I heard this, I burst into tears to see how these gentiles were setting an example for us Christians. Of the many cases which have occurred in this mission, I shall tell of only two about which it is very necessary that Your Reverence should know, particularly the last one which I shall relate.

First Case

One day about the first of August of the present year of 1772, I went to the Indian village nearest the mission, which is about fifty paces from here, and the Christian Indians said to me, "Father, there is an unmarried woman here who is pregnant." "Well, how can this be?" I said to them. "Have not you told me many times that you do not have sexual intercourse with any woman except your own wife?" "That is true, Father," they said to me. "We do not do so, nor have any of us done so with this woman. On the contrary, according to what the woman says, she was coming from the Rincon village (which is about a league and a half from this mission) when a soldier named Hernández and a soldier named Bravo and a soldier named Julián Murillo seized her and sinned with her, and although she was getting away, she is almost blind and could not run very fast, and so it is that she is in this condition without being married." They told me, furthermore, that she was ashamed to be in this condition without being married, and that for this reason she had made many attempts to have an abortion but could not, but that as soon as the creature was born she would kill it. I told her through the interpreter (for, although I understood her some, I used the interpreter so that she could understand better) that she should not do anything so foolish, for God would punish her in hell, that she should bear the little one and we would give her clothing for it to wear, and we would baptize it, etc. Several times I made this and other exhortations to her so that she would not carry out her evil intentions, but it was to no avail. When the time came for the child to be born, she went to the said Rincon village, where she bore the child and killed it without my being able to baptize it. The child was killed about the middle of August of this year. The Indians who saw the little boy told me that he was somewhat white and gave every indication of being a son of the soldiers.

Second Case

On the eleventh day of September of the present year, there went to the Indian village called El Corral the soldiers Casteló, Juan María Ruiz, Bravo, and another who, although the Indians did not know his name, they knew his face well, and a sailor named Ignacio Marques. When they arrived at the said Indian village, they asked the Indian women for prickly-pear apples, which they graciously gave to them. They then asked them to give them some earthen pots, and when they would not do so, the soldier Casteló went forward to take them by force in front of Marques, the said sailor, and boldly seized one of the women by the hand. The said sailor left the soldiers, giving them to understand that he did not want to cooperate in such iniquity as the soldiers were going to commit, and in fact did commit, as soon as the said sailor left them.

Before the said soldiers sinned with the women, the soldier Casteló and the soldier Bravo threatened a Christian Indian named José Antonio who happened to be at the said Indian village, so that he would say nothing about what he had seen. Soldier Casteló carried a gentile woman into a corral which serves as a part of the enclosure surrounding the said Indian village, and inside the corral the said soldier had sexual intercourse with the woman and sinned with her. When he had raped her, the said soldier came out of the corral, and the soldier Juan María Ruiz entered the same corral and sinned with the said woman. After this they released the woman and went to the Indian village, and the soldier whose name is not known seized another woman violently and carried her into the same corral and sinned with her there. He came out, and the soldier Bravo entered and sinned with her. He came out and the soldier Juan María Ruiz entered and did the same. He came out and the soldier Casteló entered and did the same. They went to the Indian village and the soldier Casteló gave this last woman two tortillas and some red ribbons. The soldier Juan María Ruiz also gave this same woman some ribbons. The two said soldiers also gave the first woman some ribbons. In order that these outrages should not become known, soldiers Casteló and Bravo told José Antonio, the Indian (who is the one already mentioned above, he having been at the Indian village while all this was taking place) that if he told the Father they would punish him. The said José Antonio arrived here at the mission and the soldier Casteló gave him two tortillas, warning him not to tell.

On the afternoon of the same day, the two women came to tell me about what had happened. They came into the mission weeping, and were seen by many soldiers who were inside. Guessing why they had come, I sent them to the Indian village next to the mission so that the case would not become known to the public. I went to the Indian village after a little while and learned about everything that had happened from the same women with whom the said soldiers had sinned, Diego Ribera serving as my interpreter for greater clarity, he being the one whom I use to teach the Christian Doctrine.

I was informed of this case twice by the said two women, and three times by José Antonio, the said Indian, and they always agreed on everything. This evil was followed by another which, *abisus abisum invocat,* * was that this same Indian who had told me about this case was placed in stocks without my being notified, and I took him out in defiance of the corporal of the guard, for I judged, and rightly so, that they were going to punish him so that he would not confess the truth concerning the said case. I am not writing you all the details. I beg Your Reverence to do everything possible (as I suppose you will) so that this conquest will not be lost or retarded because of the bad example of these soldiers, also so that it may be materially restored.

In the *memoria* I am asking for a little sundial adjustable to any latitude, one like the one which Your Reverence had made for Father Antonio Paterna when he was in the Sierra Gorda. I should appreciate it if Your Reverence would send for it or have it made. Enclosed you will find the *memoria* from the Fathers at Mission San Luis Obispo, which, since they neglected

---

* "Deep is calling to deep." This is a quotation from Psalm 43, a psalm of exile and of longing to be delivered from a terrible and alien situation.

to include it among their papers, they forwarded to me so that I could submit it to Your Reverence with mine.

I remain, Your Reverence, as ever, praying that God will watch over you and preserve you for many years in His Divine Love and Grace. From this Mission of San Diego, October 17, 1772.

Kissing the hands of Your Reverence, always your most affectionate friend and faithful, humble subject,

Friar Luis Jayme

1773
The Presidio at Monterey

Pedro Fages

The *presidio* was the cornerstone of Spanish military presence in California. The construction of the original structures at San Diego and Monterey was supervised by the engineer Miguel Costansó. Those initial efforts in San Diego were probably nothing more substantial than a collection of tents and huts and a makeshift stockade the soldiers threw up around the camp after the Portolá party left for Monterey in 1769. The next year, in Monterey, Costansó measured out the *presidio* site on a slight hill about a musket-shot distance from the beach. Construction of a log stockade, a chapel, various warehouses, and a few quarters was completed by July. Costansó then departed with Portolá, and Fages was left in command. He supervised the construction of a number of additions to Costansó's design over the next few years. In the meantime, Serra moved the mission to Carmel in 1771, seeking better agricultural land, more water, greater proximity to the neighboring Ohlone people, and greater distance from the *presidio* and the soldiers. The following report, which Fages sent to the viceroy in 1773, described the way the *presidio* developed in its first three years.

FROM A REPORT BY PEDRO FAGES

The *presidio* came into existence on June 3, 1770, when it was founded along the shore of the beach of the said port (of Monterey), not very far away from where the packet boats anchor. It commands a view of the roadstead. At its shoulder is an estuary of salt water. On its sides are forests of pine and at its right is Point Pinos.

The *presidio* is about fifty *varas* square. At its center is a base of adobes four *varas* square consisting of four steps half a *vara* in height, on top of

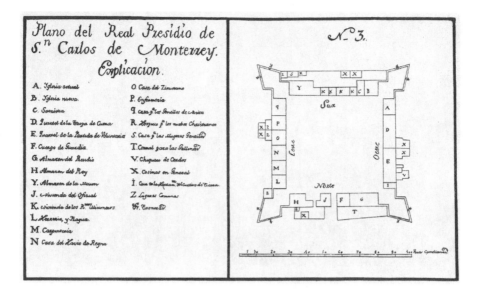

Plan of the Monterey presidio prepared by Miguel Costansó around 1770. The letters are: A, present church; B, new church; C, sacristy; D, quarters for the leather-jacket troops; E, quarters for the volunteer troops; F, guard room; G, presidio warehouse; H, king's warehouse; Y, mission warehouse; J, officers' dwelling; K, missionaries' dwelling; L, blacksmith shop and forge; M, carpenter's shop; N, house for the pack-train drivers; O, surgeon's house; P, infirmary; Q, house for the visiting gentiles; R, hospital for the new Christians; S, house for the gentile women; T, chicken yard; V, pig-pen; X, common kitchens; I, storage room for farming implements; Z, privies; Vr, embrasures. Reproduced from Irving B. Richman, California Under Spain and Mexico, 1535–1847.

which is a cupola in the shape of a half-orange, on which stands the Holy Cross of hewn wood, seven *varas* tall, whose trunk and arms are one-fourth of a *vara* wide. The entire base is plastered with a mixture of lime and sand.

In the wing of the *presidio* on the south side facing the base is an adobe church whose foundations are of stone set in mortar. These foundations extend two-quarters above the surface and are a *vara* and a half in width. Upon these foundations rise the (adobe) walls five-fourths in thickness. The church is fifteen *varas* long, seven *varas* wide, and seven *varas* high. Twenty hewn beams, each a palm in width and ten *varas* in length, have an overlay of cane, and upon this rests the roof, which is flat. This has a cover of lime. The roof has four spouts to carry off the rainwater.

Joined to the right of the chapel is a tower six *varas* square, also built of adobe. It is fifteen *varas* high and contains two terraces, in ascending proportion in which to hang bells. The tower is surmounted by a cupola in the

The text of Fages's 1773 report indicates that not all the elements of Costansó's 1770 plan were carried out precisely. This is how the presidio *and its environment appeared to José Cardero in September 1791. Courtesy of the Museo Naval, Madrid (MS 1723-3).*

shape of a half-orange, and upon this rises an iron cross a *vara* and a half in height which also has a weathervane to show the direction of the wind. This tower has its foundation of stone mortared with lime and protrudes from the ground for three-fourths of a *vara*. The church and tower are plastered with lime within and without.

To the left of the church is an adobe dwelling for the Reverend Fathers who come here to administer to our spiritual life. This dwelling is about twelve *varas* long and about six *varas* wide. It has its small outside corridor along its length with its pillars and wooden corbels, upon which lies the beam supporting the roof. The roof is flat and is covered with lime. The corridor has fifteen hewn beams ten *varas* in length. This building communicates with the church. It is plastered with lime in its entirety.

Along the east wing of the *presidio* there are six rooms, five of which are eight *varas* square, the other eight by five *varas*. One is used by the mail couriers and the blacksmith, another serves as the carpenter shop, the third contains the gear of the muleteers, the fourth is the dwelling of the servants, and the fifth is for the use of Indians who happen to sleep at the *presidio*. The sixth room is used to store building tools and field implements. All these rooms are built of poles of pine and are plastered, their roofs being of earth. Behind the servants' dwelling is their kitchen, eight *varas* square, with an inside connection. It is built of the same construction.

In the west wing there are two quarters for soldiers, the one fifteen *varas* long and eight *varas* wide, which is used by the volunteers (of Catalonia). The other, twenty *varas* long and eight *varas* wide, is used by the leather-jacket soldiers. To the rear of these quarters are two kitchens, each four *varas* square for the use of the two aforementioned groups. There are inside connections between the kitchens and the respective quarters. At the head of the wing of the *presidio* facing the south there is a dwelling place eight *varas* square which serves as a pharmacy, containing the medicine chests. All these constructions are the same as those in the aforementioned wing. The two entrances to the garrisons face the plaza of the *presidio*.

In the north wing there are two storehouses for food and for royal property. Attached to this are two small rooms occupying the space of the width of the wing of the *presidio*, both of which are four *varas* wide and six *varas* long. The first serves as a prison, the second as a guardhouse and as sleeping quarters for soldiers (on guard duty), with a rack for firearms inside and with another outside. Next, one comes to a large main entrance which is four *varas* wide. Next to it is a small room with its display table and shelves with a stock of goods, made of wood. This is the storeroom and salesroom for clothes that are sold and distributed to the dependents of these establishments. There is a door connecting it with the main entrance and an inside connection to the door of the Commander. This room is about six *varas* in length and eight *varas* in width. Along it is a corridor six *varas* in length and three in width, with two pillars and their corbels of cypress supporting the roof beam. Behind this is a kitchen with a chimney to carry off the smoke. It measure four *varas* square.

Then, one comes to the second storeroom, which is ten *varas* long and eight *varas* wide. To one side is a storage bin five *varas* square. Almost all of this wing is of adobe, its foundation being of stone. The walls of the buildings are five *varas* high and three-fourths in thickness. The beams are hewn and are covered with a roof topped with lime, which has its corresponding spout to carry off the rainwater from the *presidio*.

Most of the doors of the dwellings of the *presidio*, which number about thirty, are of pine. Some are of redwood, which is very similar to cedar, while still others are of cypress, sawed and fashioned at the *presidio*. At the four corners of the *presidio* are ravelines with two embrasures each, containing batteries with a bronze campaign cannon placed in each. One of the ravelines is of adobe with a sentry box facing the Point (Pinos), together with three trenches which command the front of the *presidio*. At the front the foundations are of stone, while on the other three sides they are constructed of logs of pine wood. However, stones have already been cut and adobes fashioned which will be used to build walls similar to that in front, because the humidity of the place tends to rot and destroy the wood. Consequently, buildings so constructed have little advantage.

For the east and west wings of the *presidio*, one hundred beams have already been hewn. They are ten *varas* long and a quarter of a *vara* wide. They are roof supports so that these sections of the *presidio* will be the same as the others. The kitchens will be incorporated with them in a corner of the *presidio* leeward to the northwest. There is a very large cesspool, a subterranean outlet going toward the estuary. In another place there are three hogsties for the sows, with the doors facing the open country. And at a distance of forty *varas* there is another large one. The roofs are covered with lime. Outside the stockade, at a distance of forty *varas*, there are two corrals fifty *varas* in circumference which are for the cows and mules. Next to the first is a hogsty for breeding purposes.

At about a fifteen-minute walking distance from the *presidio*, on the other side of the estuary, is the powder magazine, four *varas* square, built of poles plastered inside and out. It has its door and lock. At a distance of four *varas* there is a stockade of poles four *varas* high. At a musket shot away leeward to the northwest, in which the wind prevails for the greater part of the year, is a small house four *varas* square for the soldiers who stand guard.

For labor service at the *presidio* I had ordered to be made two *carretas,* one for transporting poles, the other being of the ordinary type. Both are now in service. They have been used to haul all the stone used for the foundations of the structures of the *presidio*. Mules are used for hauling. The *carretas* were built also to haul the goods brought by the ships from the beach to the *presidio*, a musket-shot away and this is over level land. They also transport salt from the salt beds located to the northeast about three leagues away over good land which the *carretas* can negotiate. This year I ordered about two hundred loads of salt to be dug up. This I had piled up and refined. Lest the rains deteriorate it I intend to build a house with a good roof in which to store it. The salt marshes are located in estuaries which are about nine in number and which, each year in the months of June, July, August, and September, are filled with very good salt that looks like stone. If this were sought each year, one could obtain hundreds of loads. Also, I have appointed six transport teams to conduct the salt hither, with one man in charge of each for supplying the establishment.

To the Mission San Carlos by the Carmel River, I will give a *carreta*. I shall do the same for Missions San Antonio and San Luis Obispo when they are made. The terrain is accommodated to their use. I have also constructed a launch of eight ribs at its keel with its sail and oars to aid in disembarkment to shore and for the transportation of salt should this be necessary, as well as for the transportation of logs. These latter are obtainable along the seashore about six leagues from the *presidio*. The frame and keel had already come from San Blas. I also had a mast altered which rises from a basket seven *varas* in length and three-fourths in width for use at the *presidio*, should it be needed.

At a distance of half a league from the *presidio* is a garden one hundred and twenty *varas* in length, its width varying from seventy to eighty *varas* in places. It decreases even to forty *varas* at its narrowest. Therein have been sown and harvested various vegetables. At present we are gathering many of them by means of irrigation. Next to it is fallow land which I shall order to be sown with two and a half *fanegas* of wheat, all to be under irrigation. On one side of the garden is a house, four *varas* square, for two of the Catalonian volunteers. It has its door and lock and a battery embrasure within for whatever contingency may arise. The roof of the house is of earth. About an eight-minute walk from the *presidio* there are some fallow lands which were sown during the past year with about four *fanegas* of wheat, and I shall see if it can be sown again.

Next to the *presidio* on the side in the direction of the church is where the mission of San Carlos was founded. There it remained until May of 1771, when an order came from His Excellency the Marquis de Croix, your predecessor, to transfer the mission site to the banks of the Carmel River, since it is only one league away from the *presidio*. Moreover, the site offers better lands for cultivation than those which the port has.

The transfer was soon effected, the change of the mission from one site to the other having been accomplished by the end of December of the said year, although the Reverend Father President with his companion went out to the Carmel River to that mission earlier to administer it. He left at this *presidio* the two missionaries destined for the founding of Mission San Luis Obispo, who were to remain here until that mission would be actually established. So they remained, administering and saying Mass at the *presidio*, until the beginning of June 1772, when they went to found said mission.

From that time on, the *presidio* has been without a resident priest, although on Sundays and holy days one of the two missionaries from Mission San Carlos comes over to say Mass.

Now that the Reverend Father President Fray Francisco Palóu has arrived from Lower California with five additional religious to found the other three missions ordered to be established, he offered to me one of the religious to stay at the *presidio*. This I considered very proper, for it has been my experience that in years of heavy rain it is impossible to travel over the roads.

In consideration of the fact that the same original church was destined for the royal *presidio* and for mission purposes, although the order came for their separation, there did not come for the *presidio* church any church goods or other items useful for the church and sacristy. For the *presidio* church there were only those things that belonged to the missions which have been ordered to be founded. Wherefore I beseech Your Excellency to deign to order that the church be furnished with everything necessary to celebrate the Holy Sacrifice of the Mass and to administer the Sacraments. Meanwhile, those things will serve which belong to the missions as they have supplied up to the present. The same holds true for bells.

Royal *Presidio* of San Carlos de Monterey
September 29, 1773
Pedro Fages

1773
Trip to Mexico City

Junípero Serra

Serra and Fages exemplified the tension between the military and the missions. They quarreled over various issues in Monterey in 1770 and 1771, including the way the missionaries treated the soldiers in the mission guard. In 1772, their disagreements came to a head over the question of the size of the mission guard to be assigned to the new mission at San Buenaventura. Serra wanted twenty soldiers there, and Fages said he could not spare that many. They also had words over the number of mules and other items that were to be assigned to the mission. Serra decided that he would have to go to Mexico City himself and lay his case directly before the new viceroy, Antonio María de Bucarcli y Ursúa. He left for Mexico City on October 17, 1772, and arrived in the capital on February 6 , 1773. He soon had an audience with Bucareli and followed it with a formal written document. The following is an excerpt from that document. Serra asked that Fages be removed as Monterey commander, suggesting that he be replaced by Sergeant José Francisco Ortega, whose California performance Serra praised. His description of Ortega provides an excellent overview of the many duties of a presidial soldier. Serra also made a number of suggestions for the management of the missions and the lines of authority between the missionaries and the soldiers.

As a result of Serra's requests and effective lobbying by the Franciscans in Mexico City, Bucareli did decide to replace Fages, whose stern disciplinary methods had not endeared him to his own soldiers either. But the viceroy balked at promoting Ortega all the way up the ranks from sergeant to commander of Monterey. Instead, he appointed Fernando de Rivera y Moncada, who had returned to Baja California after he had been passed over as commander of Monterey by Portolá. Rivera arrived to assume his duties in 1774.

From a Report by Junípero Serra

A ppreciating the great favor Your Excellency deigns to show me, without any merit on my part, because I have had a share in all that has been accomplished in these new establishments since the first day they were begun; and, in that I have been an eyewitness of all the events which have taken place there, and can explain to Your Excellency everything that, in my judgment, seems necessary and fitting to procure the fulfillment of the pious projects of our Great Monarch—whom God prosper—who is desirous of introducing, and spreading, in these extensive territories our Holy Catholic Faith, I, with all submission due to Your Excellency, wish to present the following suggestions....

A measure that seems to me of special importance is the removal, or recall, of the officer Don Pedro Fages from the command of the *Presidio* at Monterey, and the appointment of another in his place. Otherwise there will be no stopping the desertions of soldiers and others who, up to the present time, have caused so much trouble and will continue to do so. Nor can matters remain as they are, as far as those who still stay on are concerned—they stay because they cannot get away. Every one of them is extremely wrought up. Their grievance is not only because of long hours of work and a lack of food—as I have on numerous occasions heard them declare—but because of the harsh treatment and unbearable manners of the said officer.

Independently of what I already knew from long experience, I have just received, along with my last bundle of letters, copies of what, on the one hand, the volunteer soldiers of that *presidio* write to their Captain, Agustín Callis, whom they suppose to be at your Court, and on the other hand, what the leather-jacket soldiers think, as they write to their officer, Don Fernando de Rivera—whom, also, they suppose to be in Mexico. Both groups of men ask their respective officers to free them in any manner they can from such harsh treatment and oppression. In the said writings there is no other complaint except that they have over them Don Pedro Fages.

If I were called upon to tell not of the annoyances he has caused me and the rest of the religious—a story that shall remain untold—but of the damage his conduct has continually done to the missions, it would be a long story. If details are required to supply further arguments to bring about the result desired, Your Excellency has only to say the word. But if what has already been said, as well as the information given in writing by the Reverend

The central plaza of Mexico City in the eighteenth century. It was in the large building on the left, the official residence of the viceroy, that Serra met with Bucareli. Drawn by Fernando Brambila, 1791, Malaspina Expedition. Courtesy of the Museo Naval, Madrid (MS 1726-57).

Father Guardian of our College, and by me by word of mouth, be sufficient for the purpose we have in mind, I beg and beseech Your Excellency that he may be discharged honorably, and without any humiliation whatsoever; and I pray God to bless him....

Appreciating fully the great compliment Your Excellency pays me in permitting me to suggest a candidate suitable for the place, I say that, as far as I can judge, among those belonging to the company there is no more suitable man than the company sergeant, Don José Francisco Ortega.

The reasons for my choice are his record and his ability to take charge of such a command.

First, his record. After he had served the King for some years as a leather-jacket soldier in California during the time of the Jesuits and was promoted to the rank of sergeant, he left the service to spend all his time in the mines in the southern part of the peninsula. At that time he, being clearly the man best suited for the post in that department, was appointed

Associate Judge for all the King's mines there and administered justice with equity for a number of years.

When the new Governor, Don Gaspar de Portolá, came to take command of the province at the time the Jesuits were expelled, he met him for the first time, and had numerous dealings with him, and insisted that he join the service once more with rank as sergeant. Ortega accepted and went in the Governor's company to Loreto. He served the said Governor and the King in the management of the royal warehouse, being put in charge of all correspondence, accounts, and administration for more than a year, while the said royal *hacienda* was under the control of Señor Portolá.

Then the new Commissary, Don Francisco Trillo, came, who employed him as secretary as long as he needed him. When the expedition to Monterey got under way, the sergeant was appointed to the second part of it, with which I went myself, as well as the Governor. We set out on our way and when we began to enter the gentile country, we received the last letters from the Most Illustrious Inspector General. In the letter addressed to the Governor, which was read in my presence, His Most Illustrious Lordship said that Sergeant Ortega should follow the expedition with the assurance that, on his return, he was keeping for him his promotion as Lieutenant officer of the company, for Don Blas Somera was leaving this post, having asked for his retirement. We all celebrated the good news and promise, repeatedly offering him our congratulations.

When the expedition started on its way, as soon as the short stretch of the road familiar to some of the soldiers who had passed that way before came to an end, the Governor instructed the sergeant, accompanied by only one soldier, to explore ahead, daily, the road we had to follow the next day. And so, for the period of more than a month that our journey lasted, he continued to go ahead the whole time, covering more than three times the distance that the rest of the expedition had to cover. He forged ahead in search of watering places and camping spots; then he would come back with the information and guide us to the spots he had discovered. The single soldier who was his companion was sometimes changed, but the sergeant never.

The risks he ran in going among so many gentiles, which became evident by what we saw later, kept me in continual anxiety; and, as a matter of fact, at times it was only thanks to the protection of his favorite saints that he escaped unscathed.

After our arrival at San Diego, everyone was elated, telling one another what a marvelous trip we had made. At that time the search for the port of Monterey was decided upon. The sergeant went along with the others. Fathers Crespí and Gómez, who accompanied the expedition as far as the port of San Francisco, told me that during all the trip, the part taken by Señor Ortega was most remarkable. Even though Captain Rivera was appointed as first explorer, the sergeant was always employed in the same capacity, especially when they tried to find the port in various directions. And he was the man that went the farthest in exploring the estuaries of San Francisco in search of a crossing to the other side, which was never found.

Antonio María de Bucareli y Ursúa, Viceroy of New Spain, 1771 to 1779. Courtesy of The Bancroft Library, University of California, Berkeley.

When the expedition came back to San Diego, the Governor was informed of what had happened to us on the feast of the Assumption of Our Lady—that the gentiles had killed one of our men, wounded others, and tried to kill all of us. And while the return to Monterey was under consideration—as actually happened after the arrival of the boat—he decided it was desirable that a man especially adapted to the work should take command of the escort and remain in the mission of San Diego. Accordingly the Governor appointed the said sergeant. As for me, since I was going to Monterey with the greatest anxiety at leaving the two poor Fathers exposed to so many dangers and as many hardships, the great consolation I had as regards their dangerous position was that the sergeant was there to defend them; and my confidence was not misplaced.

The expedition being at an end, he was sent to California. The Governor employed him in carrying provisions from Sinaloa, in going to and from San Diego, and in discovering and pointing out the proper sites for the five missions that are to be founded in the stretch in between. During these explorations, while he was climbing mountains and crossing valleys, over and above what he had principally in mind, he discovered a way from Velicatá to San Diego which saves a distance of some fifty leagues; and this he will soon shorten still more, I assure you.

This, Most Excellent Lord, is a short sketch of the record of the man I am recommending to Your Excellency.

Now, as regards his fitness for the position, I can say that, as far as I have seen, in command of soldiers he is firm without rigidity and has prudence and common sense. I believe they will love him without ceasing to fear him; they will fear him sufficiently without ceasing to love him. Since, in all the duties with which he has been entrusted and which I have just now described, he has acquitted himself with honor, I feel confident that he will do the same with all future appointments. In his youthful days, in the town of Zelaya, his native place, he had the management of a storehouse and shop; he is alert and capable in the management of business. He writes a good hand, and I am sure that the storehouse will be well administered; and since he is most conscientious, the accounts will be as the law requires. When Pedro Fages got his appointment to the office in question, he had only the title of Lieutenant. With the same title this most deserving man could be given the same office. But let it be as Your Excellency shall decide; in any case you will decide what is for the best.

I suggest that Your Excellency give strict orders to the officer who will be sent that, as soon as the missionary Father of any mission requests it, he should remove the soldier or soldiers who give bad example, especially in the matter of incontinence; he should recall them to the *presidio* and send, in their place, another or others who are not known as immoral or scandalous. And even when the Father does not specify the sin of the soldier, his request for removal should always be heeded, since in certain cases it is not advisable to give the reason, either to prevent making public a hidden sin, or for other reasons that can easily be imagined. As for the soldier who does not give grounds for complaint at the mission, you may be very sure the Father will not ask for his removal; and if the request is made, it is very evident that there are good reasons; and so it is right that his request should be granted. This is what a number of the most excellent predecessors of Your Excellency have decided upon, at the suggestion of our College.

Your Excellency should notify the said officer and the soldiers that the training, governance, punishment, and education of baptized Indians, or of those who are being prepared for baptism, belong exclusively to the missionary Fathers, the only exception being for capital offenses. Therefore no chastisement or ill treatment should be inflicted on any of them, whether by the officer or by a soldier, without the missionary Father's passing upon it. This has been the time-honored practice of this kingdom ever since the conquest; and it is quite in conformity with the law of nature concerning the education of the children, and an essential condition for the rightful training of the poor neophytes. Having these as his basic reasons, as well as others that might be adduced, the Most Illustrious Inspector General gave instructions to this effect before leaving California. Yet the contrary practice has prevailed, which has resulted in the worst of evils. I had intended to explain myself at greater length on this most important topic but I leave it for later, should circumstances make it necessary.

Concerning the number of soldiers required in the missions as escort, I give my opinion as follows:

> For Mission San Carlos de Monterey, established on the banks of the Carmel River, in consideration of its proximity to the *presidio,* eight leather-jacket soldiers are sufficient.
>
> For San Antonio de Padua de los Robles: ten leather-jacket soldiers.
>
> For San Luis Obispo de los Tichos: ten leather-jacket soldiers also.

For San Gabriel de los Temblores: likewise ten leather-jacket soldiers.

And for San Diego of the Port: thirteen or fourteen leather-jacket soldiers also.

The reason for this increase in number is that, from this mission, very frequently a courier has to start, either for [Baja] California or for Monterey. If the number were less, what occurred when the boat last came there might happen again. Captain Don Juan Pérez found so few soldiers in the mission that he deemed it advisable to order a number of sailors to disembark for the proper protection of the mission. This I mentioned in my letter to Your Excellency, if my memory serves me well.

As for the missions of San Buenaventura and Santa Clara, at first sight it would seem to me that there should be twenty for the first mentioned, on account of its closeness to the Santa Bárbara Channel, and for Santa Clara, fifteen....

It is of no less importance that, when the livestock arrives which Your Excellency, in virtue of your decree, orders to be forwarded from California for the equipment of the Monterey missions, some Indian families from the said California should come of their own free will with the expedition, and that they should receive every consideration from the officials. They should be distributed, at least two or three being placed in each mission. By taking such measure, two purposes will be accomplished. The first will be that there will be an additional two or three Indians for work. The second, and the one I have most in mind, is that the Indians [here] may realize that, till now, they have been much mistaken when they saw all men, and no women, among us; that there are marriages, also, among Christians. Last year, when one of the San Diego Fathers went to California to get provisions, which had run short in that mission, he brought back with him along with the rest of his company two of the said families. At his arrival, there was quite a commotion among the new Christians, and even among the gentiles; they did not know what to make of these families, so great was their delight. Just to see these families was a lesson as useful to them as was their happiness at their arrival. So if families other than Indian come from there, it will serve the same purpose very well—that is, if we can provide for them.

1775

Encounter in San Francisco Bay

VICENTE DE SANTA MARÍA

For the first few years of Spanish Alta California, Monterey was the effective northern boundary. A new mission was founded at San Luis Obispo in 1772. In the meantime, a series of expeditions was organized to learn more about the huge inland body of water which the Portolá party had seen in 1769. It was first thought to be part of an estuary that led to Drake's Bay, which Cermeño had called San Francisco Bay, and it was accordingly dubbed "the estuary of San Francisco." Fages led a small party up the east shore of the bay in 1770, and his group managed to get slightly farther north than Ortega's group had done the year before with the Portolá expedition. Fages and Crespí undertook another journey up the east shore of the bay in 1772. They reached the Carquínez Strait and discovered that Point Reyes and Drake's Bay (still called San Francisco Bay then) could not be reached by this route. In 1774 Rivera and Palóu headed up the peninsula on the west side of the bay, and they reached the location of the current city of San Francisco.

In 1775, the *San Carlos* was ordered to enter the bay directly and investigate. Under the command of Juan Manuel de Ayala, it reached the Golden Gate on August 5. Pilot José Cañizares and ten men were dispatched in the ship's longboat to scout out a place to anchor. The strong tides made it impossible for them to return, and the *San Carlos* had to fight its way in against strong winds. It finally managed to reach shelter at Richardson's Bay, on the north side of the channel, where it remained until September 18. For most of that time, it was anchored off of Angel Island, and Cañizares directed explorations and soundings from the longboat. His reports and maps were the first that referred to this area as the "port of San Francisco," and the name stuck.

The *San Carlos*'s chaplain and occasional passenger in the longboat was the Franciscan Vicente de Santa María. A Spaniard, he had served in the missions of Baja California from 1771 to 1773 and then returned to Mexico City. He was appointed chaplain the next year and boarded the *San Carlos* in San Blas at the beginning of the journey. His account of his close and amicable interactions with the Huimen and Huchiun peoples of the bay, both in their villages and aboard the ship, as well as his attempts to learn their languages and teach them his, and his obvious respect for their abilities, make his journal a unique document in the early history of California. He later served at the missions of San Francisco and San Buenaventura until his death in 1806.

FROM A REPORT BY VICENTE DE SANTA MARÍA

R ash, seemingly, was what I did with five sailors and the surgeon on the afternoon of August 9: we decided to go as far as an Indian *ranchería* that was about a league from the shore and with a poor approach. We were sustained only by our Catholic Faith and were impelled by Godly zeal lest our gains be lost. It so happened that the Indians had assembled with their usual daily present, but had not been able to go over to get it, because the dugout, inadequate though it was as a conveyance, was not available, being in immediate need of repair. About midday, twelve Indians had appeared with the new supply and though they had called repeatedly to us, it was not feasible for us to respond to them; we lacked the means, since the longboat had not yet returned from its first [extended] expedition. Tired, at last, of pressing us and seeing that we did not comply with their requests, they all began putting on a dance. When they were done, they returned to calling us over to where they were waiting for us; and then, as we could not give them that pleasure for want of a boat, they went away as if with hurt feelings, showing by the speed of their departure that they had begun to feel worried at so decided a change in our behavior.

When we had about given up hope of satisfying our Indians, the longboat returned to the ship with the sailing master, José Cañizares. Day and night, he had gone exploring what parts of the harbor he could. This time he had come upon the real circular bay, satisfying himself that it was not the one earlier conjectured; and of this bay, as of what else he had explored, he brought some rough drafts of maps. This would have been about a quarter past six o'clock in the evening, and the Captain, as a mark of kindness, asked if I should like to take a walk along the shore. The surgeon and I accepted the favor and, setting out in the longboat, we went ashore without delay. We were mindful that the Indians might have gone away offended; so, like the hunter, fearless of dangers, who leaps over the rough places and forces his way through obstacles until he meets his quarry, we went up the slopes, taking chances, hunting for our Indians until we should find them. In pursuing this venture we did not share our intentions with the Captain because, if we had, from that moment he would have had nothing to do with it, in view of the risks involved in our desire to visit the *rancheria* at so unseasonable a time and in so remote a place. Notwithstanding all this, and even though we had no notion of how soon we might reach the Indians, we were nevertheless making our way by their very path. As night was now approaching, we were considering a return to the ship and were of two minds about it, when we caught sight of the Indians. At the same time, seeing us, they began inviting us with repeated gestures and loud cries to their *rancheria,* which was at the shore of a rather large round cove.

Although we might on that occasion have succumbed to dread, we summoned our courage because we had to, lest fear make cowards of us. We thought that if we turned back and for a second time did not heed the call of the Indians, this might confirm them in their resentment or make them believe that we were very timid—not an agreeable idea, for many reasons. As none of those who came along declined to follow me, ignoring our weariness, we went on toward the *rancheria.* As soon as the Indians saw that we were near their huts, all the men stood forward as if in defense of their women and children, whom undoubtedly they regard as their treasure and their heart's core. They may have thought, though not expressing this openly to us, that we might do their dear ones harm; if so, their action was most praiseworthy.

We were now almost at the *rancheria.* As we were going to be there awhile, an Indian hustled up some clean herbage for us to sit on, made with it a modest carpet, and had us sit on it. The Indians sat on the bare ground, thus giving us to understand in some degree how guests should be received. They then made quite clear to us how astonished they had been that we had not joined them at the shore; but we succeeded in giving them some reassurances. When I saw there was so large a gathering, I began to speak to them for a short time, though I knew they could not understand me unless God should work a miracle. All the time that I was speaking, these Indians, silent and attentive, were as if actually comprehending, showing by their faces much satisfaction and joy. When I had finished speaking, I said to those who had come with me that we should sing the *Alabado*. When we had got as far as the words *"Pura Concepción,"* there was a great hubbub among the Indians, for some of them had come with two kinds of hot *atole* and some *pinoles,* and they gave all their attention to urging our participation in the feast. So our chorus stopped singing and we gave the Indians the pleasure they wished, which was that we should eat. After the sailors had finished with the supper that our hosts had brought, I called to the Indian who seemed to me the headman of the *ranchería* and, taking his hand, began to move it in the sign of the Cross, and he, without resisting, began repeating my words with so great clearness that I stood amazed, and so did those who were with me.

One of the sailors had brought a piece of chocolate. He gave some of it to an Indian, who, finding it sweet, made signs that he would go get something of similar flavor. He did so, bringing back to him a small tamale that has a fairly sweet taste and is made from a seed resembling *polilla*. We gave the Indians, as usual, some glass beads, and received their thanks; and as they saw that the moon was rising they made signs to us to withdraw, which we then did.

Because there was not much daylight when we got to the *ranchería,* we could not take note of the appearance and the features of the Indian women, who were at some distance from us; but it was clear that they wore the pelts of otters and deer, which are plentiful in this region. There were a number of small children about. Many of the Indian men we had seen at other times, including some of the leaders, were not present. We headed back for the ship, and as we reached the shore we came upon the usual present, which the disquieted Indians had left in the morning. After having made them this visit, we were without sight of the Indians for four days, that is, until the thirteenth of August....

We did not think their nonappearance very important, for we supposed that the distance to the ship and the Indians' apprehensions about coming on board explained why they did not care to waste time on visits that would not gain them the object of their desires; and furthermore, this was in any case an advantage to us because, the longboat being engaged in its explorations, we were spared the distress of not being able to make visits in return for theirs.

However, their great liking for us from the time of the first visit made them forgo their fears and come to see us on board at a time when we were least expecting them. It would be about ten o'clock in the forenoon of August 23 when, towards the point of the Isla de Santa María de los Angeles

[Angel Island] near which we stayed, two reed boats were seen approaching, in which were five Indians. As soon as the Captain was informed of this, he directed that signs be made inviting them aboard, to which they promptly responded by coming, which was what they wanted to do. Leaving their boats, they climbed aboard quite fearlessly. They were in great delight, marveling at the structure of the ship, their eyes fixed most of all on the rigging. They wondered no less at the lambs, hens, and pigeons that were providently kept to meet our needs if someone on board should fall sick. But what most captivated and pleased them was the sound of the ship's bell, which was purposely ordered to be struck so we could see what effect it had on ears that had never heard it. It pleased the Indians so much that while they were on board they went up to it from time to time to sound it themselves. They brought us, as on other occasions, gifts of *pinoles,* and they even remembered men's names that we had made known to them earlier. They brought among their party an Indian we had not seen before. Soon after receiving our greetings, he went away alone in his boat, leaving in another direction than the one they had taken. We thought he had been sent by the others to bring us back a present; but when he did not return even after the others had gone away, we dismissed this unworthy thought from our minds.

Throughout the time the Indians were on board, we tried to attract them to Christian practices, now having them cross themselves or getting them to repeat the *Pater Noster* and *Ave María,* now chanting the *Alabado,* which they followed so distinctly that it was astonishing with what facility they pronounced the Spanish.

The Indian chieftain, less reserved than the others, showed how much pleased he was at our warmth of feeling; more than once he took to dancing and singing on the deckhouse. I paid close attention to their utterances that corresponded with their actions and found that their language went like this: *pire* means, in our language, "Sit down"; *intomene,* "What is your name?"; *sumite,* "Give me"; and this last is used with respect to various things, as, a man on the ship having given an Indian a cigar, the Indian said, "*Sumite sot sintonau,*" which means "Give me a light to start it with." They call the sun *gismen,* the sky *carac.* And so on. Close on midday they took to their boats again, bidding farewell to us all and promising to be back on the morrow, and they made good their promise so effectually that at seven o'clock the next morning they were already aboard. They had no sooner arrived than I went to meet and welcome these guests, although I did not stay with them as long as they wanted me to because I was about to say Matins and prepare myself for celebrating the Holy Sacrament of the Mass. I made signs to them to wait for me until I should be through and those who occupied the cabin should get up; but they could not hold their expectations in suspense so long, for while I was at my prayers in the deckhouse the Indian chieftain, seeing that I was putting them off, began calling the surgeon by his name and saying to me, "Santa María, Vicente, Father, *ilac*," which means "come here"; and seeing that the surgeon did not leave his bunk, and that I did not come down, he came up to where I was reciting my prayers and, placing himself at my side on his kneecaps, began to imitate me in my manner of praying, so that I could not keep from laughing; and seeing that if the Indian should continue I would not be getting on with my duty, I made signs to him to go back down and wait for me there. He obeyed at once, but it was to set out in his boat with a chieftain, not known to us before, whom he had brought to the ship, and, as if offended, he left behind the daily offering of *pinoles.*

Word of the kindliness with which those on the ship dealt with these heathen was spread so quickly from *ranchería* to *ranchería* that it served to dispel the fears of a number of Indians not hitherto seen by us, so that they hastened to come aboard. They came, at the same time, to offer us (perhaps depriving themselves) the food of their daily sustenance. This event, which set before our eyes a new spectacle, took place that same day, August 24, two and a half hours after those Indians I have just told about had gone away. These others came in two *balsas* [tule boats] and numbered about eight in all. When they were in sight close by and we made signs to them to come to the ship, one of them, who doubtless came to the bow of his boat for the purpose, began to make a long speech, giving us to understand that it was the headman of the *ranchería* who came, and that he was at our service. This visit was not a casual one, for all of them appeared to have got themselves up, each as best he could, for a festive occasion. Some had adorned their heads with a tuft of red-dyed feathers, and others with a garland of them mixed with black ones. Their chests were covered with a sort of woven jacket made with ash-colored feathers; and the rest of their bodies, though bare, were all worked over with various designs in charcoal and red ochre, presenting a droll sight.

As soon as they left their boats, it was made clear to them who it was that commanded the ship, and they endeavored to point out their leader to us. The chieftain of the *ranchería* had all his men, one after another, in the order of their importance, salute our Captain; and when this ceremony was completed he begged us all to sit down, as the Indians also did, for distribution among us of their offering, which they brought to us in all tidiness. All being in their places in due order, the second chieftain who was among the company asked of another Indian a container made of reeds that he carried with him, in which were many pats or small cakes of *pinole*. It was given him, and having placed it beside him, he indicated that he was to be listened to. With no lack of composure, he spoke for quite a while and then, opening the container, handed the *pinole* cakes to the first chieftain, who, as soon as he received them, handed them to our Captain, making signs to him to distribute them among all the men of the ship, insisting, moreover, that he be the first to taste the *pinole*. The second chieftain was now very watchful to see if by chance anyone of the ship's company had missed partaking of the bread of hospitality; he went up to the deckhouse and several times stuck his head in the after hold; there was no limit to his painstaking inspection. After this, our Captain directed the steward to bring some pieces of pilot bread and gave them to the Indian headman, who distributed them with all formality among his party.

We gave them glass beads and other little gifts, which they put in their reed container. This done, I brought out a representation of our Holy Father St. Francis, most edifying, and upon my presenting it to the Indians to kiss they did so with so much veneration, to all appearances, and willingness that they stole my heart and the hearts of all others who observed them. Then I had them make the sign of the Cross and repeat the *Pater Noster,* which they did very clearly, showing in their faces that they took pleasure in such things although they lacked comprehension because the Spanish language was beyond them.

They left us about one o'clock in the afternoon, taking to their boats and heading toward the island contiguous to us. On it were some casks with which our supply of water aboard was in part replenished, and a board and some tools that had been taken off the ship for making certain repairs to the dugout. The Indians went ashore, and our Captain, on seeing them do so, prudently entertained doubts of their trustworthiness, thinking that, if not through self-interest, at any rate from greed, they might take some of the things we had on the island. The Indians, however, were of quite another mind: as soon as they saw the dugout approach land, they all headed for it, bent on catching up with it and helping our men to run it ashore. Next, after seeing that it was intended to take aboard the things that were on shore, the Indians, supposing that the sailors were going after wood, went to a tree that was lying at the waterside and exerted their strength prodigiously to put it aboard the dugout. Then our men came, loaded down with the water casks on their shoulders, and going to meet them, two of the Indians took the casks on their own backs, carried them to the dugout and stowed them in it. They all helped to get the dugout afloat again to return to the ship.

I watched all this from the ship, and as the Indians remained seated on the shore I could not bear to lose the rest of the afternoon when I might be communicating with them; so, setting out in the dugout, I landed and remained alone with the eight Indians so that I might communicate with them in greater peace. The dugout went back to the ship, and at the same time they all crowded around me and, sitting by me, began to sing with an accompaniment of two rattles that they had brought with them. As they finished the song, all of them were shedding tears, which I wondered at for not knowing the reason. When they were through singing they handed me the rattles and, by signs, asked me also to sing. I took the rattles and, to please them, began to sing to them the *Alabado* (although they would not understand it), to which they were most attentive and indicated that it pleased them. I gave them some glass beads that I had had the forethought to bring with me, and they made me hang them in their ears, which most of them had pierced, with my own hands. Thus I had a very pleasant afternoon until, as nightfall neared, our Captain sent the dugout for my return to the ship.

I came back well pleased, reflecting on how quick-witted the Indians were and how easy the acquisition of their language—as we all put to the test when, early next morning, the Indians came back to the ship. We designedly put before them several objects, asking what these were called in their language, to which they answered with great care; seeing that what they said was put down on paper, they came near and repeated the word as if anxious not to give occasion for any blunders in the writing. With this good opportunity we improved the occasion to acquaint ourselves with some words that tallied with what was presented to their attention; thus, their manner of counting is as follows: *imen,* one; *utin,* two; *capan,* three; *catauas,* four; *misur,* five; *saquen,* six; *quenetis,* seven; *osatis,* eight; *tulau,* nine; *iguesizu,* ten; *imeniluen,* eleven; *capanuya,* twelve; *imenaye,* thirteen; *catsuya,* fourteen; etc. We learned other words, but lest I grow tiresome I do not put them down. I shall record only some names that, like baptismal names, distinguish them one from another. Thus, the eight Indians who came to us on this occasion were named as follows: their chieftain was called Sumu; the second chieftain, Jausos; the others, Supitacse, Tilacse, Mutuc, Logeacse, Guecpostole, Xacacse. To give an example of Jausos's liveliness: on being taught to say "*piloto* Cañizares" he made signs that Sumu be taught to say the same thing. When Sumu mistakenly said "*pinoto*" instead of "*piloto*," Jausos corrected him, laughing so hard as to astonish all of us.

They are very fond of trading. All of them hanker for our clothes, our cloaks most of all, and so as to move us to make them warm they show us with sad gestures how they suffer from the cold and even say the words *coroec cata,* "I am cold," and the like.

Soon after these Indians came to the ship, there came eight others of our new friends, and at first it appeared that those of the one and the other *rancheria* did not look on each other with much friendliness, but our treating them all as equals made them friends and on speaking terms with one another.

We taught all of them how to cross themselves; and although those who came under Sumu's command were better disposed toward these pious observances, the Indians who came under the command of the other *rancheria's* headman became compliant, and all of them came to me to be instructed. Among all these Indians, Mutuc is noticeably clever, so perceptive that he not only grasped at once what we said to him in Spanish and repeated it exactly, but also, as if well versed in our language, he showed how the Spanish terms we asked about were expressed in his. On this day it came off colder than usual, and of the poor unfortunates on board, those who could do so took refuge under my cloak, showing with piteous looks how keenly, being stark naked, they felt the chill. Luck, it seems, offered a sailor's long coat to Supitacse, the oldest and least forward of them all, as soon as he came on board, and he took it at once and kept himself warm in it, huddling in corners. When it was time to leave, he most considerately put the garment back where he had taken possession of it. True, the first day that Sumu's party came aboard, most of his Indians, especially Jausos and one other, were somewhat troublesome because they had a fancy for everything. Everything looked good to them and they all wanted to barter with their feathers and little nets, but once we had given them to understand that this was doing wrong, they behaved quite differently thereafter, so that two who had been wandering all over the ship did not now leave my side unless they were called. This was a striking example of how tractable they were.

1775
Rebellion at San Diego

VICENTE FUSTER

In the early morning hours of November 5, 1775, a group of Kumeyaay from at least fifteen nearby villages attacked and burned Mission San Diego, which had recently been moved from its location near the *presidio* to a site about six miles away. The movement of the mission site had been accompanied by an increase in conversion efforts among a number of settlements south of the San Diego River. It appears that the attack on the mission complex originated in these villages. As had been the case in Baja California in 1734, local leaders and shamans were able to mobilize large numbers of people to resist what they regarded as an incursion into their way of life. Fr. Luis Jayme was killed during the attack.

While the mission was eventually rebuilt, it was never able to attract large numbers of native people, and its influence was limited to its more immediate surroundings. Spanish and Mexican control of the frontier between the two Californias, especially east and south of San Diego to the Colorado River delta, always remained very tenuous.

The account that follows is taken from a letter written to Serra by Jayme's companion at San Diego, Fr. Vicente Fuster.

FROM A LETTER BY VICENTE FUSTER

Hail Jesus, Mary, and Joseph!
Reverend Father President Fray Junípero Serra
My ever revered Father:

With emotions that stir my innermost being I face the duty of informing Your Reverence of the sad state and ruin of the mission here, in which undeservedly I am a minister. It is something to be grateful for to Almighty God that one of the Fathers can give you an account of what happened. That certainly was not the intention of those wicked men. They meant to exterminate the entire white population and the Fathers in particular. But why was such a fate not to be mine? The answer must be left to the inscrutable decrees of God. For my part I merely say that His Infinite Mercy and Kindness were made manifest for the betterment of my faulty life. And I acknowledge that in return for such goodness the balance of my life will be insufficient for all the gratitude and thanks which I owe. Hence I call upon Your Reverence to help me give thanks to God.

On the fifth day of this present month of November, about one o'clock at night, there was such a throng of Indians, both gentiles and Christians, who came to the mission, that as far as the soldiers could judge they must have numbered more than six hundred. The first thing they did was to circle the *rancheria,* then the mission, from the four sides; then they pillaged the church of its precious articles, and after that they set fire to it. Next came the guardhouse and building where Fray Luis had his quarters. I slept in the storehouse or granary, which was the last place they set afire. Amid the yelling and discharges of the guns, half asleep, I made my way out of the building, hardly knowing what it was all about. Since I had to cross over to the other side, God kindly kept watch over me. I made a dash for it and got there safely. Then I asked the soldiers, "What is this about?"

Hardly were the words out of my mouth than I saw on all sides around me so many arrows that you could not possibly count them. The only thing I did was to drop my cloak and stand flat against the wall of the guardhouse, and use the mantle as cover so that no arrows might hit me. And this, thanks be to God, is what I succeeded in doing.

There we were, surrounded on all sides by flames. Seeing that we were all in a bad way, I said to the soldiers, "Let us go to my house, and perhaps there we will put up a better fight." Off we went. The soldiers did not come to the house itself, but remained in a room we had just finished making the day before adjoining my house, about fourteen paces separating the door of the one from the other. From there they began to fire their guns. I shut myself in the house along with two boys, and with them I started to implore the Divine Mercy through the intercession of Mary Most Holy, San Diego, and many other saints to free us from the hosts of enemies besetting us on all sides—namely, the Indians and the flames.

While occupied with these prayers, I could not help but feel uneasy for the safety of my dearly beloved Fray Luis, so I made up my mind to dash through the flames and see if he was in his house. Out I went, and pausing to take a deep breath, I hurriedly darted inside and felt all over his bed, but could not find him. And so I turned back to get away at top speed. It so happened most fortunately that the roof beams had not yet fallen. They were all ablaze, however, and yet I got away unscathed.

I made for my own house, sad of heart, and when I saw it was already on fire I turned to the soldiers and told them to see if they could not put the fire out. But they either could not do so or did not hear me. When I realized that I was surrounded by fire, the thought struck me to see if I could not get hold of some of the packing cases of clothes, not to save them but to form a barricade out of them. So with the help of the two boys, I rescued three cases from the house.

While I was thus busily engaged, a soldier came up and asked for the gunpowder that was in the mission. This put new heart into me, and it seemed nothing less than the Providence of God, because in that very house or granary which was already on fire there was a trunk containing two *arrobas* of powder in a bag. I dashed off to get it and handed it over to him with the injunction to take all they wanted and to place what was left over in the middle of the courtyard so as to keep it away from the fire, lest we should be burned by its explosion. Seeing that fire was leaping at me on all sides, I ran with my boys to where the soldiers were stationed. Scarcely had I got there when I heard a gunshot in the smithy and saw the blacksmith Felipe Romero running towards us. He told us that we should commend the soul of the other blacksmith, José Arroyo, in our prayers to God, because they had already shot and killed him. The said Felipe managed to escape because he shot his gun at a gentile and killed him; whereat the others scattered, and he had a chance to join the rest of us.

I have already stated that the spot where the soldiers stopped when we left the guardhouse was near the house or granary where I took refuge. And very soon the flames reached that place. Hence it was necessary to move elsewhere; but in the whole of the mission there was nowhere to go, because everything was on fire, and not even the smallest building escaped. Seeing that we were all lost and could not escape in any direction, I said to the soldiers, "Let us go to the cookhouse and barricade ourselves with these bales of clothes that I have here."

The cookhouse is about four or five paces square, closed in on three sides with loose adobes, one on top of the other, and open in front. It seemed a good idea to the soldiers. They got together their bags of bullets and other implements of war, and in a body we ran for it. When we reached the cookhouse two soldiers set about dragging the bales so as to close off the front part. While busy with that work they were badly wounded by the Indians, but God granted that the entranceway could be blocked to mid-height. The said cookhouse had no other roof than some loose reeds that the helpers had put there to shade themselves from the sun. These immediately took fire, but the soldiers at once quenched it.

As soon as we reached the cookhouse our enemies saw us, and with united forces they hurled such a storm of arrows, rocks, adobes, and fire-brands that it seemed they were determined to bury us under them. The two soldiers who alone were fit to fight kept up a constant fire, and just eight paces away we could see a gentile stretched out dead from their bullets. The walls of the Father's buildings, already afire, served the Indians as a protection. The buildings were quite close at hand; hence the enemy could fire on us with more precision.

I could not possibly give Your Reverence any adequate account of the arrows which came singing straight for my head and stuck in the adobes. Thank God not one of them hit me. But this much I can say: one arrow hit square into the pillow I was holding up as a protection for my face. I immediately removed the arrows from the pillow—the one I was using to protect myself.

As some relief to their jangled nerves, the soldiers handed over to me the sack of gunpowder. Your Reverence can well understand the strain under which we all were when we could see fire all over and around us from the firebrands they were hurling at us and the danger of an explosion from the gunpowder. In this extremity I exclaimed to the soldiers, "Friends, our plight is a bitter one, our enemies are many, we are few. Let us turn to God and to Mary Most Holy. Let us offer our prayers to Our Heavenly Queen and ask her to look with a favorable eye upon us, to slacken the fury of our enemies and give us victory over them. With this intention, for my own part, I propose to fast nine Saturdays and offer up my Mass in her honor nine times," etc.

The soldiers and everyone else there heartily agreed to this, and the Heavenly Lady seemed perceptibly to hear our prayers, because many a time I snatched the firebrands from the very mouth of our gunpowder bag. At this juncture I received a terrible blow from a piece of rock that caught me on the shoulder. Although it gave me plenty of pain, I pretended that it was nothing so as not to upset the others. I did not mention it until two days afterwards, when I had to rub it with oil. And, thanks be to God, by using this simple remedy it has got better.

We were all longing for daylight—there was plenty of the other kind—and that night seemed to us as long as the pains of Purgatory. The arrows stopped coming for a while, but not the rocks and firebrands. Yet this very cessation caused me anguish, because I reckoned they were merely resting up to make a more furious attack at dawn. And sure enough, my suspicions were well grounded. Scarcely had dawn appeared than they let loose such a storm of arrows as to overwhelm us. I could hear numbers of the enemy, who until recently had been my trusted children, giving orders that now they should once and for all make an end of us, and encouraging their own ranks for the final charge. But God so decreed that a discharge of our guns just in the nick of time disheartened them and caused them to scatter.

At the sight of so many of their enemies in flight, the Christians of the mission—those from *ranchería* San Francisco, our Father, and from *ranchería* Nuestra Señora de la Soledad, who at that time were encamped at the mission to hear Mass on that day—set off with their arms to pursue them. Those of their stories that have reached me assert that they shot some with their arrows, but in any case they did not pursue them any great distance from the mission. They did not come to our rescue earlier for fear of the dark.

As soon as the gentiles had taken flight, we saw a [Baja] California Indian shouting at us—his name was Ignacio and there was another, from here, called Roque but known under his other ill-sounding nickname, Barrabás—and they were calling out that we should not shoot at them, that the gentiles had gone off, that we should not have any fear. We let them come up, and immediately I asked them, "My sons, where is Father Luis?"

They each replied, "Father, I do not know."

And their response was like a sharp sword going right through my heart.

Then came all the Christian women, sad-faced and dejected. At the sight of them I was both sad and glad. I can assure Your Reverence that my mind was tottering and weak, with all sorts of pictures disturbing it. Then, one after the other, the Indians who live regularly at the mission came along, and those from the two *rancherías* I have mentioned. And I noticed those from the mission came without their arms, while the others had them. I began to suspect a trap. But this was quickly dispelled when they began to speak and tell me they had chased away the enemy and that I should have no fear or misgivings.

I came out from that ill-fated cookhouse then and stood in front of them. They all came up and embraced me and acknowledged me as their Father. Just what my feelings were, I cannot properly describe, hardly knowing whether anguish or joy was uppermost in my mind. As soon as my thoughts cleared somewhat, my first anxiety was for Father Luis. And so I told the Indians to go and see where the Father was; others I told to look for the horses, and others to go to warn the *presidio,* others again to fetch water for the wheat granary, which was still on fire. All this they did with the utmost dispatch, dividing themselves off into groups to do my bidding. Those who went in search of water were the first to come across the Father. One of them dashed up to me and announced that the Father was lying in the *arroyo.* I asked, "Alive or dead?"

"Dead," he replied.

Just think, Your Reverence, what must have been my grief and sorrow at hearing that he was already dead. But since God so wished it, I told them to go and bring him up. Very soon they had done so. If the news that he was already dead was a blow to me, how much harder was it to bear when I saw he was quite unrecognizable. He was disfigured from head to foot, and I could see that his death had been cruel beyond description and to the fullest satisfaction of the barbarians. He was stripped completely of all his clothing, even to his undergarments around his middle. His chest and body were riddled through with countless jabs they had given him, and his face was one great bruise from the clubbing and stoning it had suffered. The only way my eyes could recognize him to be Father Luis was from the whiteness of his skin and the tonsure on his head. It was indeed a stroke of fortune that they did not take his scalp off with them, as is customary with these barbarians when they have killed their enemies.

At the very sight of my dead Father and comrade I fainted, from which I did not recover for a long time. I do not know what would have happened if a number of Indian women had not taken hold of me as I fell across the body of the dead Father. There they held me until some water was brought for me to drink; they bathed my temples in it and brought me back to consciousness. What anguish and sorrow were mine my pen cannot describe. How much difference there is between a fact and its description! Before my eyes was the comrade I had lost, and whom I loved and revered so much. I could see, to my shame, how shining were his virtues and what a weak imitation were my own poor efforts. But *Dominus dedit, Dominus ab-stulit: sit nomen Domini benedictum.* *

When I was once more myself, I looked up and saw the soldiers from the *presidio,* and among them the corporal. They reassured me and set about making all necessary arrangements. They put together five stretchers, two for the two who had been killed, the other three for the two soldiers and the master carpenter who were seriously wounded. The carpenter died five days later. The other two soldiers, although suffering from many a wound, rallied themselves sufficiently to get to the *presidio* on horseback. When everything was in readiness, the Indians took charge of the dead and wounded, and by slow stages we arrived at the *presidio.* I made my way on foot, walking by the side of the dead.

We reached the *presidio,* and the many sighs and tears of the people there brought a fresh tide of sorrow to my own heart. I at once asked for a habit, girdle, and underwear for the deceased Father, and with great generosity one good fellow brought them all to me. As for myself, I only had the habit and tunic I was wearing. But gladly would I have given these except for the generosity of this good man. But anyway, I wish to declare openly how generous he was.

In the afternoon I called together my sad-faced Indians, and we went to the church to recite the Rosary for the dead Father. Next day I celebrated the Holy Sacrifice of the Mass with a set of vestments which, as they say, was for all colors†—it was kept here in the *presidio* for the celebration of Mass, and I did not have any other vestments—and gave church burial vested in these to the aforesaid Father Luis Jayme in the church of the *presidio* here. Likewise I buried the master blacksmith. I recited a number of psalms and prayers for the dead, from memory because I was without a Manual. And so, Reverend Father President, these were the terrible happenings which took place in this poor mission here.

---

* "The Lord gave, the Lord has taken away: blessed be the name of the Lord," a quotation from the first chapter of the Book of Job expressing resignation in the face of suffering.

† Normally, the priest wore vestments of different colors for different types of liturgical celebrations: white for joyous feasts, red to commemorate the feasts of the martyrs, black for funerals, etc. The single set of vestments kept at the *presidio* was pressed into service for all manner of liturgical occasions.

1776
The San Francisco Bay Region

Pedro Font

Spanish colonial officials could not expect colonization to prosper if all communication between the Californias and the Mexican mainland had to take place by sea. Eusebio Kino and the Jesuits on both sides of the Gulf of California had long dreamed of establishing a land route between Sonora and California. Gálvez, too, believed that Alta California could never fully develop without a secure land route to Mexico. Fr. Francisco Garcés undertook an eight-hundred-mile journey through the desert regions around the Colorado and Gila Rivers in 1771. The good relations he was able to establish with the peoples of these areas impressed Juan Bautista de Anza, commander of the *presidio* at Tubac, south of Tucson. Anza received permission from viceroy Bucareli to attempt to forge a trail to Alta California.

Anza was joined by Sebastián Taraval, a Cochimí from Baja California who had been brought to San Gabriel. He had escaped from there with his wife and a brother and crossed the mountains, desert, and dunes before reaching Tubac. His companions, however, did not survive the harrowing trek. Anza and Garcés, swayed by the magnitude of the journey he had made, recruited Taraval as a guide for their own attempt. The thirty-four-man party left Tubac on January 8, 1774. After ten terrifying days lost in the dunes west of the Colorado River, Taraval guided them over the mountains to Alta California. They reached San Gabriel on March 22.

Bucareli then approved a second journey. Its purpose was to bring enough colonists to Alta California to establish a *presidio* and two new missions to the north of Monterey and to put the new colony on a more secure long-term footing. Anza recruited soldiers and settlers from the frontier. His group of two hundred and forty men, women, and children and over a thousand animals left Tubac on October 23, 1775. When they reached the Colorado River, they heard about the Kumeyaay attack on San

Diego from the Quechán people there. Continuing across the desert and through the snow-covered mountains, they reached San Gabriel on January 4, 1776. Responding to Rivera's request for assistance in subduing the Kumeyaay, Anza detoured to San Diego and did not reach Monterey until March. From there he led a party of twenty men, including Fr. Pedro Font, to the San Francisco Bay region to investigate possible sites for the new *presidio*.

Font was born in Catalonia, Spain, and came to the New World in 1763. He became a missionary in Sonora in 1773. He was serving there, at San José de los Pimas, when his religious superior assigned him to accompany the second Anza expedition in 1775. At the conclusion of this journey to the bay, Font accompanied Anza back to Sonora. On June first they reached the starting point of their journey, San Miguel de Horcasitas. Font returned to his missionary work and died at Mission Pitic in Sonora in 1781. The following account, which begins on the peninsula south of San Francisco, is from his diary. He took copious notes on the trip itself and put the diary into final form after he returned to Sonora.

From the Diary of Pedro Font

F*riday, March 29 [1776].* We traveled through the valley some four leagues to the southeast and southeast by south, and crossed the *arroyo* of San Mateo where it enters the pass through the hills. About a league before this there came out on our road a very large bear, which the men succeeded in killing. There are many of these beasts in that country, and they often attack and do damage to the Indians when they go to hunt, of which I saw many horrible examples. When he saw us so near, the bear was going along very carelessly on the slope of a hill, where flight was not very easy. When I saw him so close, looking at us in suspense, I feared some disaster. But Corporal Robles fired a shot at him with aim so true that he hit him in the neck. The bear now hurled himself down the slope, crossed the *arroyo,* and hid in the brush, but he was so badly wounded that after going a short distance he fell dead. Thereupon the soldiers skinned him and took what flesh they wished. In this affair we spent more than an hour here. The Commander took the hide to give as a present to the Viceroy. The bear was so old that his eye teeth were badly decayed and he lacked one tooth, but he was very fat, although his flesh smelled much like a skunk or like musk. I measured this animal and he was nine spans long and four high. He was horrible, fierce, large, and fat, and very tough. They found several bullets they had fired at him between his hide and his flesh, and the ball that entered his throat was in his neck between the hide and the muscle, with a little piece of bone stuck to it....

We came to the camp at the *arroyo* of San Mateo. The Indians of this village were very attentive and obliging, and even troublesome, for they had so attached themselves to the camp that when it was already very late it was necessary to drive them out in order that we might get some sleep. So I think that it would be easy to establish them in a mission.

Saturday, March 30. On setting out, we retraced our outward road some six leagues and passed by the same villages, whose Indians were very gentle and friendly. Those of the third village came out to the road and were very sad because we did not go to their huts, to which they invited us. We went as far as the *arroyo* of San Francisco, on whose bank is the very tall redwood which I mentioned yesterday. I measured its height with a graphometer which they loaned me at the mission of San Carlos del Carmelo, and I found it to be, according to the calculation which I made, some fifty *varas* high, a little more or less. The trunk at the foot was five and a half *varas* in circumference, and the soldiers said that they had seen even larger ones in the *sierras*.

At this place, with the plan of going to explore the large river which was called San Francisco and was said to empty into the port on the north side, we left the road which we had followed in coming. Changing our direction, we traveled along the water but apart from it about a league, and in places more on account of the marshes, going some three leagues to the east. Then, beginning to go around this extremity of the port, we traveled for about three leagues to the northeast, finally winding around all the way from west to east in order to ford the river and reach the camp site. All this road goes through very level and low land and therefore miry, so that when it rains heavily it becomes impassable. For this reason, the experienced soldiers told us that to go to the other side it would be necessary to make a detour almost to the *Arroyo de las Llagas,* but God willed that we should come out well by the shortcut through here, by which we saved several leagues and discovered the Guadalupe River, of which the soldiers had not heard.

Because the river was so deep, it cost us more than an hour to find a ford across it. We wished to cross at the place where we first struck it, because at that place there was a bridge consisting of a tree lying athwart it. On the

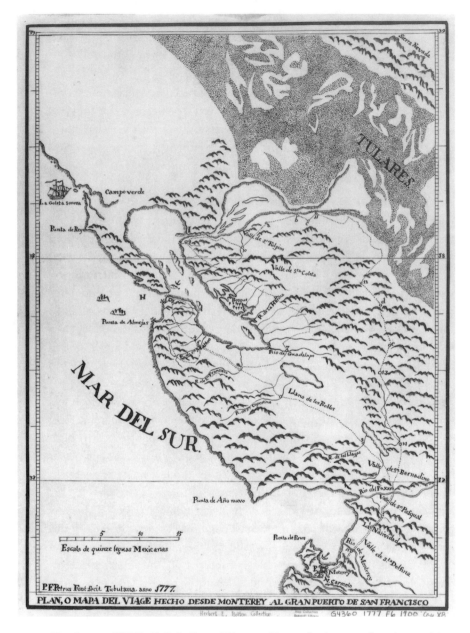

Map drawn in 1777 by Fr. Pedro Font at Tubutama, Mexico, after his return from the second Anza expedition. In the corresponding excerpt from Font's diary, he and the others were between camp-sites 5 and 6. They were a bit to the west of the spot where the two paths north of campsite 4 intersect, and they were heading south through the San Andrés Valley. They crossed the River of San Mateo (now called San Mateo Creek). The bear was killed in the vicinity of what is other side there was a village whose Indians manifested great fear as soon as they saw us. The Commander quieted four of them who were there by giving them glass beads; but it was not possible to cross, because the banks were very high. A ford was now sought lower down, but the farther we went toward the estuary and its mouth the worse it became, so it was decided to take the packs and everything over the bridge and to swim the animals across; and since the banks were so high and so overgrown with trees, a beginning was made by cutting branches and digging into the banks to make a path to the river. Then a soldier went to seek a ford higher up, and after a short time returned, reporting that he had found one, and in fact we were able to cross over there very well by merely cutting a few branches.

This place is one of very level land, well covered with pasturage, but it is lacking in firewood, for there is no other timber than the growth along the river, which is of cottonwoods, sycamores, ash, and laurels; and in all that region there is not a single stone. The Indians afterward were somewhat obliging, bringing some brush for firewood, and were not so much afraid as they had been at first. On the way here we had the *Llano de los Robles* on our right. On beginning to go around the head of the estuary we found another village whose Indians showed great fear as soon as they saw us, but it was greatly lessened by giving them glass beads. One of the women, from the

---

now Crystal Springs Reservoir. Then they turned northeast and went back to the creek, where they camped (6).

On March 30 they headed down the peninsula to the San Francisco River (now San Francisquito Creek). They crossed it and traveled through the Llano de los Robles (Plain of Oaks), now called Santa Clara Valley, to the Guadalupe River, on whose banks they camped (7).

On March 31 they started up the east side of the bay, staying close to the coastal hills. After crossing Encarnación Creek (now Scott Creek), they reached a lagoon slightly north of Irvington in modern Fremont. The creek to which Font refers is now called Laguna Creek. Continuing north, they reached Alameda Creek, which is where they encountered the Indians slapping their thighs. They made camp at Río de la Harina, now called San Lorenzo Creek (8).

On April 1 they resumed their march, once again staying close to the hills. They first came to San Leandro Creek, where they met the bears. The dry creek that Font mentions is near the campus of Mills College in Oakland. The peninsula he saw in the distance and termed the forest (bosque) is modern Alameda Island. From there they headed straight to "the mouth of the port," the Carquinez Strait, where they camped along Rodeo Creek (9).

The next morning they turned toward the south shore of Carquinez Strait. The Indian village was in the neighborhood of Tormey and the midday camp was close to the southern end of the present Carquinez Bridge, across the strait from where Font has drawn the letter "I." Courtesy of The Bancroft Library, University of California, Berkeley.

time when she first saw us until we departed, stood at the door of her hut making gestures like crosses and drawing lines on the ground, at the same time talking to herself as though praying, and during her prayer she was immobile, paying no attention to the glass beads which the Commander offered her.

From here I viewed the course of the estuary and saw that it ran east-southeast, just as I noted yesterday. Likewise I sketched the island which is seen at this end near the shore, as I said on the twenty-seventh. In this place we were very cold, and likewise were molested somewhat by the mosquitoes that live on the banks of the river. This stream appears to have some fish, for we saw there some small *mojarras,* and some nets with which the Indians fish; but I think it all amounts to very little, for I noticed that the Indians who live around about the estuary and the port are not fishermen, for in their villages are seen only piles of shells of mussels, which must be what they fish and eat most of.

Sunday, March 31. At first we went about a short league to the north-northwest. Then, because of the sloughs and marshes, we wound around for about three leagues to the east-northeast, twisting about until we emerged from the sloughs and lowlands where we had been, and gained higher ground at the foot of the hills which run as far as the bay and mouth of the Puerto Dulce and belong to the same range which I mentioned on the eighth.* Then we traveled far away from the water for some three leagues to the north-northwest and three more to the northwest. The Indians whom we saw along here are totally distinct in language from the previous ones. They are somewhat bearded, gentle, and very poor, but in color they are the same as all the rest. As soon as we began to travel we came to a small *arroyo* which, according to the account, is the one which Father Crespí called La Encarnación and which they crossed higher up than we.

After we had left the sloughs and taken the higher ground, we passed along the shores of a somewhat salty lagoon, which we left on our right and into which apparently flowed some *arroyos* from the canyons of the range of hills which we were following. All the rest of the road is through very level country, green and flower-covered all the way to the estuary, but with no other timber or firewood than that afforded by the trees in the *arroyos* which we encountered, which were five. All along the plain we saw occasional

---

* The "mouth" is the Carquínez Strait. The "bay" is Suisun Bay.

Indians, some of whom fled on seeing us and others who waited for us. These latter the Commander tried to win by giving them glass beads. Those whom we saw before we reached the first *arroyo* appear to be very poor and miserable, for they have not even firewood by which to keep warm, and they go about naked like all the rest in those countries and eat grass and herbs and some roots like medium-sized onions, which they call *amole** and in which those plains greatly abound. One Indian who carried his provisions on the end of a pole invited us to eat some of them.

About halfway on the road, we came to an *arroyo* with little water, most of it in very deep pools. It has on its banks many sycamores, cottonwoods, and some live oaks and other trees, and it appears to flow west to empty into the estuary toward which all the *arroyos* flow and toward which runs a thick growth of trees; but I was not able to distinguish whether it marked the course of the river or was a stretch of grove. From these trees about thirty Indians came out on the road to us, armed with somewhat dilapidated bows and arrows but in a peaceful mood and apparently very gentle. Their language is distinct from all those we had formerly heard and it is very ugly; and with the gabbling which they made, all speaking together, it was very disagreeable to the ears. Their method of greeting us was as follows: they came running, and before reaching us they raised an arm, extending the hand as a sign that we should stop. Yelling with great rapidity, they said, "Au, au, au, au, au, au, au, au, au, au, au, au, au," and then they halted, vigorously slapping their thighs. As they went yelling, one behind another, and then continued talking with great velocity and shouting, it seemed like something infernal. We stopped with them a short while and the Commander gave them glass beads. These Indians perhaps belong to that tribe of which Father Garcés makes mention in his diary, saying that when they salute they speak in this way.

A little more than two leagues farther on, we crossed two small, wooded *arroyos* which are separated only by a small hill, and between which we saw a village without people. We traveled a league more and crossed another *arroyo,* where we saw an abandoned village and, in a hut, many birds stuffed with grass, which the Indians use to hunt with. Here the soldiers got some wild tobacco, of which there was a considerable amount. Going another league we came to the fifth *arroyo,* where we halted. As soon as we crossed it we came upon a poor Indian who was coming very carelessly

---

* Probably soaproot, *Chlorogalum pomeridianum*

along, carrying a bunch of grass such as they eat, like that which at the mission of Carmelo they call *morrén*. But as soon as he saw us he manifested fright so great that it is not possible to describe. He could do nothing but throw himself at full length on the ground, hiding himself in the grass in order that we might not see him, raising his head only enough to peep at us with one eye. The Commander approached him to give him some beads, but he was so stupefied that he was unable to take the gift, and it was necessary for the Lieutenant to dismount and put it in his hand. Completely terrified, and almost without speaking, he offered the Lieutenant his *morrén,* as if with the present he hoped to save his life, which he feared was lost. He must never have seen Spaniards before, and that is why we caused him such surprise and fear.

This place is almost opposite the *arroyo* of San Mateo, whence we set out yesterday. All the way, the road is set apart from the estuary, at first about a league and then farther and farther away, so that this place where we halted is distant from the water of the estuary somewhat more than two leagues. All the country is level, clear to the foot of the hills which we have been following.

All day today, the Commander and I have been in doubt as to whether the island at the end of the estuary that I mapped yesterday is really an island or not, because aside from the fact that today it has changed its shape, we were not able to see the water on this side of it. We had the same experience with another long island which I mapped next day, and I concluded either that the water which surrounds it is small in amount and could not be seen on account of the distance, or that the passage is so miry that it may be reputed to be an island because it is impassable from the mainland. I was not able to ascertain whether or not Indians live on the islands.

Monday, April 1. The road followed the foothills of the range that I mentioned on March 8. In all its exterior this range has very few trees, except a grove of redwoods in front of the mouth of the port, although in its interior it has thickly grown groves and is quite broken, as we saw on our return when we crossed it, and at the mouth of the Puerto Dulce, where it ends in some hills that are very high and very round.

After going two leagues, we came to an *arroyo* with little water but with a very deep bed thick with cottonwoods, live oaks, laurels, and other trees, crossing it at the foot of the hills by making a detour. Before crossing it we saw on a slope four bears—which, according to all accounts, are very plentiful through here also, for we saw several Indians badly scarred by bites and scratches of these animals. After going about two more leagues, we crossed a small *arroyo* without water and almost without trees. Then, a little further on, we ascended a hill that is in a straight line with the mainland and the plain which runs toward a very thick grove of oaks and live oaks on the banks of the estuary, and is almost made into an island by two arms of the estuary. From there I mapped this grove and the two arms of the estuary, and I am inserting the map here on the back of this sheet. Then, descending the hill, we crossed another *arroyo* almost without trees and with some little pools of water that did not run. This appears to be the *arroyo* which Father Crespí called the *Arroyo del Bosque* and which empties into the extremity of one arm of the estuary.

We continued the journey over hills and plains, crossing two more *arroyos* with little water, deep beds, and a heavy growth of trees, the second one having more than the other, both of them flowing into a bay which the arm of the estuary forms on this side. Afterward we entered a plain in which we crossed two small *arroyos* without water. From this plain we clearly descried the mouth of the port, and when the point of the red cliff on the inside was in line with the outer point of the mouth, I observed the direction in which they ran and saw that it was to the west with some declination to the south. It appeared to me that the estuary in front of the mouth must be some four leagues wide. Our road ran apart from the estuary about two leagues.

Then we crossed an *arroyo* with a small growth of trees and very little water, which appears to be the one Father Crespí called the *Arroyo de la Bocana*. Further down this *arroyo* there is a grove or growth of not very large timber. Having seen tracks of the large deer whose hoof tracks are almost like those of cattle, the soldier went to hunt for them in the brush, but although they found them, they were not able to get any. Then we continued over level land and some small hills. Along here we saw an Indian in the plain who, as soon as he saw us, was so frightened that he ran up a hill and hid behind some rocks. Afterward we ascended some hills and came to a rather deep *arroyo* with a growth of trees and little water, on whose banks we saw an abandoned village.

From here we continued, now in the plain and now over hills. Seven Indians came out to us on the road. The Commander gave them glass beads, and they followed us to the next *arroyo*, which was not very far away. We crossed it with some difficulty, because the bed was very deep, with a heavy growth of live oaks, sycamores, and other trees. Here we found a village

where we saw about twenty-three Indian men and some seven women, for the rest were in the woods hunting for *tule,* herbs, and roots of the kinds they eat. The Commander presented them with glass beads and they were very well content and obliging, giving us *cacomites,* half roasted or roasted.*
On the way I mapped the large and very long island that is on this side, close to the land, and from the end of which begins the large bay.

From here we traveled northwest, over hills, up and down. Having passed two or three small *arroyos* without water, we came to an *arroyo* with very little water on whose banks we found a fair-sized village whose Indians, both men and women, were very happy to see us and very obliging. They presented us with many *cacomites,* which is a little bulb or root almost round and rather flat, the size and shape of a somewhat flattened ball, and likewise with a good string of roasted *amole,* which is another root, like a rather long onion, all well-cooked and roasted. I ate some of it and liked the taste, and the Commander gave the Indians glass beads. The *amole,* which is their most unusual food, tastes a little like mescal. It is the food which most abounds, and the fields along here are full of it.

We continued on our way over hills and through valleys, and having passed a small *arroyo,* we halted on the next little rivulet. This place is about a league before reaching the mouth of the Puerto Dulce or the mouth of what they called the *Río Grande de San Francisco,* which I greatly desired to see, but which finally I did not see because there is no such river, as I shall show tomorrow.

As soon as we halted, thirty-eight Indians came to us unarmed, peaceful, and very happy to see us. At first they stopped and sat down on a small hill near the camp. Then one came, and behind him another, and so they came in single file like a flock of goats, leaping and talking, until all had arrived. They were very obliging, bringing us firewood, and very talkative, their language having much gabbling, nothing of which was understood. They go naked like all the rest, and they are by no means white but are like all those whom we saw on this journey; and they are very little bearded, not so much, indeed, as those whom we saw on the other side, near the mouth of the port. After they had been a while with us they bade us goodbye and we made signs to them that they should go and get us some fish with two hooks that I gave them. They apparently understood us clearly, but they brought us nothing and showed very little appreciation for the hooks, because their method of fishing was with nets.

---

* Possibly brodiaeas or other edible bulbs known generically as Indian potatoes.

From the camp, the roar of the sea was heard somewhat, for in the bay the waves break a little on the beach, although not very much. From a high hill, before reaching the camp, we looked out at the bay, for from that place most of it is visible. I saw that it is surrounded by hills and mountains on all sides, except for a large opening which lies almost west by north, in which direction for a good stretch runs a tongue of lowland, behind or beyond which it looked white like water, extending to another range which at the end and very far away looked blue. I surmised that perhaps in that direction the bay might communicate with the port of Bodega, for on account of the currents which he saw in it when he was there, Captain Don Juan de la Quadra was not able to say whether it was sea or a river; and that port lies not very far from the bay in that direction, as I understand, although this is only a conjecture.

Tuesday, April 2. I said Mass. The night was serene and not very cold, and day dawned very clear and beautiful. It remained clear all day and was somewhat hot, which tempered the fresh wind which blew softly from the northwest. We set out from the little *arroyo* at seven o'clock in the morning and passed through a village to which we were invited by some ten Indians who came to the camp very early in the morning, singing. We were welcomed by the Indians in the village, whom I estimated at some four hundred persons, with singular demonstrations of joy, singing, and dancing.

Their method of welcoming us was like this: at sunrise the ten Indians came, one behind another, singing and dancing. One carried the tune, making music with a little stick, rather long and split in the middle, which he struck against his hand and which sounded something like a castanet. They reached the camp and continued their singing and dancing for a little while. Then they stopped dancing, all making a step in unison, shaking the body, and saying dryly and in one voice, "Ha, ha, ha!" Next they sat down on the ground and signaled to us that we must sit down also. So we sat down in front of them, the Commander, I, and the Commissary. Now an Indian arose and presented the Commander with a string of *cacomites,* and again sat down. Shortly afterward he rose again and made me a present of another string of *cacomites* and again sat down. In this way they went, making us their little presents, another Indian giving me a very large root of *chuchupate* which he began to eat, telling me by signs that it was good.

This compliment being over, they invited us to go to their village, indicating that it was nearby. The Commander consented to give them this pleasure, and at once we began to travel. They followed after us with their singing and dancing, which I interrupted by chanting the *Alabado,* as we did every day on beginning the journey, but as soon as I finished they continued their singing and shouting with greater vigor and in a higher key, as if they wished to respond to our chant. After going a short distance we came to the village, which was in a little valley on the bank of a small *arroyo,* the Indians welcoming us with an indescribable hullabaloo. Three of them came to the edge of the village with some long poles with feathers on the end, and, hanging like a pennant, some long and narrow strips of skin with the hair on that looked to me like rabbit skin, this being their sign of peace. They led us to the middle of the village, where there was a level spot like a plaza, and then began to dance with other Indians of the place with much clatter and yelling.

A little afterward a rather old Indian woman came out and, in front of us, for we were on horseback, nobody having dismounted, she began to dance alone, making motions very indicative of pleasure, at times stopping to talk to us, making signs with her hands as if bidding us welcome. After a short while I said to the Commander that that was enough. So he gave presents of glass beads to all the women, they regaled us with their *cacomites,* and we said good-bye to everybody in order to continue on our way. They were apparently sad because we were leaving, and I was moved to tenderness at seeing the joy with which we were welcomed by those poor Indians. Their color and other qualities of nakedness, slight beard, etc., are the same as those seen hitherto, and the same as those we saw farther on. Some wear the hair long, others short, and some have beards rather long and heavy.

We continued about a long league to the north and northeast and at nine o'clock arrived at the shore of the water near to and inside the *Boca del Puerto Dulce,* indicated on the map by the letter "I," which hitherto has been considered as a large river but which is not, according to the experiments we made, and for reasons which I shall set forth. Here the Commander decided that we should halt until after midday in order to calculate the latitude of this place.

1776
The Beginnings of San Francisco

Francisco Palóu

The formal purpose of Anza's 1776 journey through the San Francisco Bay region was to select the site of the new *presidio*. Anza chose a site close to the coast, near the mouth of the Golden Gate. In June 1776 an expedition headed by José Joaquín Moraga and including Fr. Francisco Palóu left Monterey to establish the *presidio* and a mission. Moraga decided to construct the *presidio* a bit farther inland, away from the foggy and windswept point Anza had recommended. The mission was placed near a stream about three miles away, which Anza and Font had identified as a good location. The stream was named Our Lady of Sorrows *(Nuestra Señora de los Dolores)*, and over time the church became known as Mission Dolores. In the excerpt that follows, Palóu describes the founding of the mission and the first encounters with the people of the vicinity.

FROM *Historical Memoirs of New California*

It was then decided that the formal act of possession should take place, the day appointed for it being that on which our Mother Church celebrates the impression of the stigmata of Our Seraphic Father San Francisco, that is, the seventeenth of September, a most appropriate day, since he is the patron of the harbor, the new *presidio*, and the mission. And for taking formal possession of the mission, the fourth of October was designated, which is the day dedicated to Our Seraphic Father San Francisco. The Commander of the packet, his two pilots, and the greater part of the crew were present at the ceremony of taking formal possession, with only those who were absolutely necessary having remained on board; and with the people from the *presidio*, troops as well as citizens, they made up a goodly number of Spaniards. There were also present four friar priests, all of our College, that is, the two missionary ministers of this mission, the chaplain of the bark, and Father Fray Tomás de la Peña, who had come from Monterey to examine the site for the second mission, of which he had been named minister.

A solemn Mass was sung by the priests, and when it was concluded, the gentlemen performed the ceremony of taking formal possession. This finished, all entered the chapel and sang the *Te Deum Laudamus,* accompanied by peals of bells and repeated salvos of cannon, muskets, and guns, the bark responding with its swivel guns, whose roar and the sound of the bells doubtless terrified the heathen, for they did not allow themselves to be seen for many days. The ceremony concluded, the Commander of the *presidio* invited to it all the people, conducting himself with all the splendor that the place permitted and supplying with his true kindness what would have been missed in other parts, for which all the people were grateful, expressing their gratitude in the joy and happiness which all felt on that day. . . .

The chapel was blessed with all ceremony on October 3, the Eve of Our Seraphic Father, it being our intention to celebrate the occasion on the following day with all solemnity. But, as the Lieutenant had not returned from his expedition at the end of the day, it was agreed to postpone the founding and merely to sing a Mass on the day of Our Seraphic Father, as was done.

On the eighth of the same month, the Lieutenant having arrived the previous afternoon, the ceremony was performed in the presence of the gentlemen of the bark and all the crew, except those required to take care of the vessel, and of the Commander of the *presidio,* with all the troops and citizens, except that those who were absolutely required remained in the fort. I sang the Mass with the ministers, and at its conclusion a procession was formed in which an image of Our Seraphic Father San Francisco, patron of the port, *presidio*, and mission, was carried on a frame. The function was celebrated with repeated salvos of muskets, rifles, and the swivel guns that were brought from the bark for this purpose, and also with rockets. All the people who were present at the ceremony remained at the mission to dine, two cows having been killed for their entertainment. In the afternoon the men returned to the *presidio* and the crew went aboard, the day having been a very joyous one for all. The heathen were the only ones who did not enjoy this happy day, as I shall relate at length in the next chapter.

The founding of the *presidio* and mission concluded, the Sea Commander decided to prepare the bark for its return to San Blas, ordering wood and water taken on and the necessary ballast loaded. Everything being finished and the weather favorable, it safely left this harbor on the morning of October 21. The mission had been successfully founded, not only through the presence of the gentlemen at the function, but also with the aid of some sailors who assisted in the building, and of the carpenter, who made the doors of the church and house, and a table with two drawers for the altar. Besides this, a gift was made of a *cayuco* and a net for fishing. At the same time it was arranged that four sailors should remain as laborers, completing the number of six who were allowed by His Excellency. With this reinforcement, the work proceeded on the buildings and in preparing the land for planting. Crops were put in, and a good stream of water for irrigating was conducted by a ditch that passes close to the houses.

The heathen of the village near this place made frequent visits and were apparently pleased with our arrival, although through lack of interpreters and our ignorance of their language, we could not tell them the purpose of our coming. They went on in this way until August 12, when the heathen of the villages of San Mateo, who are their enemies, fell upon them at a large town about a league from this lagoon, burned it, and had a fight in which there were many wounded and dead on both sides. Apparently the Indians of this vicinity were defeated, and so fearful were they of the others that they made tule rafts and all moved to the shore opposite the *presidio*, or to the mountains on the east side of the bay. We were unable to restrain them, even though we let them know by signs that they should have no fear, for the soldiers would defend them.

After their removal their visits were very rare, and only now and then some men and boys came, and then only because they happened to come to this lagoon to hunt ducks. They generally gave us some of them, and we returned the gifts with beads and some of our food. In the last visits which they made, early in December, they began to disgrace themselves, now by thefts, now by firing an arrow close to the corporal of the guard, and again by trying to kiss the wife of a soldier, as well as by threatening to fire an arrow at a neophyte from the mission of Carmelo who was at this mission.

The Sergeant who was at this mission in the middle of December learned of all this, and one day when five heathen came to visit us and one of them turned out to be the one who a few days before had threatened, or made a gesture, to fire the arrow at the neophyte, he caused him to be arrested and given a flogging in the guardhouse. On hearing his cries, two heathen who were hunting on the lagoon ran up, and they were bold enough to try to avenge the injury, making ready to shoot arrows at the soldiers, who fired two gunshots only to frighten them, and in fact they fled without any injury having occurred. The Sergeant followed them and, seeing that they entered the wood toward the beach, he returned to the *presidio*, where he was in command as a substitute for the Lieutenant.

Fearing that the Indians would cross the bay, on the following day the Sergeant went to the beach with some soldiers to order the two Indians who had fired arrows at the mission flogged, to frighten them. On the beach, he found a band of heathen. When they were asked which ones had fired arrows at the mission, they pointed out two, and although those two denied it, the others accused them. The Sergeant alighted, and when they saw the movement the two guilty ones fled, and two of the soldiers followed them. The rest of the Indians withdrew and began to shoot arrows, wounding a citizen who had gone without his leather jacket, and also a horse, although they were not seriously hurt.

The Sergeant, seeing this and seeing that they did not stop shooting, ordered the men to fire, and the wounded citizen brought down one with a ball, and he fell dead in the water of the bay. The rest ran to take refuge among some isolated rocks not far away, whence they continued to shoot their arrows. The Sergeant fired at them, and at one shot the ball went through the leg of one of them and then pierced the rock, for they found the hole the next day, and signs that the Indians had taken out the ball, doubtless to see what it was that had made such havoc among them. As soon as the Indians among the isolated rocks saw one of their number dead and the other so badly wounded, they asked for peace, making the gesture of throwing their bows and arrows on the ground. The Sergeant did the same with his gun, upon which they became quiet, but they did not wish to go to the beach when the Sergeant called them to collect their things.

The soldiers caught the two who had run off to the woods, and the Sergeant went to them and charged them with having dared to fire arrows at the mission, caused them to be whipped, and told them by signs that if they did it again he would kill them. He told them to gather up all the things they had there, their own as well as those of their companions, and to tell the others not to do any harm and they would be friends.

Because of this misadventure they became panic-stricken and absented themselves to such an extent that they did not dare to approach the mission or the *presidio* and did not permit themselves to be seen for three months, up to the beginning of March. Thereafter, now and then one came to the mission, and little by little they yielded themselves up, so that on the day of San Juan Bautista, June 24, 1777, the first three were baptized, they being adults, but the rest of the heathen came no more.

1779
Rules for Towns and Missions

FELIPE DE NEVE

Despite Fages's removal from the post of commander of Monterey and hence of Alta California, the relationship between the military and the missionaries in Alta California did not improve. Even though Fages's replacement, Fernando de Rivera y Moncada, had maintained fine relationships with the Jesuits in Baja California for many years, his experience with Serra was basically the same as Fages's had been. The issues were varied but the underlying point of contention was constant: what type of place was Alta California to become? Serra wanted the resources of the province—its soldiers, supplies, stocks, and laborers—deployed in a way that would serve the interests of the missions to the virtual exclusion of all else. Rivera, on the other hand, viewed the needs of the missions as simply one set of needs among many. He viewed his job as strengthening the entire Spanish presence in this remote region; the missions would have to compete with the *presidios* for their sustenance. In 1774, for instance, Rivera refused to provide a mission guard for the proposed Mission San Buenaventura. This effectively killed the project. In 1775, Rivera became upset when, without clearing the matter with him, Serra sent two soldiers from the Carmel mission guard after some Indians who had fled. The following year, Rivera entered the *presidio* chapel at San Diego and arrested an Indian whom he was seeking in connection with the attack on the mission the year before. The Indian was being sheltered by Fr. Fuster, who told Rivera that the Indian was entitled to asylum in the chapel. Rivera nevertheless took the Indian away, and Serra, in Carmel, declared that Rivera's action warranted his being excommunicated. This tense situation was resolved when Felipe de Neve, appointed governor of the Californias in 1775, was ordered to move his headquarters from Loreto to Monterey in 1777. Rivera was sent to Baja California as lieutenant governor.

Neve, a Spanish army officer, had come to New Spain in 1764 as a minor officer in the coterie of José de Gálvez. He spent seven years on duty in Zacatecas, where, among other responsibilities, he administered the assets and endowment of the former Jesuit college in that city. Like his king and like Gálvez, who by this time was serving as minister of the Indies in Madrid, Neve was a man of the Enlightenment. He was not sympathetic to the mission system he encountered in California. He clashed with the Dominicans in Baja California, and his experience with the Franciscans in Alta California was stormy. Sometime after he arrived, he asked Serra and Fr. Vicente Mora, the president of the Dominican missions in Baja California, to submit mission inventories to him. Mora sent his along, but Serra refused, saying that he would continue to send his to the College of San Fernando, without sharing them with the governor. The two men argued over this, and Neve complained to the viceroy that he could not do his job if he remained ignorant of the total population and property holdings of the missions. But he never received any reports from Serra.

When Serra informed Neve that he had received permission from Rome to administer the sacrament of Confirmation (a privilege normally reserved to a bishop, but occasionally conferred on the ranking clergyman in the absence of a bishop, especially in missionary areas), Neve demanded to see the original document so that he could check, he said, that it had the appropriate signatures. Serra told him that it was at the college in Mexico City. Neve in turn told Serra that he would refuse to allow him to administer the sacrament until he produced the actual document.

It was in this context that Neve determined to push forward and establish towns in Alta California. Gálvez's vision had included towns in California, and Neve had begun planning the establishment of Indian secular settlements in Baja California before he came north. He brought the same desire to Alta California and lost little time in beginning to implement it—for, besides producing food for the *presidios*, the towns would also function, he hoped, as important civil counterweights to the missions. He chose two sites. One was near the Porciúncula River, in southern Alta California, and the other was near the Guadalupe River, in the north. Since the northern site was nearer to Monterey, and two *presidios* were at hand to provide a core of initial settlers, Neve chose that one first. Sixty-eight men, women, and children under the command of José Joaquín

Moraga, who laid out the central plaza and allotted the land, founded San José de Guadalupe on November 29, 1777. The settlers first threw up temporary shelters fashioned from woven branches and rough clay. Later, they gradually replaced these with structures of more solid adobe. Within five years, the *pueblo* was supplying food to both San Francisco and Monterey. Neve also began planning for the second *pueblo,* in the south.

In 1779 Neve drew up a set of regulations for the government of the Californias. The section on towns went into great detail on the distribution of lands, the arrangement of the plaza, the necessity of trying to ensure a basic equality among the settlers, and the measures to be taken to enhance the production of food and the care of the livestock. The section on the missions, which came significantly after the section on towns, was much shorter. Neve envisioned the number of missionaries at each establishment gradually being reduced, diminishing their importance and influence. In addition, he omitted any references to supplying the missions with farming implements and the like. The thrust of the regulations was that the missionaries would be permitted to administer the churches, but that there were to be no more large mission estates built on the labor of the converts.

From Regulations Issued by Felipe de Neve

Title Fourteen
Political Government and Instructions for Settlement
1. Since the most important aim for the fulfillment of the pious intentions of our Lord, the King, and to perpetuate His Majesty's dominions over the extensive territory embraced for more than two hundred leagues by the establishment of the *presidios* and the respective ports of San Diego, Monterey, and San Francisco is to advance the reduction* and to make this exceedingly vast country as useful as possible to the State, inhabited as it is by innumerable heathen, excepting the 1749 Christians of both sexes at the eight missions on the road between the first and last *presidios*; and also to erect *pueblos* of white people who, being gathered together, shall promote the planting and cultivation of crops, stock raising, and in succession the other branches of industry, so that in the course of a few years their population

---

* Reduction, or *reducción,* the process of congregating the Indians into compact settlements at the missions.

Alta California Missions, *Presidios,* and *Pueblos*

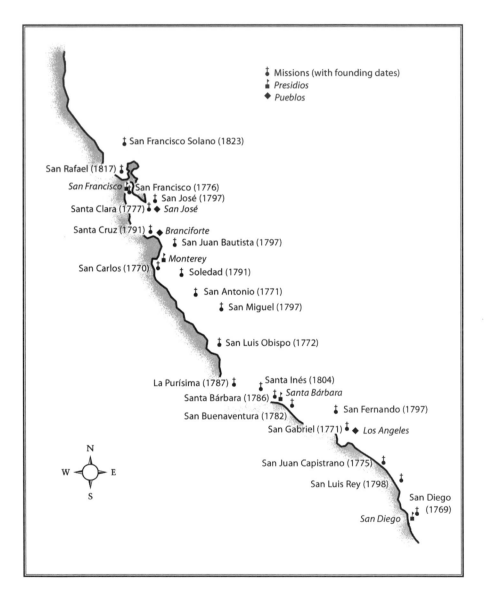

Missions (with founding dates)
Presidios
Pueblos

San Francisco Solano (1823)

San Rafael (1817)

San Francisco San Francisco (1776)
San José (1797)
Santa Clara (1777) *San José*

Santa Cruz (1791) *Branciforte*
San Juan Bautista (1797)

Monterey
San Carlos (1770)
Soledad (1791)

San Antonio (1771)

San Miguel (1797)

San Luis Obispo (1772)

La Purísima (1787)
Santa Inés (1804)
Santa Bárbara (1786) *Santa Bárbara*
San Fernando (1797)
San Buenaventura (1782)
San Gabriel (1771) *Los Angeles*

N
W — E
S

San Juan Capistrano (1775)

San Luis Rey (1798)
San Diego
(1769)
San Diego

may suffice to supply the *presidio* garrisons with provisions and horses, thus avoiding the long haul, risks, and losses under which these things are brought at the expense of the Royal Exchequer (with which fit idea the *pueblo* of San José is already founded and settled, and the establishment of another is determined upon, for which settlers and their families must come from the Province of Sonora and Sinaloa, that their progressive increase and that of the families of the troops will provide for the establishment of other settlements and supply recruits for the *presidio* companies, and thus free the Royal Exchequer from the inevitable costs which it is now under to gain these ends), since to secure these things it is desirable to establish regulations, the following instructions shall be observed....

3. To each settler and to the common fund of the *pueblo*...there shall be given two mares, two cows with one calf, two ewes, and two she-goats, all pregnant, one yoke of oxen or bullocks, one ploughshare or tip, one hoe, one spade, one ax and one sickle, one field knife, one lance, one shotgun and one shield, two horses, and one pack mule. Likewise, and to the common charge, shall be given sufficient sires for the number of head of stock in each kind in the whole community; one master burro and one common one and three she-burros, one boar and three sows, one forge equipped with an anvil and other corresponding tools, six crowbars, six iron spades, and the tools needed for carpentry and wagon making.

4. The lots granted to the new settlers must be determined by the Government as to location and size according to the extent of land where the new *pueblo* may be established, so that a plaza and streets shall be left as provided by the laws of the realm; and in the arrangement there shall be marked out sufficient common land for the *pueblo,* and pasture lands with the suitable arable lands for individuals.

5....There shall be allotted to each settler two fields of irrigable land and two more of dry. Of the royal lands there shall be set aside such as are deemed proper for the community, and of the remainder, and also of the respective building lots, grants shall be made by the Governor in the name of His Majesty to those who come newly to settle, particularly to soldiers who, by having served the time of their enlistment or because of advanced age, are retired from the service, as also to the families of those who die. These shall carry on their farming with the funds each should have, without assistance from the Royal Exchequer in salary, rations, or livestock, this privilege being limited to those who emigrated from their own country with that understanding to colonize this one.

Drawings of a Monterey soldier and his wife in 1791, copied by the Malaspina expedition artist José Cardero from sketches made by Tomás de Suria, his fellow artist on the voyage. They may portray Gabriel Moraga and Ana María Bernal. Courtesy of the Museo de América, Madrid.

6. The houses erected upon the lots granted and set aside for the new settlers, and the fields embraced in their respective grants, shall be entailed in perpetuity on their sons and their descendants or on daughters who marry useful settlers who have no allotment of fields themselves, all such complying with the conditions which will be set forth in these instructions. And in order that the sons of the possessors of these grants may have the obedience and respect they owe their parents, the latter, if they have two or more sons, shall be free and empowered to choose which one, if secular and lay, shall be heir of their houses and fields. And likewise they shall be free to dispose that the fields be divided among the children, but not that one single field be divided, for these, all and each, must be indivisible and inalienable forever.

7. Neither the settlers nor their heirs shall lease, entail, bond, mortgage, nor place other encumbrance whatsoever upon the houses and fields granted to them, even though it be for a pious cause. If anyone should do so in violation of this just prohibition, he shall irredeemably be deprived of the property, and because of that very act his endowment shall be given to such other settler as may be useful and obedient.

8. To maintain their livestock, the new settlers shall enjoy the common privileges of water, pasturage, firewood, and lumber from the public lands, forests, and pastures to be assigned to each *pueblo,* and each shall also enjoy exclusively the grazing of his own lands....

11. When the droves of swine and burros shall have multiplied, and the necessary burros adopted for the service of the mares, if the division of each of the two kinds be feasible, said division shall be made by common consent of the settlers among themselves as equitably as possible so that from the first herd each shall have two head, a male and a female, and one from the second herd. When this is done, the animals should be marked and branded by their owners....

15. The maize, beans, garbanzos, and lentils produced by the crops of the *pueblos,* after the citizens have reserved the amount necessary for their own subsistence and planting, shall be bought for the provision of the *presidios* and paid for in cash at the prices established....

16. Every settler and resident, head of a family, to whom has been granted or in the future shall be granted building lots or fields, and their heirs, shall be obliged to keep themselves equipped with two horses, a saddle complete, a shotgun, and the other arms which have been mentioned. These must be furnished them at cost in order that they may defend their respective districts and lend aid without abandoning their first obligations wherever with grave urgency they may be ordered by the Governor....

18. And as it is meet for the good and proper government of the *pueblos,* the administration of justice, direction of public works, apportionment of water, and careful watchfulness over whatever has been provided in these Instructions that the *pueblos* be given, in proportion to the number of inhabitants, ordinary *alcaldes* and other magistrates yearly. These for the first two years shall be appointed by the Governor, and in following years the settlers shall nominate by and from themselves the public officials that shall have been arranged for. These elections must pass for their confirmation to the Governor, by whom said nominations shall be continued in the three following years if he deems it expedient.

Title Fifteen

Erection of New Reductions

The eight missions already established shall retain the two priests that each now has, but vacancies by death or retirement shall not be filled until they are reduced to one each, excepting the missions close to *presidios*, in which two priests must be maintained, as one of them is obliged to serve the *presidio* as chaplain until such a time as it shall be decided to provide the *presidios* with secular chaplains. Consequently, if a vacancy occurs in these missions or in those at the Channel, a priest shall come from one of the missions of San Juan Capistrano, San Gabriel, San Antonio, or Santa Clara to fill it or, as aforesaid, one from these shall aid in the founding of new missions.

1779
Adapting to the Governor's Regulations

Junípero Serra

One of the controversies in which Serra and Neve engaged revolved around the role of the Indians at the mission communities. The missionaries had been criticized for keeping the indigenous people in too dependent a position and failing to introduce them to the forms of self-government they would need if they were to become productive citizens of the Spanish empire. In an attempt to force the missionaries to develop this consciousness of representative government among the Indians, Neve decided to require them to have the Indians elect *alcaldes* and *regidores* at each mission. This had been the rule in various Indians towns in New Spain since the middle of the sixteenth century, and Neve wanted to apply it to the missions. The missionaries in Alta California resisted these commands. They regarded them as an intrusion into their sphere of command and thought that the real reason for Neve's decree was to weaken the mission Indians' respect for the authority of the fathers.

In the excerpt which follows, Serra, writing to his friend and fellow California missionary, Fr. Fermín Francisco de Lasuén, describes an argument he had with Neve before Mass a few days earlier. In the opening of the letter, Serra describes a tense and heated discussion on a topic the nature of which is not entirely clear. He relates how intensely Neve's order agitated him. He has realized, however, that this order will be impossible to resist, so he urges his fellow missionary to try to manipulate the system by seeing to it that only mission Indians who have already been given offices in the missions can be elected to these positions. Or, Serra suggests, make sure that those who are elected *regidores* are from different villages, so that they will find it more difficult to act together against the mission.

Following Serra's lead, the missionaries henceforth generally accepted Indian officials at the missions. These indigenous officers usually supported the missionaries, although there were exceptions. For instance, the *alcaldes* Andrés at Mission Santa Bárbara in 1824 and Estanislao at Mission San José in 1829 both led resistance movements against their missions.

FROM A LETTER BY JUNÍPERO SERRA

March 29, 1779
Hail Jesus, Mary, Joseph!
Reverend Father Preacher Fray Fermín Francisco Lasuén
Well-beloved and dear Friend:

I hardly think that the misfortunes of your missions—if your worries can be so designated—can be compared to the misfortunes that happen to me every time I take a step to help you. I have not been able to get out of my mind the answer I received when I was so insistent on having escort soldiers in sufficient numbers for what Your Reverences declared to be your needs at that time.

At the present time, I have put in claims for rations and for the suspension of those elections. Yesterday was Palm Sunday, and I said Mass at the *Presidio*. Before Mass we exchanged a few words, and he [Neve] brought up something so flatly contrary to the truth that I was shocked, and I shouted out, "Nobody has ever said that to me, because they could not say it to me!"

He answered, smiling, that he too was a logician and gave me thereby to understand that what he was telling me was inferred, even though in itself it was not [stated]. My reply was that his logic was very faulty, because such an inference was not there but leagues away from it. And that is the way it is. He told me with irony in his voice not to worry and that the information was entirely confidential between us. I told him that it outraged me even if only a single individual knew of it.

And so our exchange of words came to an end. That was the preparation I made for Mass on so solemn a day. I stood for a long time in front of the altar trying to calm my emotions. I said my Mass, after which I had a short chat about routine matters, and I came back to join the others in singing the Passion. They were already waiting for me. The whole affair was concerning the question of *alcaldes*.

During the rest of the day I felt wretched, being quite incapable of throwing off the obsession, and arguing with myself in a thousand ways as

The first page of the Confirmation Register at Mission Santa Clara. Against Governor Neve's wishes, Serra administered the sacrament there in 1779. Courtesy of the Santa Clara University Archives.

to what I should do. I started a letter to the said Señor, having in mind to enclose Your Reverence's and Father Fray Juan's letters in which you both asked me for permission to resign in case the said elections were held, although it had been expressed in conversation with many other things.

Yet with every sentence I wrote, something came up against it. So I stopped. I went over the matter again and again in my mind and attributed my difficulty to my upset condition, and after wrestling with that letter until about midnight, to see if I could not calm myself, I took a fresh piece of paper and started to write a letter to Father Sánchez. It was a long one. I finished it and sealed it, wrote the address, and put it aside. Then I began anew to argue, and the same thing happened to me as before.

The thought came to me that the night was far spent and that if I did not lie down for a while, even though I did not feel sleepy, I would be useless for anything today. So I made up my mind to lie down, fully dressed as I was. I got to the alcove with the idea of finding some rest in sensible reflection and in fixing my mind on some religious subject. But it was all to no purpose. I just had to break out with, "What is the meaning of it all, O Lord?"

And a voice within me seemed to reply in very clear words: "Be prudent as serpents and simple as doves."* And I felt a new man again. "Yes, Lord, yes, Lord," I said, "thus it will be with Your grace." I fell off to sleep. At the usual time I arose to say my Office. Immediately afterward, I sang a Mass of thanksgiving for the birth of a daughter to His Highness, the Prince of Asturias, named María Luisa, a favor Your Reverences may also perform, without making mention of the President.

And so the program I have outlined is this: whatever the gentleman wishes to be done should be done, but in such wise that it should not cause the least change among the Indians or disturb the routine Your Reverences have established.

Let Francisco, with the same staff of office he uses and his coat, be the first *alcalde*. All we have to do is to change the name. Another *alcalde* might be the chief from one of the *rancherías,* of those that visit the mission every fifteen days. As for the *regidores,* who carry not staff, let one be from that *ranchería,* and the other from another. Whether they be chiefs or not is of little importance, but it is better if they are. In this manner everything will be settled without causing any great upset. For that purpose, much help may be derived from the manner in which the Lieutenant explains to them

---

* This was Jesus's advice to his disciples in Matthew 10:16.

their various functions when he installs them into office. For my sake and for Your Reverences' sake, I beg of you for the love of God to use your influence with him. Ask him to carry out this function so that, without failing in the slightest degree in his duty towards his superior officer, the Indians may not be given a less exalted opinion of the Fathers than they have had until now. The diploma which is used in conferring these offices on them may be as solemn as they wish, provided Your Reverences are the only ones to get it and read it.

I hope to God that in this way the disadvantages will not follow which under the other circumstances would, almost of a moral certainty, ensue. The gentleman prides himself on being clever, but with God's help and in the interests of His cause, it may also be true of us: "but the serpent was still more cunning." Since this quality may be joined—and we have the word of the Holy Gospel for it—with the simplicity of the dove, what more could we ask for?

1782
Neve's Instructions to His Successor

FELIPE DE NEVE

After San José had been founded, Neve turned his attention to the southern *pueblo* site. He wished to have it established before the founding of a new *presidio* near the Santa Barbara Channel, so that the *pueblo* could begin supplying food to this new establishment as well as to the *presidio* at San Diego as quickly as possible. The founding of San José had been made possible by the presence of settlers who had come on the Anza expedition, and if a new *pueblo* were to be started, a new group of settlers would be needed. Rivera, who was at Loreto, was ordered to proceed to the mainland and recruit settlers as Anza had done. He journeyed as far south as Mazatlán and enticed a substantial group of soldiers and civilians to join the colonizing effort. He assigned all the civilians—twenty-three adults and twenty-one children—and about one-third of the soldiers and their families to José de Zúñiga and Ramón Laso de la Vega. He told them to cross to Baja California by sea and then to follow the trail he had blazed a dozen years earlier to the north. He kept with himself forty-one soldiers and their families and more than one thousand animals he had collected. This group set out on the Anza trail.

Many members of the Zúñiga-Laso group contracted smallpox in Baja California, so they marched north in two groups, the healthy first and later those who had recovered from their illness. The land group arrived at the Yuma crossing and rested at two missions that had recently been established there. One of the missions was headed by the intrepid Fr. Garcés. Rivera's men picked up indications of local resentment toward the new Spanish presence. The livestock that had been introduced to the region by the missions were damaging the environment on which the indigenous people depended for food. The huge number of animals with Rivera's party exacerbated matters. In addition, the Rivera party treated the local Quecháns more harshly than the more polished and diplomatic Anza had allowed his soldiers to do. Rivera sent most of the soldiers and their families ahead while he and a small detachment remained behind to allow the most exhausted animals to rest. This detachment was all killed, along with Fr. Garcés and his fellow missionaries, when the Quecháns fell upon them.

In Alta California, Neve ordered José Darío Argüello to lay out the plaza for the new *pueblo* and divide the lands, and he did so. The formal date of the founding of the *pueblo* of Our Lady Queen of the Angels of the Porciúncula, or, as it quickly became known, Los Angeles, was September 4, 1781. The original population of thirty-two included men and women of Spanish, Indian, and African backgrounds. The next year Neve was promoted to the position of commanding general of the internal provinces, the chief military office in the northwest of New Spain. The instructions he left to his successor left no doubt that he believed that the future of Alta California depended on the growth and prosperity of its towns. An excerpt from those instructions follows.

FROM A LETTER BY FELIPE DE NEVE

The continued growth of the towns is very important to the colony. Very soon their harvests and those of the missions will be able to supply the *presidios* with corn, wheat, and beans, relieving us from the need of transporting these foodstuffs from San Blas. This will be a precaution against such a total failure of shipments from that department as occurred last year. Despite that failure, no shortage was observed in the *presidios* of Monterey or San Francisco. They were completely fed by the town of San José, whose harvest exceeded thirteen hundred *fanegas* of grain. The same thing was true of the *presidio* of San Diego; the missions of San Gabriel and San Juan Capistrano supplied it abundantly, as well as the troops and families destined for Santa Bárbara *presidio*, and the soldiers who came into California and stayed more than five months.

The fostering of these towns demands very special attention. They will not lack difficulties, and only the vigilance of the government can overcome these. It is most essential that special watchfulness be maintained with respect to the *pueblo* of Nuestra Señora de Los Angeles. Its location, like that of the town of San José, its plentiful water, land, and everything else necessary for progress, are advantageous, but it is necessary to have an

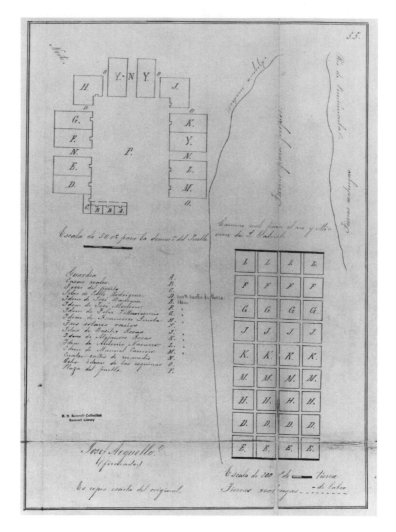

Map of Los Angeles, drawn by José Darío Argüello, a soldier at Santa Bárbara in 1786. Argüello had gone with Rivera to recruit settlers for Los Angeles in 1781. He was one of the soldiers Rivera had sent ahead with most of the party before being surprised by the Quecháns and killed. In 1786 Pedro Fages ordered Argüello to oversee the division of the lands in Los Angeles, and this map is the result. It shows the city laid out around a central plaza, with house lots adjoining the square. Farmlands were located on the outskirts of the town, in the lower right-hand corner. The letters indicate: A, guardhouse; B, royal houses (for officials and soldiers); C, part of the well; D, Pablo Rodríguez; E, José Banegas; F, José Moreno; G, Félix Villavicencio; H, Francisco Sinoba; Y, three vacant house lots; J, Basilio Rosas; K, Alejandro Rosas; L, Antonio Navarro; M, Manuel Camero; N, four streets running through the middle of the pueblo; O, eight streets along the corners of the pueblo; P, plaza of the pueblo. Courtesy of The Bancroft Library, University of California, Berkeley.

active and exacting man there who will bestir the settlers to cultivate their lands, care for their crops, and do everything else connected with farming. The slight care they took in watching over the wheat harvest reduced the yield from a possible four hundred *fanegas* to two hundred and sixty. Through the same neglect, they lost their first crop of corn. The plants, already sprouted, dried up because of their carelessness in not opening up the irrigation ditch soon enough to water them. They then had to make a second sowing, which was in good shape but will produce a smaller yield. It seems they may raise from three to four hundred *fanegas*, however, notwithstanding the fact that they lost some sections because they did not plow the ground well enough and it did not get the benefit of the irrigation water. Since in this case they did take advance precautions to avoid this, and these did not suffice, presumably there was carelessness on the part of the corporal in charge of the town. He is sufficiently experienced in farming, but he needs to be supervised to keep him at his job if success is to be achieved to the benefit of both the settlers and the colony.

The last brandings and the records which are in the hands of paymasters of Monterey and San Francisco respectively will make clear which of the cattle belong to the Royal Treasury. The records and the brandings of cattle in the aforementioned *pueblos* will also show which cattle there belong to the Treasury; these should be brought to Monterey so that the recording of their increase will not have to be dependent on the reports of the corporals of the town guards. For the guidance of the people, a reminder should be given of the amount of land and the number of cattle each town is allowed to possess and the ox teams they are required to maintain, as well as the tools and other equipment needed in agriculture. They should be reminded, too, of the order with which they ought to market their produce, here as well as in other sections to which the said instructions refer. It is desirable, for the better administration, safeguarding, and development of these towns, that the settlers be made to observe and carry out these measures to their due and genuine effect. They should not neglect the building of granaries, nor, so far as San José is concerned, the construction of a stone dam. In the latter place, carts are being constructed for the carrying of the stones, and they have already made a start in building a bin which will serve as a granary.

1784
The Death of Junípero Serra

FRANCISCO PALÓU

When Junípero Serra died in 1784, relations between the missionaries and the military authorities were, if anything, more tense than they had been when he was put in charge of the California missions. Nine missions had been founded, but the missions were sharing the province with two *pueblos* and four *presidios*. Neve's regulations had been formally approved in 1781, and the missionaries were very worried that these other establishments would overwhelm the missions and become the preeminent centers of influence in Alta California. Rather than submit, the Franciscans decided not to found a mission at Santa Bárbara under the conditions established by Neve. Eventually, by dint of hard lobbying in Mexico City, the College of San Fernando was able to see to it that Neve's instructions on the missions were not implemented.

These controversies between the missionaries and the governor were by no means over when Serra died. The College of San Fernando decided to use Fr. Serra's death as an opportunity to forward its own agenda in California. Fr. Francisco Palóu's biography of Serra was part of the process. Another part was that Palóu was brought back to Mexico City and elected guardian of the College of San Fernando. His own health was such that he could not be more than a ceremonial figure at the helm, but that did not matter; the frankly hagiographic and apologetic character of Palóu's work on Serra and Palóu's elevation to a position of authority in the capital of New Spain were both designed to publicize and further the missionary version of California history.

The following excerpt from the biography is a case in point. It describes Serra's death, in a manner which is obviously modeled after the edifying accounts one finds in devotional lives of the saints written during the Middle Ages. The tone of the work, whose full title was *Historical*

226

Account of the Life and Apostolic Labors of the Venerable Father Friar Junípero Serra, was designed entirely to further Serra's legend.

Palóu's life of Serra was hardly the only instance of this in California mission history; a Jesuit wrote a highly laudatory and inspirational life of Fr. Salvatierra in the eighteenth century. Nor was this type of enterprise limited to missions. In the United States, the very popular 1805 biography of George Washington by Parson Weems was in exactly the same vein. Palóu's work was undoubtedly one of the most successful works of its kind ever to be printed, from practically the moment it was published, and the Junípero Serra whose statue adorns the United States Capitol and every Alta California mission is the man who was substantially created by his Majorcan friend and fellow priest.

It is always dangerous to be turned into a saint; one's virtues and short-comings both tend to be greatly exaggerated; one is simultaneously turned into a perfect icon by one's admirers and a perfect demon by one's detractors. The unique individuality of the person is lost—and Serra was nothing if not a commanding individual. Small people do not inspire great emotions, and Serra's presence, from Majorca to the Sierra Gorda to the Californias, called forth the enormous admiration of those who called him teacher, preacher, and friend, likewise eliciting the enormous scorn of those who considered him arrogant and self-centered.

Like all people, Serra was a mix of light and darkness; he was a man of great vision and great blindness, of immense zeal and immense stubbornness. In his own mind, his goals justified his treatment of the Indians, whom he loved as the children he did not have and whom he disciplined with the same ardor with which he disciplined himself. His vision, like that of many of his eighteenth-century contemporaries, demanded intolerance against those with different ideas about this world and the next. These qualities do not make him an angel or a devil; they simply make him a man of his time and place. His time and place were, like ours, far from perfect.

From *The Life of Junípero Serra* by Francisco Palóu

W hen I read the letter of the Reverend Father President in which he asked me to come to Monterey, though he did not tell me to hurry, I set out overland because I foresaw that the ship would delay in sailing. I arrived on August 18 at his Mission San Carlos. There I found His Paternity in a very weakened condition, although he was up and around, and with great congestion of the chest. This condition, however, did not prevent him from going to church in the afternoon to recite the catechism and prayers with the neophytes. He concluded the devotions with the tender and pious hymns and versicles composed by the Venerable Father Margil in honor of the Assumption of the Blessed Virgin, whose octave we were celebrating. When I heard him sing with his voice as strong as usual, I remarked to a soldier who was talking to me, "It does not seem that the Father President is very sick." The soldier, who had known him since 1769, answered me, "Father, there is no basis for hope: he is ill. This saintly priest is always well when it comes to praying and singing, but he is nearly finished."

On the following day, August 19, he told me to sing the High Mass in honor of the Most Holy Patriarch St. Joseph, which was customarily sung each month, because he said he felt quite bad. And so I did. However, His Paternity did not fail to sing in the choir with the neophytes or to recite seven times the Our Father and the customary prayers. In the afternoon he was present at prayer and the singing of the versicles in honor of the Blessed Virgin. On the following day, a Friday, he made the Stations of the Way of the Cross in the church in company with all the people.

We spoke leisurely on the matters for which he had called me, until the ship arrived. However, I was always in fear he would shortly die, for whenever I would enter into his little room or cell of adobes, I always found him quite interiorly recollected, although his companion told me he had acted this way ever since his faculty to confirm had expired.* This, as I have stated before, was on the very day the ship anchored at these missions [of San Francisco]. Five days after I arrived at Monterey, the packet boat anchored at that port. Immediately, the royal surgeon went over to the mission to visit the Reverend Father President. Finding his chest in so bad a condition, he suggested hot poultices to expel the phlegm that had accumulated in the chest. The Father President told him to apply whatever remedy he chose. He did, but with no effect other than to cause further pain to that already worn-out body. But he did not show the least sign of pain, either at this strong application or at the agonies he was suffering. He acted as if he were not sick at all, always up and about as if he were well. When some of the cloth from the supplies of the ship was brought over, he began to cut it up with his own hands and distribute it to the neophytes to cover their nakedness.

On August 25, he told me he was disappointed that the Fathers from Missions San Antonio and San Luis Obispo had not arrived, and that possibly the

---

* "Faculty" is a term for ecclesiastical permission.

letters he had written them were delayed. I immediately sent word to the *presidio*, and the letters were brought over with the information that they had been overlooked. As soon as I saw their contents, an invitation to the Fathers for a final farewell, I sent a courier with them, adding a message that the Fathers should come posthaste, for I feared that our beloved Superior would not be long with us, because of his very weakened condition. And although the priests set out as soon as they received those letters, they did not arrive in time. The one from Mission San Antonio, which was twenty-five leagues away, arrived after his death and could assist only at his burial. The one from San Luis Obispo, fifty leagues away, arrived three days later and was able to be present at the commemorative services only on the seventh day after his death, as I shall point out later.

On August 26, he arose weaker still. He told me he had passed a bad night. As a result, he desired to prepare himself for whatever God might decree with regard to him. He remained secluded the entire day, admitting not a single distraction. That night he made his general confession to me amid many tears and with a clear mind, just as if he were well. When this was over, after a brief period of reflection he took a cup of broth and then went to rest, his wish being that no one remain with him in his little room.

As soon as morning dawned on the twenty-seventh, I went to visit him and found him saying his breviary, since it was his custom always to commence Matins before daybreak. On the road he always began it as soon as morning dawned. When I asked him how he had spent the night, he answered, "As usual." Nevertheless, he asked me to consecrate a Host and reserve it, and he would let me know when he wanted to receive. I did, and after finishing Mass I returned to tell him, and then he said he would like to receive the Most Holy Viaticum, and that for this he would go to the church. When I told him that was not necessary, that his cell could be fixed up in the best way possible and that the Divine Majesty would come to visit him, he said no, that he wanted to receive Him in church, since if he could walk there, there was no need for the Lord to come to him. I had to give in and grant his holy desires. He went on his own to the church (more than a hundred yards distant), accompanied by the Commandant of the *presidio*, who came to the ceremony with part of the soldiers (who were joined by the soldiers of the mission); and all the Indians of the town or mission accompanied the sick and devout priest to the church, all of them with great tenderness and piety.

When His Paternity reached the step of the sanctuary, he knelt down before a little table prepared for the ceremony. I came out of the sacristy vested, and on arriving at the altar, as soon as I prepared the incense to begin the devotional ceremony, the fervent servant of God intoned in his natural voice, as sonorous as when he was well, the verse *Tantum ergo Sacramentum,* singing it with tears in his eyes. I gave him the Holy Viaticum, according to all the ceremonies of the ritual.

When this very devotional function was over, which I had never seen in such circumstances, His Paternity remained in the same posture, kneeling, giving thanks to the Lord. When he was finished, he returned to his little cell accompanied by all the people. Some shed tears from devotion and tenderness, others out of sadness and sorrow, because they feared they would be left without their beloved Father. He remained alone in his cell in meditation, seated on the chair at the table. When I beheld him thus absorbed, I saw no reason to enter to talk to him.

I saw that the carpenter from the *presidio* was about to go in, but I stopped him. He said the Father had called for him to make a coffin for his burial, and he wanted to ask him how he wished it made. This affected me. Not permitting him to enter and talk with the Father, I gave him orders to make it like the one he had made for Father Crespí. The Venerable Father passed the whole day in profoundest silence and deep recollection, seated on the chair, taking no nourishment all day other than a little broth; nor did he take any rest.

During the night he felt worse, and he asked to be anointed. This Holy Sacrament he received seated on an *equipal,* a little stool made of rushes. He recited with us the Litany of All Saints and the Penitential Psalms. He spent the entire night without sleep, the greater part of it on his knees, while he pressed his chest against the boards of his bed. When I suggested that he lie down awhile, he answered that in that position he felt more relieved. Other short periods of the night he spent seated on the floor, leaning against the lap of some of the neophytes. All night long, his little cell was filled with these neophytes, drawn there by the great love they had for him as for the Father who had begotten them anew in the Lord. When I saw him in this state of exhaustion and leaning against the arms of the Indians, I asked the surgeon how he thought he was. He answered (since the Father appeared to be in a very critical state), "It seems to me that this blessed Father wants to die on the floor."

I went in soon after and asked him if he wished absolution and the application of the plenary indulgence. He answered yes, and prepared himself. On his knees he received the plenary absolution, and I gave him also the plenary indulgence of the Order, with which he was most happy. He passed the entire night in the manner described. The feast of the Doctor of the Church St. Augustine dawned, August 28, and he appeared relieved. He did not experience so much congestion in his chest. During the whole night he had not slept or taken anything. He spent the morning seated on the rush stool, leaning against the bed. This bed consisted of some roughhewn boards covered by a blanket serving more as a covering than as an aid to rest, for he never used even a sheepskin covering such as was customary at our college. Along the road he used to do the same thing. He would stretch the blanket and a pillow on the ground, and he would lie down on these to get his necessary rest. He always slept with a crucifix upon his breast, in the embrace of his hands. It was about a foot in length. He had carried it with him from the time he was in the novitiate at the College, nor did he ever fail to have it with him. On all his journeys he carried it with him, together with the blanket and pillow. At his mission and whenever he stopped, as soon as he got up from bed he placed the crucifix upon the pillow. Thus he had it on this occasion when he did not wish to go to bed during the entire night or next morning, on the day when he was to deliver his soul to his Creator.

About ten o'clock in the morning on that feast of St. Augustine, the officers of the frigate came to visit him. They were the Captain and Commandant, Don José Cañizares, very well known to His Paternity since the first expedition in the year 1769, and the Royal Chaplain Don Cristóbal Díaz, who also had met him in this port, in the year 1779. He received them with extraordinary greetings and ordered that a solemn ringing of the bells be given in their honor. Standing up, he gave them a warm embrace as if he were well, giving them their due and customary marks of respect. When they were seated, His Paternity sat down on his rush stool, and they told him of the voyages they had made to Peru since their last meeting in that year of 1779.

After listening to them, he said, "Well, gentlemen, I thank you that after such a long time during which we have not seen each other, and after making such a long voyage, you have come from so far off to this port to throw a little earth upon me." On hearing this, the gentlemen and all the rest of us present were surprised, seeing him seated on the little rush stool and hearing him answer everything with full mental faculties. But, scarcely concealing

Painting of Father Serra receiving communion shortly before his death, commissioned by the College of San Fernando and executed by Mariano Guerrero. Courtesy of the Santa Barbara Mission Archive Library.

their tears, which they could not restrain, they said, "No, Father, we trust that God will still make you well and enable you to continue this conquest." The servant of God (who, if he did not have a foreknowledge of the hour of his death, could not but know that it was near at hand) answered them, "Yes, yes, do me this favor and work of mercy; throw a little bit of earth upon my body, and I shall be greatly indebted to you." And casting his eyes upon me, he said, "I desire you to bury me in the church, quite close to Father Fray Juan Crespí for the present; and when the stone church is built, they may put me wherever they want."

When my tears allowed me to speak, I said to him, "Father President, if God is pleased to call you to Himself, it will be done as Your Paternity wishes. In that case, I ask Your Paternity, out of love and the great affection you have always had for me, that when you arrive in the presence of the

Most Blessed Trinity, you adore the Same in my name, and that you be not unmindful of me; and do not forget to pray for all the dwellers in these missions, particularly for those here present." He answered, "I promise, if the Lord in His infinite mercy grants me that eternal happiness, which I do not deserve because of my faults, that I shall pray for all and for the conversion of so many pagans whom I leave unconverted."

Within a short time he asked me to sprinkle his little room with holy water, and I did. When I asked him if he felt some pain, he said no; but he asked me to do it so he would have none. He remained in profound silence. All of a sudden, very frightened, he said to me, "Great fear has come upon me; I have a great fear. Read me the Commendation for a Departing Soul, and say it aloud so I can hear it." I did as he asked, while all the gentlemen from the ship assisted. Also present were his priest companion, Fray Matías Noriega, and the surgeon, and many others, both from the ship and from the mission. I read for him the Commendation for a Departing Soul, to which the Venerable Father, though dying, responded as if he were well, just sitting there on his little rush stool, moving the hearts of us all to tenderness.

As soon as I finished, he broke out in words full of joy, saying, "Thanks be to God, thanks be to God, all fear has now left me. Thanks be to God, I have no more fear, and so let us go outside." All of us retired to a little outside room with His Paternity. When we noticed this change, we were at one and the same time surprised and happy. The captain of the ship said to him, "Father President, now can Your Paternity see what my devoted St. Anthony can do? I have asked him to make you well, and I hope he will, and I trust you will be able to make some more journeys for the good of the poor Indians." The Venerable Father did not answer him a word, but with a little smile he made it very clear to us that he did not expect this, nor did he hope to get well.

He sat on the chair by the table, picked up his diurnal, and began to pray. As soon as he was finished, I told him it was already after one o'clock in the afternoon and asked him if he would like a cup of broth. He said yes. He took it and, after giving thanks, said, "Now, let us go to rest." He walked to his little room where he had his bed. He took off only his mantle and lay down over the boards covered with a blanket, with his holy crucifix mentioned above, in order to rest. We all thought he was going to sleep, as during the whole night he had not slept any. The gentlemen went out to eat. Since I was a little uneasy, after a short time I returned and approached his bed to see if he was sleeping. I found him just as we had left him a little before, but now asleep in the Lord, without having given any sign or trace of agony, his body showing no other sign of death than the cessation of breathing; on the contrary, he seemed to be sleeping. We piously believe that he went to sleep in the Lord a little before two in the afternoon on the feast of St. Augustine in the year 1784, and that he went to receive in heaven the reward of his apostolic labors.

1785

The Trials of a Frontier Woman

EULALIA CALLIS

Neve's successor as governor of the Californias was Pedro Fages, who had been removed as commander of Monterey at Serra's behest. Fages had first gone to Mexico City, where he spent a year before being appointed a commander in Guadalajara. His detachment was soon ordered to Sonora to conduct operations against the native peoples there. In 1774 he had started wooing sixteen-year-old Eulalia Callis, the daughter of his old commander, and they were married in 1780, when Fages was fifty and she was twenty-one. The couple then moved to Arizpe, the capital of the Internal Provinces. Fages commanded troops sent to reestablish Spanish control in the Colorado River region after the 1781 Quechán revolt.

Appointed governor when Neve was promoted in 1782, Fages moved directly to Monterey. Once there, he prevailed upon Eulalia to join him with their young son. She agreed and they rendezvoused at Loreto in May 1783. They journeyed together overland and she suffered a miscarriage on the way. They reached Monterey in January 1784. In August she gave birth to a daughter. Early the next year she accused her husband of having sexual relations with an Indian girl, a servant in her preteens. A priest tried to get her to withdraw her accusations. She refused and demanded to be released from her marriage. When her husband had to travel south on official business, she was locked up at Mission San Carlos to keep her from spreading her story. In April she addressed the following petition to José Antonio Rengel, acting commandant general of the Internal Provinces in Arizpe. Callis was acutely aware of the fact that as a woman she had little legal recourse. However, determined to seek justice, she prepared a written testimony using formal and somewhat legalistic terminology to detail the steps the men of power in the province had taken to vilify her for having raised the issue. Ultimately, she begged for protection and justice.

Eulalia Callis eventually went back to live with her husband. Nicolás Soler, assistant inspector of *presidios* and a friend of both her and her husband, intervened and apparently convinced Fages to make some sort of amends to Eulalia. His interventions are summarized in the excerpts that also follow. In 1787, Fages told Palóu that Eulalia had withdrawn her accusations. In any event, they lived together for the remainder of Fages's term as governor. She acquired a reputation around Monterey as a woman of great charity and generosity to the poor. Her appeal, which is given below, is one of the most unusual documents from the early history of California.

The summaries of the Soler letters come from the "Archive of California," a 63-volume summary of nearly three hundred thousand pages of documents that come from Spanish and Mexican California. These documents were copied or summarized in the 1870s from the originals, which were in repositories in San Francisco, by Hubert Howe Bancroft's fifteen-man staff as part of the research for Bancroft's *History of California*. The particular staff member who came across these two letters by Soler did not think they were worth much, so he merely summarized them. Unfortunately, all of the original documents were destroyed in the San Francisco earthquake and fire of 1906. Thus, these tantalizing summaries are all that we have.

The bulk of the documents about this case ended up in the archives of the Mexican government. The following summary was written and attached to the pile of all the documents relating to the case by a secretary in the archives when the papers were filed, probably in the late 1780s.

PETITION BY DOÑA EULALIA CALLIS, THE WIFE OF DON PEDRO FAGES, GOVERNOR OF THE CALIFORNIAS, THAT HER CASE BE HEARD AND THAT SHE BE FREED FROM THE OPPRESSION FROM WHICH SHE IS SUFFERING (SUMMARY)

Doña Eulalia Callis, wife of Don Pedro Fages, the current Governor of the peninsula of the Californias, seeking Your Honor's most benevolent and superior protection, submits this petition for your fair ruling. She appeals to your benevolence because she is a helpless woman. She calls upon your superior protection so that justice may be served. Justice seeks out the guilty parties and recognizes the one who has been wronged. Justice must protect the weaker party because that is the law.

It is the case that I found my husband physically on top of one of his servants, a very young Yuma Indian girl. Well-founded suspicions and the girl's easily obtained confession put me in the position of being the sentinel who discovered the incident. Even though prudence should have prevailed (this is my crime), I was overcome by passion, which fueled the flames of my rage, which caused me to cry out publicly against this infamy. Your Honor, what person would not acknowledge the wrong that had been done to them even though the pain had passed? A few hours later this guilty party was besieged with an onslaught of advice and words of persuasion for her to return to her husband. It was all very well-meaning. However, the wound was still fresh and since the medicine was applied at the wrong time, it had no effect. Thus, drastic measures were taken. It is from the pain of these measures that I seek Your Honor's magnanimous mercy.

Reverend Father Fray Matías Antonio de Noriega, the priest at the nearby mission, ordered that the offended party be locked in a room guarded by soldiers from the troop. Placed there incommunicado, she began to prepare her case. The most important piece of evidence in this case was the girl's statement. Kneeling before the judge, the girl uttered what she could, constrained by her fear of the punishment she faced. This testimony was followed by cries to restore her [Callis's] husband's reputation (as if he had lost it with just that one woman). The judge forgot to obtain statements from everyone at the *presidio* who had evidence, according to the girl. In cases such as this, the law requires that the testimony be from credible witnesses, such as midwives or others who have knowledge of the situation. The proceedings of this case have been drawn up as best as can be expected under the circumstances and they have been sent to the Illustrious Bishop of Sonora. We await news of his decision with regard to the offended party. Was it not important for Your Honor to allow this woman of sound mind to be heard? Apparently not. Perhaps one fears what she will say in her defense.

There is further evidence: on Ash Wednesday in the *presidio* church, the priest who celebrated Mass also was the judge on the case. After reading from the Gospel and preaching the sermon, he ended by vilifying me and had the soldiers throw me out of the church. This is what he said: "Detain that woman so I can put a gag over her mouth." He made it known that he would excommunicate anybody who spoke to me or who spoke about the matter. The error of these peoples' ways is due to their ignorance with regard to the matter. On my saint's day they tied me up and transferred me to

Mission San Carlos. The cloister was rigorous. There were few candles. They stood watch over me and forced me to eat even though I was sick. I conclude this wretched tale of suffering with the threats of the aforementioned Father, who said he would have me flogged and placed in shackles.

I shall consider the first insult to my person as my cross to bear. I am told that the crimes committed against me were not that serious and my desires for satisfaction are merely earthly and transitory. Hence, I am told that I should forgive my husband and return to him, a surrender that would force the most innocent party to suffer the greatest losses. If he (Fages) insists that he has suffered from my outrage, then keep me imprisoned at the disposal of the priest who can restrain me more or less according to his nature. He will not, however, close the doors to my honor and noble birth. These doors shall remain open to receive a lawful defense and Your Honor's protection.

I humbly beg you to agree to hear this petition in the form that it is presented. Justice will grant me a pardon. I swear to accept what I am given. The laws that protect me will save me from poverty. I will not give up my rights during the course of the proceedings of my case.

Mission San Carlos
April 12, 1785
Eulalia Callis

Summary of a Letter from Nicolás Soler to Eulalia Callis: Observations with Regard to her Behavior

Monterey, April 9, 1785

In a personal letter he advises her on the manner in which she should behave in the future, indicating to her that she should restrain or suppress her strong desires to obtain satisfaction with respect to matters of sensual pleasures. She should control herself in her dealings with the priests and patiently suffer the insults that were hurled at her publicly in the church. Her husband showed him the proceedings that are being sent to the Bishop, but he did not want to read them, because he is uncertain as to the jurisdiction under which they were formulated.

Summary of a Letter from Nicolás Soler to Pedro Fages with Regard to the *Gobernadora's* Right to Speak

Monterey, April 14, 1785

He tells Fages that everyone has become interested in reuniting husband and wife. However, to attain this he did not count on Fages's inflexible nature. Once he arrived at the *presidio*, he (Soler) could not ignore the scandals at the church. As a means of subduing the *Señora Gobernadora,* the priest had her placed in seclusion. He threatened her with even further seclusion, excommunication, whippings, and shackles.

Assuming that her crimes or slanderous comments are irrefutable, Fages's prestigious position as Governor does not diminish the severity of his actions. This behavior by a Governor who publicly offends his wife cannot be tolerated. He (Soler) offers to help rid her of her rage, but has not proposed the idea to her yet. He leaves it up to Fages's discretion. He will neither speak with her nor go to see her until Fages wants him to do so.

"The way a California Soldier and his Daughter are Dressed." Fr. Ignacio Tirsch, S.J. Courtesy of the National Library of the Czech Republic.

1785
Between Baja and Alta California

JOSÉ VELÁSQUEZ

The Dominicans entered Baja California in 1773 and took control of the existing missions. They discovered that these establishments were not so fully equipped as they had thought they would be, and some bitterly accused the Franciscans of despoiling them in order to support the Alta California venture. The Dominicans also continued the process of pushing the mission frontier to the north. By 1797 they had founded five new institutions along the Pacific coast, from El Rosario, about thirty miles northwest of San Fernando de Velicatá, to San Miguel, about forty miles south of San Diego. They also established two missions inland, including Santa Catalina, located about forty miles east of the Colorado River delta. This establishment pointed to another aim of the colonial authorities in northern Baja California at the time: the discovery of a land route from Sonora to California.

Since a reliable land route between Mexico and California was widely regarded as indispensable to the prosperity of the province, the Quechán revolt and resultant closing of the Anza route in 1781 had been very problematic. Explorations in the Colorado River region were planned in an attempt to discover a route that skirted the territory of the Quecháns. Pedro Fages led one such expedition in April 1785. (At the time, his wife, Eulalia, was being held at Mission San Carlos.) The group started from Mission San Vicente Ferrer, near the Pacific coast about one hundred miles below San Diego. They proceeded east into the territory of the Cocopah people of the delta, then north along the eastern face of the mountains into what is now the Imperial Valley. Then they turned west into San Diego.

The expedition's diarist was José Velásquez. A native of Sonora, he served at the Loreto *presidio* from 1751 to1769. He accompanied Rivera on his march to San Diego and then participated in both of Portolá's land journeys to find Monterey. He returned to Baja California in 1770 and served for a decade as commander at Mission San Fernando de Velicatá. In that capacity, he conducted a number of surveys to assist the Dominicans in locating sites for their new missions. Velásquez was assigned to San Diego in 1780. His account of this expedition is significant. He describes, for instance, how the rough frontier soldiers related to their Spanish commander. He served at times as the leader of the advance scout party on the expedition and was thus often the first to encounter the inhabitants of a new region. He tells how the soldiers devised a complex plan to enter an Indian village only to find that the residents had already slipped away. Above all, his close attention to cultural as well as physical geography provides us with an intimate picture of what it meant to be a frontier soldier in colonial California. The excerpt below begins with the expedition's departure from Mission San Vicente Ferrer.

FROM THE DIARY OF JOSÉ VELÁSQUEZ

On the eighth of the current month, His Lordship ordered that Sergeant Mariano Verdugo should go ahead with the horse herd and some loads of supplies to wait for us at the watering place of La Calentura. His Lordship (Fages), two soldiers, and I went out the same day toward the south along the *Camino Real* of the missions for two leagues. Leaving the *camino*, we turned southeast and went downward through a pass. We came to an *arroyo* which took us upward to the east and to the said watering place, about five leagues. Once there, His Lordship directed that I should take six soldiers and two Indian interpreters to repair the trail if necessary: we had the requisite tools. He ordered that if I encountered any heathens I should let them know that we would not harm them, but rather that they would be friends to whom I would give presents. He had given me some packages of seeds for that purpose. That same evening I marched up the *arroyo* four leagues to the east. We made camp in the same *arroyo* on the eighth and ninth of April.

[The ninth] Immediately at dawn I resumed the march. Soon we came to the beginning of a grade which had to be fixed up a little. I left a note for the said Señor [Fages] to tell him to water the animals there. I continued on up the grade and then followed a small *arroyo* down from the summit. Near its end there was pasture and water where I left a cross made from sticks to show the Señor that this was the place to spend the night, as he had told me to do. Along the banks of the stream we saw some deep pits which the Indians had made to catch deer, so I directed that willow branches be set up as a warning sign, lest the horses fall in. A little earlier I had left a note for the Señor so that he would stop where the cross was found, but for fun the soldiers made a cross among the branches at the pits, which caused a certain ambiguity on account of which he stopped halfway between the two crosses. Today I probably traveled six leagues....

On the fourteenth, as soon as it was light, I noticed a little range of hills near the river; I had passed near its foot before. We resumed our march on a line toward the north. After we passed over the plain, some low dunes lay across our path. Once these were passed, we found a very wide alkali flat, very muddy, from which we learned that there the tide ebbed and water came from underground. We crossed over this difficult alkali flat and found the point of the range. We were comforted by the thought of drinking water, because I had seen a little good water here before, but not finding any, we were obliged to stop without water.

When the heat of the sun had subsided, as we were already near the river, His Lordship decided that I should go ahead to see if water could be found in a field of reeds which I had seen before, well away from the river. For this purpose he gave me some beads and ten men to accompany me.

Having marched a little way over the plain near the range mentioned above, I saw some Indians on a little hill. Here I stopped and called them through the interpreter. They came in a friendly fashion. After giving them some strings of beads, I asked them if there was water among the reeds. They answered that there was some in the wells, but that in their village there was much water easily obtained, and pasturage.

On receiving this information, I told them to lead on. About a cannon-shot away, a large crowd of people were coming, more or less five hundred, some armed and some not, with three others on horseback riding about among them as if preparing for a skirmish. When I saw this, I pretended that I was about to give them some beads, but I told them that anyone who came armed would get nothing but a lance. All this was to keep them occupied while my soldiers remounted. As soon as they told me that they were ready, I went ahead looking for water, keeping the Indians ahead of me without allowing them to mingle with our men. Those that persisted in approaching too close, I charged with my horse, and so I continued to drive toward the water. I had noticed before that those who were armed were displeased and drew apart. The three on horseback were Juilica men.

In 1791, as part of a five-year scientific expedition, Alejandro Malaspina spent two weeks in Monterey. The expedition consisted of two vessels, the *Descubierta* and the *Atrevida,* and approximately two hundred men, including scientists and artists. Sailing from Acapulco to Monterey, the artists sketched a variety of animals. The result of their labors is a lively portfolio that includes an engaging record of Monterey's natural and social environment in the late eighteenth century.

Butterflies, worm, caterpillar, and other insects. Drawing by José Guío. Courtesy of the Museo Naval, Madrid (MS 1726-29).

Top: Unidentified bird, most likely a jilguero, *or goldfinch. Drawing by José del Pozo. Courtesy of the Museo Naval, Madrid (MS 1725-89). Bottom: "Gracula," red-winged blackbird* (Agelaius phoeniceus). *Drawing by José Cardero. Courtesy of the Museo Naval, Madrid (MS 1725-85).*

Top: "Nodí," *brown noddy* (Anous stolidus). *Drawing by José Cardero. Courtesy of the Museo Naval, Madrid (MS 1725-70). Bottom:* "Tetrao Regio-montanus," *California valley quail* (Lophortyx californica). *Drawing by José Cardero. According to Donald Cutter, this is the second known drawing of this bird. The first was done in black and white in September 1786 by an artist with La Pérouse. Courtesy of the Museo Naval, Madrid (MS 1725-63).*

Suria fecit.

"*Salmon of Acapulco.*" *Drawing by Tomás de Suria. Courtesy of the Museo Naval, Madrid (MS 1725–48).*

"Roedor Esciurido," squirrel. Drawing by José del Pozo. Courtesy of the Museo Naval, Madrid (MS 1726-14).

Coati (nasua sp.) *Drawing by Tomás de Suria. Caption in bottom left corner reads,* "Especie de oso que en Acapulco llaman tejon" *(type of bear that is called tejon in Acapulco). Courtesy of the Museo Naval, Madrid (MS 1726-6).*

*Mapache, raccoon (*procyon sp.*). Drawing by José Guío. Courtesy of the Museo Naval, Madrid (MS 1726-15).*

Coyote (Canis latrans). Drawing by José del Pozo. Courtesy of the Museo Naval, Madrid (MS 1726–7).

I remained only with the Cocopahs, who had their village on this shore of the lagoon. As soon as I saw water, I made the Indians draw to the side. We watered the horses one by one.

When this was completed, the Indians came to me with gifts of squash, beans, fish, and different kinds of meal. I said that they should keep them until the great chief who was coming behind us should arrive, and that they should go to meet him with water, which they did. I soon saw the Lord Governor coming. He was following me, not holding back, so as to give assistance where it might be needed. He traveled into the midst of everything. When I saw him, I went to meet him, telling him what was taking place. Then we withdrew a short distance into the plain. There we halted; then he went with eight men and the interpreter to talk with the Indians of the village. He ordered me to send the horse herd along and said that he would not leave until the horses had finished drinking. The watering completed, he withdrew to the camping place, telling me that the Indians had given him many little presents. They urged him to rest there two or three days. To all this he had answered yes, but he gave orders that all should sleep with their horses saddled. Secretly he ordered me to pack up at dawn. Before daylight we were to begin the march along the edge of the plain close to the sierra, to avoid getting ourselves into some lagoon or estuary, and to pass the many villages which might be there, judging from the great number of smokes we saw.

After this order was given and we were at rest, at the beginning of prayers, some old Indians came with women, who carried a basket of seeds and some jugs of water. The Governor, in his turn, gave them trinkets and told them to return to their village to sleep. They might come again the next day....

We skirted a hill and began the march westward. There were some *arroyos* that lay across the trail. After prayers we found the placed called La Palma, with water and pasturage. When we stopped, we sensed the presence of heathens on the opposite bank of the *arroyo*. In view of this, His Lordship gave me orders that at dawn six men and I should surround the village and call its chief, because on one occasion when the Governor had passed by this place, horses had been stolen. By this evening we had made four leagues.

The eighteenth, at dawn, I surrounded the village and found no one in it except a woman with a child. She made signs to point out a range of small hills nearby. We scanned with our eyes and saw people on the top, whereupon

I returned, reporting to His Lordship what was happening. Then he ordered us to load and saddle up. He ordered three soldiers with two sluggish beasts to go ahead. We followed behind, then the pack animals, and finally the horse herd, all going toward the west.

Soon after starting, the sergeant counted the horses and found one missing. He went back to recount, which gave the Indians time to drive another horse off and kill it with *jara* blows. While he was counting, about thirty Indians appeared. When the soldiers learned of the missing horse, they hunted for it diligently. The trail could not be found, because the Indians who had led it off had covered its tracks. While the soldiers were hunting for it, the Indians followed them in a friendly fashion, calling them to their village to give them food. The soldiers would not pay attention to them. Finally, they saw a horse's footprint where the Indians were trying to cover the trail. They followed the trail diligently until they found the horse, dead from the blows. Seeing this, the Indians ran up the hill. The soldiers immediately returned.

We reached the San Felipe Valley about eleven or twelve in the morning, six or seven leagues from where we had slept. The sergeant came last and told us about the Indians who had killed the horse. The sun had already set, and some heathens who had come to visit us had already gone when His Lordship ordered me to take twelve soldiers and the interpreter. Since night had fallen, we were to march silently, each one taking a well-trained horse. We left our mules tied up a long way from the village; the horses were saddled very quietly. We had been ordered to surround the village of these rascals and, when it became light, to speak to them through the interpreter. He would order the chief to be bound, and whoever appeared to be his second man was to be told to come with him because the great chief wanted to talk to them. For the rest of those who seemed to be most guilty, he would order that they be given six lashes, letting them know that it was for the damage they had done before and on this occasion. To the others—women and children—he would give presents of beads.

All this was carried out to the letter, but having surrounded the village when it became light, we found only empty houses. Straining eyes to all sides, we saw a fire about a musket-shot away, at the foot of a hill to the north; the hill was much cut by ravines and surrounded by the plain. As the fire was so near, I considered that if the Indians were not spoken to, they would think that we were afraid; it is unimaginable that the Indians could believe this about the King's troops.

In the end we hurried to surround the hill; I called the interpreter to tell them not to be frightened and that I wanted to talk to them without making any trouble, although our arms were in hand. The Indians rushed to the crest of the hill and began to run away. Running toward an Indian soldier, Corporal Olivera raced his horse at high speed. As I was going around the hill to place the men, the corporal shouted to me, "Señor, they are running away, what shall I do?" I stopped and ordered the corporal and another to fire on those who were on the hilltop.

When the shots rang out, one of the Indians fell; the rest threw themselves into the gullies. Seeing this, I ordered the interpreter to speak to them. Their answer was that they did not want to talk. They kept on lashing out with *jaras,* wounding two horses. I ordered the corporal to keep up a steady fire. After a short while, I ordered the interpreter to tell them, for the third time, that they must make peace, and that I would not do them any harm. They answered no, that they would not. In attempting to flee, they were blocked by the soldiers behind the hill, but the Indians did wound a soldier. When we opened steady fire on them, some fell, and they returned to the gullies.

One of them fought more than all the rest. For the fourth time I gave an order to speak to this one, who was pointed out to be the chief. He answered the interpreter that he would not surrender, that he did not know how to die. Some soldiers called to him, making signs that they would not do anything at all to him. His answer was to throw darts, whereupon I ordered the soldiers to fire until he was killed. All became silent. The remainder, with the women and children, were hidden in ravines. I ordered the interpreter to assemble them while I inspected those who came out wounded, but there were only three, none serious.

This done and the people already assembled, I asked one of them who had killed the horse. By a sign he pointed to where the dead chief was. When asked who had killed a soldier in this same *arroyo* in which they were, he replied he did not know. Noticing that the women were talking in signs, I asked the interpreter what they were saying. He replied that they were saying that the chief had collected men together and they had killed people, including a soldier. This was Hermenegildo Flores, who had deserted last year from the *presidio.* It was while I was going toward the summit that I heard the news that they had killed him, and I had to report this to the *presidio.*

Returning to the Indian women who were at the beginning of the *arroyo,* I asked them, through the interpreter, who had killed a Christian man and a Christian woman of the mission of San Diego. They answered, "the dead chief." When asked who had killed an Indian from San Sebastián who had served as a guide on the trip which I made there, they answered that "those yonder" had killed him.

It is a common rumor that these same Indians had killed another soldier, a deserter, a long time ago. The Indian interpreters of the mission of San Diego, according to information of those from the sierra, consider the Nuzes as spies or bandits, and these are the same kind. The soldier, Solís, heard a woman, half-Spanish and half-Indian, say that they had killed the late Flores, from which it was inferred that it was God's will and that they have paid what they owed....

1785
Rebellion at San Gabriel

Toypurina

In 1785 a group of Indians from different *rancherías* in the San Gabriel area attacked the mission. The plan had apparently been discovered beforehand by the soldiers, and the participants were captured soon after beginning the attack. The leaders, a woman named Toypurina (a shaman who had not become a Christian) and Nicolás José (a Christian convert), were brought to trial. After hearing the testimony of various witnesses, Toypurina and Nicolás José were convicted, along with two other men. The men were sent to work duty at San Diego. Toypurina was imprisoned at Mission San Gabriel. Eventually she converted to Christianity, which enabled her to move to another mission and live as a free woman. She was relocated to Mission San Juan Bautista, where she married and had at least one child. She died in 1799.

The joint leadership of a neophyte and a gentile in this rebellion points to an important aspect of the ways the indigenous peoples of California, in common with those throughout New Spain, responded to Spanish culture. The Christian imaginative world was remarkably flexible. It contained a host of narratives that celebrated resistance to oppression. Some native groups adapted Christian symbols to their own circumstances and used them in their own struggles for autonomy and freedom.

Toypurina's interrogation at the trial was largely directed at determining which of the conspirators was responsible for various parts of the plot. In her responses, she is revealed as a person of authority in the Gabrielino communities, one who could give orders to chiefs. Her insistence that the reason she helped organize the attack in the first place was that the Spanish were living on the Indians' land stands as the most fundamental reason for the attack on the mission.

From Investigations of Occurrences at Mission San Gabriel on the Night of October 25, 1785

I the sergeant ordered that the gentile Indian woman named Toypurina appear before me. She was accused of being the instigator of an Indian rebellion that took place the night of October 25. She was persuaded by the interpreter to reply truthfully to the questions asked.

Question 1: Previously, when it was discovered that they (the Indians) were plotting to kill the *Baja Californio* as well as the priests and soldiers, had they not been warned by the Governor, the Lieutenant from San Diego, and by the very same priests that if they tried to commit a similar act they would be severely punished?

Reply: She responded that she knew nothing about that.

Question 2: After they had been warned and advised repeatedly to keep the peace, why did they come here armed to kill the priests and the soldiers who had never harmed them?

Reply: She responded that it was true that she had ordered Chief Tomasa-jaquichi to come and persuade the Christians to trust her and not the priests. She said that she advised him to do this because she was angry with the priests and all the others at the mission, because we were living on their land.

Question 3: What prompted them to come here, knowing that it would be impossible to kill the soldiers, for with one shot from the cannon many Indians would die?

Reply: She responded that the Indian Nicolás José had persuaded her by giving her some beads. She joined the others to encourage them to be brave and fight.

Question 4: Have they been harmed in any way at the hands of the soldiers, priests, or other Christians which would make them want to kill them?

Reply: She responded that the only harm that she had experienced was that we were living on their land.

Question 5: Who conspired to plan the assault and who was the leader?

Reply: She responded that Nicolás José was the first one to bring the chiefs together, and he persuaded her to influence them.

Question 6: Who was the Christian they obeyed the most and who was the first to suggest the attack?

Reply: She responded that it was Nicolás.

Question 7: Were the sheep and goats they killed at night stolen from the corral or the fields? Who committed these acts? Did the shepherds allow this or not?

Reply: She responded that Nicolás had sent the others out to steal the lambs. However, she knew nothing about the shepherds. Nicolás also ordered that three sheep be brought back, but it was not done.

Question 8: What weapons did they bring for fighting, and who provided them?

Reply: She responded that she did not bring any weapons.

Question 9: How many and which *rancherías* banded together and where?

Reply: She responded that six *rancherías* came with their chiefs, as well as some other Indians from other *rancherías*.

Question 10: Do they understand why they are imprisoned and why the Governor, the Lieutenant, the priests, and all the soldiers are so angry with them? Are they aware of the just punishment they deserve?

Reply: She responded that she understood everything. When she was asked if she had anything else to add regarding Nicolás or the other Christians, she responded that she did not, and that everything she had said was the truth. When the inquiry was finished, I signed and dated it at the aforementioned mission, as did the assistants and the interpreter. I swear to this.

José Olivera (Sergeant)
Manuel de Vargas (Assistant)
José María Verdugo (Assistant)
José María Pico (Interpreter)

1796
Judicial Proceedings against Silberio and Rosa at San Luis Obispo

FELIPE DE GOYCOECHEA

A murder trial in the 1790s throws considerable light on the development of the mission communities among the indigenous peoples. It appears that in 1796, as part of his effort to root Christianity more deeply in the Chumash community at San Luis Obispo, Fr. Miguel Giribet decided to require a number of the single women in the mission community to marry. This presented something of a problem for two of the mission Chumash, whose Christian names were Silberio and Rosa; although Silberio had contracted a Christian marriage to a woman name Rebeca, he and Rosa were lovers. The two of them were afraid that Rosa would be forced to marry another mission Indian, named Anselmo, a widower who was interested in her. Silberio and Rosa schemed to kill Rebeca so that the two of them could marry before the priest forced Rosa to marry Anselmo.

Silberio convinced Rebeca that the two of them ought to go outside the mission to gather seeds. When Rebeca heard that Fr. Giribet had given Silberio permission to take her along on his seed gathering trip, she told a cousin of hers that she did not think she would return alive from this journey. To protect herself, she induced her mother to accompany her and Silberio. The mother did so, but on the way back, for some reason, she stayed in a Chumash village near Santa Margarita.

On the trip back to the mission, Silberio reported that his wife had been killed by a bear. After an investigation revealed discrepancies in this story, he and Rosa were put on trial. They were both convicted. Silberio was sentenced to a work gang at the San Diego *presidio* for eight years, and Rosa was sentenced to be a domestic servant for an equal amount of time at the house of the commander of the San Francisco *presidio*.

The following selections from the trial consist of the testimony of four people: the indigenous blacksmith at the mission, Tiburcio Jecha; a woman from the mission named Edicta who knew Rebeca; and the accused, Rosa and Silberio. The testimony reveals a number of interesting things about mission life some twenty-five years after this particular church was started. The mission Indians regularly participated in the traditional seed gathering activities of their people. To do so they traveled considerable distances to various indigenous villages. Also, many of the mission Indians appeared to know of the tension between Silberio and Rebeca and of the potential for violence, yet it seems that no one had told the priest. In fact, the priest seems to have been the only one in the mission who did not know that Silberio and Rosa had an ongoing, long-term relationship with each other. The transcript reveals that the native community continued to function very effectively in the mission setup, and that the Spanish priest was, in many ways, as much an unknowing outsider as he was the leader of the community. But his insistence on imposing the Christian concept of marriage on the native community could be very destructive.

From the Criminal Case against Silberio and Rosa

Testimony of the first witness: Tiburcio Jecha

On October 11, 1796, at Mission San Luis Obispo, Don Felipe de Goycoechea had Tiburcio Jecha, a neophyte at the mission, appear as the first witness in this proceeding. He stood before me (the scribe), and Goycoechea had Tiburcio raise his right hand and make the sign of the Cross. Through the interpreter, Goycoechea impressed upon Tiburcio his obligation under oath. When he was asked, "Do you swear before God and this Holy Cross to tell the truth about what I am going to ask you?" he replied, "Yes, I swear."

He was asked to state his name, his occupation, if he knows Silberio, and if he knows where Silberio is at the present time. He said that his name is Tiburcio Jecha and he is the blacksmith at Mission San Luis Obispo. He knows Silberio, who is a Christian at the mission. He also knows that he is a prisoner in the soldiers' guardhouse.

He was asked if he knows why Silberio is being held prisoner. He said that he had heard Gaspar Lechagua, Casimiro, Liberatto, and Rugelio Nipoguo say that the wounds on Rebeca's body were not made by a bear;

Silberio must have killed her. Corporal Briones had ordered that the body be uncovered so her wounds could be seen. After he left, the body was uncovered four more times. Everyone at the mission had inspected it and agreed that the wounds were not made by a bear.

He was asked if he knows or has heard any Christians say that Silberio had been angry with his wife, Rebeca. He replied that he did not know, and he had not heard anyone say that. He was asked if he knows why Silberio fled the day after he brought back his wife's body. He replied that he knew why. Simeón had told Silberio that the soldiers were going to kill him, and that is why he fled.

He was asked if he knew whether Silberio had been angry with his wife, Rebeca, before she died. He said that when the Christians and gentiles were out gathering pine nuts and seeds, Silberio, Rebeca, and Rebeca's mother also went out to do the same thing. About a league from the mission, Silberio beat his wife. His mother-in-law was not too far behind them. When she came to defend her daughter, Silberio said to his wife, "I have to kill you. You have no relatives who can defend you." As soon as the mother-in-law heard him say he had to kill her daughter, she rushed to her daughter's defense. Silberio proceeded to beat her as well. He left them at that spot and then headed for Laguna Larga. Rebeca and her mother went to the place where most of the people were gathering seeds and told all those Christians what Silberio had done to them.

The witness was asked if he knew or had heard either his fellow Christians at the mission or the gentiles say anything else about Rebeca's death. He replied that the week Rebeca died, Silberio asked for permission to go and spend time in the mountains. As soon as the priest gave him permission to go, he informed his wife that they had to go to the mountains. When Rebeca asked Silberio where they had to go, he told her wherever they could find seeds to collect. After saying this, Silberio left the house. Finding herself alone, Rebeca began to cry. At that moment, Ponposa, her cousin, who is also a Christian, entered the house. Rebeca told her to sit down and said, "Take good care of my children, because by Saturday I will no longer be alive. Feed them well with what the Father gives you and with what you have." After she said this, Silberio came back inside the house, and then they went to the Chumash village of Santa Margarita, five or six leagues from the mission. They stayed there for two days. While there, Silberio told his wife, "Let's go closer to the mission, because there are plenty of *quiotes* there and we can take some back for our children." They set up camp about one league from the mission with other women who were camping out there. They spent two more days there collecting seeds. On the third day, Rebeca died.

The witness was asked if he knows if Rebeca had shared with these women her suspicions regarding her husband. He replied that she had told everybody at the mission that her husband was going to kill her. She also said the same thing to the women with whom she stayed this last time. He knows that on the day Rebeca died, Silberio went to see his own mother, who was with those women who had camped out with them. He called her aside, and the two of them, mother and son, spoke at a distance from everyone else. From there, they went together to the spot where Rebeca's body lay. A while later Silberio's mother arrived with his two children at the place where they had camped with the other women. Silberio also arrived, carrying Rebeca's body. He threw her body on the ground so hard it was as if he were throwing a deer carcass. When they heard moans coming from the deceased, it was assumed that she had not finished dying yet. Silberio then went to inform the Father that a bear had killed his wife. He left the body at the location previously mentioned.

When the witness was asked if he knew whether Silberio had sought refuge in the Holy Church, he replied that he did not see him, but Casimiro told him on the road to Monterey that Silberio had taken sanctuary.

Once his statement had been read back to him, the witness was asked if he had anything to add or delete. He replied that he also had heard Anselmo say that when his wife had died, he was planning to ask the Father for permission to marry Rosa, who was a widow. When Silberio had found out that Anselmo was going to ask the Father for Rosa, Silberio had said that he would have to kill his wife in order to marry Rosa.

The witness was asked if he knows who Silberio spoke to about this. He replied that he does not know who he talked to, but he heard everyone at the mission say that this is what Silberio had said. That is why he (Tiburcio) is saying it now. And, that is all he has to add according to the oath he took, which he maintains and accepts. He said that he does not know his age. He appears to be about twenty-eight years old. Since he does not know how to write, he made the sign of the Cross with his hand. The previously mentioned Señor (Goycoechea) and the scribe signed the declaration.

Felipe de Goycoechea
Before me, José Tades Sanches

Testimony of the third witness: Edicta

At the previously mentioned mission, same day, month, and year, Don Felipe de Goycoechea, Lieutenant of the Cavalry, had Edicta, a neophyte Indian woman at the mission, appear before him as the third witness in this trial. She stood before me (the scribe) and Goycoechea had Edicta raise her right hand and make the sign of the Cross. Through the interpreter, Goycoechea impressed upon Edicta her obligation under oath. When she was asked, "Do you swear before God and this Holy Cross to tell the truth about what I am going to ask you?" she replied, "Yes, I swear."

She was asked her name, if she knows Silberio, and if she knows where Silberio is at the present time. She said that her name is Edicta. She knows Silberio, who is also a Christian at the mission. He is a prisoner in the soldiers' guardhouse.

She was asked if she knows why Silberio is a prisoner. She replied that it is because he killed his wife.

When she was asked how she knows that he killed his wife, she replied that the day Rebeca died, she (Edicta) and the other woman who is testifying went out with Silberio and three other women. Rebeca told them, "Don't leave me alone with my husband, because he is going to kill me." And whenever they were about to leave, she would say the same thing over again. A short distance from the *rancho,* Silberio and his wife separated from the group. Edicta and another woman also separated from the group and headed in another direction, over to a hill, so they could see what Silberio was doing to his wife. Edicta and her friend had not been on top of the hill for very long when Silberio and Rebeca passed by where they were standing. Rebeca said to them, "Don't leave me." Edicta and her friend did leave and go back down to the campsite, because they heard a little boy crying from thirst. At about noon, Silberio arrived, shouting, "We have died." One of the women asked him what had happened to him and Silberio said that a bear had killed his wife. He said, "Come and help me bring back what the bear has left of her." Edicta replied, "How can we go there? The bear that killed her could still be there and might kill us, too." Silberio repeated, "Let's go, come and help me bring back her remains." Edicta replied, "I don't have a deerskin in which to wrap her. We can wrap her in my blanket." They went with him, and when they arrived where she lay dead, they noticed that neither her body nor her clothing were torn to pieces. They looked all over her body and at her blouse but saw no slashes or scratches that could have been made by a bear. The body was face up. There were two wounds on each side of her neck and another near her throat. There were two more wounds about three fingers wide on each side of her spinal column. They appeared to be deep. She lost a lot of blood when they carried her. The wounds on her neck seemed to be made with the point of a stick that Silberio always carried on his head. Edicta does not know if the wounds on Rebeca's back were made with a knife or with the same stick. From there, Edicta carried her to the place where they had the campsite. Some Christians had arrived, and in their presence Silberio wrapped Rebeca in two blankets, and they carried her back to the mission. Edicta stayed at the campsite. Shortly after everyone had left with the body, Edicta went back to the mission with some other women.

The witness said that she had nothing more to say and what she had said is the truth. She swears to it. When her statement was read back to her, she said she had nothing to add or delete. She does not know her age. She appears to be about thirty years old. Since she does not know how to write, she made the sign of the Cross with her hand. The previously mentioned Señor (Goycoechea) and the scribe signed the declaration.

Felipe de Goycoechea
Before me, José Tades Sanches

Confession of the accused accomplice: Rosa

At the previously mentioned mission, same day, month, and year, Don Felipe de Goycoechea, Lieutenant of the Cavalry, had Rosa, a neophyte Indian woman at the mission, appear before him. She is accused of being Silberio's accomplice in the death of his wife, Rebeca. Both are neophytes at the same mission. Rosa stood before me (the scribe), and Goycoechea had her raise her right hand and make the sign of the Cross. Through the interpreter, Goycoechea impressed upon Rosa her obligation under oath. When she was asked, "Do you swear before God and this Holy Cross to tell the truth about what I am going to ask you?" she replied, "Yes, I swear."

She was asked her name, age, where she is from, and her religion. She replied that her name is Rosa and she is about forty years old. She is from the Chumash village called El Morro, which is about five leagues from the mission. She is a Christian at the mission.

She was asked if she knows why she is being held prisoner. She replied that it is because Silberio's wife died. He is also a Christian at the same mission.

She was asked if she knows how Rebeca died. She replied that she does know. Rebeca's husband (Silberio) killed her.

She was asked if she knows why he killed her. She replied that she does know. Silberio told her that if the Father told her to marry someone, she was to tell him that she did not want to. He (Silberio) would go down and kill his wife, because he had a strong feeling in his heart about this. Someone had told him that his wife was behaving badly with another man, and he (Silberio) wanted to marry Rosa.

She was asked how she responded when Silberio said that he wanted to marry her. She replied, "The Father is not going to say anything to me, because I am an old woman. He gives husbands to the young girls."

She was asked how Silberio reacted to this. She said his response was, "I have been told that the Father wants to give all the adult women a husband. This is causing me so much distress that I cannot sleep at night."

She was asked how she responded to Silberio. She replied that she said, "Well, why can't you sleep at night?" And Silberio told her, "If the Father gives you a husband, I won't see you anymore and I won't go to your house."

She was asked if she and Silberio were involved in a "bad friendship." She replied, "Yes."

She was asked how long she and Silberio had been involved in this "bad friendship." She replied that it had been for a long time.

She was asked if she is still living this "bad life" with Silberio. She replied, "Yes."

She was asked if she saw Silberio on her way to the Chumash village of El Morro, the Sunday before they killed Rebeca. She replied that she had seen him. However, before leaving the mission on that same day, she told her friend not to tell Silberio, because he would catch up with them. Rosa and her friend had come to get some meat. When Silberio saw them, he asked if they were going for a walk. Rosa's friend told Silberio that they were. Silberio then grabbed Rosa's blanket and took it to the Chumash village. When Rosa asked him to give it back to her, he put the blanket in one of the houses. The two of them stood there arguing about the blanket. In the end, Silberio kept it. After Rosa and her friend left, Silberio went after them along the path to give the blanket back to Rosa. That is where Silberio told Rosa that he had to take his wife down below and kill her.

She was asked if Silberio had asked her for some *quiotes*. She replied that he did not ask her for anything.

She was asked at what time Silberio had caught up with her at that location, and when he left. She replied that he arrived about midday and that when he left the sun had gone down some.

She was asked if she had promised to marry Silberio or had given him hope that she would. She replied, "No."

She was asked why Silberio said that she had ordered him to kill his wife. She replied that even though he might be saying that, she had not ordered him to do anything.

She was asked if she recognized the knife that was being shown to her. She replied that she did not recognize it. They should ask her friend if she ever saw the knife at Rosa's house.

She was asked if she knew if Rebeca's unhappiness with her life was because of Rosa. She replied that the dead woman was someone who never got angry with anyone. She had never been angry with Rosa, as far as she knew. That is why Rosa thinks that Rebeca did not have an unhappy life on her account.

She was asked if she had anything else to say or declare about the matter. She replied, "No," and what she had said under oath about what she knows was the truth. When her statement was read back to her, she approved and agreed. Since she does not know how to write, she made the sign of the Cross. The previously mentioned Señor (Goycoechea) and the scribe signed the declaration.

Felipe de Goycoechea
Before me, José Tades Sanches

Confession of the accused: Silberio

At Mission San Luis Obispo, on October 12, 1796, Don Felipe de Goycoechea, Lieutenant of the Cavalry and Commander of the Royal *Presidio* of Santa Bárbara, with the assistance of the scribe, went over to the soldiers' guardhouse to take down the confession of Silberio, the accused in this trial. Silberio was informed that he should choose someone to defend him in the case. A list of all the people who could serve in this role was read to him by me (the scribe). After he had heard it and had been well informed about everything, he appointed Mariano Cota, a soldier at the Royal *Presidio* of Santa Bárbara. Cota signed it so it would be formally on record. I, the undersigned scribe, swear to this.

Immediately following, the Judge had Silberio raise his right hand and make the sign of the Cross. Through the interpreter, Goycoechea impressed upon Silberio his obligation under oath. Then he was asked, "Do you swear before God and promise the King to tell the truth about what I am going to ask you?" He replied, "Yes, I swear."

He was asked his name, age, where he is from, his religion, and his job. He replied that his name is Silberio. He is thirty years old and he is from Laguna Larga. He is a Christian at Mission San Luis Obispo, and his job is that of farmhand.

He was asked if he knows why he is a prisoner. He said that it is because he killed his wife.

He was asked why he killed Rebeca. He said that it was because Rosa, who is also a prisoner, told him to kill her so he could marry her.

He was asked where they were when Rosa ordered him to kill his wife, and how many times she ordered him to do it. He said that on two occasions she ordered him to do it; the first time was at Rosa's house, and the second time was on the way to El Morro.

He was asked if he knew the person who was with Rosa on the day he saw her heading to El Morro. He said that a woman was with Rosa, but he does not know her name. It was on Sunday, around 10:00 or 10:30 in the morning.

He was asked how long he was with Rosa at that place on that day and where he went when he left her. He replied that when he headed back to the mission, it was not very late, because the sun was still high.

He was asked where he went after leaving the mission and on what day. He replied that he left the mission with his wife the following day, Monday, near this side of the Santa Margarita area, about four leagues away. They spent three days there. On Thursday they came in closer to the mission. They only spent one night there. The next day, Friday, he killed his wife at noon.

He was asked what weapon he used to kill her. He said that he killed her with a knife.

He was asked if the knife he used to kill her was the same one they were showing him. He said, "Yes."

He was asked what else he did to the body after he wounded her. He said that after he killed her, he carried her a short distance and left her there. He then went over to where her friends Edicta, Petra, and Ponposa were. Another woman and a man were there, too, but he does not know their names.

He was asked if he took sanctuary in the church, as well as where and how he did it. He said that when he was headed back to the mission, he intended to turn himself in. He was saying to himself, "What am I going to do? I am going to die." As he approached the church, it seemed as if someone were whispering in his ear, telling him to get inside the church. When he looked towards the church, he saw that it was open, and he went inside.

He said that he had nothing to add and what he had said under oath was the truth. When his confession was read back to him he approved and agreed. Since he does not know how to write, he made the sign of the Cross with his hand. The previously mentioned Señor (Goycoechea) and the scribe signed the declaration.

Felipe de Goycoechea
Before me, José Tades Sanches

1797
Treatment of the Indians at Mission San Francisco

José María Fernández

When Serra died, he was succeeded as mission president by Fermín Francisco de Lasuén, a Spaniard from the region of Alava who had worked in both the Sierra Gorda and Baja California before coming to Alta California in 1773. A less driven and more politic man than Serra, Lasuén ably directed the missions until his death in 1803. The position of governor of the Californias also saw changes. Fages resigned in 1790 and was replaced by José Antonio Romeu, a veteran soldier who died shortly after arriving in Monterey. The commander at Loreto, José Joaquín de Arrillaga, served as interim governor for two years until the arrival of Diego de Borica, a soldier who had served for many years as a *presidio* commander in Nueva Vizcaya. Like Lasuén, Borica was from the Spanish region of Alava.

A census of the province taken in 1790 revealed approximately one thousand persons with some amount of Spanish blood (called *gente de razón,* literally "people of reason," to distinguish themselves from the Indians), up from a total of about 170 in 1774. The figures continued to grow over the decade, and by 1800, Alta California numbered some eighteen hundred *gente de razón.* Indians congregated at the missions also grew in numbers. From the 462 in five missions which Palóu had reported in 1773, the nine missions in 1785 housed 5,123 Indians.

Indigenous groups were often drawn to the missions by the desire for technology, food, or protection from disease. There were many other reasons as well, each one as unique as the individual or family or village that decided to enter a mission and be baptized. They often did not understand, however, that the fathers considered the entrance to the mission a one-way door. Once in, the missionaries considered that the neophytes had made a permanent commitment, an irrevocable choice for Christianity. The neophytes often did not see things that way, and trying to track down Indians who had left the missions (the fathers tellingly called them "fugitives") became one of the main tasks of the *presidio* soldiers and the mission guard.

The situation in San Francisco in the 1790s offers a close picture of the multiple pressures faced by the indigenous peoples in what one anthropologist has called a "time of little choice." As a mission, San Francisco had experienced modest success until the mid-1790s. It reported 215 neophytes in 1783 and experienced more or less steady growth for the next decade. Then it underwent a tremendous population jump in the early 1790s. From 623 neophytes in 1792, it recorded 918 in 1794. The reasons for this increase most likely had to do with drought, diseases, and crop failures. Then, just as suddenly, a number of Indians began to leave the mission. The immediate cause was probably an epidemic that broke out at the beginning of spring in 1795. One of the priests, Fr. Antonio Dantí, organized an expedition of mission Indians to bring the runaways back. When the posse reached the *ranchería* where many of the fugitive Indians had gone, violence broke out and seven members of the posse were killed. Although Dantí tried to suppress word of the killings, more mission Indians found out about it, and groups continued to flee San Francisco over the summer. By the end of summer, at least 280 had fled. Dantí, who already had a bad reputation among some of the mission Indians, and who had been rebuked for his treatment of the Indians by Borica, was removed from San Francisco by Lasuén in June 1796. In his place, Lasuén named a newly arrived priest, José María Fernández. The new priest soon began to complain to his brethren at San Francisco about their treatment of the Indians. His disagreements with them became public and caught the attention of the soldiers at San Francisco and the governor. Lasuén had to travel to San Francisco himself. He ordered the other priests to be more lenient in their treatment of the Indians, and he ordered Fernández not to carry his grievances against other Franciscans into the public realm.

Matters remained fairly calm among the priests for almost a year, but they heated up again in early summer 1797. The two priests with Fernández at San Francisco, José de la Cruz Espí and Martín de Landaeta, decided to send an expedition of mission Indians to the east shore of the bay to retrieve more fugitives. The two hoped that this foray would succeed where the one organized the year before by Dantí had failed. They undertook the expedition in spite of Borica's decree strictly prohibiting such excursions, entrusting the leadership of the expedition to a Baja California Indian named Raymundo the Californian. This expedition was also a failure, for the Indians drove Raymundo's band away.

This affair caused Fernández to break the truce he had observed with his brethren. What follows are excerpts from two angry letters he wrote to the governor at the end of June 1797. Soon after these letters became public knowledge, Fernández was sent back to Mexico City by his superiors. The letters vividly demonstrate the tensions that always existed in a mission community among the missionaries, between them and the soldiers, and among the indigenous peoples themselves.

FROM LETTERS OF JOSÉ MARÍA FERNÁNDEZ

Very dear Sir: I have reason to suspect and I assume that Lt. Don Josef [José Darío] de Argüello has submitted a report to Your Excellency in which he tells you that without his knowledge the Reverend Fathers of this mission have sent thirty or more men to the other shore under the command of the Californian Raymundo. He sent the Fathers a report regarding this foolishness. After twenty-four hours had passed and he had not received a response, he presented Your Excellency with the report I mentioned so that you would be informed of the consequences that might ensue from the situation.

And I suspect that these consequences cannot be good, because Raymundo and many of those who accompanied him from here on the seventeenth have not yet returned. If these consequences are negative, someone must be held responsible that these men have strayed from the mission, even if none of the bad repercussions which I expect from the expedition actually happen. This expedition was conducted without my knowledge and in such a manner that I did not know anything after eight days, not even that Raymundo was missing from the mission. If I had been consulted, such an absurdity would not have been carried out, for I know very well that the fugitive Indians harbor bad feelings toward Raymundo. I also know why they have fled. It is due to the terrible suffering they experienced from punishments and work. Raymundo, the executioner used by Frs. Dantí and Landaeta, was not the only one that the Indians wanted to get; they longed for the opportunity to take revenge against those two Fathers, or at least cause some harm at the mission.

A group of native people of the San Francisco area crossing the bay in a reed boat, by Louis Choris, 1816. Courtesy of the California Historical Society, North Baker Research Library; FN-30512.

These are the reasons why I have opposed this expedition for the entire year I have been ministering here. However, Fr. Martín took advantage of the opportunity offered by a new minister who, unaware of everything that has happened here, will approve everything that on the surface might seem beneficial. This was why it was done and also, undoubtedly, to rebuke me. Thus, the information was kept from me so that such an absurd endeavor could be put into effect. I call it an absurdity, Sir, for I know much that helps me deal with the Indians. I know why they have fled. There are many of them and it is thus very risky to search for them in this manner. Since they do not want to come out, for fear of what they have already experienced, the only measure that might work could be to send out an appropriate number of well-prepared soldiers. But I doubt that even that would be successful.

In closing, Sir, I could elaborate more by pointing out other details that I do not judge useless. However, the faintness in my head and the pain in my chest that have been tormenting me steadily for eight days do not permit me to continue further. To conclude, let me only say that, if I had been listened to last year, everything could have been resolved. But I was not believed. I was considered an impostor, a troublemaker. I was accused of becoming entangled with secular elements who had sinister goals. I say this because my heart is drowning in sorrow. But I declare that I shall seek vindication in God's tribunal for all these offenses. And if God spares my health, then I shall seek vindication in the relevant human tribunal.

I had prepared the letter that I include here, dated the twenty-seventh, which has just passed. However, I have no choice but to add the following, stating to Your Excellency that yesterday, the twenth-eighth, Raymundo and those who accompanied him finally appeared at the mission. They returned, thanks be to God, after having overcome many dangers at sea. The fast-moving currents carried them outside the port and then returned them to the estuary of San Francisquito. Although they were on land, not once could they escape from the gentiles who wanted to kill Raymundo. And even though they have returned, this recourse was not necessary. In the letter to which I refer I have informed Your Excellency of everything, not omitting anything. It seems to me that the content of the letter and the repercussions that can be deduced can be useful to Your Excellency in order to handle this matter in the best manner possible.

Sir, if I am to speak as my heart dictates, I shall not restrain myself from advising Your Excellency to use all your authority to prohibit similar expeditions from being carried out in the manner in which they have been up until now. Taking note of and weighing all the circumstances, I do not know that they can be carried out in good conscience the way they have been done....

The benefits and tranquility that I seek for the Indians as well as the mission have guided my quill in this appeal. I love the Indians very much and I will feel their misfortunes even more if they are to be treated like this. I repeat, I love them very much, because they have caused me great sorrow, very bad days, many sleepless nights, some tears, and ultimately my shattered health.

In return and with good will I dedicate what little health I have left and shall expend it to help them until not one drop of blood is left in my veins. I have relieved them of a thousand burdens that have not been kept secret from Your Excellency. I have cared for them for one year, to the limit of my strength. And although the only consequences of this have been my infamy, my dishonor stemming from my actions which they say were based on poor judgment, false zeal, and sinister goals, I have the satisfaction of knowing that when I am judged on the scale that makes no errors as it weighs its verdicts, that scale being God, my intentions will be seen as having been honest. And if the means have not been perceived as such, it is because they have been judged based on obsession, prejudice, intrigue, lies, and flattery. Do not believe for a moment, Your Excellency, that when I make myself understood in this manner that I mean to lose due respect for my superior. I only ask God to protect Your Excellency as your loving and attentive servant so desires.

1797
Military Interrogation of San Francisco Indians

José Argüello

In the summer of 1797 Governor Borica himself authorized an expedition to the eastern side of San Francisco Bay to try to bring back some of the Indians who had fled from San Francisco. The sortie was led by Pedro Amador, and it was successful in capturing a number of Saclan and Huchuin people. They were tried at the *presidio* of San Francisco. What follows are excerpts from their interrogations, when they were asked why they had fled the mission. The excerpts offer a close example of some of the daily experiences with which mission Indians had to contend.

From Testimony of Runaway Christian Indians

In fulfillment of the decree of Governor and Inspector General Don Diego de Borica calling for testimony from the runaway Christian Indians of Mission San Francisco captured by Sergeant Pedro Amador during the recent campaign, on this day, July 21, 1797, I brought them before me. Once I figured out who was capable of testifying, I separated them out. By means of the interpreters and in the presence of the witnesses Sergeant Joaquín Pico, Corporal Claudio Galindo, Corporal José Miranda, and soldier José González, four members of the Catalonian Volunteers, I questioned each one regarding the causes and motives they had for running away from their mission without wanting to return. To these interrogations they responded in the following way:

Tiburcio: He testified that after his wife and daughter died, on five separate occasions Father Dantí ordered him whipped because he was crying. For these reasons he fled.

Marciano: He offered no other reason for fleeing than that he had become sick.

Macario: He testified that he fled because his wife and one child had died, no other reason than that.

Magín: He testified that he left due to his hunger and because they had put him in the stocks when he was sick, on orders from the *alcalde.*

Tarazón: He declared that he had no motive. Having been granted license to go on *paseo* to his land, he had felt inclined to stay.

Ostano: He testified that his motive for having fled was that his wife, one child, and two brothers had died, and because he had fought with another Indian who had been directing their work group.

Román: He testified that he left because his wife and a son had gone back to their land, because of the many whippings, and because he did not have anyone to feed him.

Claudio: He declares that he fled because he was continually fighting with his brother-in-law Casimiro and because the *alcalde* Valeriano was clubbing him every time he turned around, and when he was sick, this same Valeriano made him go to work.

José Manuel: He testifies that when they went to bring wood from the mountains, Raymundo ordered them to bring him water. When the declarant wouldn't do it, this same Raymundo hit him with a heavy cane, rendering one hand useless. He showed his hand. It was a little puffed up but had movement. That was his reason for having left the mission.

Homobono: He testifies that his motive for fleeing was that his brother had died on the other shore, and when he cried for him at the mission they whipped him. Also, the *alcalde* Valeriano hit him with a heavy cane for having gone to look for mussels at the beach with Raymundo's permission.

Malquíedes: He declares that he had no more reason for fleeing than that he went to visit his mother, who was on the other shore.

Liborato: He testifies that he left because his mother, two brothers, and three nephews died, all of hunger. So that he would not also die of hunger, he fled.

Migilo: He declared that his motive for fleeing was that Lorenzo, who had been at the house of *La Sargenta,* took him along with him.

Louis Choris sketched these faces of San Francisco-area people in 1816. The second person from the left was a member of the Huchiun group, while the two on the far right were Saclan. Courtesy of The Bancroft Library, University of California, Berkeley.

Nicolás: He says that he ran away only because his father had died. He had no other motive.

Timoteo: He declares that the *alcalde* Luis came to get him while he was feeling ill and whipped him. After that, Father Antonio hit him with a heavy cane. For those reasons he fled.

Otolón: He reports that he fled because his wife did not care for him or bring him food. The *vaquero* Salvador had sinned with her. Then Father Antonio ordered him whipped because he was not looking out for said woman, his wife.

Milán: He declared that he was working all day in the tannery without any food for either himself, his wife, or his child. One afternoon after he left work he went to look for clams to feed his family. Father Dantí whipped him. The next day he fled to the other shore, where his wife and child died.

Patabo: He says that he fled just because his wife and children died and he had no one to take care of him.

Orencio: He declared that his father had gone several times with a little niece of his to get a ration of meat. Father Dantí never gave it to him and always hit him with a cudgel. Because his niece died of hunger, he ran away.

Toribio: He stated that the motive for his having fled was that he was always very hungry, and that he went away together with his uncle.

López: He explained that his reason for having run away was the following: he went one day over to the *presidio* to look for something to eat. Upon returning to the mission, he went to get his ration, but Father Dantí did not want to give it to him, saying that he should go to the countryside to eat herbs.

Magno: He declared that he had run away because, his son being sick, he took care of him and was therefore unable to go out to work. As a result he was given no ration and his son died of hunger.

Próspero: He declared that he had gone one night to the lagoon to hunt ducks for food. For this Father Antonio Dantí ordered him stretched out and beaten. Then, the following week he was whipped again for having gone out on *paseo.* For these reasons he fled.

Having concluded the preceding declarations that were legally gathered and which follow the testimony of the interpreters, and in the belief that they represent the truth, I and my assistants sign it at the San Francisco *Presidio* on August 12, 1797.

> José Argüello
> José Miranda
> Joaquín Pico
> José González
> Claudio Galindo

1798–1801
The Mission System Evaluated and Defended

Antonio de la Concepción Horra and
Fermín Francisco de Lasuén

One of the most serious controversies in which the Franciscan missionaries were involved resulted from the actions of one of their own members. In 1798, Fr. Antonio de la Concepción Horra, who had been expelled from California by Lasuén for alleged insanity after only five months of service at Mission San Miguel, wrote a long letter to the viceroy in which he attacked the California missionaries. First, he complained about some alleged catechetical practices. He stated that the missionaries routinely mistreated the Indians. He also maintained that they ignored the long-standing colonial policy of teaching the Indians Spanish. He further claimed that some missionaries inflated the success of their efforts by baptizing the same Indians more than once. Second, Concepción Horra argued that the missionaries were not cooperative citizens of Alta California. He asserted that they overcharged for items that they were selling and that they were selfish in not helping the newer missions get sufficient provisions. They refused to extend hospitality to other *gente de razón*. Finally, he complained that he had been mistreated by his Franciscan brethren and branded insane for his effrontery in raising these issues.

This letter set off a chain of events, and Viceroy Miguel José de Azanza ordered Borica to investigate. Borica told the viceroy, "Generally, the treatment given the Indians is very harsh. At San Francisco, it even reached the point of cruelty." Borica then sent out a fifteen-item questionnaire to the *presidio* commanders in which he asked detailed questions about the treatment of the Indians and about some of Concepción Horra's other accusations. In 1801, Lasuén wrote a long reply to the commanders' responses and sent it on to the viceroy. Finally, in 1805, after getting more information, the viceroy found Concepción Horra's charges "groundless." By that time Lasuén and Borica were dead, and Concepción Horra was back in Spain.

What follows is an excerpt from Concepción Horra's letter and part of Lasuén's reply, in which he addresses the issue of the treatment of the Indians at the missions. Concepción Horra demonstrates, among other things, just how important the missions were becoming for the overall Alta California economy. Lasuén's reply contains the missionaries' assessment of indigenous culture and their reasons for trying to transform it. The issue that separated the Franciscans of the College of San Fernando from other Spaniards in Alta California was not the desirability of transforming native ways of life into Hispanic ones; all colonials agreed that such a transformation was necessary. Lasuén's frankly negative assessment was shared by most Spanish Californians. The debates between the missionaries and the military and settlers were not over ends, but means.

From a Letter by Antonio de la Concepción Horra

Your Excellency the Viceroy:

I Fr. Antonio de la Concepción, a member of the College of San Fernando of the same city in Mexico, hereby present my case before Your Excellency with the utmost humility and respect so that you may examine the charges that have been brought against me and pass fair judgment according to the law.

Your Excellency, last year I was sent to the missions of New California by His Excellency, Viceroy Juan. I established a new mission there and named it San Miguel. The Fr. President of those missions selected Fr. Buenaventura Sitjar to be my associate. This priest is completely opposed to everything that is mandated by the Royal Decrees of Our Sovereign King with respect to the care and education of the Indians. Your Excellency, a written report does not suffice as a means of informing Your Excellency of all that has transpired between the two of us with regard to this matter. In light of this, if the opportunity should so arise, I hereby request an audience with Your Excellency, at which time I shall clearly describe for you everything that has happened to me and all that transpires on that peninsula. And so that Your Excellency may reflect on the most important aspects of my case, I shall cite them in a very precise manner. The priest who is my associate not only speaks with the Indians in their own language but also is in the habit of teaching them the doctrine in their own language, and he wanted me to adopt those practices. This is contrary to the mandates of our King and I showed this priest the Royal Decrees. He baptizes them without teaching them the very explicit and essential information that one needs in order to receive this Holy Sacrament. He engaged in this practice with a number of adults the very day that the mission was founded. Evidence of this fact is the Baptismal Registry that is at the mission. This is contrary to the mandate and practices of our Holy Church. At another mission where this priest had been, it is customary for the Indians to return to the woods after being baptized. They remain there as long as they wish and after a few years return to the mission. Since it is not easy to recognize them, they are rebaptized, a practice which occurs daily. I reprimanded this priest for all these deeds and many others that I do not mention here, informing him that in all good conscience I could not allow this to continue and that I would send a complaint to the Superior Government. His anger was so intense that he burst out with many offensive words against Our King and his Ministers....

Your Excellency, I would like to inform you of the many abuses that are commonplace in that country. The manner in which the Indians are treated is by far more cruel than anything I have ever read about. For any reason, however insignificant it may be, they are severely and cruelly whipped, placed in shackles, or put in the stocks for days on end without receiving even a drop of water. With regard to the sale of cattle and other food, there is no official price list except for what suits their fancy. This occurs with every purchaser. Even though there is an official price list, they do not want to follow it, and if the purchaser challenges them, they tell him to go and buy what he wants from the Governor. The sailors are excellent witnesses of this practice because they observe it every year....

According to what the Governor told me, the majority of the complaints that I have outlined here have already been presented, but nothing has been resolved yet. At Mission San Luis, I saw with my own eyes the arrival of a weaver who was dressed in the habit of Our Lady of Carmen. I describe him this way so as not to reveal his name. He was traveling from the *presidio* of San Diego to the *presidio* of Monterey under orders from the Governor. He arrived with his wife and children and asked for some cabbages. They refused to give him any, even though the garden was full of them. The same thing happens every day to the soldiers of the escort. Even if they are dying of hunger and all they request is a morsel of bread, they will not give it to them....

On this day, the twelfth of July 1798, I ask that God our Father protect Your Excellency with His Holy Grace for many years. I remain Your Excellency's most humble servant, who kisses your hand.

Fr. Antonio de la Concepción

From the Refutation of Charges by Fermín Francisco de Lasuén

They [the mission Indians] appreciate, of course, the fruits from the forest; but in addition to the fact that they are given plenty of time to gather them, they know quite well the superiority of those we supply. Among all our Indians, ours are worth double the price of theirs. Our neophytes sell one measure of wheat, or corn, etc. (it is true; they sell them, and they even keep them in order to sell them) for four strings of beads. They can buy a like quantity of forest seeds for just two. The Indians themselves have established this rate of exchange; and they are in the habit of saying that among all the seeds of the forest there are none to equal our barley.

The effort entailed in procuring a sustenance from the open spaces is incomparably greater than what is now enjoined on them so that they can sustain themselves; but the former is free and according to their liking, and the latter prescribed, and not according to their liking.

Here, then, (and it cannot be otherwise) lies all the loss and harm which can be imagined or said to have befallen these natives through Christianity.

In their pagan state it is quite certain that they disregard the law of self-preservation which nature implants in us, a law which binds under penalty of the total destruction of the human race. Hence, as a rule, they live without providing for what is indispensably necessary for existence; they know nothing of comforts; and they enjoy life as long as they can sustain it with ease, and without having recourse to what they regard as work.

The bow and arrow, which they fashion without much effort, by and large are their only instruments of industry. The uncultivated soil supports their manner of life, which differs little from that of the lower animals. They live on herbs while they are in season, and then gather the seeds for the winter, and as a rule, they celebrate the end of it by holding a feast or a dance. They satiate themselves today and give little thought to tomorrow.

Here then, we have the greatest problem of the missionary: how to transform a savage race such as these into a society that is human, Christian, civil, and industrious. This can be accomplished only by denaturalizing them. It is easy to see what an arduous task this is, for it requires them to act against nature. But it is being done successfully by means of patience, and by an unrelenting effort to make them realize that they are men. They are treated with tolerance or dealt with more or less firmly, depending on the longer or shorter time that has elapsed since their conversion, while awaiting the time when they will gently submit themselves to rational restraint, something they had not known before. At the same time, they can see that those who are ill and those who are well receive what is necessary for their daily needs without too much effort on their part, and that they are sure of daily sustenance, when before they lived from hand to mouth.

Mission San Carlos in Carmel in 1786, with unenthusiastic native people lined up for the formal reception of the Frenchman La Pérouse. Lasuén awaits the visitor in the doorway of the church. This work was copied at the mission by Malaspina expedition artist José Cardero from a now lost original done by La Pérouse expedition member Gaspar de Vancy. Courtesy of the Museo Naval, Madrid (MS 1723-1).

Among the more pressing problems that can arise in any mission is that of not having food for the workers. This supplies a good excuse for a trip to the mountains; but no one is forced to go. Instead, for such emergencies a sufficient supply of food is purchased and brought from some other place so as to maintain all who remain at the mission, both the healthy and the sick. In addition to the three meals—morning, noon, and evening—they are seldom refused if they come to ask for something to eat, and on each of these occasions it is customary to give the Indians what they would not get perhaps in a week in the mountains. This and the distribution of meat, fruits, and raw grain are made in accordance with the capacity of each mission. The capacity varies; but what there is gets distributed among the neophytes of each respective mission.

Furthermore, it cannot be denied that, among missionaries, some are more generous and liberal in meeting the needs of their wards, just as in the case of good parents in a family. If some are poor, as they are here, they cannot but act accordingly. A hospital is not the same as a palace. The missions are communities whose resources have to come from the labor of individuals; and of the three groups that make up [a mission], one group, the aged, the retired, the children, and the sick, contribute only to the consumption.

They are helped to the best of our ability. Nothing is kept back from them, and despite that, they run away. They know very well how greatly improved is their condition as compared with that of the pagans—a condition in which many perish through want of care, and many die of hunger. Despite that, because of their untrained nature they have an affinity for the mountains that more than offsets this obvious truth. I have seen Indians run away although they were on the sick list and excused even from Sunday Mass, individuals who at the same time, in addition to the three customary rations, were being given morning and evening *atole* made from corn specially prepared for the sick, a good meat stew at midday, more than two pints of milk each day, and a good dish from the Fathers' table with a piece of bread (this is the way we do it when it appears that they have taken a fancy for something from the Fathers' table). And when such persons are returned from their flight, they intimate that they are hungry. This they have told me—I have discussed with them what they have been given—they have told me (after having eaten all or maybe most of what they were served) that they cannot swallow *atole* made from corn or flour, that what they need is fish. And if we have it, we give it to them; and if we do not have it, we go and look for it, so that we may have it for them.

On an occasion like that, when someone asked permission for some of this group who get "hungry" to go to the mountains for a week, I said to them with some annoyance, "Why, you make me think that if one were to give you a young bull, a sheep, and a *fanega* of grain every day, you would still be yearning for your mountains and your beaches." Then the brightest of the Indians who were listening to me said, smiling and half ashamed of himself, "What you say is true, Father. It's the truth." In the light of this, anyone can see whether or not complaints of this kind made by the Indians have a right to be considered by the authorities as accusations against the missionaries....

Finally, I point as tangible proof to the fact that among our neophytes the most robust, the healthiest, and the stoutest are those who absent themselves the least from the mission. I pointed out to the San Diego Indians that the occasion when vast numbers of pagans died of hunger coincided with the two years, and especially the one, when there were no seeds from the soil to give them....

We must not fail to note here how different women are in this respect. In their native state they are slaves to the men, obliged to maintain them with the sweat of their brow. They are ill treated, trampled on even to the point of death if, on returning to their huts after spending the entire night in raids or in dancing, the entire morning in play, and the entire evening in sleeping, the men find that the women have made no provision for food for them. The women never object or show any dislike for the work we assign. They are not so much given to running away. And if it were not for their husbands, if they are married; or their fathers, if they are not; or for their sons and grandsons, if they are aged, they would perhaps never leave the mission. I add the word "perhaps," for the majority of them, whether because of the example of their elders or the force of habit, often fall like the Israelites into the weakness of ingratitude. For them, not even food from heaven, enjoyed in liberty and accompanied only by work that was pleasing, could suffice to overcome the longing for grosser foods purchased at the price of cruel labor in the heartless slavery of Egypt. What food, then, will be able to overcome in these men the yearning for the brutal life they knew? It was free and it was lazy. Who can keep them from murmuring after it?

1809
Life in the Pueblo of San José

José Joaquín de Arrillaga
and José María Estudillo

The first few years in the newly founded *pueblos* of Alta California were difficult for the settlers, and growth was slow. In San José, the new residents built a dam on the Guadalupe River to help with irrigation, but it was washed away in March 1778. It was soon rebuilt and was lost again the following winter. However, by 1782, the *pueblo* was producing two thousand bushels of corn annually. This was enough to supply both northern *presidios*. Population grew slowly as occasional settlers and retired soldiers trickled in to receive their land and house lots. By 1790, the *pueblo* had reached a grand total of eighty inhabitants. The southern *pueblo* of Los Angeles grew in the same fashion as San José, with occasional retired soldiers and other assorted settlers moving in. By 1790, its population had grown to more than a hundred, and ten years later it had reached slightly over three hundred residents. By that time, Los Angeles was also producing a surplus of corn, which was used to feed the *presidio* of Santa Bárbara.

The use of *pueblo* lands was carefully regulated. About half the total land was administered by the town government, and it was divided into common pasturelands, woodlands for gathering fuel and timber, and the lands associated with the town's water supply, such as the river, the irrigation ditch, and various springs. The *pueblo* also administered the public structures around the plaza. The other half of the *pueblo* lands were distributed to private parties. These included the private buildings on the central plaza, lots for private buildings, and agricultural land for individual settlers and families.

Consistent with the Spanish municipal tradition, towns were, on the surface, self-governing, with elected *alcaldes* and town councils managing their affairs. In the frontier regions of Alta California, however, the powers of the elected officials were somewhat circumscribed. Since a primary task of the *pueblos* was to provide food for the *presidios,* the military became heavily involved in the management of town affairs. In San José, for instance, the commander of the Monterey *presidio* appointed a soldier as commissioner *(comisionado)* and for the *pueblo* of Los Angeles the commander of the Santa Bárbara *presidio* did the same. This person wielded the real authority. The *presidio* commander also had the right to veto the election of anyone as *alcalde* or to the town council.

The following correspondence was taken from a random year (1809) of San José's history, and it gives a sense of issues associated with *pueblos* in Alta California. These excerpts of letters between Governor José Joaquín de Arrillaga, Monterey Commander José María Estudillo, and local commissioner Luis Peralta involved two sets of issues. First, there was the boundary between the *pueblo* and the two surrounding missions, Santa Clara and San José. Settlers and missionaries accused each other of letting their cattle graze on the other's land. Disputes such as these were extremely common. The other item of contention in this correspondence relates to the basic function of the *pueblo:* that is, to feed the soldiers at the *presidio.* When Estudillo picked up a rumor that some settlers were secretly harvesting corn and not including it in their reports, he was quick to order that such practices be stopped. Again, such occurrences were commonplace. Both controversies demonstrate how complex and fractious were the relationships between the *presidios,* missions, and *pueblos* in colonial California. Such controversies constituted an important part of the fabric of daily life in Spanish Alta California.

The worlds encompassed by these letters indicate the kind of diverse place Alta California was becoming. The correspondents themselves came from different backgrounds. Arrillaga was a native of the Basque region of northern Spain. He had served in Texas before being appointed to Loreto in 1783. He was interim governor of the Californias for two years in the 1790s. When the governments of the Californias were separated in 1804, he was appointed the first governor of Alta California. Estudillo was also a Spaniard, and like Arrillaga, he had served in Baja California before being transferred north in 1806. Peralta, on the other hand, was from Sonora. He had accompanied his parents on the 1776 Anza expedition, and his family was among the founding group of settlers in San José. He was named commissioner in 1807.

Some one hundred and twenty settlers lived in the *pueblo* of San José, along with an undetermined number of Indians who were employed as laborers. The settlers had recruited a group of Cholvon people who lived thirty miles east of Mission San José to come to the *pueblo* to work in 1807, and they and other native peoples continued to appear in town to work, especially during harvest time. The 1809 harvest was about three thousand bushels, and the *pueblo* settlers owned over one thousand head of cattle.

More than fourteen hundred native people lived at Mission Santa Clara, just a few miles from the *pueblo*. They included an increasing number of Juña and Pala people, who came to the mission from farther and farther east as the mission gradually extended its influence. The mission was also a prosperous ranching and agricultural enterprise. It owned over eight thousand head of cattle, over two thousand horses, and over ten thousand other smaller animals, and it harvested over sixty-five hundred bushels of crops annually.

Mission San José, which had been founded only a dozen years earlier, housed over five hundred neophytes, mainly from various regions east of San Francisco Bay, as well as an increasing number of people from the San Joaquin Valley. Its ranching and farming operations, while not so large as Santa Clara's, were significant. It owned over seven thousand head of cattle, one thousand horses, and seven thousand smaller animals. The 1809 harvest, slightly over two thousand bushels, was abnormally low—the average annual harvest for the decade 1801 to 1810 was over four thousand bushels.

Another institution, the private *rancho,* was also beginning to take root in the Californias. One of the many ways the colonial government tried to develop the province was by enticing soldiers into its service by promising them land once their service was ended. Only the use of the land, not the land itself, was formally granted to veteran soldiers during the Spanish period, since all the land belonged to the king. The grants, therefore, were technically grazing permits, but the distinction was more legal than real. The granted lands were generally regarded as private family *ranchos* from the beginning, and legal private ownership was formally granted by Mexican legislation after independence. José de Gálvez distributed land to soldiers in Baja California in 1768 and 1769. Fages followed this precedent in the 1780s in southern Alta California and made grants to such veterans as Juan José Domínguez (Rancho San Pedro), José María Verdugo (Rancho San Rafael), and Manuel

German naturalist Georg Heinrich von Langsdorff, traveling with a Russian expedition, painted these Indians from Mission San José in 1806. Wearing paint for a formal dance ceremony, they were most likely celebrating having survived the severe measles epidemic that had just ravaged the mission's native community. Courtesy of The Bancroft Library, University of California, Berkeley.

Nieto (from whose sprawling, 150,000-acre grant five substantial *ranchos* were eventually carved out). Other governors followed Fages's lead, and about thirty grants were made during the Spanish period.

In short, forty years after the first Spanish expedition had passed through, the native Californians found themselves working as laborers in a *rancho* and farm landscape, producing and supporting a new set of crops and animals, and directed by groups of recently arrived Spaniards and *mestizos*.

FROM LETTERS BY JOSÉ JOAQUÍN DE ARRILLAGA AND JOSÉ MARÍA ESTUDILLO

Sergeant Luis Peralta:

The Reverend Fathers of Mission San José de Guadalupe have brought to my attention the damage caused by the livestock at that town. They have warned the townspeople that if the cattle continue to damage the fences on a daily basis, they will be confiscated and killed. They will, however, permit the livestock that is already in the field to remain, so as not to increase tensions, even though the animals are damaging the pasture land.

The townspeople responded that the owners should definitely be reimbursed for any cattle found within the fences which the mission should kill. The Reverend Fathers have told me that they are not in agreement with the proposed reimbursement. They say that they are suffering serious losses and that any cattle they find in the cornfields or pasturelands either will be killed immediately or penned up and left to die. But they are adamant that the mission will not pay the reimbursement that the townspeople have proposed.

You have been informed of this and of the fact that the Reverend Fathers have requested my opinion on the matter. I must instruct you that my position is the same as the practice that is followed in all New Spain, namely that the owner should take care of his land during the day and that from sunset to sunrise the owner should take care of and be accountable for his livestock. If during this time the cattle are penned up or killed, no claim or complaint whatsoever will be accepted. I also should warn you that the cattle that habitually break fences are exempt from similar rules. I am giving the same notice of my position on this matter to the Reverend Fathers for their information and management. It is your duty to let the townspeople know that they will not be reimbursed for cattle that are killed within the fenced area or that die penned up in the corrals. No complaint regarding this matter will be accepted from them either.

God keep you many years.

Monterey, January 28, 1809
José Joaquín de Arrillaga

Sergeant Luis Peralta:
By your letter of last August 29, I am informed of the arrest of the townsman Gabriel Amesquita, who is already in this *presidio*. . . .

The arrangement you made about the appointment of people to take care of the labors is fine. With those who resist, work rigorously to carry out the orders that I gave everyone in the community without exception. If anyone does not work when it is his turn, or demonstrates any resistance, punish him immediately and assign one of your company to take his place. Send me a note about this right away. Then send the resister, so that I can personally give him the most severe punishment.

Regarding what you tell me about the oxen of the mission, I say nothing because I have not been enlightened by the Fathers. In 1806 the present Señor Governor, together with the late Sergeant Macario de Castro and the *alcalde* of the *pueblo* (I do not remember his name), tried to put an end to the disputes between the townspeople and Mission San José regarding land ownership. The *jefe* properly designated a hill that lies to the south of the *rancho* that belonged to Josef Larios as the boundary between the *pueblo* and the mission. I remember that the Fathers agreed to put a fence from the top of that hill to the first estuary. Since you have not told me whether the Place of the Skulls is on that hill or adjacent to the *rancho* of Larios, I cannot declare who owns the place where the Fathers from Mission Santa Clara keep their livestock. Let me know the location as soon as possible. It is very good that the town's horses have been removed from the riverside, since that site belongs to the mission.

God keep you many years.

Monterey, September 15, 1809
José María Estudillo

Sergeant Luis Peralta:
I have just found out that three people already have harvested their corn crops and to this date you have not told me anything. For that reason I am instructing you to take an exact account of what these individuals have harvested, as well as what those who soon will be harvesting their corn and beans bring in. Warn them not to distribute one single grain of corn or any beans until I advise you, after I receive the urgent dispatch that you will send me.

Instruct the townsman Francisco Castro and those who already have harvested their corn to proceed immediately to dry it and sort out the grains. On the twenty-sixth of this month, without fail or excuses whatsoever, they are to appear here with as much corn as they can transport. They will be reimbursed accordingly for the cost of transportation. You will ensure that this order is carried out and you will be held responsible if this does not come to pass.

God keep you many years.

Monterey, October 14, 1809
José María Estudillo

To the Town Commissioner:

In the report you have given me, dated the twenty-ninth of last month, Reverend Father Narciso Durán, Minister of Mission San José, did not concur that the hill that you showed him was the one designated by the present Señor Governor of the province, or that the Place of the Skulls is presently a very necessary grazing spot for the work oxen from the vicinity, or that it belongs to the *pueblo*. I advise you that you can place said oxen and the military horses at the Place of the Skulls temporarily until another solution is found to remove the mission livestock.

If you should find it necessary, for whatever reason, you can order the townspeople to keep watch themselves.

God keep you many years.

Monterey, October 31, 1809

José María Estudillo

To the Commissioner of the Town of San José:

I have been informed by your report of the fourteenth of the current month that you have gone to the Place of the Skulls and have removed the livestock that belonged to Mission San José.

Maintain the guards that you have put in place, or keep a watchful eye on the oxen and horses from that vicinity that are at said location. I will let you know whom I will order to be on the lookout in case the priests at San José attempt to remove the livestock that belong to the town and replace them with their own, as they have told me they will do. If they try to do this, do not allow it. Notify me immediately if this or anything new should happen.

God keep you many years.

Monterey, November 18, 1809

José María Estudillo

1812
The Killing of Fr. Andrés Quintana at Mission Santa Cruz

LORENZO ASISARA

In preparation for his *History of California,* Hubert Howe Bancroft, in addition to having a good number of Spanish and Mexican-era documents copied or summarized, sent two members of his staff, Thomas Savage and Enrique Cerruti, to interview many old residents of California. Included in this group were scores of men and women who had lived in California before the United States takeover in 1846.

On July 10, 1877, Savage was at San Andreas Ranch near Watsonville interviewing José María Amador, who had served for a number of years as a sergeant at the San Francisco *presidio.* Also present was Lorenzo Asisara, a local Indian who was born at Mission Santa Cruz and had lived most of his life in the region. Savage also interviewed Asisara. The transcript of that interview is embedded in the larger transcript of the Amador interview. In the passage below, as translated and presented by historian Edward Castillo, Asisara tells Savage a story he heard from his father about how the Santa Cruz Indians took revenge on the resident priest, Fr. Andrés Quintana. The broad outlines of Asisara's story are confirmed by other sources. Two years after the incident, a number of Indians were arrested, whipped, and sentenced to hard labor for their part in the conspiracy. All but one of them died before they had completed their sentences.

Asisara's account chronicles one of the most dramatic episodes in the early history of Alta California. Forms of Indian resistance to the Spanish presence were varied, the most common being to simply slip out of the mission or refuse to return at the conclusion of an officially sanctioned leave. Another form of resistance was to refuse to work wholeheartedly or vigorously; frequent whippings for "laziness" and the like indicate that this was a prevalent form of resistance. Other native peoples engaged in the theft of horses, prompting regular military excursions into the interior valleys to track them down.

The killing of missionaries usually occurred in the context of a large-scale attack, as we have seen in Baja California in 1734, San Diego in 1775, and the Colorado River in 1781. But there were other instances in which a group of mission Indians plotted against a specific priest whose behavior they deemed particularly oppressive. The Santa Cruz episode recounted by Asisara was preceded by a similar happening at Mission Santo Tomás in Baja California in 1803, when a group of mission Indians, apparently led by a woman whose Christian name was Bárbara, killed Fr. Eudaldo Succora.

FROM REMINISCENCES OF LORENZO ASISARA

The following story which I shall convey was told to me by my dear father in 1818. He was a neophyte of the Mission of Santa Cruz. He was one of the original founders of that mission. He was an Indian from the *ranchería* of Asar on the Jarro coast, up beyond Santa Cruz. He was one of the first neophytes baptized at the founding, being about twenty years of age. He was called Venancio Asar and was the gardener of the Mission of Santa Cruz.

My father was a witness to the happenings that follow. He was one of the conspirators who planned to kill Father Quintana. When the conspirators were planning to kill Father Quintana, they gathered in the house of Julián the gardener (the one who made the pretense of being ill). The man who worked inside the plaza of the mission, named Donato, was punished by Father Quintana with a whip with wire. With each blow it cut his buttocks. Then the same man, Donato, wanted vengeance. He was the one who organized a gathering of fourteen men, among them the cook and the pages serving the Father. The cook was named Antonio, the eldest page was named Lino, the others were named Vicente and Miguel Antonio. All of them gathered in the house of Julián to plan how they could avoid the cruel punishments of Father Quintana. One man present, Lino, who was more capable and wiser than the others, said, "The first thing we should do today is to see that the Father no longer punishes the people in that manner. We aren't animals. He [Quintana] says in his sermons that God does not command these [punishments], but only examples and doctrine. Tell me now, what shall we do with the Father? We cannot chase him away, nor accuse him before the Judge, because we do not know who commands him to do with us as he does." To this, Andrés, father of Lino the page, answered, "Let's kill the Father without anyone being aware—not the servants, or anyone, except us that are here present." (This Lino was a pure-blooded Indian, but as white as a Spaniard and a man of natural abilities.) And then Julián the gardener said, "What shall we do in order to kill him?" His wife responded, "You, who are always getting sick—only this way can it be possible—think if it is good this way." Lino approved the plan and asked that all present also approve it. "In that case, we shall do it tomorrow night." That was Saturday. It should be noted that the Father wished all the people to gather in the plaza on the following Sunday in order to test the whip that he had made with pieces of wire, to see if it was to his liking.

All of the conspirators present at the meeting concurred that it should be done as Lino had recommended. On the evening of Saturday at about six o'clock [October 12] of 1812, they went to tell the Father that the gardener was dying. The Indians were already posted between two trees on both sides so that they could grab the Father when he passed. The Father arrived at the house of Julián, who pretended to be in agony. The Father helped him, thinking that he was really sick and about to die. When the Father was returning to his house, he passed close to where the Indians were posted. They didn't have the courage to grab him, and they allowed him to pass. The moribund gardener was behind him, but the Father arrived at his house. Within an hour, the wife of Julián arrived [again] to tell the Father that her husband was dying. With this news the Father returned to the orchard, the woman following behind, crying and lamenting. He saw that the sick man was dying. The Father took the man's hand in order to take his pulse. He felt the pulse and could find nothing amiss. The pulse showed there was nothing wrong with Julián. Not knowing what it could be, the Father returned to pray for him. It was night when the Father left. Julián arose and washed away the sacraments (oil) that the Father had administered, and he followed behind to join the others and see what his companions had done. Upon arriving at the place where they were stationed, Lino lifted his head and looked in all directions to see if they were coming out to grab the Father. The Father passed and they didn't take him. The Father arrived at his house.

Later, when the Father was at his table, dining, the conspirators had already gathered at the house of the allegedly sick man to ascertain why they hadn't seized Father Quintana. Julián complained that the Father had placed herbs on his ears, and because of them, now he was really going to die. Then the wife of Julián said, "Yes, you all did not carry through with your promised plans; I am going to accuse you all, and I will not go back to the house." They all answered her, "All right, now, go and speak to the Father." The woman again left to fetch Father Quintana, who was at supper. He got up immediately and went, where he found the supposedly sick man. This time he took with him three pages, two who walked ahead lighting his way with lanterns, and behind him followed his majordomo Lino. The other two were Vicente and Miguel Antonio. The Father arrived at the gardener's house and found him unconscious. He couldn't speak. The Father prayed the last orations without administering the oils and said to the wife, "Now your husband is prepared to live or die. Don't come to look for me again." Then the Father left with his pages, to return to his house. Julián followed him. Arriving at the place where the two trees were (since the Father was not paying attention to his surroundings, but only the path in front of him), Lino grabbed him from behind, saying these words: "Stop here, Father, you must speak for a moment." When the other two pages who carried the lanterns turned around and saw the other men come out to attack the Father, they fled with their lanterns. The Father said to Lino, "Oh, my son, what are you going to do to me?" Lino answered, "Your assassins will tell you."

"What have I done to you children for which you would kill me?"

"Because you have made a horsewhip tipped with iron," Andrés answered him. Then the Father replied, "Oh, children, leave me, so that I can go from here now, at this moment." Andrés asked him why he had made this horsewhip. Quintana said that it was only for transgressors. Then someone shouted, "Well, you are in the hands of those evil ones, make your peace with God." Many of those present (seeing the Father in his affliction) cried and pitied his fate, but could do nothing to help him, because they were themselves compromised. He pleaded much, promising to leave the mission immediately if they would only let him.

"Now you won't be going to any part of the earth from here, Father, you are going to heaven." This was the last plea of the Father. Some of them, not having been able to lay hands on the Father, reprimanded the others because they talked too much, demanding that they kill him immediately. They then covered the Father's mouth with his own cape to strangle him. They had his arms tightly secured. After the Father had been strangled, [they did not beat him but] took a testicle so that it would not be obvious that he had been attacked, and in a moment Father expired. Then Lino and the others took him to his house and put him in his bed.

When the two little pages, Vicente and Miguel Antonio, arrived at the house, the former wanted to tell the guard, but the others dissuaded him by saying, "No, the soldiers will also kill your mother, father, all of the others, and you, yourself, and me. Let them, the conspirators, do what they want." The two hid themselves. After the Indians had put the Father in his bed, Lino looked for the two pages, and he found them hidden. They undressed the body of Father Quintana and placed him in the bed as if he were going to sleep. All of the conspirators, including Julián's wife, were present. Andrés asked Lino for the keys to the storeroom. He handed them over, saying, "What do you want?" And they said silver and beads. Among the group there were three Indians from the Santa Clara Mission. These proposed that they investigate to see how much money there was. Lino opened the box and showed them the accumulated gold and silver. The three Indians from Santa Clara took as much as they could carry to their mission. (I don't know what they have done with that money.) The others took their portions as they saw fit.

Then they asked for the keys to the convent, or nunnery [women's dormitory]. Lino gave the keys to the *jayunte,* or barracks of the single men, to one of them in order to free the men and gather them together, below in the orchard, with the unmarried women. They gathered in the orchard so that neither the people in the plaza, nor in the *ranchería,* nor in the guardhouse would hear them. The single men left and without a sound gathered in the orchard at the same place where the Father was assassinated. There was a man there cautioning them not to make any noise, that they were going to have a good time. After a short time the young unmarried women arrived in order to spend the night there. The young people of both sexes got together and had their pleasure. At midnight Lino, being in the Father's living room with one of the girls from the single women's dormitory, entered the Father's room in order to see if he was really dead. He found him reviving. He was already on the point of arising. Lino went to look for his accomplices to tell them that the Father was coming to. The Indians returned, and they crushed the Father's other testicle. This last act put an end to the life of Father Quintana. Donato, the one who had been whipped, walked around the room with the plural results of his operation in hand, saying, "I shall bury these in the outdoor privy."

Donato told Lino that they should close the treasure chest: "Close the trunk with the colored silver (that is the name that the Indians gave to gold), and let's see where we shall bury it." The eight men carried it down to the orchard and buried it secretly, without the others knowing.

At about two o'clock in the morning, the young girls returned to their convent and the single men to their *jayunte,* without making any noise. The assassins gathered once more after everything had occurred, in order to hear the plans of Lino and Donato. Some wanted to flee, and others asked, "What for? No one except us knows." Lino asked them what they wanted to take to their houses—sugar, *panocha,* honey, or any other things—and suggested that they lie down to sleep for a while. Finally everything was ready. Donato proposed to return to where the Father was, to check on him. They found him not only lifeless, but completely cold and stiff. Lino then showed them the new whip that the Father was planning to use for the first time the next day, assuring them that he (Father Quintana) would not use it now. He sent them to their houses to rest, remaining in the house with the keys. He asked them to be very careful. He arranged the room and the Bible in the manner in which the Father was accustomed to doing before retiring, telling them that he was not going to toll the bells in the morning until the majordomo and corporal of the guard came and he had talked to them. All went through the orchard very silently.

This same morning (Sunday), the bells should have been rung at about eight o'clock. At that hour the people from the *Villa de* Branciforte began to arrive in order to attend the Mass. The majordomo, Carlos Castro, saw that the bells were not being rung and went to Lino, who was the first assistant of the Father, to ask why the Father had not ordered him (to toll the bells). Lino was in the outer room feigning innocence and answered the majordomo that he couldn't tell him anything about the Father because he was still inside, sleeping or praying, and that the majordomo should wait until he should speak to him first. The majordomo returned home. Soon the corporal of the guard arrived, and Lino told him the same thing he had told the majordomo. The majordomo returned to join in the conversation. They decided to wait a little while longer. Finally, Lino told them that in their presence he would knock on the door of the room, observing, "If he is angry with me, you will stand up for me." And so he did, calling to the Father. As he didn't hear noise inside, the majordomo and corporal asked Lino to knock again, but he refused. They then left, charging him with calling the Father again, because the hour was growing late. All of the servants were busy at their jobs, as always, in order not to cause any suspicion. The majordomo returned after ten o'clock and asked Lino to call the Father to see what was wrong. Lino, with the keys in his pocket, knocked at the door. Finally the majordomo insisted that Lino enter the room, but Lino refused. At this moment, the corporal, old Nazario Galindo, arrived. Lino (although he had the key to the door in his pocket) said, "Well, I am going to see if I can get the door open," and he pretended to look for a key to open the door. He returned with a ring of keys, but he didn't find one that opened the lock. The majordomo and the corporal left to talk to some men who were there. Later, Lino took the key that opened the door, saying that it was for the kitchen. He opened another door that opened into the plaza (the key opened three doors), and through there he entered. Then he opened the main door from inside, in front of which the others waited. Lino came out screaming and crying and carrying on in an uncontrolled manner, saying that the Father was dead. They asked him if he was certain, and he responded, "As this light that illuminates us. By God, I'm going to toll the bells." The three entered, the corporal, the majordomo, and Lino. He didn't allow anyone else to enter. The corporal and the majordomo and the other people wrote to the other missions and to Monterey to Father Marcelino Marquínez.* (This Marquínez was an expert horseman and a good friend.) The poor elderly neophytes, and many other Indians who never suspected that the Father was killed, thought he had died suddenly. They cried bitterly. Lino was roaring inside the Father's house like a bear.

The Fathers from Santa Clara and from other missions came, and they held the Father's funeral, all believing that he had died a natural death, but not before examining the corpse in the entrance room and opening the stomach in order to be certain that the Father had not been poisoned. Officials, sergeants, and many others participated in these acts, but nothing was discovered. Finally, by chance, one of those present noted that the testicles were missing, and they were convinced that this had been the cause of death. Through modesty they did not reveal the fact, and buried the body with everyone convinced that the death had been a natural one.

A number of years after the death, Emiliana, the wife of Lino, and María Tata, the wife of the cook Antonio, became mutually jealous. They were both seamstresses and they were at work. This was around August, at the time of the lentil harvest. Carlos Castro was with his men, working in the

---

* Fr. Marcelino Marquínez was the other priest stationed at Santa Cruz. He was at Monterey receiving medical treatment when Quintana was killed.

cornfields. Shortly before eleven o'clock he returned to his house for the meal. He understood the language of the Indians. Returning from the cornfields, he passed behind one of the plaza walls near where these women were sewing and heard one tell the other that she was secretly eating *panocha*. Castro stopped and heard the second woman reply to the first, "How is it that you have so much money?" The first replied, "You also have it, because your husband killed the Father." Then the second accused the husband of the first woman of the same crime. The war of words continued, and Castro was convinced that Father Quintana had been assassinated, and he went to tell Father Ramón Olbes, who was the missionary at Santa Cruz, what he had heard. Father Ramón went to tell Father Marquínez. The latter sent one of his pages to the orchard to warn Julián and his accomplices that they were going to be caught. At noon, at about the time of the midday meal, Father Olbes spoke to Lino and asked him to send for his wife to come there to cut some pieces of cloth. Emiliana arrived, and Father Olbes placed her in a room where there was clothing and gave her some scissors with which to cut some pieces, telling her, "you will eat here." Then he sent a page to bring María Tata to take some dirty clothing out of the church to wash. The majordomo was observing the maneuverings of the Father. He made María Tata stay to eat there. He placed her in another room to cut some suits for the pages. The majordomo and the two Fathers went to eat. After the meal, and when the two women had also eaten, Father Olbes said to Emiliana, "Do you know who eats a lot of white sugar?" She answered that it was María Tata, "because her husband had killed Father Quintana." The Father made her return to the room and called for María Tata. The Father asked her, "Tell me if you know who it was that killed Father Quintana, tell me the truth so that nothing will happen to you." Lino and Antonio often took their meal in the kitchen. María Tata replied, "Lino, Father." Father Olbes then sent the women to their houses to rest, offering them a present. Then the Father sent for the corporal, Nazario Galindo, to arrest the assassins. They began with the orchard workers and the cook, without telling them why they were under arrest. Antonio was the first prisoner. They put him in jail and asked him who his accomplice was. He said who his accomplice was, and the man was arrested, and they asked each one the name of their respective accomplices. In this way they were all arrested, except Lino, who was looked upon as a valiant man of great strength. He was taken through the deceit of his own *compadre* Carlos Castro, who handed him a knife to trim some black and white mares, in order to make a hackamore for the animal of the Father. Suspiciously, Lino said to Castro, *"Compadre,* why are you deceiving me? I know that you are going to arrest me." There were already two soldiers hidden behind the corral. "Here, take your knife, *compadre,* that which I thought is already done. I am going to pay for it—and if I had wanted to, I could have finished off the soldiers, the majordomos, and any others that might have been around on the same night that I killed the Father."

The result of all this was that the accused were sent to San Francisco, and among them was my father. There they were judged, and those who killed the Father were sentenced to receive a *novenano* (nine days in succession) of fifty lashes for each one, and to serve in public works at San Diego. The rest, including my father, were freed because they had served as witnesses, and it was not proven that they had taken part in the assassination.

All returned, after many years, to their mission.

The Spanish Fathers were very cruel toward the Indians. They abused them very much. They had bad food, bad clothing, and they made them work like slaves. I also was subject to that cruel life. The Fathers did not practice what they preached in the pulpit. The same Father Olbes was once stoned by the Indians for all his cruelties.

San Andrés Ranch/Santa Cruz
Jurisdiction of Watsonville
July 10, 1877
Lorenzo Asisara (rubric)

1815

Captivity at Mission San Fernando

Vassili Petrovitch Tarakanoff

The perceived threat of Russian expansion along the Pacific coast of North America had been one of the prime motives for Spain's expansion into Alta California in 1769. After the explorations of Vitus Bering in the northern Pacific in the 1740s, a number of Russian companies had sent expeditions into the area to hunt seals and sea otters, whose furs were an especially valuable component of the developing China trade. At the end of the eighteenth century, the Russian American Company was the sole company authorized by the Russian government to hunt and trade in North America. Using the expertise of the native people of the Aleutians and Kodiak Island, the company expanded its sea otter operations and established a base on the mainland at New Archangel (Sitka) in 1799.

Problems with the long voyages required to bring supplies from home forced the company to look to Spanish California for food. In 1806, an expedition headed by Nikolai Rezanov journeyed to San Francisco. He managed to gain the favor of the son of the *presidio* commander, Luis Antonio Argüello, and Luis Antonio's sister Concepción, and he returned to New Archangel with food supplies. This encouraged the company to think about establishing its own base in Alta California. After examining and then rejecting a location at Bodega Bay as being too vulnerable in case of Spanish naval attacks, the company established a post farther north. This became known as Fort Ross. It was constructed from timber by about twenty-five Russians and eighty Aleuts. The design was along the lines of the New Archangel outpost.

The fort soon became a base for sea otter expeditions all along the northern California coast, but it never became the source of food for Alaska that the company had envisioned. The coastal fog inhibited the growth of crops, although some private ranches a bit farther inland had better yields. Stock raising proved to be more consistently profitable, and wool and hide and tallow products were eventually shipped to Alaska. A lively though illegal trade developed between the Russians and the northern Spanish settlements around the San Francisco *presidio,* as farm implements and household goods manufactured at the fort were exchanged for grain, other food products, and permission to hunt for sea otters.

For the Russians, the timing of their arrival in California was fortuitous. The Napoleonic Wars preoccupied Spain, and in New Spain, on September 16, 1810, Fr. Miguel Hidalgo y Costilla sparked an insurgency against the colonial authorities with a fiery speech in his church in Dolores (now Dolores Hidalgo, about two hundred miles northwest of Mexico City) that initiated a decade of turbulence and instability. Hidalgo's troops quickly captured a number of cities north of the capital. When he was captured and executed in 1811, the leadership of the insurgency passed to José María Morelos. He was executed in 1815, and the next five years saw intermittent but persistent guerrilla fighting. As a result of this warfare, the colonial officials had more urgent things to worry about than California. The supply ships from San Blas to Alta California virtually ceased after 1810, and foreign vessels, generally English, American, or Russian, gradually filled the void. Trading with foreigners remained technically illegal, but it became necessary if any supplies were to be purchased. Governor Arrillaga allowed Luis Antonio Argüello to engage in fairly regular trade with Fort Ross. When Arrillaga died in 1814, he was succeeded by Pablo Vicente de Solá, a Basque who had served in the royal army of New Spain since 1796. Solá at first tried to compel Argüello to observe the Spanish trading laws, but he quickly realized the practical necessity of acquiescing, and the commerce continued. The Russians also continued to be welcomed in Baja California, where José Darío Argüello succeeded Felipe Goycoechea in 1815 and served until 1822.

It was the sea otter trade that brought the Russians into California in the first place, and they engaged in it continually. In the mid-1810s a number of Russian hunters were captured by the Spanish along the central California coast. The following account was provided to Hubert Howe Bancroft by Ivan Petroff, who did research in Alaska for Bancroft's *History of California.* Ascribed to Vassili Petrovitch Tarakanoff, a Russian hunter who worked for the Russian-American Company, it represents a summary of these captivity experiences.

FROM REMINISCENCES OF VASSILI PETROVITCH TARAKANOFF

We still kept on to the southward, and one day the skipper sent two boats ashore with some sailors, myself, and eleven Aleuts, to get some fresh meat if we could. We saw some cattle grazing on the hills, but before any of us could reach the place, we found ourselves surrounded by soldiers on horseback, and our sailors ran back to the boats and pushed off without waiting for us or trying to rescue us. The soldiers, who were Spaniards, spoke to us very roughly in their own language, shaking their fists at us, flourishing long knives, and nearly frightening the Aleuts to death. They then tied us all together with ropes made of rawhide and took us away a long distance, more than two days' travel, resting at night but keeping us tied hand and foot. At last we came to a place with some grand houses and a Spanish church, and at that place were nearly a thousand natives, or *Indios* as the Spaniards called them, living in great misery.

I saw many soldiers with lances and always mounted on horseback. I and the Aleuts were put into a big house without windows, and our feet were kept tied. Some of the *Indios* brought us some maize and one melon, and that was all we had to eat for two days. Then an officer or commander of some kind came to the place, and we were taken before him. He asked many questions in Spanish, but we could not understand, and he could not speak a word of our language. At last he ordered the ropes taken off our feet, but the rawhide had cut into our feet so that we could not walk. After a few days our ankles healed, and the Spaniards made us work in the field with the *Indios*. Soldiers and some men who I found out to be priests watched us all the time, and whoever did not work to suit them was beaten.

One of the Aleuts became very sick, and the Spaniards thought he was going to die. The priest came every day to see him, but he gave no medicine and only wanted him to kiss a cross. He also tried to make the man cross himself in a different way from the manner in which he had been taught by our Orthodox missionary. The sick man would not do it, and the priest scolded very much, but the man recovered.

After a time, most of us got to understand some of the Spanish words, and one day a great officer with many soldiers came to the place which the Spaniards called a mission, and he and the priests talked about me and the Aleuts. The officer seemed to wish to release us or take us away from the priests. I heard the word the Spaniards use for "Russian" and I walked up to the party and pointed to my breast and said, "I am a Russian," but the priests shouted, *"No, Indios, Indios,"* and we were all sent out to the field.

On that evening, one priest told me that unless I kissed his cross and crossed myself in his way I would be punished in this world and the other. I said nothing, but I was sick at heart.

Vassili, one of the Aleuts, came to me one night and said, "Our people have all gone away and forgotten us—we shall never see them anymore. Let us do like the natives, the *Indios,* do. Most of them have their wives—we can take wives from among them and perhaps the Spaniards will treat us better."

I said, "You must not do that. If you do that, the Spaniards will surely call you their own, and they will make you pray in their church."

Vassili said he did not care; he would just as soon cross himself one way as another, and if he only had a wife he would feel better and would try to be as happy as the *Indios* were. I told him that it would be a sin to do that, as he had a wife at home on Ounalaska, but he thought that his wife must think that he was dead anyhow, and if they were ever to go to heaven, they could all live together. All my remonstrances went for nothing, though I told him he could never go to heaven if he left the Orthodox Church. He went to one of the chiefs of the natives, who gave him a young girl, and on the next Sunday one of the priests married them, and Vassili went to live among the natives, away from us.

The priests told us we might all do the same, but I advised the Aleuts not to do it. In course of time, however, four more followed Vassili's example. Two of them had left wives at home; two on Ounalaska Island, one at Ounga, and one at Novo Arkhangelsk [Sitka].

At one time some of the *Indios* became dissatisfied, and overnight they all left, except our men who were living among them. The *Indios* had been away several days when a great number of soldiers came to the mission, and they and some of the priests went out and stayed away many, many days, and when they came back they brought most of the natives. They were all bound with rawhide ropes, and some were bleeding from wounds, and some children were tied to their mothers.

The next day we saw some terrible things.

Some of the runaway men were tied on sticks and beaten with straps. One chief was taken out to the open field, and a young calf which had just died was skinned, and the chief was sewn into the skin while it was yet warm. He was kept tied to a stake all day, but he died soon, and they kept his corpse tied up. The Spaniards must have put some poison on the calfskin that killed the man.

After that time the Spaniards treated us all much worse. Our Aleuts who had taken wives had not gone with the *Indios,* but that made no difference—they were treated just the same.

The Spaniards used wooden plows to plow the fields, and when I told them that I could make iron plowshares, they took me to a forge they had at the mission, but they had scarcely any tools and no iron but what was in use, and the priest got very angry and sent me to the fields again.

When I had been with the Spaniards about a year, they received new supplies and some carpenters' tools, and I and one of the Aleuts were set to work making boxes and chests and some beds and chairs. We also made some benches for the church. From that time I worked in the field no more and was treated somewhat better.

1818
The Attack on Monterey
by Hipólito Bouchard

PABLO VICENTE DE SOLÁ

The only time during the Spanish period when Alta California was actually attacked by a hostile power from the sea occurred during Solá's tenure as governor. In 1818, a French privateer under the flag of the United Provinces of the Río de la Plata (Argentina) appeared off the coast after a journey around the world. Commanding a ship named the *Argentina,* Hipólito Bouchard had harassed Spanish ships in the Philippines and then traveled to Hawaii, where he obtained another ship, the *Santa Rosa,* a Buenos Aires privateer whose crew had mutinied. He put it under the command of Peter Corney, an Englishman who had worked for a British trading company but was stranded in Hawaii after his ship was sold there. The two ships headed for California together to harass Spanish interests and to encourage Alta California to join the revolution against Spain that was spreading throughout South America.

Bouchard arrived in Monterey Bay on November 20, 1818, and after some artillery exchanges and negotiations in the bay, he landed near Point Pinos, marched overland to Monterey, and took the *presidio* on November 24. The defenders, led by Governor Solá, retreated to the Rancho del Rey, near Salinas. Bouchard remained at Monterey for five days, repairing his vessels and destroying the fort. He departed on November 29. He then headed down the coast and stopped at Refugio, where he skirmished with troops from the Santa Bárbara *presidio.* After a prisoner exchange at Santa Bárbara, he sailed to San Juan Capistrano, where his troops looted the mission. He then went to the Isla de Cedros, off Baja California, blockaded San Blas, and raided Spanish shipping off Central America, ending his journey at Valparaíso in Chile. He later served in South America under José de San Martín and was rewarded with land in Peru. He settled there and was killed by one of his slaves in 1837.

The following selection is from the report Solá wrote to the viceroy after Bouchard departed. His report is inevitably defensive, for he was unable to prevent his capital city from being occupied and burned. Solá's plaintive remarks ("But what could this officer [José Estrada] do, without cannons, to prevent the landing?" and "What could I do, Your Excellency, in such a situation?") underscored the military weakness of this Spanish outpost. This situation would continue when Alta California became a part of the independent Mexican nation.

FROM A LETTER BY PABLO VICENTE DE SOLÁ

To His Excellency Viceroy of New Spain, Don Juan Ruiz de Apodaca
From the Señor Governor of Alta California, Don Pablo Vicente de Solá

Excellency: I am presenting to the superior knowledge of Your Excellency the news about what happened in the *presidio* of Monterey with two frigates belonging to the rebels from Buenos Aires.

On November 20, the lookout, who is always on duty at Point Pinos, reported sighting two vessels. I immediately issued orders to all the settlers and militiamen from around fifteen miles to gather at the battery site. This has been my custom since I took command of this province. With the *presidio* company troops and four veteran artillerymen, I gathered forty men in total; twenty-five were from the *presidio* company, four were the artillerymen, and eleven were militiamen. After reminding them of their duties and exhorting them to fulfill their obligations, I sent them to the battery under the command of the Second Lieutenant of Artillery Don Manuel Gómez, and the Ensign of the *presidio* company, Don José Estrada. One of the frigates anchored at eleven at night. From the battery we asked where they were coming from, the identity of the vessel, and other such questions, but they answered in English, which nobody could understand. We insisted that they answer our questions and launch a boat to bring ashore the papers or passports with which they were navigating. Finally we could understand that they were in the process of mooring the ship, and since the night was dark, in the morning they would send a boat ashore with the requested papers.

But imagine my surprise, Your Excellency, when the next morning, instead of launching the boat, she started firing at the battery with cannonballs

Hipólito Bouchard. Courtesy of the City of Monterey Colton Hall Museum Collection.

and shrapnel. This was returned in kind by our battery, and after two hours of stubborn combat by both sides, the enemy hauled down their flag, begging the battery not to fire anymore, as they were surrendering. Just before hauling down the flag, they launched six boats in the water. After the flag was hauled down, we noticed many people embarking in the boats and heading toward the other frigate, located on the opposite coast.

The frigate that anchored [near the battery], called the *Santa Rosa*, carried twenty-eight cannons of substantial caliber, while the battery of the *presidio* had eight cannons of eight and six inches. The battery guns were fired by the two artillerymen and their ensign in such a vigorous and accurate manner that they inflicted much damage to the frigate. In this they were helped by the soldiers of the *presidio* company, who, during the attack, remained in their posts with remarkable calm in spite of the many cannonballs falling on it.

As soon as the *Santa Rosa*'s flag was hauled down, she was ordered to send her commander ashore, but the answer was that he had escaped with most people to the other frigate, called *Argentina,* which carried thirty-eight cannons. Her commander was Hipólito Bouchard, a Frenchman with the title of General who was at the head of both ships. I ordered that whoever was now commanding the frigate [*Santa Rosa*] should come ashore, otherwise the firing would continue. The second in command, an American, and two sailors, one from Buenos Aires and the other from Guinea, came ashore. As I was unable to get anything out of them other than lies and frivolous excuses, I had them put in the guardhouse. At the same time, the large frigate was approaching at full speed, so I gave the orders to receive her. However, she anchored at a point where she could not be harmed by our battery. From there, Bouchard sent me a note with one of his officers carrying a flag of truce, suggesting that I surrender the entire province. To this I answered that the Governor of this province looked with due contempt on everything said in that note: that the great Monarch whom he was serving entrusted to his authority the preservation of the province to remain under his domain; that, since he was threatening with the use of his force, I would with mine make him know the honor and firmness with which I was ready to repel him; and that as long as there remained a man alive in this province, he would not succeed in his intent, because all the inhabitants were loyal and loving servants of the King, and they would spill their last drop of blood in his service.

Despite a heavy rain, the troops remained alert at their post all night. At eight in the morning it was noticed that the large frigate was moving against the battery. At the same time, nine boats full of people, four with a small cannon each, were heading toward Point Potreros. I soon realized, Your Excellency, that the intent of the enemy was to disembark in Point Potreros and fire on the battery. I ordered Ensign Don José Estrada, along with the twenty-five men from his company, to observe the boats. But what could this officer do, without cannons, to prevent the landing? They disembarked by placing the boats on the beach near each other to protect the landing. Receiving instant updates about the enemy movements, I learned that they had disembarked with four hundred men and four cannons. Seeing at the same time the two enemy vessels dueling with our battery, what could I do, Your Excellency, in such a situation? I immediately ordered Ensign Estrada to fall back to the battery, and if he had to retreat farther, to spike all cannons, remove all gunpowder, and blow the little that would remain. One cannon was placed on a cart and I ordered it to be taken away. As the enemy saw few of our troops where they landed, they marched in a column toward the battery, using a path where they could not be harmed. Assessing the recklessness of waiting for them, the officers carried out my orders to spike the cannons and dispose of the rest, and then retreated to the *presidio,* where I was located. From there some resistance was offered, although it was fruitless because of the large enemy numbers. Therefore, I retreated with the ammunition and troops to *Rancho Real Hacienda,* thirteen miles from the *presidio.* I was able to save two boxes of gunpowder, six thousand rifle cartridges, one cannon of gauge two, and the paper archives of the province. But first I ordered the families of the troops and the few neighboring settlers to retreat to Mission Soledad.

It is known from the declarations of the second commander [of the *Santa Rosa*] and his two companions that on the day of the battle with the frigate *Santa Rosa,* she suffered five dead and a major number of wounded. The frigate was badly battered, and had there been more artillerymen, useful cannons, and sufficient ammunition, she would have been sunk, for it was not possible to board her for lack of my people and small boats. In spite of the active fire of two hours, no men were lost on our side, which can almost be considered a miracle.

After doing the wicked things the rebels do by custom, like relieving their rage by shooting the animals they found because they could not do that with people, they stole whatever they found useful in the midst of the poverty in which these inhabitants live. They left on November 25, at night. But first they set the *presidio* on fire, reducing to ashes the row of houses facing north and three more houses facing south. The construction is all of adobe, with walls sixteen to nineteen feet high and a wooden skeleton on top to hold the tiles, which all collapsed as the wood burned. Likewise, they set afire and ruined the house of the artillerymen at the battery, as well as the wooden platform on top of which the cannons were resting. We could only save two cannons in working conditions: one of gauge six and the other of gauge two. They took two iron cannons of gauge eight and destroyed the remaining ones. Three days after leaving, they cast anchor at the *Rancho del Refugio,* in the jurisdiction of Santa Bárbara at a distance of twenty-three miles from it. The ranch is located four hundred and sixty yards from the beach, and they made the same landing as at Monterey. As they did not find anybody because the inhabitants had retreated to the nearby Mission Santa Inés, they removed all the goods they could, set the ranch houses afire, and stole some seeds. They also killed cattle, since they ran out of time to remove them all. At this place we seized three of their men. One was a lieutenant of American nationality named Guillermo Tela.

From here, they set sail on the second day and anchored the next day with a flag of truce in the bay of the *presidio* of Santa Bárbara. They agreed to an exchange of prisoners with the Commandant, Captain Don José de la Guerra [y Noriega], even though they did not have any prisoners, other than a peasant from Monterey who got drunk the day they departed and whom they took aboard. They were boasting that this man was a prisoner. They set sail on the second day of their arrival, having first promised to Captain de la Guerra not to stop at any other point of the coast. This promise they did not fulfill; after two days they anchored again by the beach of San Pedro, where they left the next day, and then again they stopped at the anchorage of the mission of San Juan Capistrano. Here they did not find anybody but the Ensign, Don Santiago Argüello, in command of thirty soldiers from the *presidio* of San Diego who, in anticipation, I had sent there, fearful about the damage the enemy could cause. The enemy came ashore with four hundred men and with the same cannons [as at Monterey]. They sent the attached note to the majordomo of the mission. It was received by Officer Argüello, who answered that he did not have anything but gunpowder and bullets to give them. Having advanced toward the mission, the rebels burned some wood and straw houses of neophytes and then returned aboard. As a result of my orders to the Commandant of the *presidio* of Santa Bárbara, Captain Don José de la Guerra, the next day twenty-five soldiers and twenty-nine settlers arrived. An enemy drummer with his box and three soldiers with their rifles, bayonets, and cartridge belts came forward to ask for forgiveness; they told Officer Argüello that they came in those ships against their will and were submitting themselves to the mercy of the King. The next day, Captain de la Guerra arrived there with thirty men. He challenged the enemy to come ashore, but instead, the same night, they weighed anchor, and the next morning they were nowhere to be seen.

I must bring to the attention of Your Excellency the enormous hardships suffered by the worthy and loyal troops in such long marches with critical time constraints, crossing large rivers with the desire to fight the enemy, but the places where the enemy anchored were so far away from one another that as soon as we got a group together to face them, even if their numbers were half those of the enemy, they would immediately retreat to their ship and sail away. The distance between the first and second inlet or port where they anchored is 218 miles, second to third 23 miles, third to fourth 120 miles, and from the fourth to the last stop is 73 miles. Because of these distances, it was impossible for the troops that gathered at the first stop to reach [the second stop] before they did, even though I had lookouts posted all along the coast who were providing me with the necessary news.

In the *presidio* fire we lost some two thousand *pesos* in soap, tallow, butter, corn, beans, blankets, cloth, rice, and some other things of little value belonging to our soldiers. I lost all my furniture and other things that I need very much.

May God our Lord keep the important life of Your Excellency for many years, which I wish for the good of this province.

Pablo Vicente de Solá
Monterey
December 12, 1818

1819
A Bear Hunt

Juan Bautista Alvarado

At the time of Bouchard's attack, future governor Juan Bautista Alvarado was a boy of nine living at the Monterey *presidio* with his grandparents, Sergeant Ignacio Vallejo and María Lugo de Vallejo. They were evacuated to Mission San Juan Bautista. Ignacio María Ortega, owner of nearby Rancho San Ysidro, offered to let Alvarado and his mother and stepfather stay with him. Ortega, the son of Portolá expedition veteran José Francisco Ortega, had been granted this *rancho* by Arrillaga in 1808. Later in his life, Alvarado recalled a bear hunt he experienced during that time.

From the Reminiscences of Juan Bautista Alvarado

My stepfather was a famous hunter and had good friends in the countryside, and for this reason he had two good shotguns of the kind that were then in use. Don Ignacio Ortega, one of the ranchers who lived near Mission San Juan Bautista, invited him to come to his ranch for some time to hunt bears, which were very abundant and which were doing a great deal of damage to his livestock; and he offered him food and lodging for his family. My stepfather considered this to be a very profitable deal; and when he consulted my mother and me, it was jointly decided to accept Don Ignacio's invitation, on the condition that the skins of the bears would belong to us and that Don Ignacio would supply the old mares that we would need as bait for those beasts. These conditions were accepted by the rancher, who immediately sent some oxcarts to take us to his ranch. With this help we undertook the trip, carrying along our household furniture, which we had salvaged in the stampede from Monterey caused by Commander Bouchard.

As for me, I was delighted to become an apprentice rancher, because up to then I did not know how to ride a horse or do farm work; and bear hunting also appealed to me, since the skins were sold for six to ten *pesos* each, depending on their quality, to the captains of the ships that brought the annual accounts. They took them to the coast of Mexico, where they sold them at a great profit because they were used to decorate saddles and riding chaps, for which the Mexicans prepared them so as to make them very black and very pliable.

We reached Don Ignacio Ortega's ranch, which was called San Ysidro. This old man had a family, horses, and much other livestock, and he gave us a lodging suitable for bear hunters....

On the days when the rain did not keep him at home, my stepfather used to scout the countryside to choose the best hunting posts, so that the hunt could begin as soon as the worst of the winter was over. He had a very trustworthy horse that he called Coyote and that he always took on all his hunting expeditions. It was so used to gunfire that he could shoot over any part of its body without its making the slightest movement. He always kept it in the house and was so concerned about its fodder and water that he would not eat until Coyote had eaten. He gave it sugar candy, tortillas, and other food from the kitchen; and so this animal always stayed close to the house, and if it did wander, it would only be a little way. My stepfather began by having me mount Coyote, and then he took one of the ranch horses and told me that he would lead me to the place where he was to begin the hunt.

We reached the edge of a wood, about a league from our house, where there stood a sturdy live oak all by itself; and my stepfather told me, "This is the starting point for our operations. I have already made a wattle, or platform of woven twigs and branches, in this tree. When I decide on the right days, you will bring me out here, leave me, and then go back home; and at a set time, you will come for me again, because the bears usually come out of their lairs at nightfall, so that there is no point in waiting for them once it gets very late. The wattle has been set on two branches of the tree, and the palisade has been firmly lashed on. I will have to spend whatever time is necessary on the platform with my two guns, and the bait for the bears has to be down below. That way I shoot from very close to the animal, so that my shots hit right by the foreleg and enter the heart. Just the same, when you come to take me home, do not come up close to the tree.

You will whistle to me from a distance, and I will answer you; and only if I do can you come as close as you like."

All these instructions, together with those he gave me at home, taught me what I had to do in this bearish enterprise. We returned home very late, and my mother asked me what I thought of the bear business; and I told her that I already had all my instructions and that I was determined to go ahead with it, since this business was lucrative and was going to make some money for us to take back to Monterey....

Early in February we began our hunting operations; and so my stepfather spent the day cleaning his guns and preparing the ammunition, and I saw to it that Coyote was well saddled and fed. Don Ignacio had a mare taken out and killed, according to my stepfather's instructions, beneath the platform in the tree. Everything was well prepared. We set out at sundown, with my stepfather in the saddle and me behind him; and he told me once again, as he had before, how I was to come for him at midnight, and how, before coming up to the tree, I was to whistle according to his instructions and then wait for his reply. My stepfather climbed up to his platform, which I would say was no more than eight feet above the ground; and I went home to return at the time agreed on. He had chosen the second quarter of the moon so that I could have good light in which to get used to night riding.

Although at my age it was difficult to undertake so unaccustomed a chore, I got up at midnight to fetch my stepfather, because I was anxious to know the results of the first night's hunting; and so I started off on Coyote at a full gallop. Before reaching the tree I whistled as agreed, and he answered me; and hearing that, I pushed on as much as I could, because the horse balked at going up to the tree, as if something were holding it back.

My stepfather climbed down and came straight toward me, and I asked him, "How is our business doing?"

He answered me, "Just fine. I have killed three very big bears, the kind that do so much damage attacking Don Ignacio's cattle. Let's go now, and we will come back tomorrow to skin them."

The next day we took our knives and went to skin the bears. Don Ignacio went with us and was greatly pleased with the success of the first night's hunt, because he could tell that the dead bears were some of the old ones that hunted down and destroyed his cattle. My stepfather told me that the skinning had to be done without detaching the claws from the hides, because this increased the value of the skins when the Mexicans made their chaps, letting the natural claws of the bearskin hang down from the bottom part of those chaps. Once we had stripped the bears, we laid the skins on a sledge of green boughs; and with Coyote pulling the sledge, we took them to our house. Then we immediately washed them very well with water in order to get rid of all the ticks and other creatures that might be on them, and we stretched them on a square wooden frame to keep them good and clean.

My stepfather told Don Ignacio that on that night he would not go to the platform but would let the bears come and eat the whole mare without the least interference, so that they would grow confident (this he called baiting the bears); but that the next day he should put out another mare in order to continue the hunt. In the course of the month of February, and following this strategy, my stepfather killed twenty-five bears in that first place and when he saw that he had to find another location because the bears were not coming any more, he chose a new spot some two miles from the ranch houses. I was delighted with the building of this second platform because it was closer to home, and so my nocturnal voyages would be shorter; but at any rate, patience was the word if we were to keep making money, and so I decided to work harder and more diligently.

In this second hunting post I proposed to my stepfather that I go with him to the blind to see how he killed the bears; and he answered me, "You will have to be very calm and brave to do that, because you have no idea what it is like in these places the first time you do it. Bears are very cautious,

A bear chained to a tree near New Almaden in the late 1840s or early 1850s, sketched by Fritz Wikersheim. Courtesy of The Bancroft Library, University of California, Berkeley.

and they have a very sharp sense of smell and hearing, and they observe everything very carefully before coming up to the bait. When the bear draws near, you have to keep absolutely still, because at the slightest suspicion of danger he will run off and not come back, even if that means going hungry."

After telling me these things and giving me due warning, my stepfather agreed to take me with him to the blind; and we climbed up into the tree, asking Julián Cantúa to bring Coyote at midnight to take us home. I had along a blanket which my mother had given me to wrap myself in, because it was very cold.

After night had fallen, my stepfather said to me, "There comes a bear." As I said before, this platform, like the earlier one, was probably no more than eight feet above the dead mare; and looking at the way it was made, I thought the bear could smash it with one blow of his paw. This thought was very vivid in me as I saw that beast draw near the tree, and right away my whole body began to shake with an uncontrollable fear.

My stepfather touched me with his hand and in a very low voice told me, "Keep still." But I could not help it; panic had seized me, and my fear grew as the bear drew nearer; and as a result, the branches supporting our blind were moving in a way the bear could clearly hear, just as my stepfather had told me. The bear seemed to be coming up with a good deal of suspicion, because he stopped several times, which showed that he suspected danger in the place where the dead mare, the bait, was lying. The bear stopped some twenty paces from us because the leaves of the tree on which we were sitting kept moving with the trembling of my body. He moved in circles around the tree, and in my fear I came to believe that he was looking for a way to attack us on the tree and preparing to climb up the trunk of the oak. My stepfather did not for a moment stop watching these movements; and at last, the bear withdrew without coming to eat any of the bait, and my stepfather said to me, "We have lost a fine skin."

Very soon after this a female bear began to draw near us with two little cubs; and my stepfather told me, "This female is going to replace what we have lost with the male. She is coming with her hungry cubs and will not pass up a chance to eat or take notice of any danger." To be sure, as soon as the bear came close to the bait and the cubs smelled the dead mare, they moved ahead of their mother to start eating; and, either because she was as hungry as her cubs or because she saw that they met with no obstacle, she advanced to the spot with no caution whatsoever. At this point my stepfather got ready to shoot, in spite of the fact that I kept on trembling, though less violently than when the male bear had come. The shot was true, for it entered by the foreleg and hit the heart, instantly killing the bear. When they heard the noise of the gunfire, the cubs fled a short distance off; but, seeing that their mother was not following them, they came back to the bait. Now I recovered my spirit; and once rid of the fears which had gripped me earlier, I said to my stepfather, "Don't kill them; let's catch them alive and take them back to the house." But he answered me, "They are already too big and would defend themselves against us if we tried to do anything like that, and I could not be sure that they would not bite us and also scratch us with their claws—enough to lay us up in bed for a while. They have to be killed, so that when they are grown up they will not destroy Don Ignacio's livestock."

And at that point he fired on one of the cubs and killed it. The third bear drew back a bit; but seeing that his mother and brother were not following him, he came back and kept on eating, while my stepfather reloaded his gun; and at the end, all three bears had been instantly killed. Just then Julián Cantúa came with Coyote, and we went back to the house.

I told my mother the whole story of what had happened at the hunting blind, leaving out nothing; and she said, "Now you know how to kill bears; you have satisfied your curiosity, and it would be better for us to pay Cantúa to go at night for your stepfather. You have lost a lot of sleep and you are not used to this kind of work. I am afraid you will get sick. You had better help me with other things, without having to go after bears...."

My stepfather began to wonder what he might best do with the bearskins, since in Monterey he would have no place to keep them, and it would not be a good idea to leave them in the mission, either. While he was thinking about these things, there appeared a Spaniard, a merchant of sorts, one of those who came to this country and enjoyed the protection of their compatriots, the missionaries, and who carried on a trade, buying and selling things that might yield some profit. Taking advantage of this opportunity, my stepfather negotiated with that Spaniard, who could safely deposit the skins in the mission warehouses and wait to sell them at the right time to the officers who came on the ships with the King's accounts. My mother and he decided to sell the skins to the Spaniard for two hundred *pesos,* and thus they avoided having to take such a troublesome load to Monterey. The deal was made, and with this money we bought all that the family needed from the mission trading post....

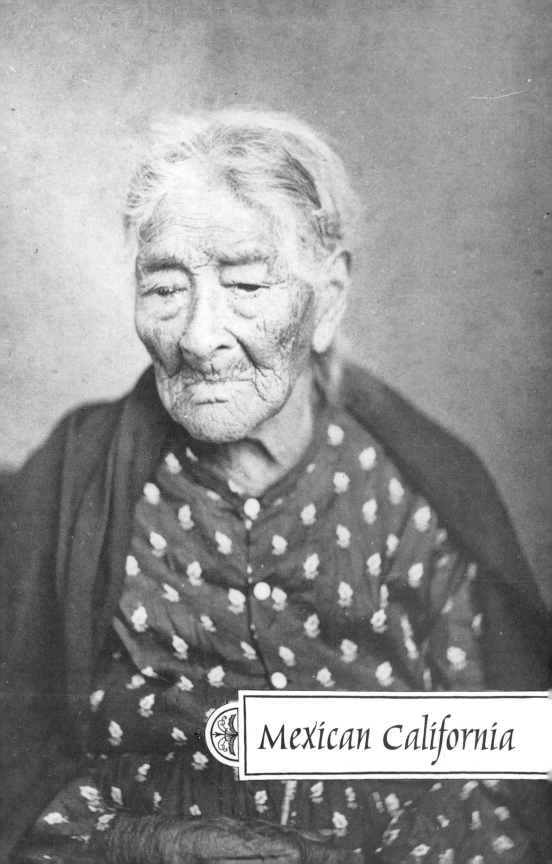

Mexican California

Mexican California

The movement for Mexican independence culminated in 1821 in a series of events that would have been difficult to predict. While Viceroy Juan Ruiz de Apodaca was reporting to King Fernando VII in 1819 that the insurgency was basically under control, events in the mother country were about to undermine that promise: the very next year, a military force bound for the New World rebelled at Cádiz and marched on Madrid. There they were joined by other garrisons and by veterans of the 1808 to 1812 struggle against the French. They demanded that the king pledge allegiance to the liberal constitution of 1812. This document, composed during the tumult of the Napoleonic conflict, affirmed the sovereignty of the people. It also contained a bill of rights and some anticlerical provisions. The king acquiesced.

The conservative *criollos* (people born in New Spain who claimed to be descended directly from peninsular Spanish families), fearful that the more radical elements of the 1812 constitution would make their way across the ocean to New Spain, decided to follow the lead of army officer Agustín de Iturbide, who was trying to negotiate a more conservatively based independence agreement with insurgent leader Vicente Guerrero. In 1821, Iturbide and Guerrero agreed on the Plan of Iguala, which contained the "three guarantees" for Mexico: independence, Catholicism, and equality. The last viceroy, Juan de O'Donojú, agreed to the terms of the plan. Even though, over the next decade, Spain would periodically send forces to try to retake Mexico, independence was now a fact. However, the liberal-conservative alliance that had gained it would not last long. The Plan of Iguala called for a kind of constitutional monarchy, and Iturbide was named emperor in 1822. He was overthrown within a year, and a more liberal, federalist constitution was adopted in 1824.

California eventually became a territory of the new Mexican republic. Three changes that accompanied this transition would alter the territory's economy permanently. First, Mexico repealed a number of the restrictive Spanish laws regarding foreign trade, and ships from England and the United States began to call at California more frequently. This occurred not only at Monterey, but also at the other three *presidios,* and at some missions that had fairly easy access to the water, such as San Juan Capistrano and Santa Clara. Beginning in the 1820s, agents of commercial firms in England and the United States began to enter into contracts with the missions for the hides and tallow of the mission cattle. Vessels sailed up and down the coast, filling their holds with this precious cargo.

Second, the missions were secularized. This was an outcome of long-standing developments in both Spain and Mexico. In Spain, it had long been understood that the missions were not to be permanent institutions. The missions now became churches without extensive lands attached to them, and the mission Indians were legally emancipated and no longer tied to a particular church complex. A new group of Franciscans, mostly born in the New World, arrived to shepherd about half of the former missions into this next phase in their history.

The third development was closely related to secularization of the missions. As ownership of the lands was taken away from the missions, it was generally distributed over the next few years to the *Californios* and their families. On these lands, the elite of this generation built their *ranchos* and took over the already profitable hide and tallow trade.

The native Californians were profoundly affected by these developments. Despite promises that went back practically to the beginning of the mission system in New Spain, very few of them received any share of the mission lands. Those who stayed at or near the missions found that the new social order allowed them roles only as wage laborers in the fields and on the *ranchos.* Some moved to the *pueblos,* where they tried to hire themselves out as unskilled labor. Those who moved farther away generally found that the changes in the human and physical geography of Alta California had made it very difficult to resume their more traditional ways. In the interior of the territory, especially in southern Alta California and northern Baja California, indigenous groups that had been largely untouched by mission life continued their resistance to European domination, raiding the more isolated *ranchos* and churches for livestock.

By 1836, secularization was complete. In the face of these rapid changes, one basic problem remained: lack of population. In the 1830s, the Mexican government made a serious attempt to bring a large group of new settlers into Alta California and establish them as farmers and ranchers. However, the *Californio* elite chose to interpret this endeavor as an attempt to deny them access to the mission lands which they had so long coveted. They accordingly resisted the colony and prevented it from establishing itself. As a result, they paradoxically destroyed any chance that the territory would develop into the kind of liberal society they had professed to desire. Property remained very unequally distributed, and formal education continued to be underdeveloped. In this context, no professional class ever emerged to challenge the foreigners for dominance in the crucial commercial sector.

This last development is more obvious in hindsight than it was at the time. The *Californios* tried their hardest to develop their land, to increase its productive capacity, and to construct a liberal, modern, Mexican identity. They were not allowed to complete the experiment.

1824
The Sea Otter Hunts

Zakahar Tchitchinoff and Antonio María Osio

When Mexico gained its independence from Spain in 1821, the new government of Agustín de Iturbide sent Agustín Fernández de San Vicente, a priest from Durango, to Baja and Alta California to manage the transition from Spanish to Mexican government. Fernández's reputation as a womanizer and a gambler did not sit well with the conservative California elite, but he managed to win them over by naming California-born Luis Antonio Argüello as first Mexican governor of Alta California. He adopted the same strategy in Baja California, selecting veteran soldier Fernando de la Toba and then José Manuel Ruiz as governor. Fernández also convened a rudimentary gathering representing the various interests of Alta California, which elected Pablo Vicente de Solá as Alta California's representative to the new Mexican congress. In Baja California, Fernández set up three elected municipal governments, at Loreto, San Antonio, and San José del Cabo.

As we have seen, Argüello had considerable dealings with the Russian American Company when he was commander at San Francisco. As governor he went even further and negotiated a contract with the company for the hunting of sea otters, with the profit to be shared by the company and the territory. The sea otter trade was by then fairly well established: the Russians had entered into a contract with an American boat to hunt sea otters off the Baja California coast as early as 1806, and Russian forays into California had extended from Eureka in the north to San Francisco Bay and even farther south. The Russians established a base at the Farallon Islands, just outside the Golden Gate, where they usually stationed at least ten Aleuts and a Russian foreman. The two following accounts detail this aspect of Alta California's past. The first, ascribed by Petrov to Zakahar Tchitchinoff, describes a journey in 1824 to the area north of Fort Ross. It highlights the interactions between the Russians and the indigenous peoples of the northern coastal areas. The second account is by Antonio María Osio, a native of Baja California who came to Alta California in 1825 and who had observed the Aleut fishing methods firsthand.

FROM THE REMINISCENCES OF ZAKAHAR TCHITCHINOFF

In the summer of 1824, sea otter seemed to be getting scarce in the vicinity of the Ross settlement and along the coast southward from there. An order came from Sitka to outfit a large *baidarka* expedition for the purpose of hunting in a northerly direction from Bodega Bay. A man by the name of Tarakanoff was placed in command of the expedition, which consisted of over fifty *baidarkas* containing two men each. I was sent along to help Tarakanoff to keep the journal. We set out at the beginning of June. The first day, we had to return to the bay about noon on account of northerly wind, but the second day we paddled all day, and some of the party killed a few sea otters. In the evening we could not make a landing on account of the steepness of the shore, and though tired out already, we were compelled to keep on until daylight showed us a strip of sandy beach on which we could haul up our canoes. We then ate up nearly all the provisions we had started out with and slept all day.

Late in the evening we set out again, and the weather being calm, we made good progress. The hunters found us more sea otters, and all we could do was to catch fish enough for our own subsistence. On the third day from that we passed an Indian village. The place did not look promising for sea otter and Tarakanoff concluded to pass by without stopping. When the Indians saw us, many of them jumped into their canoes and tried to come out to us, but we were too fast for them and kept a long distance away from the beach. The next evening we camped on the beach, but just when we had gathered wood for our fires and caught some fish, some Indians appeared on the bluffs above us, and though they gave no signs of hostile intentions, Tarakanoff made us embark at once and travel on for three or four hours more.

On the sixth or seventh day, we entered a very large bay. It ran in the same direction with the sea coast, and the entrance was about the middle. Several large rivers emptied into this bay, and as the rocks about the entrance looked promising, Tarakanoff concluded to stay there and hunt.

For the first few days we saw no signs of natives, and the men of the party killed over forty sea otters. On the mouths of the rivers there were sand bars and big meadows on either bank, but farther inland and on part of the coast we could see forests of very large trees. There was any amount of fish in the bay, and we should have liked very much to hunt there all summer, but Tarakanoff wished to go up the rivers as far as he could, and the whole party (except ten men who were left at the entrance of the bay to fish) entered the largest river. While crossing the bar, some of the *baidarkas* were upset, but no lives were lost. When we had advanced up the river for several hours, we stopped on the bank to rest, and as the water in the stream was not fresh, we sent five or six men out to look for water to drink. In a few minutes they came back running and said there was a large Indian village just around a bend of the river. Tarakanoff was afraid to go on, and though we were suffering for the want of fresh water, he made the whole party stop there, hidden in the high grass, until dark. Then we went in carefully in the middle of the river. When we came abreast of the village, some dogs began to bark, and then we could hear some Indians shouting to each other. Our party all moved close into the opposite bank of the river, and as our paddles made no noise, the Indians could not notice us, and we went by unseen. In the morning we hid ourselves in the grass again and speared some fish from the bank of the river. As we neither saw nor heard anything of the natives, Tarakanoff concluded to move on. We had the current and the tide against us and made but slow progress. About noon we came upon a village suddenly. About fifty men came running down to the beach, and all the women and children ran into the houses and into the brush to hide. The men shouted and began to shoot arrows and spears. Tarakanoff saw that the river branched out a little above the village, and hoping that we could get back to the bay by another arm without passing the village we had avoided during the night, urged us to paddle ahead as fast as we could. Some of the Indians jumped into wooden canoes and tried to follow us, but we were too fast for them—we turned into the other arm of the river and went down rapidly with the current. We could hear the shouts of the Indians for a long time.

We had four muskets in the party, but as the agent at Ross had furnished us but very little ammunition, it was thought best to wait for real danger before making use of them. The channel we had fled into was very crooked, and we rested once during the afternoon and caught some fish, which we were compelled to eat raw, as we could not dare to make any fires and betray our whereabout to the Indians. An hour before sunset, while we were

Kodiak Aleut dressed for the sea otter hunt, 1778. Sepia and watercolor drawing by John Webber.
Photo by Hillel Burger. Courtesy of the Peabody Museum, Harvard University.

moving along fast, we suddenly came into the main stream again, just above
the village which we had passed during the night. The Indians living there
had been alarmed and were waiting for us. Ten or fifteen canoes were in the
water, across the channel, and armed men were on both banks. They began
shooting arrows as soon as we came in sight. The Aleuts who had the guns
and Tarakanoff, who had a pistol, began to fire, but it did not seem to

greatly frighten the Indians, who continued to throw arrows, spears, stones, and clubs. A stone hit me on the shoulder and almost made me drop my paddle. Some of the *baidarkas,* avoiding the canoes in the stream, got into shallow water, and some of the Indians waded out and captured them with their hands. Four *baidarkas* and their occupants were lost in that way.

After escaping from this dangerous ambush, the whole party encamped at the very mouth of the river. Tarakanoff posted lookouts some distance back, along the stream, in order to guard against surprise. No fires were made at all, and the whole party was obliged to subsist on raw fish alone. In the morning the captured *baidarkas* were seen floating down the stream, bottom side up. They were secured, but they had been cut and slashed by the Indians beyond repair. The party remained two more days at the mouth of that river, suffering great hardship from exposure and hunger, in order to ascertain whether any of the captured Aleuts had made their escape, but the men were probably murdered or carried off into the interior.

Finally, the party went on to the entrance of the bay, where the men left behind had, in the meantime, secured quite a large amount of fish. While the fish were drying, a number of *baidarkas* were sent out to hunt, and in ten days over eighty sea otters were killed. As soon as the fish were dry enough, Tarakanoff, who was always expecting an attack from the natives, hurried up our departure.

At first we skirted the coast northward for three days, but not finding any indications of sea otter grounds, Tarakanoff concluded to turn about. On the way down the coast, our Aleuts were very fortunate, killing nearly one hundred sea otters. We arrived at the Ross settlement late in the month of July, and as we brought plenty of sea otters, Tarakanoff was not censured for losing some men and *baidarkas.*

From *The History of Alta California*
by Antonio María Osio

The Kodiak canoes are made with strong, flexible branches. When they are tied together well, they create the approximate shape of a *chalupa.* Next, they line this frame with sealskins, well prepared with the oil of the same animal. The skins are sewn together with sinews fashioned into cord for this purpose. Depending on its size, each vessel has two or three openings on top of the covering. The Kodiak inserts almost half his body through the

Malaspina expedition artist Tomás de Suria drew this sketch of a baidarka-*like boat off the northwest coast of North America, 1791. Courtesy of the Museo de América, Madrid.*

hole and sits with his legs stretched out forward. Because they are accustomed to it, they are the only ones who can tolerate up to ten or twelve continuous hours in that uncomfortable position. Each person usually wears a shirt made from seal gut. When he sits in the manner that has been described, he ties the flaps of the shirt to a type of rim on the canoe openings. So, even though water might wash over them, not one drop makes its way into the canoe. They also carry a musket to defend themselves and to hunt, and they feel no repugnance eating the animals that they kill. If the animal is large, they use the guts to store their drinking water, no matter how bad tasting it might become. Because their palates are already accustomed to decay, only one who suffers from a cold can bear being close to them, since the stench that they give off is intolerable even at a considerable distance.

Their skill in catching otters seems incredible. They have a type of arrow which they hurl accurately, without a bow, from a distance of up to eighty yards. They insert about half of the arrow, or slightly less, into a shaft two yards long which is grooved along the top. When they hurl the arrow, it runs backward along the groove until it hits the back part. Then it recoils and shoots out with great force, leaving the shaft behind in the individual's hand. The arrow carries a bladder hanging from a cord of sinews. When the otter is struck, the bladder detaches from the arrow. The tip of the arrow, which usually is made from bone and shaped like a harpoon, remains buried in the animal. Due to the force that the animal exerts when it swims, the arrowhead remains lodged in it. The bladder hinders the animal's ability to dive, because the pain that it feels does not allow it to garner enough strength to submerge the bladder. Meanwhile, in their swift vessels, the Kodiaks approach the animals and club them to death. Whenever two of them jointly pursue an otter, it will not escape, because they quickly tire the animals, get near them, and strike them as has been described. When a storm catches the Indians off guard and they cannot land, they protect themselves by joining together three or four canoes. They tie one to the other in the middle and on the ends, and thus form a raft so safe that it cannot capsize.

1824
The Chumash Revolt

Rafael González

By the 1820s, most of the Chumash people had been incorporated into the mission system. Disease, starvation, and violence had reduced their population, which had probably stood at about 18,500 in the eighteenth century, to just a few thousand. In the face of such devastation, a movement to reassert indigenous traditions and to free their people from the restraints of colonialism and Christianity gathered force among the Chumash. By the early 1820s, tensions were running high in the Chumash region: according to oral tradition that the linguist John P. Harrington encountered in 1914, rumors of violence to come abounded among the soldiers and the indigenous people. Soldiers and neophytes alike were hearing that the other group was planning to kill all of them.

The actual revolt was apparently planned over a period of some months, and it was executed with an impressive mixture of organizational precision and operational flexibility. The plan seems to have called for a coordinated attack on the missions of Santa Inés, La Purísima, and Santa Bárbara on Sunday, February 22, as the Mass was being celebrated. However, events at Santa Inés on the previous day upset the plans and initiated the revolt prematurely. On that day, a Chumash man from La Purísima arrived at Santa Inés and requested from the corporal in charge of the mission garrison permission to visit one of his relatives, who was imprisoned there. When the corporal in charge refused to grant permission, the Chumash retorted, "Is it perhaps that the king deprives relatives from speaking with prisoners?" The soldier shot back, "There is no longer any king except the captain," and ordered the man whipped for insolence. This act apparently so inflamed the Santa Inés Chumash, who were already set to start the rebellion the next day, that they spontaneously began the uprising then and there. They burned down most of the mission complex, but

they spared the church itself. Only the chance arrival of military reinforcements prevented the Chumash from taking complete control of the
mission. They instead withdrew to La Purísima, where, after an intense
firefight, they forced the garrison to surrender. The Chumash allowed the
soldiers and their families, along with the mission priest, to be evacuated
to Santa Inés.

When news of the outbreak at Santa Inés reached Santa Bárbara, the
leader of the Chumash there, the *alcalde* Andrés Sagimomatsee, realized
that the element of surprise had been lost. He was forced to improvise
and did so quite creatively. On Sunday morning, he told the mission
priest, Father Antonio Ripoll, that the Santa Bárbara Chumash were
terrified that the mission guard (which consisted at the time of only three
soldiers) would take revenge on them for the attacks at the two other missions. Andrés convinced Ripoll that the only way to keep the situation
calm was to convince Santa Bárbara commander José de la Guerra y Noriega to remove the garrison from the mission and thus allay the Chumash
fears. Ripoll agreed to go to the *presidio* and present this request.

While the priest was gone, the Chumash quickly armed themselves as
they had planned to do all along. When Ripoll returned after having convinced the commander to order the soldiers back to the *presidio,* he found
the Indians fully in control of the situation. All he could do was negotiate
the peaceful withdrawal of the soldiers. Guerra y Noriega soon attacked
the mission but retired from the field without being able to dislodge the
Chumash. The defenders then abandoned Santa Bárbara and headed into
the hills for the interior.

During March, a military expedition led by Mariano Estrada managed
to retake La Purísima. Then the attention of the authorities turned to subduing the Santa Bárbara rebels, who were encamped near Buena Vista
Lake, about sixty miles from Santa Bárbara. An expedition was sent out
under the command of Narciso Fabregat, but the fugitives defeated the
soldiers and forced them to return. A second expedition, composed of
two parts, was then planned. One force, commanded by Captain Pablo de
la Portilla, left from Santa Bárbara. Ripoll and Fr. Vicente Sarría, president
of the missions, accompanied this group. Another force, commanded by
Antonio del Valle, left from San Miguel. The two contingents joined up
before finally setting out for the interior. When this expedition reached
the Chumash camp, it was able to negotiate their return to the missions
with the promise of amnesty from the governor. The Chumash revolt was

the largest organized resistance movement to occur during the Spanish and Mexican periods in California.

Rafael González, a native of Santa Bárbara and a corporal at its *presidio,* participated in these events. When the revolt began, he was stationed at an outpost at Point Rincón, south of Santa Bárbara, and he heard the distant sounds of the fighting. He reached La Purísima soon after it was recovered by the Mexicans. He was also a member of the expedition that went into the interior and negotiated the return of the Chumash to the missions. His account, more than fifty years after the rebellion, portrays these events through the eyes of an ordinary soldier. His description of the internal confusion, the rivalries among the soldiers of the *presidios,* and the swift and deadly punishment meted out to those accused of leading the revolt offers a unique window into the experiences of a Mexican soldier in California.

From the Reminiscences of Rafael González

We arrived back here at the beginning of February 1824, and within six or eight days at the most, the uprising of the Indians of the Santa Inés and La Purísima missions occurred on Saturday, and of Santa Bárbara on the following day.

I was acting as corporal of the cavalry at El Rincón when, during the night, I received two or three couriers from here going to San Buenaventura. They told me nothing, nor did they know anything here on Saturday night. In the last letter that I received from Sergeant Don Carlos Antonio Carrillo, he told me, "Tomorrow you will come here with all the horses and have the soldiers round up all the horses that may be along the way."

When I arrived here opposite the beach, we saw far behind us a corporal coming with two soldiers who we thought must be the ones from San Buenaventura. It turned out that it was not them, but Vicente Valencia and two other soldiers who had been dispatched to see what had become of the mounted men. We heard cannon shots, and that sound surprised us, because we did not know that it was a holiday or feast day.

Those men caught up with us, and one of them, who was a relative of mine named Antonio Germán, told me that the Indians had rebelled in Santa Bárbara. When we arrived, I presented myself to the sergeant at headquarters, gave my report, and acquainted myself with everything. Captain de la Guerra [y Noriega] called me and told me he had not expected to see me, due to what had happened. Many days later, they ordered me to get ready, and I went with others under the immediate command of Captain de la Guerra to the Santa Inés mission, where we found that the Indians had already surrendered.

At La Purísima, the men of the guard with their corporal, Tiburcio Tapia, had surrendered after a long battle because their ammunition ran out, but the Indians harmed no one in the mission except a woman whom they had shot with a dart. But in the night during the battle, two or three travelers from Los Angeles arrived, coming from the north. One was named Dolores Sepúlveda and another Ramón Sotelo. In the skirmish, the Indians killed those two and another one, also, who was named Isidoro, I think.

Sergeant Don Anastasio Carrillo brought the first force that arrived in Santa Inés. Almost all the Indians of the mission were probably at La Purísima. Carrillo arrived at Santa Inés on Sunday about sunrise. The news of Carrillo's arrival in Santa Inés with troops reached La Purísima. At that place there was an Indian named Patricio, of whom it was said that he was the son of a well-to-do man called Cota. I learned through Anastasio Carrillo that on Monday, Father Blas Ordaz, coming from the north, arrived, and finding the Indians in control of the mission of La Purísima, he surrendered also.

The following day, Fr. Blas and Corporal Tapia came from La Purísima to Santa Inés as agents sent by the said Patricio (who I judge was the leader of the rebels) to Sergeant Carrillo to tell him that no soldier should go there (to La Purísima). Carrillo replied that the Indians had better not harm any soldier, woman, or child.

When the Captain and we arrived in Santa Inés, we found Anastasio Carrillo there with the ten or twelve men he had taken with him. It was around three or four in the afternoon. Carrillo urged the Captain to take us immediately to Santa Rita, near La Purísima. At that time, the Governor was Don Luis Argüello, who sent a troop and auxiliary citizens under the command of Ensign Haro (a drunkard). This troop arrived at La Purísima before we did.

The Captain told Carrillo that he agreed with the Governor that we should join Ensign Haro and go together to La Purísima. Carrillo told him not to pay any attention to Haro or his men, because we were accustomed to regard the people of Monterey as outsiders, and we did not like the idea of the Montereyans claiming the honor of having subdued the rebelling Indians. Carrillo wanted the men of Santa Bárbara to avail themselves of the opportunity to receive the credit for having alone put down the rebels.

When we reached Santa Inés, they made me corporal of cavalry to care for the horses that there were for such a large number of people. The following morning at dawn, I came to report to the sergeant that there was no news about the horses, and at the same time I started to warm a chicken over the fire for lunch. At that moment, we heard a cannon shot in the direction of La Purísima, and right away I was ordered to assemble the horses.

The mail carriers traveled from San Luis Obispo to Santa Inés by the Los Alamos road (not entering La Purísima). To effect this service, ten men came and went. As soon as the cannon shot was heard and the horses were ready, the men of Monterey began to seize their horses, mount, and ride off toward La Purísima, one by one, two by two, or in small groups.

Those of us from Santa Bárbara also got ready for the march, but when we reached La Purísima, the Montereyans had already taken it, which caused us Santa Barbarans to be greatly chagrined, because Captain de la Guerra wished to respect the orders of the Governor to the letter.

A few days afterward, an indictment was drawn up against the Indian ringleaders who turned out to be the ones who assassinated Dolores Sepúlveda, Ramón Sotelo, and the other one. The crime was proven before a council of officers, and seven Indians were sentenced to death. They were made ready for execution, and after being given unction by the priests, they were shot to death. I was in the formation and saw the act. Some of the doomed men were about half dead and had to be almost carried to the place of the execution. The executioners were from the company of Mazatlán. The next day, Haro and his troop marched north, taking with them some fifteen or twenty Indian prisoners.

A day or two later, Captain de la Guerra returned to Santa Bárbara with the troop and auxiliaries, leaving at La Purísima a detachment of fifteen men (for the most part Mazatecans) under the command of a corporal. He considered that under those circumstances the usual guard of a corporal and five soldiers would be inadequate.

When the campaign was over, several Indians from Santa Inés and La Purísima, and all those from Santa Bárbara, left for the tule region. A mixed expedition of calvary scouts, Mazatecans, and citizens of the *pueblo* of Los Angeles went out in search of the fugitives who were with the heathens in the tule region. Lt. Narciso Fabregat commanded the expedition. He had a battle with the Indians but could not defeat them, because he ran into very foul weather, including heavy windstorms and a great deal of dust. The expedition returned to Santa Bárbara.

A short time later, I was part of another force that went out. Father Commissioner Prefect Sarría and Father Antonio Ripoll, Minister of the Mission of Santa Bárbara, accompanied us. We reached the tule region and stayed there some distance from the tules for about two or three days.

We were camped there when, one morning between six and seven, two Indians representing their people came with flags of truce. One of the Indians was called Jaime and the other Francisco. Both were neophytes from Santa Bárbara and very good fellows. They came to a place about halfway between the tules and our camp. The two missionaries and Captain de la Portilla, who had come from San Diego and commanded the expedition, went out to hold a parley with them. The discussion lasted three days.

Three other officers on the expedition were the Lieutenant of Mazatecans, Juan María Ibarra, the Lieutenant of Infantry of San Blas, Don Antonio Valle, and the Ensign from Santa Bárbara, Domingo Carrillo. Ibarra was a dark man, and he had a reputation for energy and valor. He was accustomed to wearing a cloak and his sword even right here in this town [of Santa Bárbara]. On the third day of the parley (according to what Ensign Domingo Carrillo told me) the following took place: Captain de la Portilla could not explain himself very well. They said that he was a man of few words. Ibarra was walking near the parley, and finally he went up to those in the conference, which included the two Indians, the Fathers and Captain Portilla. As he was coarse and foul-mouthed, he said, "For almost three days I have been exposed to the weather night and day. If they do not decide to surrender before tomorrow dawn, I am going to lead the charge."

By afternoon, the Indians had already begun to approach us. Father Sarría and Father Ripoll won over the Indians with a few well-chosen words. Sarría said to them: "Come now, come along, for we have to sing the *Corpus* tomorrow." With the revolution, the Indians had taken away all the musicians. By that same afternoon a great many of the Indians raised in the mission had come over to us. The next day, the Indians made a large *ramada* for the ceremony of the *Corpus,* which was celebrated right there in camp. A day or two later, when all of the Indians had come over, we all went back to Santa Bárbara, except Valle and the Monterey troop and artillerymen, who went directly from the tule region to San Miguel [mission]. The men from San Diego came back here and afterward returned to their destination.

1820s
Indian Life at San Luis Rey

Pablo Tac

Pablo Tac was born at Mission San Luis Rey in January 1822. The priest at the mission was Fr. Antonio Peyri, who had worked there continuously since its founding in 1798. Peyri left the mission at the beginning of 1832, taking Tac and another Indian boy, Antonio Amamix, with him to Mexico. They remained at the College of San Fernando for a year, and then Peyri and the two boys went to Europe. Peyri returned to his home country of Spain and sent the two boys to a seminary in Rome, where they were to study for the priesthood. Both of them died before finishing those studies. At some point after his arrival in Rome, working with the chief custodian of the Vatican Library, Tac began to prepare a grammar of the Luiseño language. Before his death at the age of nineteen, he also composed the following narrative of life at Mission San Luis Rey. Tac's account is one of the few firsthand accounts by an Indian of life at a California mission. In it he illustrates the wide range of responses which the Spanish and Catholic presence elicited from the native peoples of California.

FROM THE REMINISCENCES OF PABLO TAC, WRITTEN IN ROME IN THE 1830s

When the missionary arrived in our country with a small troop, our captain [headman] and also the others were astonished, seeing them from afar, but they did not run away or seize arms to kill them—but having sat down, they watched them. But when they drew near, then the captain got up (for he was seated with the others) and met them. They halted, and the missionary then began to speak, the captain saying perhaps in his language *"hichsom iva haluon, puluchajam cham quinai."*

(What is it that you seek here? Get out of our country!) But they did not understand him, and they answered him in Spanish, and the captain began with signs, and the Fernandino,* understanding him, gave him gifts and in this manner made him his friend. The captain, turning to his people, (as I suppose) found the whites all right, and so they let them sleep here. There was not then a stone house, but all were camps (as they say). This was that happy day in which we saw white people, by us called Sosabitom. O merciful God, why didst Thou leave us for many centuries, years, months, and days in utter darkness after Thou camest to the world? Blessed be Thou from this day through future centuries.

The Fernandino Father remained in our country with the little troop that he brought. A camp was made, and here he lived for many days. In the morning he said Mass, and then he planned how he would baptize them, where he would put his house, the church, and as there were five thousand souls (who were all the Indians [Luiseños] there were), how he would sustain them, and seeing how it could be done. Having the captain for his friend, he was afraid of nothing. It was a great mercy that the Indians did not kill the Spanish when they arrived, and very admirable, because they have never wanted another people to live with them, and until those days they were always fighting. But thus willed He who alone can will. I do not know if he baptized them before making the church or after having made it, but I think he baptized them before making it. He was already a good friend of the captain, and also dear to the neophytes. They could understand him somewhat when he, as their father, ordered them to carry stone from the sea (which is not far) for the foundations, to make bricks, roof tiles, to cut beams, reeds, and what was necessary. They did it with the masters who were helping them, and within a few years they finished working. They made a church with three altars for all the neophytes (the great altar is nearly all gilded), two chapels, two sacristies, two choirs, a flower garden for the church, a high tower with five bells, two small and three large, the cemetery with a crucifix in the middle for all those who die here.

Let us begin with the tower. The tower is placed on the right side of the church with five bells, two small and three large, whose voice or sound is heard from afar, sometimes from Usva, four or five leagues distant from the Mission of San Luis Rey de Francia.

Of the church I have already spoken. After the church comes the place of the masons; here they leave the mortar, lime, etc. After this comes the

---

* Franciscan from the College of San Fernando.

storehouse for wine. Within are two hundred casks of wine, brandy and white wine, four hundred barrels, for Mass, to sell to the Spanish and English travelers who often come to the mission to sell cloth, linen, cotton, and whatever they bring from Boston—and not for the neophytes, which is prohibited them because they easily get drunk. 5 is the place where the wine is made.* 7, the window of the room of the General of California when he comes to the Mission. 8, the door of the Fernandino Father. There are four rooms for travelers. In the middle is the reception room, with three portraits—one of the St. Louis King of France, the second of the Good Shepherd, the third of the Virgin of Guadalupe. In one corner is a clock, and beyond, the refectory. 9, glass window of the missionary. 10, a small door for the missionary to get out easily in case of earthquakes. 11, room of the servant of the missionary. 12, house for travelers. 13, door which called the biggest of all. Through her the neophytes enter and leave for work. 14, 15, 16, 17, 18, 19, houses for the Spanish majordomos of the mission. 20, large room for the neophyte boys with its patio and two gardens. 21, soap house. 22, room for the girls. 23, corral for the stock. 24, mill. 25, enclosure for the lambs. 26, house of the shepherd. 27, corral. 28, granary. 29, granary. 30, place for the horses of the missionary and of the travelers and also for the sacks of fodder. 31, infirmary for the women. 32, infirmary for the men. 33, cemetery. 34, place where *pozole* and *atole* are made. 34, rooms for the majordomos. 35, barracks. 36, *fopanco.*† 37, granary. 38, granary. 39, place for the baker. 40, clock. 41, kitchen. 42, chambers for travelers. 43, storehouse. 44, garden. 45, storehouse for blankets, storehouse for flour. 46, mill. 47, small loom. 48, large loom. 49, place where oil is made. 50, blacksmith shop. 51, granary. 52, shoemaker's shop. 53, place of the ass keepers. 54, second biggest door. 55, room of the majordomo of Pala. 56, carpenter shop. 57, place for the presses. 59, place for skins. In a few years, all was done.

Toward the south there is a very big kitchen garden with a pasture to the side. We said that the mission was placed on a hillock. Below this hillock there is an ever flowing fountain from which the neophytes and the missionary bring water to drink. They made two fountains before the gate of

---

* These numbers refer to a plan of San Luis, possibly drawn by Pablo Tac himself, which was obviously appended to this narrative but which has now been lost.

† This is the word in the manuscript, but its meaning cannot be determined. Minna and Gordon Hewes, who first translated this document into English, speculated that it was a variant of *tapanco,* which means a small shed.

the garden, and between them a stairway to go up and down, which is made all of bricks. The entering gateway has three thick timbers in the middle. One of them, driven into the earth, reaches high above the wall, the other two are more or less fastened on it, making a cross of all parts, if you would like to see it, and the water carrier, wishing to pass, pushes a timber, and the two turn, and in this way he passes with ease, raising the pitcher above his burdened shoulders stronger than those of asses themselves. The stairway is so very high that one cannot ascend by it in the same trip, and it is necessary to rest in the middle. It happens many times that they get tired in vain (as it is said), because when they arrive at the gate and wish to pass through it with haste, the pitcher is broken, and they return to the house without water or pitcher, dripping with water.

The timbers were placed in order not to let in the bulls and horses, spirited when there is bullfighting, though they come in often and frighten the old women who wash their clothes here. Beyond the two fountains is the gate of the orchard. The water from the two fountains passes down through a little door, running toward the west as in a ditch, and irrigates another garden almost a league distant from the mission.

The garden is extensive, full of fruit trees, pears, apples, or *perones,* as the Mexicans say, peaches, quinces, pears, sweet pomegranates, figs, watermelons, melons, vegetables, cabbages, lettuces, radishes, mints, parsley, and others which I don't remember. The pears, apples, peaches, quinces, pomegranates, watermelons, and melons are for the neophytes, the others that remain for the missionary. The gardener must bring something each day. None of the neophytes can go to the garden or enter to gather the fruit. But if he wants some he asks the missionary, who immediately will give him what he wants, for the missionary is their father. The neophyte might encounter the gardener walking and cutting the fruits, who then follows him to punish him, until he leaves the walls of the garden, jumping as they know how (like deer in the mountains).

Once a neophyte entered the garden without knowing the gardener was there, and as he was very hungry, he climbed a fig tree. Here he began to eat with all haste a large ripe fig. Not by bits, but whole, he let it go down his throat, and the fig choked him. He then began to be frightened, until he cried out like a crow and swallowed it. The gardener, hearing the voice of the crow, with his Indian eyes then found the crow that from fear was not eating more. He said to him, "I see you, a crow without wings. Now I will wound you with my arrows." Then the neophyte with all haste fled far from the garden.

Mission San Luis Rey in the late 1820s, by French visitor Auguste Duhaut-Cilly. Courtesy of The Bancroft Library, University of California, Berkeley.

Toward the west of the garden is the pasture for the horses of the Fernandino Father and for those of the Anglo-American travelers. It is as large as the garden, full of water underneath, and so it has green grass. There are many trees, very many birds. A great many crows arrive in the evening to sleep, and they let themselves fall from the height, turning somersaults until they come to the trees. Here too the workmen found a California lion, which is the same as the cat of Europe but more powerful than a tiger, not for its strength, but for its agility. It is very difficult to kill. It kills the horses, seizing them with a leap. Then it beheads them; for this it is feared. The workmen found it, and because they were many, the lion was afraid of them and the cries which they let out following it. It ran leaping here and there around the pasture. The Indians, hidden behind the trees, threw stones at it until one struck the middle of the forehead and soon, weakened, falling, he then died. Here they make bricks and tiles for the mission. Deer are not found. Beyond the garden runs the road to the *presidio* of San Diego, where the General of California is.

Not to speak much of the gardens of the Mission of San Luis Rey de Francia of Alta California, the Fernandino Father made five big gardens, that is to say, three in the mission itself, one in the district we call Pala, the fifth in another district whose name I do not now remember, all very fruitful with what is sown. Four districts, the Mission, Pala, Temeco, and Usva, three *ranchos*. The Mission of San Luis Rey de Francia, thus the Fernandino Father named it after having completed all the houses, because our patron is St. Louis the King.

But we call it Quechla in our language. Thus our grandparents called it, because in this country there were a kind of stones that were called *quechlam* in the plural, and in the singular *quechla,* and we inhabitants of Quechla call ourselves *Quechnajuichom* in the plural, *Quechnajuis* in the singular, meaning inhabitants of Quechla. In Quechla not long ago there were five thousand souls, with all their neighboring lands. Through a sickness that came to California two thousand souls died, and three thousand were left.

The Fernandino Father, as he was alone and very accustomed to the usages of the Spanish soldiers, seeing that it would be very difficult for him alone to give orders to that people, and moreover, people that had left the woods just a few years before, therefore appointed *alcaldes* from the people themselves that knew how to speak Spanish more than the others and were better than the others in their customs. There were seven of these *alcaldes,* with rods as a symbol that they could judge the others. The captain dressed like the Spanish, always remaining captain, but not ordering his people about as of old, when they were still gentiles. The chief of the *alcaldes* was called the general. He knew the name of each one, and when he took something he then named each person by his name. In the afternoon, the *alcaldes* gather at the house of the missionary. They bring the news of that day, and if the missionary tells them something that all the people of the country ought to know, they return to the villages shouting, "Tomorrow morning."...

Returning to the villages, each one of the *alcaldes,* wherever he goes, cries out what the missionary has told them, in his language, and all the country hears it. "Tomorrow the sowing begins, and so the laborers go to the chicken yard and assemble there." And again he goes, saying these same words, until he reaches his own village to eat something and then to sleep. In the morning you will see the laborers appear in the chicken yard and assemble there according to what they heard last night.

With the laborers goes a Spanish majordomo and others, neophyte *alcaldes,* to see how the work is done, to hurry them if they are lazy, so that they will soon finish what was ordered, and to punish the guilty or lazy one who leaves his plow and quits the field, keeping on with his laziness. They work all day but not always. At noon they leave work, and then they bring them *pozole.* (*Pozole* is what the Spaniards of California call maize cooked in hot water.) They eat it with gusto, and they remain seated until afternoon, when they return to their villages. The shoemakers work making chairs, leather knapsacks, reins, and shoes for the cowboys, neophytes, majordomos, and Spanish soldiers, and when they have finished, they bring and deliver them to the missionary to give to the cowboys. The blacksmiths make bridle bits, keys, bosses for bridles, nails for the church, and all work for all.

We have said that Quechla was the first of the districts, this being the first place of the Fernandino Father, and the mission itself. Around it are located the other districts and *ranchos* of the Mission of San Luis Rey de Francia. To the east is the *rancho* of San Marcos and the district called Pala and another *rancho*. To the north is Temeco, Usva, and a *rancho*.

In the Mission of San Luis Rey de Francia, the Fernandino Father is like a king. He has his pages, *alcaldes,* majordomos, musicians, soldiers, gardens, *ranchos,* livestock, horses by the thousand, cows, bulls by the thousand, oxen, mules, asses, twelve thousand lambs, two hundred goats, etc. The pages are for him and for the Spanish and Mexican, English, and Anglo-American travelers. The *alcaldes* help him govern all the people of the Mission of San Luis Rey de Francia. The majordomos are in the distant districts, almost all Spaniards. The musicians of the mission are for the holy days and all the Sundays and holidays of the year, with them the singers, all Indian neophytes. Soldiers so that nobody does injury to Spaniard or to Indian; there are ten of them and they go on horseback. There are five gardens that are for all, very large. The Fernandino Father drinks little, and as almost all the gardens produce wine, he who knows the customs of the neophytes well does not wish to give any wine to any of them, but sells it to the English or Anglo-Americans, not for money but for clothing for the neophytes, linen for the church, hats, muskets, plates, coffee, tea, sugar, and other things. The products of the mission are butter, tallow, hides, chamois leather, bearskins, wine, white wine, brandy, oil, maize, wheat, beans, and also bull horns, which the English take by the thousand to Boston.

What is Done Each Day

When the sun rises and the stars and the moon go down, then the old man of the house wakens everyone and begins with breakfast, which is to eat *juiuis* heated and meat and tortillas, for we do not have bread. This done, he takes his bow and arrows and leaves the house with vigorous and quick step. (This is if he is going to hunt.) He goes off to the distant woods, which are full of bears and hares, deer and thousands of birds. He is here all day, killing as many as he can, following them, hiding himself behind trees, climbing them, and then, loaded with hares, he returns home happy. But when he needs wood, then he leaves the house in the morning with this tumpline on his shoulders and his ax, with companions who can help him when the load is very heavy, and in the afternoon he returns home. His old woman, staying at home, makes the meal. The son, if he is a man, works with the men. His daughter stays with the women, making shirts, and if these also have sons and daughters, they stay in the mission, the sons at school to learn the alphabet, and if they already know it, to learn the catechism, and if this also, to the choir of singers, and if he was a singer, to work, because all the musical singers work the day of work, and Sunday to the choir to sing, but without a book, because the teacher teaches them by memory, holding the book. The daughter joins with the single girls, who all spin for blankets for the San Luiseños and for the robe of the Fernandino Father. At twelve o'clock they eat together and leave the old man his share, their cups of clay, their vessels of well-woven fiber which water cannot leak out of, except when it is held before the face of the sun, their frying pans of clay, their grills of wood made for that day, and their pitchers for water, also of clay. Seated around the fire they are talking and eating. Too bad for them if at that time they close the door. Then, the smoke rising being much, and the opening which serves as a window being small, it turns below, trying to go out by the door, remains in the middle of the house, and they eat then speaking, laughing, and weeping without wishing to. The meal finished, they return to their work. The father leaves his son, the son leaves his sister, the sister the brother, the brother the mother, the mother her husband, with cheer, until the afternoon. Before going to bed again, they eat what the old woman and old man have made in that time, and then they sleep.

Of the Dance of the Indians

Each Indian people has its dances, different from other dances. In Europe they dance for joy, for a feast, for any fortunate news. But the Indians of California dance not only for a feast, but also before starting a war, for grief, because they have lost the victory, and in memory of grandparents, aunts and uncles, parents already dead. Now that we are Christians, we dance for ceremony.

The dance of the Yumas is almost always sad, and thus the song; the same of the Diegueños. But we Luiseños have three principal kinds for men alone, because the women have others, and they can never dance with the men. Three principal ones, two for many, and the other for one, which is more difficult. Many can dance in these two, and in this kind it is possible to dance day and night, and in the other only at night.

First Dance

No one can dance without permission of the elders, and he must be of the same people, a youth of ten and more years. The elders, before doing the dances publicly, teach them the song and make them learn perfectly, because the dance consists in knowing the song, because they act according to the song. According to the song he makes as many kicks, as many leaps as the singers make, who are the old people, the old and others of the same people. When they have learned, then they can perform the dance, but before this they give him something to drink, and then that one is a dancer; he can dance and not stop when the others dance.

On this occasion the clothing is of feathers of various colors, and the body is painted, and the chest is bare, and from the waist to the knees they are covered, the arms without clothing. In the right hand they carry a stick made to take off the sweat. The face is painted. The head is bound with a band of hair woven so as to be able to thrust in the *cheyatom,* our words. This *cheyat* is made of feathers of any bird, and almost always of crow and of sparrow hawks, and in the middle a sharp stick in order to be able to insert it. Thus they are in the house, when immediately two men go out, each one carrying two wooden swords and crying out, without saying any word, and after stopping before the place where they dance, they look at the sky for some time. The people are silent, and they turn, and then the dancers go out. These two men are called by us *Pajaom,* meaning crimson snakes. In California there are large red snakes. These do not bite but lash out at those who come near them.

The dancers in this house can be as many as thirty, more or less. Going out of the house, they turn their faces to the singers and begin to give kicks, but not hard ones, because it is not the time, and when the song is finished the captain of the dancers, touching his feet, cries "hu," and all fall silent. He again comes to the singers and sings, and all dance, and at last cries "hu," and the singers fall silent, and they make the sound of the horse who is looking for his son. The sound "hu" means nothing in our language, but the dancers understand that it means "be silent." When the captain does not say "hu," the singers cannot be silent, and they repeat and repeat the song until the captain wants them to stop. Then they go before the singers and all the people who are watching them, and the captain of the dancers sings and dances, and the others follow him. They dance in a circle, kicking, and whoever gets tired stays in the middle of the circle and then follows the others. No one can laugh in this dance, and all follow the first ones with head bent and eyes toward the earth. When this stops, all take off the *cheyat* to end the dance and, holding it in the right hand, they raise it to heaven, blowing at each kick that they give to the earth, and the captain ends the dance with a "hu," and all return to the houses of the costumes, and at this the old men begin to suck or smoke, and all the smoke goes up to heaven three times before ending the dance. This done, it ends. The old man returns to his house tired, because the dance lasts three hours, and it is necessary to sing for three hours. It is danced in the middle of the day, when the sun burns more, and then the shoulders of the dancers look like fountains of water with so much sweat that falls. This dance is difficult, and among two thousand men there was one who knew how to dance well.

Second Dance

The second dance never pleases me, because whoever can cry more, cries; whoever can leap, leaps, but always according to the song; and it very much resembles the Spanish dance. There is an old singer who has a dead tortoise with a little stick in the middle, and the hands, feet, head, and tail are stopped up, and little stones are put inside, and thus moving it gives it sound. And always they dance through the night. They can dance among many. When they dance the old ones throw wheat and maize at them, and here the women can dance too.

Third Dance

The third is the most difficult, and for this reason, the dancers of this kind are few. In this dance one person dances. Before the dancer goes out, two men who are called red serpents (as we have said) go out. The dancer wears his *pala* from the waist to the knees, made of feathers. On his head he wears a long eagle feather, in his hands two well-made sticks, thick as a reed, one and one-half hands long, and all his body painted. The circle in which he dances is eight steps in circumference, more or less according to the place, and at four to seven steps there is an old man who watches so that the dancer cannot fall, which is very easy, because he must look at the sky, one foot raised, the other on the ground, one arm in the air, and the other to-ward the earth, and thus he must walk around that circle. This circle is made of people who want to see the dance.

Let us begin. The serpents go out, and the people are silent, and then two singers begin to sing with the *cheyat* at the mouth, saying "hu" three times. We said that it means nothing. Then the dancer goes out and begins to run along that circle. The singers sing. He dances according to the song, as we have said, and when dancing he approaches an old man, he says "hu" to him, and raises his hands, and the dancer follows his road. He can neither laugh nor speak. It ends. The old men smoke and they return to their vil-lages. Let us leave the other dances and also those of the women. Now let us see the games that the Luiseños play, and let us tell the main ones, and we play many of them. There is the game we call *uauquis*, that is to say, the game of the ball with the stick, or rather cudgel. Let us begin with it.

Ball game

The place where they play is all level, in length a quarter and half a league, in width the same, the players all men of thirty to sixty years. In all they can be seventy or eighty—thirty or forty men on one side, thirty or forty on the other. They choose two leaders from this and from that side. Each one of the men holds his stick, which is four hands high, five joined fingers thick, arched below. The ball of the game is of wood, bigger than the egg of a turkey. There are two marks where they must throw the ball, and when the enemy crosses this mark, he has won.

The rule is that they cannot carry it in the hand very long, but on the ground with the stick. In the middle of the game they bury the ball, and the two leaders must get it out with their sticks, each one staying toward his mark, and his companions behind with sticks raised, waiting for the ball, and when it goes out, each one wants to carry it to his mark. And here tu-mult, shoves, the strength of Hercules is necessary if one by chance gets the ball, hurling it with all force to his mark, throwing it in the middle of the mark. The enemies follow it. Others hinder others. One falls running, hav-ing slipped. One with equal running comes up to the ball, and from there carries it to the other part, running for fear that they will take it from him, and seeing his companion at a distance, throws him the ball through the air. They carry it to their mark, running at all haste. The enemies attack them, and here riot, running like a deer to flee so that they do not catch up or reach them, and this game lasts three or four hours.

The women also play this each Sunday with permission. The Luiseños know how to play well, strong men. Once thirty Luiseños went off to San Juan, another mission near the Mission of San Luis Rey de Francia, our mission. They arrived there and were invited to play ball. They said, "We want to, but let us make a rule that you cannot carry the ball in your hand." Those indeed said, "Thus we will do. We will play with all justice." Sunday during the afternoon, the Luiseños took their sticks and went off to the place for the game.

They went out to meet them and brought them to the place for the game. They began to play with the same rule as the Luiseños, as we have already said before. All the people of this district were watching the game, and the captain of the district too was watching on horseback. All thirty Luiseños played well and were speedily defeating the Sanjuaneños, when one Sanjuaneño took the ball and carried it in his hand. Then a Luiseño came up and, seizing him by the waist, threw him up and made him fall. Another Sanjuaneño came to defend his countryman. Other Luiseños went to help the first. After these came the captain, and he beat a Luiseño. Then one of the Luiseños, stronger and with a huge body, gave a leap, knocked him down. The horse stepped on him and dragged him beneath his feet. He was not able to get up. Attracted by the uproar, the people came up with sticks in hand. The women followed a Luiseño who had no stick but could defend himself well with leaps, although they might be warded off, and the women threw stones anywhere, but they did not hurt him.

The Sanjuaneños fled with their split heads. The Luiseños remained alone. One wanted to give a blow to another, believing that he was a Sanjuaneño. Such was their rage, they did not recognize each other, and they were afraid of nothing. The Spanish soldiers arrived, although the uproar was ended, because they too were trembling, and they wished to end the tumult with words. The chief of the thirty Luiseños was an Indian and spoke like the Spanish. The Indian said to him, "Raise your saber, and then I will eat you," but in his language, and afterwards there was no trouble.

1825
The New Governor Brings Liberal Ideas

MANUEL CLEMENTE ROJO
AND ANGUSTIAS DE LA GUERRA

When the Iturbide empire collapsed, an elected constituent congress
drew up a new constitution. This document organized the country, which
was formally named the United Mexican States *(Estados Unidos Mexicanos)*,
into a federalist republic of nineteen states and four territories (including
Baja California and Alta California), with a bicameral congress and a president elected by the state legislatures. Freedom of speech and of the press
were guaranteed. The more conservative centralists, however, were able
to maintain the Catholic Church's monopoly on spiritual matters as well
as exemptions for the clergy and military from standing trial in civil
courts. Insurgent leader Guadalupe Victoria was elected president. In
1825 he appointed Colonel José María Echeandía, an engineer who was
involved in surveying the area of the Federal District in Mexico City, as
governor of both Californias.

Word of the partial triumph of liberal ideas preceded Echeandía to the
Californias. When the liberal Spanish parliament *(cortes)* of 1813 had
called for the secularization of the missions in the New World, a hope had
developed in California that this would be on the agenda of the new
regime. Secularization would be part of a larger liberal project that would
include freer trade, widespread private land ownership, and representative political institutions based on legal equality. Echeandía did begin this
process as he formally established a representative assembly *(diputación)* in
both Baja and Alta California.

The next two accounts, both composed decades later, captured the
spirit of the new beginning that the arrival of Echeandía symbolized for
many in both Californias. The first account was written by Manuel
Clemente Rojo, a native of Peru who was an important political figure in

341

Baja California after the North American invasion in 1846. Rojo, relying on stories he heard from others, described the spread of these liberal ideas among the indigenous people of Baja California. The story Rojo relates occurred as Echeandía was proceeding north through Baja California to take office in Monterey. At Mission San Vicente Ferrer, the resident Indians complained to him about their treatment at the hands of Fr. Antonio Menéndez. Echeandía swiftly removed Menéndez from San Vicente, ordered him to proceed north with him, and replaced him with Fr. Félix Caballero. The Indians expressed their gratitude by giving Echeandía an escort to San Diego. This also was a way to assure themselves that Menéndez was actually leaving. The second account was composed by Angustias de la Guerra, the daughter of José de la Guerra y Noriega, longtime commander of Santa Bárbara. Her reflections on what Echeandía brought to Alta California are less favorable.

From "Account Gleaned from the Verbal Reports Taken from the Old Men Don Santiago Domingo de Arce, Don Guadalupe Melendres, Don José Luciano Espinosa, and Don Pedro Eulogio Duarte" in the Reminiscences of Manuel Clemente Rojo, 1879

In the year 1825, there passed through the Frontier the first General who was known in it, who had disembarked at the port of Loreto, the former capital of Lower California, and who was traveling by land to Upper California, having been named Governor of both countries by the Government of Independence, and whose name was Don Manuel [sic] Echeandía; he brought in his company the Reverend Fathers Félix Caballero and Tomás Mansilla, whom he left in the missions of this Frontier, and took with him to San Diego Father Menéndez, who was administering Mission San Vicente Ferrer, on account of certain accusations of a private nature which an Indian of that same mission made against him; and since before that date no one had ever seen any missionary removed from his charge, this removal caused a great deal of surprise, especially because it was being done by the Governor, whose authority the Frontier people did not believe to be greater than that of a missionary, because they had so long been accustomed to the unlimited authority of the missionaries, who not only governed ecclesiastically, but also directed to a certain extent the

Left: José de la Guerra y Noriega, long-time commander of the Santa Bárbara presidio. Right: Angustias de la Guerra. Courtesy of The Bancroft Library, University of California, Berkeley.

military leaders who garrisoned the missions and the principal command post itself. This astonishment grew when it was considered that the removal of Father Menéndez stemmed from the simple accusation of an Indian, given the fact that the Indians had considered themselves up to that point as beings destined to suffer all the labors to which they were assigned by force, and who were absolutely subject to the will of the missionaries, whose iron will was now being bent easily in the modest presence of the republican General, who arrived treating everyone courteously, instilling in them by his example a new disposition unknown up to that time, because not only did he treat them with republican equality, but also took the trouble to explain to them the new principles of the Government of Independence, promising them that he would see to it that they were fulfilled, and that from then on the sorry condition of the Indians would improve, and they would receive all the aid and protection which was their due.

With these manifestations, the Indians took him in triumph from mission to mission all along the Frontier; he also offered the soldiers of the escort, who had suffered so much in years previous, and with respect to whose loyalty and constancy he was completely satisfied, that he would do as much as possible on his part so that the Supreme Government would pay them all their salary and that in the future none of it would remain due them.

From *Occurrences in Hispanic California*
by Angustias de la Guerra, 1878

I forgot to say with respect to Sr. Echeandía, that when he arrived in California in 1825 he came speaking of the republican and liberal principles which filled the heads of Mexicans in those days. He was a man of advanced ideas, enthusiastic and a lover of republican liberty. Certainly he put these ideas into practice; in fact, he had been sent to California to implant the new regime. Up until then, during the administration of Argüello, the regime of government had been the same as existed under Spanish domination except for the constitutional *Diputación* and the *Ayuntamiento*.

Echeandía made the Indians of the missions know that they also were free men and citizens. This produced a harmful effect in the Indian mind. They began to demand the practice of these rights. At once a relaxation of discipline became apparent, and the Indians did not obey the missionaries with their accustomed submission. Before this, an Indian obeyed his pastor like a child his father. I am referring to the respect and obedience of children toward their parents in those times, because paternal authority was unlimited and did not cease, even after the children married or even when they had their own children.

1827
A Young Californio Embraces the New Liberalism

Pío Pico

The liberal ideas represented by the Mexican constitution of 1824 and
José María Echeandía were especially attractive to the generation of young
men who were just coming of age in Alta California. Most of this new
generation had been born in California, and they took to calling themselves "sons of the country" *(hijos del país),* or "Californians" *(Californios),* to
underscore their own sense of ownership of the land and its future. This
younger group was anxious to break with the past represented by the
colonial missions and even with the colonial military in which their fathers had served, and to establish California as a place of liberal institutions and commerce. They quickly came to dominate the territorial assembly, and it gave voice to their concerns. In one such resolution in
1832, for instance, the *diputación* spoke of "the detestable system of the
missions," which had "oppressed" the Indians. This denunciation of the past
was coupled with calls for republican institutions such as "an organic constitution for our territory" and schools and "teachers to cement the advantages of the republican system."

The 1820s and 1830s were a heady time for this group. Many of them
could trace their roots to the rough frontier towns and *presidios* of Sonora
and Sinaloa. Their grandfathers or fathers had been corporals or sergeants,
yet they were rising to positions of authority and eminence in this new
land. For them and their families, Alta California was a place of fabulous
upward mobility. They were anxious to seize the moment and develop
their land.

Pío Pico was one of the leaders of this generation. His father, José
María, had served at the San Diego *presidio* and in the mission guard at San

Luis Rey. Pío Pico grew up at the mission. By the time he was in his twenties, he was a member of the *diputación,* and he proved to be one of its most effective leaders. Later in his life he remembered how important these new ideas had been in the formation of his political consciousness.

FROM *Historical Narrative,* BY PIÓ PICO, 1877

In 1827 or 1828, I was named scribe or secretary to Captain Don Pablo de la Portilla, who was named Attorney General, to take down declarations from one Señor Bringas, a Mexican. Señor Bringas was a merchant established in Los Angeles, and it was said that the merchandise he sold belonged to Don José María Herrera, principal Subcommissioner residing in Monterey, who was accused of misappropriation of public funds and of having purchased this merchandise with government money which had been given him in Mexico to pay the troops in California.

Captain Portilla and I arrived at Los Angeles and arranged a meeting with Señor Bringas at an office that had been established by the Captain in the home of Don Antonio Rocha, situated where the city jail is now. Señor Bringas presented himself. The Captain informed him of the object of his commission, to which Bringas answered that he respected and esteemed him very much as a private individual and as a friend, but as a Captain of the Mexican Army he was nothing more to him than the sole of his shoe. This reply impressed me profoundly, because we considered a Captain a personage of high rank and distinction. Not only Captains, but all officials, and even sergeants and corporals, and even the lowest of soldiers were treated with consideration.

I was even more surprised when I heard Bringas tell Portilla that the civilians *[paisanos]* were the sacred core of the nation, and that the military were nothing more than servants of the nation, which was constituted of the people and not of the military. Bringas declared he would not give his statement except in front of a person in civil authority, even if he were an Indian *alcalde* from the mission, but not before a military man, whatever his rank. Convinced, Señor Portilla decided to send a message to the Commandant General and another to the Commandant of San Diego, Captain José María Estudillo, laying before them Bringas's reluctance.

I offered to take the communication to the Commandant of San Diego, and my offer was accepted. I arrived at San Diego and delivered the document and was told by Señor Estudillo that I should go to my home to rest

Pío Pico and his wife, María Ignacia Alvarado. Reproduced by permission of The Huntington Library, San Marino, California.

until the next day, and that I should return to take the reply back to Los Angeles. By then I was beginning to feel the effects of Señor Bringas's words.

My mother and my family were all in need of my services in San Diego and made it plain to me that, for this reason, they were opposed to my return to Los Angeles. I wanted to please my mother and at the same time show my sense of independence. I now considered myself a "sacred vessel"—words which sounded very good to my ears. I presented myself to Estudillo. He had the official letter ready in his hand, and he asked me if I was prepared to depart as he handed me the letter. I told him that I was not able to return to Los Angeles, as I was needed at home. Then Señor Estudillo issued orders to the sergeant that I should be taken to the jail. They imprisoned me in a cell with other prisoners, though I had the luck not to be placed in iron. I was there all that day and that night, and the next morning Estudillo ordered my release, and that I should be taken to the Commandant's office. I went there and he asked me to excuse the manner in which I had been treated—that it had been a hot-headed action, and that I should go and look after my mother. I retired to my home and stayed at my mother's side, but always it appeared to me, deep in my soul, that the citizens were the nation and that no military was superior to us.

1827

A Mission-Oriented Proposal for Alta California

ENRIQUE VIRMOND

Under Spanish rule, trade with foreign vessels had been forbidden, although soldiers, settlers, and missionaries all traded with the foreign ships that called with increasing frequency in the early nineteenth century. Governor Solá had even worked out a tariff schedule on this trade. By the end of the Spanish era, vessels from anywhere were welcome to trade in Alta California. When Mexico gained its independence, the new government regularized the situation and began to remove the controls on commerce that were still on the books.

As the Mexican government worked out its trade policy it sometimes veered toward greater restrictions and control. In 1826, for instance, one set of regulations ordered that all goods were to be unloaded only at Monterey, and that tariffs and anchorage fees were to be increased. Merchants and ship captains protested, and Governor Echeandía suspended the regulation for California. This and other rules, however, mirrored an ongoing discussion in Mexico City and California about how the California economy might be most fruitfully promoted and exploited.

The following selection deals with this question. It was written by Enrique Virmond, a German-born trader who operated from Acapulco. It was addressed to an unnamed high governmental official.

Virmond had long had a close relationship with the missionaries, especially with Fr. Narciso Durán of Mission San José. In Virmond's vision of California's future, the missions would continue to predominate, a gradually increasing number of private *ranchos* would help to diversify California agriculture, and the Mexican government would undertake to stimulate trade between the Mexican mainland and California—and on Mexican ships sailing between California and the rest of the world. Virmond's vision was one of gradual growth that did not represent a dramatic break with California's mission past.

FROM A REPORT ON ALTA CALIFORNIA
BY ENRIQUE VIRMOND

The bay of San Pedro could be converted into one of the best ports if its sand bar were removed. If someone were willing to make the effort required, it could become one of the principal harbors in the country. Agricultural enterprises have been fostered considerably by the missionaries during the last few years, and perhaps they could be increased even more if there were a market for what they grow. Up to now, the Russians have been the only purchasers of wheat. I would estimate that they purchase from twelve to fifteen thousand *fanegas* of wheat at a price of three *pesos* per *fanega* to send to Sitka, which is the capital of their possessions along the northwest coast. It is not worth sending the wheat in bulk to Peru, Guayaquil, or any other place in the Pacific. However, if water or windmills could be built, I believe that California could secure the greater part of the flour business in those countries.

Up to now, English, Anglo-American, and Russian ships, as well as some Mexican ones, have been the only traders in the country. The English bring some goods, and also money, and exchange them for hide and tallow. The Anglo-Americans sail out of Boston with a perfectly supplied storehouse on board, and they take away hide, tallow, and whatever money the country has. This commerce seems to me to be quite harmful, since the outcome is that the country is left almost entirely without money. The retail sales they make in their one-and-a-half to two-year treks from port to port along the coast of both Alta and Baja California hinder the *criollo* merchant who wants to purchase these items. As a result, he cannot prosper.

Commerce with the Russians is quite advantageous. They come in search of grain and meat. They bring very few goods. They trade mostly in hard cash.

Recently, a ship arrived looking for horses for the Sandwich Islands. Until recently, the few national [Mexican] ships that have come up generally have brought goods and products of the Republic and some money. However, they have made some miscalculations with respect to their cargo.

Assuming that certain items prohibited by the laws would be scarce, they have discovered instead that there is an abundance of these items, since foreigners have been allowed to bring them in.

The national merchants could provide the same items more cheaply with some protection from the Supreme Government and strict observance of the laws. The number of national ships would increase, and a more regular type of commerce beneficial to the country could be established. I, myself, in place of the one ship I now have, would buy more in order to send these products in a national ship all the way to Europe.

To link Alta California to this Republic, it seems to me that the fortification of the port of San Francisco should be a primary focus of Your Excellency. Two strong batteries—one on the side of Point Bonita and the other where the *castillo* is presently located—would render the port secure against an attack from the sea, since the entrance is very narrow. In addition, there are three islands within the same port, and if they were well fortified they would provide security to the entire bay.

It seems to me that this port is suitable for a gunnery site that could be established in the northern part of the port, where there are many appropriate locations. The climate there is less harsh and there is also an abundance of timber. I cannot tell Your Excellency with certainty that the timber is adequate for the construction of ships. However, I should assume that it is, since the spot borders the Bodega River, which is where the Russians have constructed war and merchant brigantines. Also, the launches which go from mission to mission within the port of San Francisco have been built at that river. With such an enterprise in this port it might finally be given its due. People have been avoiding it up to now because of its cool climate, which is also immensely healthy. I dare say to Your Excellency that perhaps nowhere else in the entire Mexican Republic can one find another place that is so useful and that has all essential materials so near at hand as this port.

I should bring another matter to Your Excellency's attention. The majority of the *hijos del país* who are in the military have asked to be discharged, but the Señor Commander General has refused to grant these requests. If these men did retire from the service, it would be a great good for the country in many ways. Their military knowledge does not extend beyond perhaps knowing how to rope a bull. Since almost all of the soldiers are married and their families are growing very rapidly, it is a heavy burden for the state and the missions that have to support them. And they inevitably end up in miserable circumstances. If they were free they would be able to

Vista de la Bahía y Puerto de Acapulco, desde el alto de el Ospital de los PP.s Ypolitos.

Acapulco, the home base of Enrique Virmond, as rendered by Tomás de Suria during the Malaspina expedition, 1791. Courtesy of the Museo Naval, Madrid (MS 1726-44).

take advantage of the land, work in the fields, and consequently make life much more comfortable for themselves and their families. The unmarried soldiers who would be sent from here to replace them would be like trees planted for future settlement. It would be much less burdensome to replace them. In case of need, the Government would be able to count on them more, since they would be experienced soldiers. The Indian and the soldier who is an *hijo del país* are enemies who will never become allies. Generally, the soldiers were born at the missions where their fathers were stationed. They have grown up with the Indian children and have acquired some of their gentile customs as well as their vices. They never forget, however, that they are white and they never forget the notion that the Indians were born to be their slaves. Since the soldiers have had and still have power in their hands, at times passion has wielded authority over justice. The Indian, who has no other safeguard than the Father, has had to suffer many times even though he was innocent. He resents this treatment even more because it comes from his childhood companion, the person with whom he played games and got drunk, than if he had received this treatment from a stranger. Believe me, Your Excellency, the unrest that has occurred in California and that can still occur has no other basis than the quarrels an Indian has with a soldier over unjust treatment and from the resentments that inevitably follow.

Because of the great scarcity of missionary Fathers and the advanced age of those who serve, some missions are visibly declining. I cannot recommend to Your Excellency strongly enough that California needs more clergymen. It is not yet possible for the Indians to govern themselves. If there are no Fathers, most of the Indians will return to being gentiles and will abandon the missions and their work. Consequently, the country will be ruined and without labor, for in California, the Indian is the only one who works.

Finally, if Your Excellency would permit me to say two words in favor of these religious who have spent the greater part of their lives in these remote regions trying to convert some of the unfaithful to Christianity and to render the gentiles useful to the nation. The fact that some of the Fathers have refused to swear allegiance to the constitution of this Republic is a matter of conscience for them. It is not up to me to become involved in this. However, I can assure Your Excellency that I have dealt with most of them for a number of years, and I have found them to be very moral, selfless, and simple men. Their only concern is the preaching of the Gospel and the management of the temporalities of the Indians. On every occasion, they have shown themselves obedient and ready to contribute in any way to the needs of the troops. At times this has meant even depriving themselves and their Indians of what they themselves needed. Even though since 1811 they have been paid basically nothing of the four hundred *pesos* a year the King of Spain annually allotted to each of them for their work, they have always been content to fulfill their duties.

Your Excellency might be able to find other people of equal virtue and honesty to administer these temporalities, but never any people with more of these qualities. Some people talk about the great riches some missions possess, but believe me, Your Excellency, these are just tales. I have dealt with these Fathers on business matters, and I have seen that everything they have bought from me has been divided among the Indians and the needs of the Church and the missions. This country is currently flourishing, and that is because of the Fathers. They have been tireless in their work and they will continue to be so, if they can rely on the protection of the Supreme Government. They encourage every class of industry and they freely lend their efforts to all public works and to the construction of homes for private individuals. They practice every type of virtue and charity toward their neighbors. They care for and clothe a large number of unclothed people. There is no one, rich or poor, who has not been received in their residences with the greatest generosity and openness while, at the same time and without self-interest, freely supplied with provisions, mules, horses, servants, and whatever else they needed for their journey.

Such has been the conduct of the missionary Fathers of Alta California. It is deeply gratifying for me to have this opportunity to inform Your Excellency of the services they have rendered and provided to the nation every day, which makes them worthy of gratitude and public respect.

1828
North American Trappers Intrude into Alta California

Luis Antonio Argüello

Foreign residents began to trickle into the Alta California coastal area in the 1820s as increased commerce made the presence of resident agents desirable for traders. William E. P. Hartnell, a British subject who had resided in South America, arrived in 1822 and acted on behalf of traders in Lima, Liverpool, and Edinburgh. William A. Gale of Boston, a super-cargo, had a number of extended stays in Alta California in the 1820s, and Henry Fitch of New Bedford arrived aboard Virmond's ship in 1826. Alfred Robinson arrived in 1829 as agent for a Boston firm. There were others as well. Generally, these early arrivals became Catholics, acquired Mexican citizenship, learned Spanish, and married into *Californio* families. They tried, in other words, to assimilate into Mexican California.

Another group of foreigners arrived in the late 1820s and beyond, and their presence was more destabilizing. They arrived overland from the Rocky Mountains and employed a network of trails that would ultimately fulfill the age-old dream of creating an overland route to California, but one that would connect California to the United States more than to Mexico. The hub of these routes was the New Mexican *pueblo* of Santa Fe. A land route from the Chihuahua area to Santa Fe had existed since the beginning of the seventeenth century. By the time of the colonization of Alta California, Santa Fe contained over twenty-three hundred people and regular supply caravans plied the *Camino Real** from there to Chihuahua and ultimately to Mexico City. From the north, various Indian trails led

---

* Major roads in New Spain were often called *Camino Real,* or Royal Road. *El Camino Real* in Baja and Alta California was only one of many trade routes to be so designated in the New World.

Map of Alta California in 1830 by José María Narváez. The territory was divided into four districts corresponding to its four presidios. Courtesy of The Bancroft Library, University of California, Berkeley.

into Santa Fe, and they were used in the eighteenth century by traders and soldiers. The vast majority of these and other trails that were "blazed" in both the Mexican and U.S. frontiers followed existing Indian trails. A journey north from Santa Fe in 1776 by Silvestre Vélez de Escalante reached the territory of the Utes.

In 1821, the Santa Fe Trail was opened to Missouri. At many points, the trail simply used routes established in connection with the fur trade between Santa Fe and the Plains Indians on the eastern side of the Rockies. In the 1820s, fur trappers from the United States entered the Rockies in considerable numbers, and the annual "rendezvous," a gathering of trappers and Indians, became a major event from 1825 to 1840.

After the 1826 rendezvous, Jedediah Smith and a small group of trappers seeking furs headed southwest through the valleys of the Sevier, Virgin, and Colorado Rivers. Smith was guided into California by two Indians who had escaped from Mission San Gabriel. Governor Echeandía detained him and ordered him to leave California by the same route he had entered. Instead, Smith headed up the Central Valley and trapped his way north. Leaving a band of his men at the Stanislaus River, he crossed the Sierra Nevada by the river's north fork, crossed the Great Basin, and arrived in the Rockies in time for the next rendezvous. He soon returned to California with a larger party and rejoined his men along the Stanislaus River. The Mojave Indians had attacked him and seized his supplies, so he went to Mission San José in search of more. There he was jailed and questioned by Ignacio Martínez of the San Francisco *presidio*. The authorities were especially worried about any illicit trading Smith might have been conducting with the Yokuts of the Central Valley—over the preceding two decades, Spanish and Mexican forces had fought at least six military engagements with them. Smith was then sent to Monterey and questioned by a very skeptical Echeandía. He was released only when a group of Anglo-American merchants of the town posted bond for him. Echeandía ordered that Smith be taken to Sonoma under military guard and from there be escorted out of California. Former governor Luis Antonio Argüello, also at San Francisco, assisted Smith in arranging for supplies for the journey at Mission San José. When Smith expressed a desire to return through the fur-rich Central Valley, rather than on the route Echeandía had prescribed, Argüello insisted that he had to follow the governor's orders. So Smith simply snuck out of San José one night on his own. In the following letter to Echeandía, written a few days after Smith's unauthorized departure, Argüello poured out his feelings of having been used and disrespected by the American.

From a Letter by Luis Antonio Argüello

January 2, 1828

I have not the least doubt that these foreigners have illegal plans to upset the harmonious purposes of our nation. They only care for themselves. They have convinced me of their design, because they are not grateful for the favors given to them. Abusing those favors, they mock the authorities.

After having been treated with the kindness characteristic of our nation, they have left owing debts against the sale of their furs (which, if I am not mistaken, they usurped), import duties, and other taxes that they should have paid for goods purchased from the frigate *Franklin,* and other private debts, including one to me—they owe me some forty *pesos.* The worst is that I fear that after all these deceits they will not leave our territory, and that they will return by the same routes that they wished, concealing themselves among the treasures that attract them (as I understand it), and again will gather as many furs as possible and will remove them from our territory, in which they are abundant. In the meantime, we repose in our confidence.

I have considerable evidence to convince me of this point. I believe, however, it is more prudent to restrain myself in order not to overwhelm Your Excellency [with information]. I will conclude only by saying that Smith's farewell was to send me a letter from San José that I could not understand, because it is in his language and because I do not have an official interpreter to translate it. Smith sent another letter for Your Excellency that I believe will treat the permit that you agreed to. But be that as it may, I do not wish to be anything other than a loyal executor of commands and higher orders in everything that concerns the best interest of the nation and the fulfillment of my obligations.

Perhaps this is a point of honor. On various occasions, Captain Smith and other foreigners have insulted me, threatening [to report me] to Your Excellency only because I have upheld higher orders. Perhaps because I communicate them verbally, the foreigners believe that they are promulgated by me. So, too, the English expeditionary frigate *Blossom* tried to intimidate me, but they miscalculated, because my character is not that of one who surrenders, except in justice and in reason to the voice of legitimate authorities.

I certainly hope that my suspicions, based on my limited knowledge, will not come back to haunt me after a few days. I say this in respect to *Caudillo* Smith and his party based on their conduct, and I do not know if my suspicions can be deduced from [the behavior of] his countrymen or fellow countrymen who live among us in the guise of mediators. They alone know their motives, while we [remain] full of the utmost trust in their actions and conduct, contracts, arrangements, and friendships. Only experience itself and knowledge of their language (allowing oneself to understand) can remove doubts. We overlook their not infrequent deceits, and in no way would I, and much less Your Excellency, want anyone to treat our nation, and the authorities that represent her, with such contempt. Things experienced firsthand make, no doubt, a greater impression than those heard from afar. Perhaps since Your Excellency has to listen from afar to my version, this will convince one who vacillates between whether it could or could not be as I tell it. But I am confident of your broad grasp and I have no doubt that Your Excellency will treat the matter with the urgency that its seriousness deserves.

Meanwhile, whether or not the deception occurs, I remain wishing Your Excellency all happiness. With the truest expressions of high solidarity, your loyal *compañero* who appreciates you, respects you, and kisses your hand.

Luis Antonio Argüello

1829
The Missions in Their Last Years

ALFRED A. ROBINSON

Alfred A. Robinson was born in Massachusetts in 1806 and came to California in 1829 as a clerk for the Bryant and Sturgis Company. He engaged in the hide and tallow trade for a number of years. In 1836, he married Ana María de la Guerra, daughter of José de la Guerra y Noriega of Santa Bárbara. He returned to the East in 1842, and four years later anonymously published *Life in California,* which became an important North American account of Mexican Alta California. Robinson returned to California in 1849 as an agent for the Pacific Mail Steamship Company. He lived in Santa Bárbara and San Francisco for the remainder of his life. He died in 1895.

This passage, taken from *Life in California,* is the account of a trip Robinson, William A. Gale, Manuel Domínguez, and Domínguez's servant Chulo took to Missions San Juan Capistrano (where the account begins) and San Gabriel. Robinson describes a mission system at the height of its development, with extensive lands and cattle, well-ordered gardens, friendly and contented padres, and assimilated Indians. As we have seen, however, such a picture could be applied to the missions for only a very limited portion of their existence. The California missions existed for over sixty years. For most of that period they struggled with ill-constructed buildings, contentious indigenous and Spanish neighbors, and an uncertain future. Their apparent prosperity resulted only from a temporary conjunction of fortunate circumstances in the 1810s—unrest in Mexico and a growing demand for their hides and tallow. These very circumstances also sowed the seeds of their destruction when the Mexican republic followed through on the Spanish program of secularization and *ranchos* took over the profitable hide and tallow trade. Throughout California's Spanish and Mexican periods, mission prosperity was more often the exception than the rule.

FROM *Life in California,* BY ALFRED A. ROBINSON

A corpulent old man received us at the door, bade us welcome, and appeared delighted to see my companion, with whom he had formed an acquaintance in former years. It was the superintendent of the mission, who seemed superannuated yet, from long experience in the situation, was still capable of fulfilling the duties of his office; he gave us a room within the square, where we proceeded to take possession and found the furniture, like the building, fast tumbling to decay. Two aged missionary friars resided here, but one alone attended to the temporal concerns of the mission; this was Padre Gerónimo Boscana. The other, Padre José María Zalvidea, though at this time secluded and apparently weak in mind, once took an active and laborious part in the management of the missions. This establishment was founded in the year 1776, and though in early years the largest in the country, yet is now in a dilapidated state, and the Indians are much neglected. There yet remain the ruins of an immense church which was destroyed by an earthquake in 1812, when many Indians were buried in its fall. It still bears the appearance of having been one of the best finished structures of the country, and the workmanship displayed in the sculpture upon its walls and its vaulted roof would command admiration in our own country.

The arrangement of the mission of San Juan is similar to that of San Luis; in fact, all these establishments are formed upon the same plan, and much resemble each other, varying only in their extent and population. In many of the villages the residences consist of straw huts of an oval form, which, when decayed, the Indians set on fire and erect new ones. Here, however, they are built of unburnt brick, tiled and whitewashed, feigning five or six blocks, or streets, which present a neat and comfortable appearance.

It was not until evening (suppertime) that we saw the padres, who were then seated at the table, unconscious of our approach till announced by the old majordomo. Immediately they arose, embraced us, and welcomed us to their hospitable board. During the meal our conversation turned on the political state of Europe, in regard to which they seemed to be very well informed, and they found an absorbing topic in the prospect of Spanish influence in Mexico.

The following morning we started for San Gabriel, distant twenty leagues. As we proceeded, our course was through a long and narrow defile between the hills, having before us the high, snow-capped mountains of

Mission San Gabriel in 1832, by Ferdinand Deppe. Courtesy of the Santa Barbara Mission Archive Library.

San Juan, till at length we left them on our right, and a short gallop soon brought us to an extensive plain. The road was level, and Chulo, elated with the prospect of soon reaching the habitation of his "ladylove," resumed his whistling and shouting and, dashing forward among the animals, drove them furiously along the track. We followed swiftly at his rear, our horses being unwilling to be left behind, and a few hours brought us to the farm or Rancho de Santa Ana.

The proprietor, Don Tomás Yorba, a tall, lean personage dressed in all the extravagance of his country's costume, received us at the door of his house. He came toward us, embraced G. and his *compadre* Don Manuel, took me cordially by the hand, and invited us to enter. Arrangements were soon made for dinner, which, notwithstanding the haste with which it was served, did much credit to the provider, as did our appetites to its excellent qualities.

Don Tomás and friend G. then commencing a business conversation, I got up from the table and retreated to the corridor, where I could study, unobserved, the character and appearance of our host. Upon his head he wore a black silk handkerchief, the four corners of which hung down his neck behind. An embroidered shirt, a cravat of white jaconet tastefully tied, a blue damask vest, short clothes of crimson velvet, a bright green cloth jacket with large silver buttons, and shoes of embroidered deerskin comprised his dress. I was afterwards informed by Don Manuel that on some occasions, such as some particular feast day or festival, his entire display often exceeded in value a thousand dollars.

The day was wearing apace, so we hastened our departure and mounted again for the journey. Don Tomás had prepared to accompany us to a river that crossed our route which at some seasons of the year proved dangerous to travelers unacquainted with the pass. This was a thoughtful precaution on his part and received from us due acknowledgment. We rode along slowly through the sandy soil till at length we saw the rapid stream, which, by our friend's guidance, was easily forded, and he bade us farewell.

The journey continued across a plain where thousands of cattle were grazing, and immense herds of wild horses which fled swiftly to the mountains on our approach. We soon reached the river of San Gabriel, and having forded this stream, Don Manuel, who had accompanied us thus far from San Diego, left us to pursue our journey alone to the mission, which was now just in sight, whilst he proceeded for *El Pueblo de los Angeles,* where his wife's family resided and where he had for some time past made his permanent home.

It was Saturday evening, and as we approached the buildings of the mission, the chapel bells tolled the hour for prayer. Hundreds of Indians were kneeling upon the ground, and as the tolling ceased, they slowly rose to retire, and a merry peal announced the coming of the Sabbath.

The director of San Gabriel was Father José Sanches, who for many years had controlled the establishment, which, through his management, had advanced to its present flourishing condition. Possessing a kind, generous, and lively disposition, he had acquired, in consequence, a multitude of friends who constantly flocked around him, whilst through his liberality the needy wanderer, of whatever nation or creed, found a home and protection in the mission.

In the morning, at six o'clock, we went to the church, where the priest had already commenced the service of the Mass. The imposing ceremony, glittering ornaments, and illuminated wall were well adapted to captivate the simple mind of the Indian, and I could not but admire the apparent devotion of the multitude, who seemed absorbed, heart and soul, in the scene

Alfred Robinson. Courtesy of The Bancroft Library, University of California, Berkeley.

before them. The solemn music of the Mass was well selected, and the Indian voices accorded harmoniously with the flutes and violins that accompanied them. On retiring from the church, the musicians stationed themselves at a private door of the building, whence issued the Reverend Father, whom they escorted with music to his quarters; there they remained for a half-hour, performing waltzes and marches, until some trifling present was distributed among them, when they retired to their homes.

As is usual on all their *días de fiesta,* the remaining part of the Sabbath is devoted to amusements, and the Indian generally resorts to gambling, in which he indulges to the most criminal excess, frequently losing all he possesses in the world—his clothes, beads, baubles of all kinds, and even his wife and children! We saw them thus engaged, scattered in groups about the mission, while at a little distance quite an exciting horserace was going on; the Indians betting as wildly on their favorite animals as upon the games of chance which found so many devotees.

There are several extensive gardens attached to this mission, where may be found oranges, citrons, limes, apples, pears, peaches, pomegranates, figs, and grapes in abundance. From the latter they make yearly from four to six hundred barrels of wine and two hundred of brandy, the sale of which produces an income of more than twelve thousand dollars. The storehouses and granaries are kept well supplied, and the corridor in the square is usually heaped up with piles of hides and tallow. Besides the resources of the vineyard, the mission derives considerable revenue from the sale of grain; and the weekly slaughter of cattle produces a sufficient sum for clothing and supporting the Indians.

The two *ranchos* of San Bernardino and Santa Anita are included in the possessions of the mission; the former of these has been assigned by the padres for the sole purpose of domesticating cattle and is located some leagues distant, in a secluded valley among the mountains; the latter is for cultivation, and is one of the fairy spots to be met with so often in California. On the declivity of a hill is erected a *molino,* or grist mill, surrounded with fruit trees and flowers. A beautiful lake lies calm and unruffled in front and all around, fresh streams are gushing from the earth and scattering their waters in every direction. It would be a magnificent spot for a summer retreat and much reminded me of many of the beautiful locations to be met with in the vicinity of Boston.

The Mission of San Gabriel was founded in the year 1771, and its population, including the two *ranchos* before mentioned, now numbered from twelve to fifteen hundred. It was thought at one time to possess from eighty to over a hundred thousand head of cattle, besides horses, mules, and sheep, and countless numbers which run at large. No advantage is derived from them beyond the value of their hides and tallow, and thus thousands of dollars are yearly left to perish on the field.

While here, I met with a Yankee from the interior of New England who had been a resident in the country for many years and who had become, in manner and appearance, a complete Californian. One peculiarity, however: he retained the spirit of trade, which had lost none of its original power, and to which I owed thus early my acquaintance with him. He was married and living in Santa Bárbara, where he was engaged in business in a small way, and learning that we were on our route up the coast, he had come all the way to meet us in order to gain some trifling advantage over his competitors in trade.

1829
The Revolt of Estanislao

JOSÉ SÁNCHEZ AND JOAQUÍN PIÑA

By the late 1820s, Mission San José was one of the largest indigenous population centers in Mexican California. With over seventeen hundred Indian residents (only San Luis Rey housed a greater number), its farms produced over six thousand bushels of wheat and over fifteen hundred each of corn and barley. Its lands contained over ten thousand head each of horses, sheep, and cattle. A number of the Lakisamne people (a branch of the Yokuts family), whose *ranchería* was about fifty miles east of the mission, appear to have entered the mission in the 1820s. Estanislao, who was either a *vaquero* or a mule tamer or maybe both, rose to the position of *alcalde*. In November 1828 the mission priest, Fr. Narciso Durán, realized that Estanislao and a number of other mission Indians who had left the mission to visit their *ranchería* were not going to return. Ignacio Martínez at San Francisco sent out a search party under Corporal Antonio Soto. This party confirmed that the Lakisamne were indeed "fugitives" and were constructing fortifications to repel any attempt to return them.

In the spring a military expedition of some thirty soldiers and seventy Indian allies was sent out under the leadership of veteran Indian fighter José Sánchez, but Estanislao and his group, which by now included Indians who had left Mission Santa Clara to join them, defeated the Spanish and their allies, and Sánchez had to retreat. The first document below is taken from Sánchez's report to Martínez on the failed expedition. It demonstrates the way in which Estanislao and his forces were able to isolate and immobilize the scattered soldiers of Sánchez's party.

Martínez then chose *Alférez* Mariano Guadalupe Vallejo of the Monterey *presidio* to command a combined force from the two northern *presidios* and some guards from nearby missions. Vallejo's force of one hundred soldiers left on May 26. When they arrived at the Indians' fortification, Vallejo attempted to simultaneously set part of it afire and attack another part of it. After a fierce battle, Vallejo's men were unable to dislodge the defenders. When Vallejo resumed the attack the next morning, the Indians were gone. Vallejo tracked them to another fortification they had constructed ten miles away. Another attack with the same tactics yielded the same result. The troops captured a few survivors, but most of the defenders were gone. The soldiers and their Indian allies then massacred most of the survivors, including aged men and a number of women. Then the army declared victory and returned to Mission San José.

The second document is from the diary of Joaquín Piña, one of Vallejo's soldiers. It describes the attack on the second fortification and the aftermath.

No Mexican soldiers perished in Vallejo's expedition, and the number of Indian casualties is not known. It appears that Estanislao and a number of his companions did return to Mission San José. There they were protected by Fr. Durán, who also bitterly protested to the governor about the massacre. Estanislao seems to have perished in an epidemic that struck the mission in 1839. The Stanislaus River (the site of his people's *ranchería)* and Stanislaus County are named after him.

FROM A REPORT BY JOSÉ SÁNCHEZ

I have just arrived at seven o'clock in the afternoon at this Mission of San José on my return from the campaign which you entrusted to my command. Its purpose was to make a surprise attack on the Christian Indian rebels of Santa Clara and San José, who, in alliance with the heathen Indians, have built fortifications in an impenetrable forest along the Stanislaus River. Since a detailed description would be very extensive, I shall not delay giving a report of the events and results of this campaign, or operation, for your information.

We approached the river [Stanislaus] at seven o'clock in the morning of the seventh of this month, where the Christian conspirators were located. We had heard before our arrival that they were all prepared to attack us. This we confirmed immediately, for we saw them entrenched in the woods. In consideration of this fact I ordered the mortar to be brought forward, while keeping the troops in good formation, and directed that the piece open fire. Unfortunately, at the first shot the gun carriage broke, but in spite of this, two more shots were fired. However, since I concluded that the piece was useless, I thereupon ordered fire with the carbines. I maintained this action for a considerable period of time without the enemy ceasing to reply with a multitude of arrows as well as with firearms. According to rumor, the latter were loaded with nothing but powder. They did no damage, and afterward I learned that the Indians had no bullets. However, the fierceness of the sun to which we were exposed forced the troops to abandon the thicket, and I retired about a thousand yards from the furious mob [of Indians] in the shelter of the woods from which they stubbornly refused to retreat. I camped with all the troops, with no more trouble than was caused by the excessive heat, the fatigue of the day's efforts, and the broken gun carriage, one of the wheels of which was broken, as I have said. Now there approached, always protected by the underbrush, one of the insurgent Christian chiefs, called Estanislao, to talk with the Indian auxiliaries who accompanied us on this journey. On seeing him I went toward him and called to him. Before I reached him, however, another Indian arrived and, hidden by the same underbrush, fired a shot at me. Then they left, and thereafter we passed a night through which not a sound could be heard.

On the following day, the eighth, as soon as it was daylight, the troops were formed and divided into six groups of six men each with their corporal. They were given what appeared to me appropriate instructions. One squad was to guard the horses and supplies, three were to enter the woods. The remaining two were to guard the right and left flanks, and at the same time prevent the rebels from working around the sides to the rear while the attack was being made in the interior of the thicket. This was all contingent upon the enemy's not yielding to the arguments with which I first intended to present them. Having taken all the necessary precautions demanded by the situation, I went out with only the interpreter, for the specified purpose of pleading with the rebels that they should repent and surrender. But my exhortation had no effect. Only Estanislao, the principal chief whom I have already mentioned, answered me, saying that he was not guilty because he had been advised that they should defend themselves, and consequently they would die there. Thereupon I talked to the heathen chiefs, trying to make them understand that the troops were ready to enter the thicket and that they could obviate the damage which would be done to them if they were obstinate by deserting the Christians. I was unsuccessful, for they continued to adhere to the cause of the Christians.

In view of all this, I ordered an immediate advance by the troops into the woods. They fired as they went, and when we were already committed to

Fr. Narciso Durán and an indigenous child as they appeared in a French publication in 1844. Courtesy of the California History Room, California State Library, Sacramento, California.

the engagement and the contest was going favorably for us, everything went wrong through the rashness of four soldiers. Taking no precautions, they separated themselves from the squad under command of Corporal Lázaro Piña. In spite of the fact that the latter tried to stop them, they did not obey and plunged into the underbrush to go and drink water from the river. Without doubt they were caught there unaware by the enemy, with the consequence that two of them were left on the spot badly wounded. They were rescued by Corporal Piña with only the two remaining soldiers. At the same time that they had joined the group under Corporal José Berreyesa, an Indian auxiliary arrived with the report that four soldiers were isolated and in danger. Immediately I ordered Corporals Berreyesa and Piña to proceed with their party in search of these soldiers. When they had done this they returned with only two of them. Both had been hit and were badly wounded. One had lost his weapons and the other, although he still retained them, could not use them for lack of ammunition. Meanwhile, the enemy was on them, trying to finish them off. At this juncture the party I mentioned arrived, and in their presence, those trying to kill the men fled. Forming a screen against arrows, the party brought out the wounded on their shoulders.

These two, who were among the four who detached themselves from the squad of Corporal Piña, then stated that their other two companions had remained, dead, in the hands of the enemy. This the Indian auxiliaries confirmed, adding that the enemy removed the clothing from the corpses and threw them in the river which flows through the middle of the thicket. I was convinced that it was impossible to bring out the corpses, first because all the ammunition had been used up, and second because it was already late and the troops were fatigued from fighting on foot in the impenetrable brush in the extreme heat. We had two soldiers dead and eight wounded, one mortally. The weapons were almost entirely useless: three muskets lost, two with their bandoliers. So I decided to withdraw. I retired with the soldiers and the Indian auxiliaries to the place where we had camped the previous day and where the horses were kept. I wanted the soldiers to have some rest so that I might continue the retreat. All this was done. Of the enemy, several were killed, although we could not determine the number, because the brush could not be penetrated.

Finally, I would be remiss in my duty if I neglected to commend this small contingent of troops who operated under my command for their valorous conduct in the face of all the dangers of the terrain and other advantages possessed by those savages. So I beg that you will give them your highest consideration as a whole, and in particular Corporal Antonio Soto, and soldiers Manuel Piña and Lorenzo Pacheco, who were severely wounded in the face of the enemy.

I communicate all this to you for your information.

From the Diary of Joaquín Piña

May 31, 1829: At three o'clock in the morning, the Commander ordered the troops to mount and continue the march, and at four o'clock they arrived at the aforementioned village. Here, even though they kept strict silence, the Indians noticed that the troops were coming close and immediately began to give cries of alarm. On descending to the site of the village, the troops encountered a stockade, which, it was apparent, the Indians were just beginning to construct. Now the Commander took the following measures. He ordered that immediately a corporal and ten men should watch the edge of the thicket and prevent the enemy from escaping. These men went to the right, while five others were sent to the left flank, along the river. The remainder of the troops began to set fire to the two sides, with the result that the Indians retreated to the center of the forest. During this interval, the Commander sent a civilian and the guide who we had with us with a message that the cannon, infantry, ammunition, supplies, and remaining troops in charge of the horses all should come up and join the others at the place where he was now located. This was done with the greatest celerity.

At 8:04 in the morning of May 31 we set out, and at about 11:30 we arrived at the point where the Commander was staying. He ordered the field piece to go into the forest with the troops in pursuit of the rebels. When the gun arrived in position, through the Indian captured on the thirtieth and through the interpreter, the Indians were admonished that if they would come out from the interior of the thicket, no harm would be done to them. But it was noticed that the Indian captive, instead of encouraging them to surrender, was making signs that they should retreat far into the brush and was saying that they should not come out because they would be killed, and that the artillery and the *cholos* were coming on behind him. No one responded except one Indian, quite Spanish, called Matías. He went over to where the troops were located, begging them for mercy. He declared that the Indian prisoner was a heathen and that the latter had discouraged all the others from giving up. The prisoner consequently was immediately shot.

At 1:07 p.m. the Commander ordered that the Indian Matías should accompany the troops as guide and enter the forest. When the artillery, infantry, cavalry, civilians, and Indian auxiliaries had been set in motion and had just reached the edge of the forest, Matías was told to speak to his compatriots and say to them that the troops were about to close in on them, and that they should come out. Their reply was that they would not do this, they would prefer to die on the spot. Therefore, a musketry volley was fired at them, which they immediately answered by yells and insults to the troops. As a result, all the troops, including the artillery, began to dismount and advance. The advance continued until it reached the center of the woods, where the Indians had built their trenches. At this point, the intensity of the firing increased, for the enemy were established in a position very advantageous for impeding our advance. Furthermore, the dismounted Indian auxiliaries whom we had brought with us became frightened, both because of the fury of the attack by arrows made upon us by our opponents, and because of the thunder of the cannon. As a result, we could not make them move any farther on foot. The active engagement lasted an hour and a quarter, after which we paused for a matter of an hour and a half. During this interval, an Indian was killed who was recognized by Matías as the one who had yelled the most insults at the troops. During the combat, twenty-five musket volleys had been fired.

It was now observed that to the rear and on both flanks, the entire woods were on fire. It was humanly impossible to advance directly ahead, for the dense thicket would not permit, and the conflagration surrounded us in the other directions. Consequently, the Commander ordered us to

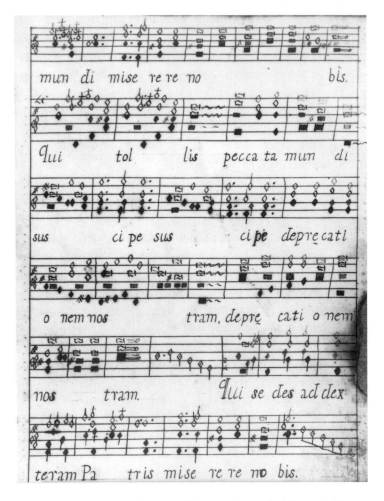

The native choir at Mission San José, organized by Fr. Durán, was highly regarded by many visitors. This piece of mission music is from the Latin Gloria, which was sung during Mass. Courtesy of the Santa Clara University Archives.

retire in good order so as to succeed in saving the cannon and its ammunition. This we managed to do, in spite of emerging nearly roasted in the tremendous blaze of the underbrush. We pulled out from the fortification until we felt we were safe from the fire, which was pressing upon us. Hearing some noise inside the forest, we fired two musket shots. These were followed by complete silence. One would not have believed so many Indians could still be inside the woods.

Immediately the Commander ordered the cavalry to surround the village completely to prevent escape, and the infantry to occupy that section of the woods known not to be on fire. This was done forthwith. In the evening not only the cavalry and civilians but also the artillery were placed on the alert to prevent the escape of the survivors. Indeed, at about 11:00 p.m. some of the rebels tried to get away along the river, but those guarding the area managed to kill some of them. The others stayed in the water [and got away] because the troops could not lose sight of their primary objective.

June 1: About seven o'clock in the morning, three women were captured, among them one quite hispanicized, called Agustina. She related in detail how on the previous day many Indians had been killed, and that there were five of the dead on the steep slope from the riverbank to the woods. The Commander ordered that the three women stay under guard in company with the Indian Matías at the ammunition park. The previous afternoon, an Indian woman had been killed who had been found at the edge of the forest and who had been about to escape.

At nine o'clock in the morning of June 1, the chief ordered the cavalry, infantry, civilians, and Indian auxiliaries to go and scout the woods and endeavor to catch all the survivors. Matías and the Indian woman Agustina were taken as guides, having been warned not to deceive the Commander, but to conduct the troops to the place which the enemy had fortified the day before. This was accomplished without expending a single shot, and the troops reached the trenches dug by the rebels. In these they found two dead Indians, another nearby, and several others through the brush. Close to the river, the wild grapevines were seen to stir. A scout was made and three old Indian women were encountered. They were immediately pulled out of the bushes and shot on the spot.

The Indian auxiliaries, in a thicket to the right of the forest, managed to find a Christian Indian from Santa Clara. After capture he confessed that he had been the one who had burned the bodies of the two dead soldiers who had been killed on the previous expedition under Don José Sánchez. On learning this, the Indian auxiliaries came out of the woods and began to beg the Commander for permission to kill the prisoner by arrows with their own hands. They were given this permission. So the Indian auxiliaries formed a semicircle, placed him in the middle, and four of them began to shoot arrows at him. But no matter how hard they tried, they could not kill him. Finally, seeing that he did not die, a cavalry soldier shot him in the head with his carbine, and only then did he die. Seventy-three arrows were counted in his body. From here they took him to an oak tree and hung him up.

After reaching the middle of the forest, inspecting the trenches, and finding no more than has been mentioned, the civilian who was conducting the bound captive Indian Matías shot him down and left him dead. The auxiliaries, together with some of the soldiers, pulled his body out of the brush and hung it to a big oak tree. On it also were hanged four other men and four women. They wanted to hang the woman Agustina and her two female companions, but the Commander would not permit their execution. Instead he placed them under guard so that they should not be harmed and should be taken back to their mission.

The previous day, during the skirmish, soldiers Rafael Contreras, Juan Gonzales, and Gil Rodríguez were wounded by arrows, as were civilians Tomás Espinosa (seriously), Melitón Soto, and José Pico. At about two o'clock in the afternoon of the same day (June 1), the Commander ordered the division to take up its march in such a direction as to bring it to San José. Hence we marched until 7:45 in the evening, when we arrived at the margin of a river in the middle of the valley where we found water and forage sufficient for the horses. At about 12:30 a.m., I awoke and saw that in the interior of the woods, close to the place where we were camped, a fire was burning and was about to reach us. Therefore, despite the late hour, I immediately went and reported to the Adjutant, Don José Sánchez. He ordered me, if the fire came any closer, to have the field gun and ammunition moved to a place which I felt the fire would not threaten. At about two o'clock in the morning of June 2, I observed that the fire was again approaching, and the wind was blowing it toward us. I immediately had the gun and ammunition moved to a spot two hundred yards distant, which seemed to me safe. There we passed the rest of the night with no further incident.

1830
A Secularization-Oriented Proposal
for Alta California

Juan Bandini

One of the principal aims of the young liberals in California was to advance the secularization of the missions. As we have seen, missions had originally been envisioned as temporary stations on the way to the full incorporation of indigenous peoples into Hispanic society. Since the history of New Spain offered ample evidence of the brutal treatment of native peoples in *encomiendas,* mines, cities, and frontier areas, many missionaries genuinely came to believe that only the missions prevented serious and sustained exploitation of the Indians. Yet the forced labor that was an inherent part of the mission system and the sustained reluctance of the missionaries to allow Indians to pass through their system into mainstream society rankled reformers throughout New Spain. They took their lead from the 1813 call of the Spanish *cortes* for an end to missions, and a new approach to Indian affairs was high on the agenda of liberals in Mexico City and California. Echeandía took some preliminary steps toward secularization and the emancipation of the Indians and issued a more formal decree on the matter just before leaving office. This stated that all the missions, starting with San Carlos and San Gabriel, were to be turned into towns within five years. They were to be settled by mission Indians and other Mexicans, and the Indians were to be provided with land and farm implements. Indian schools were also to be established.

The following report by Juan Bandini envisioned a future for California based upon the liberal ideas of private property and free trade for California. Dismissing the institutions of colonial California as having outlived their usefulness, Bandini foresaw an Alta California of private *ranchos* and commerce. His negative attitude toward the Indians anticipated the

Juan Bandini and his daughter Margarita. Courtesy of the Seaver Center for Western History Research.

manner in which their welfare would quickly be relegated to an insignificant position during the secularization process. Their legal equality would mean very little in the context of the great social and economic inequality from which they would suffer when the mission system was ended.

Juan Bandini was born in Peru in 1800 and came to Alta California with his father, a trader, in the 1820s. He was working in the customs service in San Diego when he penned this report at the end of 1830. He based large sections of it on another report on Alta California that his father had composed two years earlier.

FROM "A STATISTICAL DESCRIPTION OF ALTA CALIFORNIA" BY JUAN BANDINI

Presidios

These *presidios* were doubtless of some utility when they were built. Since they served as protection, their presence limited the power of the gentiles in the vicinity. However, since there is no longer a danger from that source, they should be demolished, because the buildings are falling into total ruin and their narrow rooms do not afford much comfort to those who live in them. Lately, some private individuals, those who are retired, and even some people who are still on active duty, have constructed simple houses in the vicinity of the *presidios*. Judging from the increase in this type of construction which takes place from year to year, it seems clear that the population of California will become quite considerable within a short time.

A short distance from the *presidios,* one finds the inappropriately named *castillos* that were supposed to protect the harbor. The *castillo* in San Francisco, which is a mile from the *presidio,* is useless because of its elevation and the way it was constructed. The *castillo* in Monterey is located at about the same distance from the *presidio* as the one in San Francisco. Even though it completely dominates its surroundings, it is of little importance, since it has no more than a few pieces of very small-caliber artillery. It does not have a tower, and the esplanades are in bad condition. In Santa Bárbara there is an esplanade which has two useless cannons. Even if it were constructed properly, the *castillo* would have nothing to protect, for it would be unable to prevent a landing. Lastly, the *castillo* in San Diego, which is about five miles from the *presidio,* could have been very useful for protecting the port if it had been built for that purpose at Point Guijarros. Ships would then have had to pass by the *castillo* at a distance of no more than twenty to one hundred *varas.* In its current state, however, it is as useless as the other *castillos.*

Pueblos

The territory has three *pueblos.* The principal one is *Nuestra Señora de Los Angeles,* located eight miles from Mission San Gabriel and eight leagues from the Bay of San Pedro. Its population is about fifteen hundred souls. It has a very good church, served at the present time by a retired Franciscan missionary. The design of this *pueblo* can be attributed to the whims of its founders as well as to those who later settled there, for they were of the same mind. The only order in the setting of the buildings is disorder, and neither proportion nor design is evident. It has an *ayuntamiento* composed of an *alcalde,* three *regidores,* and a *síndico.* Its surroundings are given over to fields and vineyards. Because of its broad plain and continuously flowing rivers, it gives every promise of being able to support a large population and extensive agriculture. This *pueblo* alone is able to supply ships with between five and six thousand hides a year, plus an equal amount of tallow.

The second *pueblo* is San José de Guadalupe, located about one league from Mission Santa Clara and twenty leagues from the *presidio* of San Francisco. It has a beautiful river which empties into the great bay of that *presidio.* Its buildings are arranged in the same way as the ones in Los Angeles. Its church, which is a shapeless hut, is served by the missionary Father from Santa Clara. Its *ayuntamiento* is the same as the one in Los Angeles. Its population is a little more than six hundred souls. The principal occupations are the cultivation of wheat, corn, and other vegetables, and the keeping of ranches for cattle and horse raising. They also engage in the hunting of a huge deer which is abundant in the vicinity. Many ranches can produce more than six *arrobas* of tallow each. This *pueblo* is located within the southern outskirts of San Francisco Bay. If the *pueblo* were to become more developed, the population of the whole area would increase greatly, for its vast plains provide everything the farmer might desire.

The third *pueblo* is the so-called *Villa de* Branciforte, which is located two miles from Mission Santa Cruz, about one mile and a half from the northern shore of Monterey Bay and eighteen leagues from the Monterey *presidio.* Perhaps slightly more than one hundred souls have settled there, and they are mainly engaged in agricultural labor. The safety of the *pueblo* has been entrusted to an auxiliary *alcalde* who reports to the military commander in Monterey. Up to the present, Branciforte's production has been insignificant.

Missions

The territory contains twenty-one missions which were founded at different times. In 1769 the first mission was established in San Diego. It is two leagues from the *presidio* of the same name. The rest were established one after the other over time as circumstances and necessity dictated. In 1822, the last mission was established, and it is called San Francisco Solano. It is the newest mission of all and is located in the northern part of the San Francisco Bay area.

The mission buildings are designed around one basic concept with little variation. They are constructed of adobe, and the size of each building is determined by its intended purpose. All of the missions contain comfortable dwellings for the Fathers, good storehouses, granaries of various sizes, areas for the manufacture of soap, workshops for weaving, carpentry shops, blacksmith works, presses, wine cellars, separate areas for indigenous youth of both sexes, large patios and corrals, and finally, any other necessary offices to complete the work. Immediately adjacent, so that it forms one body with the mission complex, is the profusely adorned church.

The Indian settlements are about two hundred *varas* from this complex. Their settlement is called a *ranchería*. Most of the houses consist of very small adobe rooms, but in some missions they have left the Indians to their primitive customs and have allowed them to construct cone-shaped *jacales* for their lodgings. At their largest, the *jacales* are over four *varas* in diameter and the vertex, or top of the cone, is two *varas* off the ground. The *jacales* are made of rough poles, which they cover with tule or *zacate* in such a way that they are perfectly protected from all types of bad weather. As I understand it, these *rancherías* are most adequate, given the temporary way that these Indians desire things. For example, when they want to renovate the *ranchería,* as they frequently do, they just burn it down, and in a short time they can easily construct another.

On the opposite side of the *ranchería,* next to the mission, there is a small barracks with enough rooms for five soldiers and a corporal of the cavalry. In the early days of the foundation of the missions and the reduction of the gentile Indians to Christianity, the aim of the soldiers was to compel respect and make the Indians avoid the disorders they might commit in their ignorant state. However, since the circumstances which first called for this permanent force have entirely changed, maintaining this military presence so firmly does not seem to be necessary any longer.

All of the missions are under the charge of the Franciscans of Propaganda Fide. At the present time there are only twenty-four of them, and most are of advanced age. Each Franciscan administers a mission and has absolute authority there. The work in the fields, the harvesting of the crops, and the slaughter of the cattle are all directed by the Father. He is the only one who can attend to the buying, selling, and other business affairs of the mission without having to go through another person. For example, if a mission has the luck of having a hardworking and capable minister, its neophytes abundantly enjoy the necessities of life. If a mission is barren and miserable, the evidence points to the ineptitude of its director.

The possessions of the missions extend from one end of the territory to the other. Their borders come right up to each other. Even though they might not need all the land they appear to have for the care of the crops and the maintenance of their herds, they have insensitively appropriated all the area. They have constantly been opposed to any private person becoming involved in the affairs of the missions. With that sinister notion, they occupy the best lands and water sources. With but a small flock of sheep they rejoice at having come into possession of everything. They desire exclusive control over the productions of the country, whose bad condition stems from that deeply rooted source.

Counting all the missions, there are about twenty to twenty-one thousand indigenous listed in the mission registers. However, they are not equally distributed among the missions. Some missions have close to three thousand souls, while others can scarcely muster four hundred. The population at a mission more or less determines its prosperity.

By their nature, the Indians are careless and lazy. Even though they are able to imitate, they are not very clever. They can be educated, of course, but that would not be the most fitting way to develop their ability to reason. It is true that their inclinations are not of the type apt to create good impressions, since thievery, treachery, deceit, and lethargy are their dominant passions. From this, one can deduce that little usefulness can be drawn out of these Indians. Because of their constant use of *temescal* [sweathouse] as well as the constant filth and poor ventilation of their dwellings, all of them are weak and lacking in vigor. The spasms and rheumatism which so afflict them are a consequence of their bad habits. However, what most destroys them and inhibits their reproduction is venereal disease, from which most of them suffer greatly. It should be noted that their bodies are prone to receiving the infections of this contagion. This accounts for the enormous gap between births and deaths.

Generally speaking, the production of all the missions is the raising of cattle, sheep, horses, wheat, corn, beans, and other vegetables. The more southern missions are extensively engaged in vineyards and olives. However, the most lucrative production is that of cattle, for there is an active, high demand on the part of the ships engaged in the coastal trade for their hides and crops. Indeed, these articles are the only items in demand which both the missions and private persons have in order to meet their needs. This is why all are anxious to stimulate this branch of trade as much as possible and why it receives the attention of everyone.

Foreign vessels have been allowed to collect hides here for the past eight years. Previously, it had been approved only on a case-by-case basis, but now those who export from the missions will deliver thirty thousand hides [annually] and about the same number of *arrobas* of tallow produced in the slaughters. And, in view of the method used in the these slaughters, it seems certain that within three or four years' time the quantity exported of one or more of these items will double.

Hemp, wine, olive oil, grains, and other agricultural products could be cultivated more extensively if there were some stimulus to export more, but since there is none, they only plant enough for domestic consumption.

Ports and Commerce

The name commonly given to the anchoring places of the four *presidios* is port. However, only San Diego and San Francisco really deserve that name, for they both afford security and protection, whatever the season and however the wind. In addition to the ease of entry, its extent, and its good accommodations, the port of San Diego has the advantage of being able to close off its entrance with a battery at Point Guijarros. It is always very calm there, and the port offers as many conveniences as a navigator could want. If the route from the Colorado River were ever opened, this port would be a major factor with respect to trade with the interior. The advantages of the second port (San Francisco) are well known, and it demands great attention. I will say without the risk of being mistaken that it is the best port in the entire country. In addition to being suitable for building docks and artillery positions, it has in its interior various inlets that would make suitable places for repairing ships. It also has abundant wood, such as pine, oak, evergreen, larch, and so forth. Its mighty rivers, some of them navigable, make possible an infinite number of enterprises.

The port of Monterey generally is sheltered from the winds, but less so from those of the north, which clearly makes it risky. Thus, its landing site is not the best for small vessels. Santa Bárbara is no more than an open bay which offers no safety. Its landing site is terrible under any circumstances.

Previously, foreign ships were allowed to anchor in the coves of Santa Cruz, San Luis Obispo, El Cojo, Refugio, San Pedro, and San Juan Capistrano.

From these places they could then load the crops from the nearby missions. However, by virtue of a superior order which the *Comandancia General* circulated, they were not permitted entrance into just any port or cove. It was ordered that Monterey remain as the designated spot for foreigners. However, in light of the significant harm the territory was going to suffer, the *Jefe Político* together with the *Excelentísima Diputación,* declared that the ports of San Diego and San Francisco and the bays of Santa Bárbara and San Pedro were to be provisionally opened for these boats. If this had not been done, all Alta California undoubtedly would have come to a complete standstill.

The only thing that makes the foreigners want to trade here is the untanned cattle hides and tallow. It is well known here that nothing else will ever be able to serve as money, for scarcely any money circulates. So it is that all who come here seek to exchange their goods for other goods. The items the ships bring as imports are designed for this kind of purchase. They know that the missionaries are not interested in money, but rather items the Indians need. Some ships that have arrived here only with cash have lost their business because they have not been able to obtain goods.

The annual take of hides in the territory is, as has been said, from thirty thousand to forty thousand, with just about as many *arrobas* of tallow. If we assume that the average value of these items is slightly less than two to one, then we can see that about 140,000 *pesos* are circulating in California. Divided among the twenty-one missions, that comes out to 6,666 *pesos* per mission. If that were turned into cash, how would the Indians be clothed? How would the missions obtain what they needed? Silver is only good for increasing investments in speculative purposes, but California does not find itself in that position as yet, because the articles produced for trading are barely enough to be exchanged for what is needed. The same can be said about the few settlers who might gather those articles. Since the articles are in short supply, the value of their exchange would be insignificant.

Therefore, if there is only one type of export, which barely produces enough to allow the settlers to purchase the absolute necessities to survive, what would happen if restrictions were placed on trading at the moment in which the exports were beginning to increase? It seems to me that the consequences would be more than obvious, yet I find it necessary to mention them here: (1) no ship would sail along these coasts, and the nation would lose the money that its wares bring in; (2) neither the missions nor private individuals would be able to obtain those articles which they most need for the field work, not to mention what they need in order to live with respectability and culture; (3) since the raising of cattle is the only useful branch of industry, and the one on which all are pinning their hopes, if harvesting the carcasses were thwarted, the populace here would once again become submerged in the poverty of eight years ago, which they attributed to this limited commerce; (4) there are many foreigners in the territory who have become naturalized citizens, but if they thought they would not be able to survive here in the future, they would abandon a country which only promised them misery. This would have an adverse affect on the whole colonization effort.

The roads in the territory are generally very good, but they are hindered by two steep slopes which are impassible for carriages and even difficult for mules. This situation is quite serious, for it prevents the missions and the principal *pueblos* from sending their goods to the port of Monterey. It is not the main reason, however. The distance between the richest missions and the port of Monterey is from eighty to one hundred and seventy leagues. It is not possible for tallow packed in wineskins to withstand the buffeting of a long journey. It is deplorable the way the wineskins and the tallow are banged around, even on short trips that have been made recently. The hides are very cumbersome and only a very unusual mule is able to carry more than eight at once. An article that is not worth very much should not incur many expenses, but if the expenses increase the asking price to more than what the article is worth, how can it possibly be sold? That is why it will always be impossible to construct favorable conditions by which one article or another can be sent all the way to Monterey.

Only a few missions can transport their goods to another port at minimal cost, and these missions are precisely the poorest ones and the ones that produce the least. The missions that are going to attract the attention of the sailors are obviously the ones that are going to suffer due to the unfeasibility of their commerce. In addition, one should not forget the *pueblo* of Los Angeles, which is worthy of consideration because it has the wealthiest population in California and a number of different foreigners also reside there. This *pueblo* is located one hundred and thirty leagues to the south of Monterey, and the course and fostering of its growth is due to the hide and tallow trade. If it becomes impossible to dispose of the hides and tallow, the city inevitably will be ruined.

As a result of this explanation, I can say with certainty that if foreigners are excluded from all ports except Monterey, I repeat, the commerce of Alta California will be completely finished.

Agriculture

Mission *ranchos,* and private ones as well, are found only in a narrow strip of the territory from north to south. Only a few are more than ten or twelve leagues inland, because the mountain range that also runs from north to south is a barrier. The missions have the best *ranchos* with the most abundant water and pastures. Private *ranchos* have had to face a thousand obstacles and barely have been able to obtain some small sites for a limited amount of cattle. Only around Los Angeles are there private *ranchos* of any consequence.

In the present year there are about three hundred thousand head of cattle, thirty-three to thirty-four thousand horses, slightly more than four thousand mules, and two hundred thousand sheep in the territory. These numbers represent the animals that have been broken and rounded up. The number of strays, especially horses, cannot be calculated.

This year's harvest has produced about thirty thousand *fanegas* of wheat, slightly more than twenty thousand of corn, about ten thousand of barley, and four thousand of beans. It should be noted that these numbers are based on rough estimates made by interested parties and in some cases the numbers are probably larger.

The climate and fertile valleys of California offer all types of vegetation a person could hope for. In addition to what has been stated previously, California produces the highest quality flax and hemp. The best vineyards are found in abundance here and there is no lack of cotton. Pear, apple, orange, and several types of peach trees abound, as well as other fruits. The olive tree is unsurpassable. It is very unusual to find a plain anywhere in the territory that is not able to produce fruitfully. In addition, all the fields and hillsides produce infinite types of wild fruit, such as strawberries and other exquisite and diverse herbs, many of which have not been botanically classified. The territory does not lack wood for the construction of ships, particularly around San Francisco, where pines and oaks are abundant everywhere around the mountains. Livestock reproduces with the most astonishing ease, especially the cattle, which become pregnant and are ready to give birth at two years of age. The wild horses are so numerous that it is necessary to round them up every year and kill a large number because of the damage they do to the fields. Also, their wildness can affect horses that already have been broken.

The sheep give the most exquisite wool and they reproduce wildly. The value of the livestock is about equal: a newly born calf is worth five *pesos,* and a horse is worth a bit more. The country also abounds in deer, rabbits, and hare. Unfortunately, there is also an abundance of bears, wolves, coyotes, squirrels, and moles, which do a good amount of damage in the fields, especially the latter three. Geese, cranes, and ducks are plentiful in season, and a unique type of quail is abundant. In sum, Alta California lacks none of the essential elements for an inexhaustible production. The only thing it does lack is people.

1831
The California Delegate Argues for Rule of Law

Carlos Carrillo

As a territory in the Mexican republic, California was entitled to send one delegate each for Baja and Alta California to the congress in Mexico City. Alta California's first delegate was its last Spanish governor, Pablo Vicente de Solá. In 1831, the delegate was Carlos Antonio Carrillo. He gave the following speech, in which he urged the congress to complete the process of establishing republican government in his territory by modernizing the judicial system. Carrillo argued, as had Bandini, that the vestiges of the colonial system had to be removed from Alta California if the territory were to advance into a prosperous future. The older system gave too much power to the whims of the military commanders, thereby preventing attainment of the ideal of equality of all before the law. The congress did not act on Carrillo's request.

Carlos Carrillo was born in Santa Bárbara in 1783. His father was a Loreto soldier who came north with the Portolá group. After a stint in the military, he served in the territorial assembly before being elected to the congress.

FROM A SPEECH BY CARLOS CARRILLO, OCTOBER 18, 1831

On October 24, 1781, the King approved a new set of regulations which remain in force to this day. These regulations, as well as those of 1772, curtailed the duties and powers of the Commandants of *presidios*. The Commandants nevertheless continued, and have in fact ever since continued, to exercise most of the functions of which they were by law deprived.

José Antonio Carrillo, brother of Carlos Carillo. Courtesy of The Bancroft Library, University of California, Berkeley.

It was all very well that in those times and circumstances the regulations [then] issued should have sufficed for the government of the new establishments and that the regulations were then thought to be fairly adequate, inasmuch as they applied (apart from matters concerning the missions themselves) only to a few military posts. Nor was there any other population to be governed than the soldiers and their families at the most, and even these had been reduced to very small numbers.

But at the present time, at least in the Territory I represent, the observance of either of the sets of regulations mentioned above is very far from adequate in matters having to do with political government. The Government of Spain, which issued the regulations, if it had disregarded the fact that they were intended for the colonies and must therefore conform with established colonial policy, either would have worded them in different terms or at least would have designated them as provisional; for it must have been apparent that in the course of time, circumstances would change, and that revisions would consequently become necessary. Precisely this state of affairs has come about in Upper California, and this is the reason that new regulations, adequate for the present situation, are needed.

The population of white, or so-called civilized people has increased considerably. To these must be added a growing number of free Indians; that is, those who for one reason or another are no longer attached to the missions or who do not live there. Thus, Indians of this kind are not subject to the exclusive authority conferred by regulations and statutes upon the missionaries in matters affecting neophytes under instruction and others remaining united with the community. The result is that the number of free Indians greatly exceeds that of the military.

Persons of this class, therefore, inasmuch as the regulations have not been changed, naturally submit to them; moreover, the military and political chiefs continue to adhere to the same regulations, not only because they conform with the dominant ideas of the military profession, but also because soldiers are unfamiliar with any other form of government.

White people and free Indians are thus subjected to the military and political authority delegated by the Commander in Chief to his subordinate Captains and Commandants of the *presidios* to such an extent that even the constitutional *alcaldes* of the *presidio* settlements are completely under the authority of the said Commandants. The *alcaldes* are thus prevented from exercising the authority vested in them by law—for such was the resolve of the next-to-the-last Military and Political Commander of the Territory under discussion; at least, so it was up to the time of my departure.

From this source has flowed the accumulation of evils inflicted upon the unhappy population, governed as they are at the discretion of Military Commanders great and small who hold in their hands all executive and judicial powers, the exercise of which no one is able to dispute. It is easy to imagine, under such conditions, the tortures endured day after day by those wretched people for lack of courts of justice. They must accept unalterable decisions from which there is no appeal, usually imposed unjustly by men who are absolutely ignorant of the simplest ideas of law.

In that unfortunate part of the Republic alone are to be found private citizens actually deprived of the civil rights proclaimed in the Constitution. There alone one sees the civilian and the soldier measured by the same standard, so to speak, because the Officer, who is (or at least considers himself) the chief of both, in every case applies military ordinances, being ignorant of any other code. Conciliatory proceedings are completely unknown, for when town councils were established in the year 1827, despite the vigorous opposition of the military authorities, the latter immediately began to undermine the powers of the constitutional *alcaldes* and succeeded in stripping away the duties and authority delegated to them by law. As I have said, the *alcaldes* were made subordinate to the Military Commandant; in short, they became nothing more than his constables.

From my remarks one can understand what the administration of justice became in that region in the past and what it still remains. It is not surprising that the Territory is backward in every respect....

1833

The Citizens of San Diego Petition for Local Government

José Antonio Estudillo, et al.

When José María Echeandía was appointed governor of both Californias in 1825, he first moved to Monterey, which had served as the capital since 1777. But because he did not care for the frequent, prolonged bouts of cold and foggy weather there, and because he felt out of contact with Baja California, he moved his residence to San Diego. Even though many of the governmental institutions, principally the customs house, remained in Monterey, San Diego functioned as the *de facto* capital of the Californias until 1831.

In Baja California, Echeandía appointed a liberal military officer, José María Padrés, as a kind of lieutenant governor. When Padrés was elected a delegate to the congress in 1828, he appointed the *alcalde* of Loreto in his stead. But the *diputación,* which earlier had stated that Baja California deserved its own governor, protested that its own senior member, José María Mata, ought to be lieutenant governor. Difficulties were avoided when Manuel Victoria arrived the next year with the title of governor of Baja California. A more conservative individual than Echeandía, Victoria tended to side with the missionaries against ranchers in the southern part of the peninsula who argued that some mission lands should be declared vacant, and hence available for development, because there were so few resident Indians on them. Victoria was soon transferred to Alta California, and he was succeeded in Baja California by José Mariano Monterde. When Monterde himself was elected to the congress, the *diputación* seized power, and each of its members rotated in and out of the post of political leader of the peninsula for a month at a time. Even though Monterde technically remained governor until 1835, Baja California experienced four years of political turmoil. Three groups—the ranchers around San Antonio and San José del Cabo, the merchants in La Paz, which became the territorial capital, and the military garrison at Loreto—jockeyed for control of the *diputación* and of the *ayuntamientos* of the territory's municipalities.

In Alta California, the governor's residence in San Diego had inevitably increased the population there, and a cluster of new buildings had sprouted around the old *presidio*. As the threat of conflict with Indians receded, settlements at all the *presidios* gradually spread outside the fortress walls. These developments accelerated a process that had been under way for some time at all of California's *presidios*: civilian participation in government. Civilians had always been a part of *presidio* life, assisting in the ordinary nonmilitary tasks that were necessary for the maintenance of the outposts. They worked in the fields, tended the livestock, and functioned as artisans. As San Diego's civilian population increased, residents were gradually given some political rights, such as the ability to participate in territorial elections. But in the early 1830s they began to seek more.

The tremendous appeal of republican self-government was not confined to elite and educated men like Pío Pico or Carlos Carrillo. The following petition by six citizens of San Diego in 1833 urged the establishment of civil government there. They used a number of republican arguments to protest their being ruled by the commander of the San Diego *presidio*, Santiago Argüello, and they appealed to liberal Spanish precedents in support of their request to have their own civilian government. The petition was sent to the governor and it was approved by the territorial assembly.

From a Petition by Citizens of San Diego, February 22, 1833

To the Honorable Head of the Superior Political Government:

The citizens José Antonio Estudillo, Juan María Osuna, Francisco María de Alvarado, Manuel Machado, Ysidro Guillén, and Jesús Moreno, for ourselves and in the name of all the residents of the port of San Diego, present ourselves before Your Excellency with due respect, with the object of obtaining protection of a right which in justice we believe ourselves entitled to as citizens of the great nation, as well as for obtaining relief from the oppression in which up to the present time this community has been submerged without even having been able to enjoy the benefits that the law confers upon it.

We are of the opinion, Sir, that whatever might be the number of individuals who live in a settlement, one way or another, they ought to have in their local government the same guarantees and the same organization as the general constitutional provisions [of the nation provide]; also, according to these [provisions], they ought to enjoy the privilege of electing their agents, and these ought to be limited in their terms of office. But if the opposite happens, and civil authority is vested in one individual who also exercises military authority and therefore force, in that case his tendency to despotism will burden the unhappy people with the heavy yoke of tyranny, without ever being able to enjoy their rights; and, moreover, there must in the natural order of things result a continual clash of opposing interests, in which the military might very well be inclined to sustain and protect the faction aligned with their profession.

Considering what has been set forth, it is deplorable to know that, while for all of the people in the Republic there is a common good, up to the present only this community is in a bad situation.

It is sad to know that in all of the *pueblos* of the Republic, the citizens are judged by those whom they themselves elect for this purpose, and that in this port alone one has to submit his fate, fortune, and perhaps existence to the caprice of a military judge who, being able to misuse his power, can easily evade any complaint that they might want to make of his conduct. Moreover, the form of this tribunal is diametrically opposed to our civil and criminal laws, for these provide for courts of conciliation, the mediation of good men, and the other legal processes designated by the Constitution; but in the former [i.e., military justice], there are no other formulas than the imperious voice: I command it; and the only order is the blind obedience that they expect for their commands; if anyone who knows his rights demands the law, in that case they succeed in avoiding the sense of [the laws], or they resort to the clever expedient of saying that they have superior orders reserved to operate according to the circumstances; the result from this is that the unhappy citizen has no other choice but to suffer, and to humble himself in his degradation, for he is always afraid to provoke further the wrath of the one who rules him by wishing to appeal to the superior tribunal, because for some reason he fears he will not find a safe means of effecting it.

Another more conspicuous evil must always result for the unhappy *pueblo* that finds itself subject to oppressive military jurisdiction, supposedly regulated in conformity with the present system of California. The reason is that the Commandant of a *presidio* is usually the Captain of the permanent company that garrisons it [the *pueblo*]; his office and command terminate logically with his existence, from which it follows that the civil jurisdiction he exercises comes to be vested in this individual during his life, a truly monstrous thing even in the most absolute government. Let us suppose that this individual is of good character and circumstances, but in spite of that should allow passions to hinder him, which will go on at an increasing rate with age. But if unfortunately the citizen has to be subject to the caprice of someone ignorant, proud, rancorous, cruel, and vindictive, then what other choice remains for him if it is not to abandon his native soil, ruin his interests, and hate his existence, since he sees clearly that his misfortune will never have a definite end?

It is certain, Sir, that it can very well happen that they suppress an abuse, [but] immediately another at the opposite extreme springs up; because all innovation, however good and plausible it may be, brings with it difficulties and obstacles; but if, because of this fear, the law does not go into effect, in this event we will never be able to enjoy our civil liberty, and there would never be any stimulus to the progress of this community, which would always remain marked with the fatal stamp of oppression.

California, Sir, demonstrates clearly the influence a liberal government has on the increase in the population; this increase has been rapid and notable for the last few years in Monterey, Santa Bárbara, and the *pueblo* of Los Angeles, making it almost possible to state as a fact that all is due to their form of local government. The settlement of San Diego shows this very clearly, because notwithstanding that it does not lack the necessary elements (less so perhaps than the former places), up to the present, no progress whatever is noted, because without doubt, under its present system all [people] fear to settle in it, since they think they will not find the necessary protection for their commerce or investment, and because they know that here, public instruction is retrogressing, and as a consequence, the individual happiness of its citizens.

Sir, the enclosed census that we respectfully submit will give you an idea that this settlement does not lack the number of inhabitants necessary to form an *ayuntamiento* in conformity with the law now in force of May 23, 1812, in the first part of Article 4.

Nevertheless, having confidence in your high ideals, your invariable observance of the law, and your continuous vigilance for the public liberty, we shall always conform with what Your Excellency may be pleased to decide about the subject set forth, since we are certain that with your wise natural fitness, and that of the Most Excellent *Diputación,* happy days will again come to this settlement which, because of its local circumstances, should have merited a better fate. For that reason:

We petition Your Excellency that in view of the fact that the Most Excellent Territorial *Diputación* is not in session, Your Excellency will receive this, our just petition, to which Your Excellency will have the goodness to give the dispensations that to you appear most conducive to our welfare and just desire, which is the favor and justice we implore.

Will Your Excellency receive this on common paper as there is no seal in this place. Port of San Diego, February 22 of 1833. [Signed:]

José Estudillo
Juan María Osuna
Francisco María Alvarado
Manuel Machado
Jesús Moreno
Ysidro Guillén

1835
Life at a Secularized Mission

José Antonio Anzar and José Tiburcio Castro

California's missions were secularized in the 1830s as a result of political developments in Mexico. In the nation's capital, a rapid-fire series of changes in leadership took place, with the ultimate victor acting quickly to put the liberal agenda in place. When President Guadalupe Victoria's term ended, he was succeeded in a disputed election by former insurgent Vicente Guerrero, the liberal candidate. Anastasio Bustamante, a conservative acceptable to many factions, was chosen as vice-president. When Guerrero refused to give up the extraordinary powers he had been granted when Spain invaded Mexico in 1829, Bustamante was able to overthrow him. After Guerrero was executed, General Antonio López de Santa Anna, a hero of the resistance against the Spanish invasion, overthrew Bustamante in 1832. Santa Anna was then elected president in 1833, with Valentín Gómez Farías, a leading liberal, as vice-president. In one of the mercurial moves that were to mark his long career, Santa Anna then retired to his estate in Veracruz, and Gómez Farías assumed the executive power.

The new executive turned swiftly to the liberal agenda. The size of the army was reduced, and officers were no longer exempt from trial in civil courts. Laws were also passed to weaken the Church: the mandatory tithe was abolished, and the government decreed that it—not the papacy—would make future clerical appointments. It was in this context that the congress voted to secularize the missions of California. Gómez Farías signed the bill on August 17, 1833.

In Alta California, Echeandía had attempted to establish Indian towns on some mission lands. This would have had the effect of loosening the missionaries' control of their vast landholdings. Echeandía's order was countermanded by his more conservative successor, Manuel Victoria. This act earned Victoria the enmity of the *Californio* elite. Knowing that this group controlled the *diputación,* Victoria refused to call it into session.

Left: A self-portrait of Agustín Zamorano, commander of the Monterey presidio and the man who brought the first printing press to Alta California. Courtesy of the California History Room, California State Library, Sacramento. Right: Fr. José Antonio Anzar. This is one of the few photographs extant of a California missionary. Courtesy of the Santa Barbara Mission Archive Library.

Opposition to his rule quickly crystalized around this suppression of representative government, and a group in San Diego organized a conspiracy against him. Their plan called for Victoria to be suspended from the government and for the *diputación* to choose two leaders, one each for military and civil affairs. Victoria marched out from Monterey to meet his opponents, and his forces were defeated by the insurgents at Cahuenga on December 5, 1831. He soon left the territory.

A period of divided rule, already the case in Baja California, then ensued in Alta California. Those in the southern part of the territory who had initiated the movement against Victoria recognized Echeandía, who was still in San Diego, as governor. The soldiers in Monterey, along with some members of the foreign merchant community there, supported Agustín Zamorano, the Monterey commander. The *diputación* argued, as its Baja California counterpart had also done, that until a new appointment was formally made in Mexico City, its senior member—at this time Pío Pico—should assume the executive authority. This situation persisted for a year, until the arrival from Mexico of José Figueroa as the new appointed governor in January 1833. A distinguished soldier, Figueroa had served as commander of Sonora and Sinaloa since 1824. With Figueroa were ten new Franciscan missionaries. All were from the Franciscan College in Zacatecas, and they were native Mexicans. Less attached to the colonial regime and to the traditional way of organizing missions to which the Fernandinos were bound, these new missionaries assumed control of the missions from Monterey north, while the old friars were reassigned to care for the missions south of the capital. The overall intent was to replace Spanish priests with Mexican ones and to move control of the mission lands out of the hands of the clergy.

Figueroa quickly solved the political instability he had inherited. Most of the *Californio* elite was tired of it by then in any event, and in a matter of months, the new governor gained widespread support. Much of this was due to his ability to consult widely and convince everyone that their own voices had been heard. He even consulted with Fr. Durán about how a gradual secularization program might be initiated. When they received word from the capital that the secularization bill had been passed, the *diputación* pressed Figueroa to accelerate the process. The governor approved a series of regulations in August 1834 that called for the appointment of commissioners to administer the possessions of the missions and for the establishment of ten Indian *pueblos* the first year, with more to follow. Figueroa quickly appointed commissioners for each of the missions. Some priests, even the recently arrived ones, found this change difficult. The following exchange between Fr. José Antonio Anzar at Mission San Juan Bautista, José Tiburcio Castro, the mission's appointed administrator, and the governor gives the flavor of the ill will of many of the priests at the loss of the missions, and of the feeling among some of the *Californios* that the missionaries were merely getting what they deserved.

FROM LETTERS BY JOSÉ ANTONIO ANZAR AND JOSÉ TIBURCO CASTRO

San Juan Bautista, January 29, 1835
Señor Governor José Figueroa,

I have been thinking about writing to you for a number of days, but when I realized that it would undoubtedly upset you, I held back. However, when I remembered that Your Honor had told me that I could communicate freely with you about anything that came to mind, I became eager to do so. This is why I am informing Your Honor in writing about what I normally could only explain face to face. At the present time, I can only say that I do not know the regulations about salaries, because as far as I can see, I am to be paid in meat and grain! To date I have not received as much as a *real* in silver. There are wages I must pay which cannot be paid in meat or grain.

In addition, I have asked for the five hundred *pesos* designated for altar wine and bread and for Divine Worship, but I have not been given anything. The reply given to me was that they would pay the sacristan. In response to that, I must say that the matter pertains to the priest and to the priest alone. This is not all I have to pay for. There are many other things that the priest must know in his capacity as minister of Divine Worship. I have told them they have no say in the matter and should turn over the designated amount of money. I must use it for the needs of the Church, which is the practice the world over. However, these men do not know anything about Divine Worship, yet they want to meddle in these matters. I hope Your Honor will order them to turn over the money to me, for I am bearing all the expenses.

Your Honor must also understand that I need servants—for example, one or two youths and one or two cooks. I have to pay them what they demand, because they will never do anything for me without receiving money. However, the settlers pursue the mission servants and this makes the servants neglect their work at the mission. Or, they go and work for the settler. This means that the settlers have all the Indians at their disposal and then the Indians completely ignore me. It should suffice for the settlers to know that these Indians are in my service and they should leave them alone, but they will not do that. If these Indians happen to approach the settlers to ask for something, the reply is, "Where do you work?" The Indians say, "I am staying with the Father." "Well then, there is nothing for you there. Come and work for us and we will give you everything you want." Is that any way to maintain order? Can there be peace with such a method? How can I remain calm? Good order, indeed!

The entire mission is supposed to be ready to serve the Commissioner and his aide at any hour, but they consistently put great obstacles in the way of the limited services I need. They coax the Indians from my own kitchen. In time I will not be able to find anybody to do my wash. As far as I can tell, it seems that they plan to undermine even the respect due me, and this worries me. Under these circumstances it will be better to surrender before something else happens. Señor, I have been very patient and have controlled myself, but I do not know how much more suffering I can endure.

Furthermore, it is necessary for me to have one or two horses. Because the number of settlers has increased, I will need to travel outside the mission to hear many more confessions. Neither the settlers nor the mission has horses. I must have horses. Since everyone will benefit from the horses, everyone should pay for them, but that is not the case. It is very difficult for me to hire a boy to take care of the horses during the day, let alone at night. I have to pay the cook to watch the horses at night. Must I be forced to have the servants also tend to the horses? This all leads to suffering. Are we to always suffer?

Señor, after the *alcaldes* have received orders to give me what I need to pay the servants, I should meet with them so we can arrive at an understanding as to how I am to meet so many needs. This order should apply to the Indians from the Tulares as well as those from San Juan Bautista, because the Indians from San Juan Bautista might say that they do not want to comply, because they are free. In fact, that is what they do say. The Indians from the Tulares say that the majordomo employs them. I, however, have to be ready to serve everyone.

Let us consider another matter. I maintain that the conversion of the gentiles is still an issue of primary importance. Although they may secularize the missions, that does not put an end to the matter. I have not seen anything to the contrary in the regulations. Instead, I understood that if any gentiles were to come to the missions, before teaching and catechizing them, the missionary would simply ask the majordomo to give each Indian a blanket or shirt and a breechcloth so they would be clothed. After baptism, the missionary would turn the Indians over to the person named by the Government. However, this has not been done. About fifteen days ago, as many as ten young and old gentiles came here as a group. I had them look after some other gentiles who had been here. I told them to bring me the orphans, two girls and two boys, who were with some other Indians. They brought them to me, but as soon as the majordomo arrived at the mission and learned what had happened, he personally took the children back to his own house. I do not know whether he has reported this or not. He has not had the courtesy and good manners to tell me anything about the matter.

Response by José Tiburcio Castro to the Governor

Señor: I have always wanted to gratify the confidence that Your Honor has placed in me by making this *pueblo* advance, giving credit to you, but I now have reached the conclusion that the ambition and malice that dominate the hearts of these men will not allow me to do this. From now on, Your Honor will see how much he will be needing. In the end this señor wants nothing more than to have me and all the natives of this population dedicate ourselves to promoting his interests, taking care of all of his needs, and doing everything according to his whim. My duty compels me to respectfully bring this to the attention of Your Honor.

José T. Castro

1835
Life in Northern California

Agustín Janssens

The major issue connected with the secularization of the missions was the distribution of the extensive network of mission lands and *ranchos*. The 1833 Mexican law had been silent on this matter, most likely because, in the eyes of Gómez Farías and his allies, secularization was only half of a larger plan for California. The other half was the first serious attempt since 1781 to send large numbers of colonists to California.

The Mexican government was just as concerned about its northern frontier as the Spanish colonial government had been. Besides the Russians, the United States was now a potential problem because of the Louisiana Purchase in 1803. The appearance, led by Jedediah Smith, of a large number of fur trappers in Mexican territory in the 1820s exacerbated concern. In 1824, President Guadalupe Victoria had created a commission for the development of the Californias, which included former Alta California governor Solá as one if its members. This body recommended a significant colonizing effort to increase the Mexican population in these territories. Although the commission's 1827 recommendations did not have much immediate effect, its ideas persisted and were adopted by acting president Gómez Farías as part of a larger effort to develop Mexico according to liberal principles. A colonization bill was introduced in the congress. Before it could be passed, the government became distracted by rumors that the increasingly conservative Santa Anna was going to try to reclaim the presidency and undo the liberal reforms. Gómez Farías decided to set up the colony on his own authority, even though the law authorizing it had not passed the congress. Santa Anna did return. He replaced a few cabinet ministers and then he departed once again, leaving Gómez Farías still in charge. Gómez Farías continued preparations for the colony and appointed Carlos Híjar of Guadalajara as director of the colony and governor of Alta California in place of Figueroa. José María Padrés, the liberal army officer who had served as *de facto* lieutenant governor under Echeandía, was chosen to be military chief. A very vague law was then rushed through the congress, and a company controlled by Juan Bandini, then serving as Alta California's congressional delegate, was designated as the supplier to the colony. The colony of 239 people—105 men, 55 women, and 79 children under the age of fourteen—left Mexico City in April 1834 and sailed for California in August.

The colonists' reception in Alta California was chilly. The fact that the full-scale colonization law had never passed the congress and the inevitably vague character of the last-minute instructions Híjar had received gave Figueroa and the *diputación* plenty of opportunities to contest its legitimacy. In fact, the government that had sent the colony no longer existed: Santa Anna had returned once again and closed the congress soon after the colonists had departed Mexico City.

Figueroa and the *diputación* piously took the position that the missionaries had long espoused: since the mission lands belonged to the Indians, they could not be colonized by others. In fact, the full colonization bill would have required Híjar and the mission commissioners to make the first distribution of all lands to the Indians before distributing the rest to the colonists.

At root, the real issue was land itself. The *Californios* did not intend to relinquish the benefits of secularization to these recent arrivals. Híjar and Padrés were arrested and expelled. The colonists scattered throughout the territory. Many of them, such as schoolteachers and artisans, had useful skills that would, over the next decade and beyond, contribute significantly to California's development.

One colonist was Agustín Janssens. A native of Brussels, he had emigrated to Mexico in 1825, and in 1833, at the age of seventeen, he was recruited for the colony. In the following selection, he describes a journey he took from Monterey to Sonoma at the end of 1834, as the colonists were waiting for the Alta California authorities to decide their fate. Janssens's stops along the way give a vivid picture of the way in which family *ranchos* were already dotting and changing the California landscape.

FROM *The Life and Adventures in California of Don Agustín Janssens*

At last I decided to go to Sonoma, and I requested a passport from Señor Figueroa to go and return. He then told me that if I thought of arriving at San Francisco before December 31, he would give me an official letter for the Commander, by virtue of which the civil authority of the jurisdiction of San Francisco would be vested in the newly appointed *Alcalde*. I answered that I would be there before January 1, 1835. He entrusted me with two official letters, one for the Commander and the other for the *Alcalde*.

On the following day, I left for San Juan Bautista and met there Don Gumersindo Flores with a part of the colonists. I departed at will without being much delayed. Don José Castro and others told me that if I should sleep in the house of Don Carlos Castro, I would find the host there an entertaining man. Although he was in the habit of discouraging travelers, I should pay no attention to him, because these ill humors left him easily. Desforges and Rojas went with me. That night we wanted to go on without knocking at the door of Don Carlos Castro, but it was very late and we had to seek lodging with him. This he gave us. We unsaddled, but as soon as we stabled the horses, Castro commenced to insult us. The first thing he said was that we came as fugitives. I said it was not so, and in proof of my assertion, presented my passport. Then he said that the General was no better than we were. He asked where the horses we brought had come from, and I answered that they were mine. To have no more words, I asked that he do us the favor of giving us our horses so that we could go at once. "No," said he, "I am in charge of my ranch and will not give you the horses." As I was not known in those places, and as I had been warned, I tried to meet old Castro's treatment with calmness, though I was tired of his unbearable insults. Indeed, he even called us *cholos*. His wife and daughters told us not to pay attention to what he said, as it was only his manner and it meant nothing.

It was after eight when the lady finally came and told us that supper was ready. We wanted to enter but we feared the old man. At last he came out and invited us to enter and eat. When we were about through with the meal, he said, "Well, they devour well; they must have been starved for many days; they stuff themselves." I was so angry that I started to walk out. My companions did the same, but Señor Castro had closed the door and we couldn't leave. "No, Señor," said he, "you shall not go until you have finished."

Resistance was of no avail. Finally, when he saw we were thoroughly aroused, he burst forth, "Come, friends, forgive all that I have said to you; I am your friend, and this is the only amusement in my life. When people are angry I am pleased with them, and so it has been with you; let us talk and eat in the bosom of my family, who likewise are embarrassed."

(On one occasion Castro thought for a moment that he was in peril of his life for having thus treated Lara, a comedy actor who had been there, and who came in the expedition. Lara, upon being abused, pretended fury and threatened to strike the old man. In this way he succeeded in calming him, and the latter closed the matter as he did with everyone.)

We had a general conversation about our trip. Señor Castro told us he had been to Mexico and talked to us of several towns as if he had been in them. However, we decided that he was speaking from hearsay and that he had never been in Mexico. He was an ancient old-timer with many memories. He offered us the hospitality of his house when we should return. Finally, a complete transformation appeared in him. While he had at first been impatient, he now changed to kindliness. The family all were most friendly.

We departed on the following day, after breakfast. (Of course they would not let us pay for anything.) At the Hernández ranch, we were asked about what had happened to us at Castro's house. We told them and they laughed heartily. There we saw Señorita Hernández, who was very kind, fine, and elegant, and also of the greatest beauty. She had all the manners of a young lady reared in the best society of city culture. I believe she was the most beautiful girl I had seen, from Los Angeles to this place.

We stopped at the home of an Ortega family before entering the *pueblo* of San José, and they received us well. They would not permit us to pay, but I made some presents to the children. In fact, we had learned from Señor Padrés in Mexico that in California one traveled without paying anything. Having been advised in Mexico, I had brought novelties such as eardrops, rings, and other little things, and glass beads to give the Indians.

We traveled swiftly in order to reach San Francisco on time with the government papers. On the night of December 30, 1834, we arrived at Mission Dolores, of which Don Joaquín Estudillo was administrator. I presented my passport to him and told him of the papers I carried and of their contents. The Judge-elect was Señor Haro. Great was the pleasure felt by Señor Estudillo on learning that they were going to have freedom from military government, for, as was known, Señor Vallejo was something of a tyrant to the inhabitants. Estudillo, his wife, Doña Juana, and their daughter,

Concepción, treated us with a kindness which no one could forget. He and others accompanied us to the old *presidio,* and when the citizens who were there learned that I had brought the orders to set up the civil government in that locality, each one was full of gladness and took pains to entertain me. They would not allow me to return to the mission. That night, in celebration, a grand ball was held and entertainment was provided.

The following day, January 1, 1835, delivery of the letters was acknowledged and authority was transferred. Don Mariano G. Vallejo, Commander, delivered the baton (insignia of the office of *Alcalde)* to Señor Haro with the customary formalities and ceremonies; speeches were made, all was well, and the people were very contented. That same afternoon at three, I returned to the mission.

On January 2, at noon, Señor Vallejo, Sergeant Dolores Pacheco with some of his family, two traveling companions, and I embarked at the place called Yerba Buena, in a launch operated by an Indian named Celso, for the estuary of Sonoma. We sailed with a good breeze, but at a little after three, the sky clouded and soon a tempest was manifest. Every moment during the night, the launch was filled with water. All helped at the oars, and even the women had to bail out water with our hats. After severe exertions and imminent danger of shipwreck, we arrived in the channel. There we landed. Señor Vallejo and the sergeant left at eleven o'clock that night for Sonoma, and the rest of us stayed in a wooden barrack there. The following day, horses were sent for us, and although the creeks were swollen, we started out and arrived safely in Sonoma. Each one of us carried on our saddle one of the young Pachecos. We rode on the croup [rump]. After my arrival at Sonoma and upon telling my companions that I had come for a brief time and must return to Monterey, they said that they would not let me go. The winter appeared very severe, and as I was afraid of crossing the bay on which we had barely escaped death, I decided to pass the winter there.

1837

A Mexican Officer Urges Defense of Both Californias

Andrés Castillero

The political stability that Figueroa brought to Alta California collapsed shortly after his death in 1835. His successor, Mariano Chico, former congressman from Guanajuato, arrived the next year, and he did not get along well with the *Californio* elite. Part of his problem stemmed from political changes in the country. For one thing, Juan Bandini, when he was in the congress, had induced that body to change the capital of Alta California from Monterey to Los Angeles. The change was not immediately effective (it was never really implemented), so Chico took up residence in Monterey, but he was nonetheless a symbol to the residents of Monterey of a change in their status that they deeply resented.

Also, Chico represented a newly conservative Mexican government. Santa Anna had finally resumed power and replaced the 1824 constitution with a much more centralist document in 1836. States and territories were transformed into military departments, with their governors appointed by the president. More stringent voting qualifications were also a part of the new order, and overall, Santa Anna's regime took on an aristocratic flavor. Disapproval of this new direction was especially acute in the peripheral areas of the country: a number of the Mexican elite in Texas joined Anglo-Americans in their successful struggle to break away from Mexico, and separatist movements also sprouted in the Yucatán peninsula, Sonora, and New Mexico.

Chico's personal behavior—he was often openly accompanied by a mistress—offended the *Californios* as well. He quickly came into conflict with the *diputación* and the Monterey *ayuntamiento*. Since he lacked any real support, he was forced to depart before the end of the summer of 1836. He

José Castro. Courtesy of the California History Room, California State Library, Sacramento.

left a senior military officer, Nicolás Gutiérrez, in charge. This officer was himself driven out of Alta California before the end of the year. A group of *Californios* led by Juan Bautista Alvarado, supplemented by a contingent of foreign residents recruited by Isaac Graham, a hunter from Kentucky who lived in the area, forced him to surrender the Monterey *presidio.* The *diputación* then met and declared Alta California an independent state. But in Los Angeles and San Diego, residents feared domination by the north and by its three young leaders, Alvarado, Vallejo, and José Castro. Alvarado managed to march a force to Los Angeles and compel adherence in early 1837, but that allegiance vanished when his forces withdrew.

While Alta California was experiencing this turmoil, Baja California was stabilizing. The central government decided to split the military and political commands, a move that the *diputaciones* in both Californias had long urged. The appointments of the talented Luis del Castillo Negrete as political commander of Baja California and of José Caballero as military commander brought an end to the factional warfare that had afflicted the peninsula since 1831. Caballero quickly became concerned, however, that Alta California's problems might spread south and threaten the stability of Baja California, so he dispatched Andrés Castillero, an officer who had served in Alta California, to try to settle things. Armed with only a vague set of instructions and little real power, Castillero nevertheless managed to bring the two sides of the Alta California dispute together. He convinced Alvarado that, in the practical order, he and the *Californios* had little to fear from the new centralist regime. Alta California was so distant from the center of Mexico that most of its officers would doubtless be *Californios,* and as a department, Alta California, once merely a territory, was actually on a par with the former states of the republic.

Further complexities arose when José Antonio Carrillo, Alta California's congressional delegate, managed to gain the appointment of his brother Carlos as governor of Alta California. After some intermittent hostilities between the Alvarado and Carrillo factions, Castillero undertook a mission to the capital that resulted in Alvarado's being confirmed as governor. With its hands already full in Texas and elsewhere, the central government had little interest in a protracted struggle in Alta California.

The following document is from a letter Castillero wrote to the minister of war in Mexico City in October 1837, after he had successfully negotiated with the various factions in Alta California. He offered a frank assessment of the situation in both Californias. He urged the government to take measures to strengthen the Mexican military presence in both Baja and Alta California. Castillero was quite aware of the growing influence of foreigners on the Pacific coast and the ease with which Mexican customs regulations could be avoided; as his letter indicates, Mexico was well aware of the dangers posed by its neighbor to the north.

From a Letter by Andrés Castillero

New California, due to its topographic situation, carries on the exchange of its products along the coast very easily. All its towns and missions are established very near to the best ports, so that the national and foreign vessels are like moving stores that remain more than a year, selling their merchandise and collecting the payments of hides and tallow to carry them to Lima and North America. Due to this custom and because it is a newly settled country, this commerce by barter has been carried on in it almost by necessity, without its being possible to enforce the law on the subject there, and to forbid it would be a hardship to the class that needs it most. In order to prevent the contraband and so that the land trade would not suffer, it would be necessary to prevent the retail trade aboard; the sales should take place on land or by consignment. The national vessels that trade on those coasts, and also the schooner *California,* should in my opinion be armed for war, for the safety of those ports and the waters of the Department. The Frontier of Lower California should have a stronger force, increasing the number in the company up to one hundred men in order to aid the Government of the Department and to prevent the raids of the savages in the southern part.

The proximity of Upper Sonora to California might serve so that the General Commandant of the former might be subject to the military command of the latter; placing in it a Principal Commander, native of the country—that is, if the former should merit the full confidence of the Government. It might also be opportune to post some force at Altar, a place close to the river road, so that, united to the Frontier company in a given case, it may aid the Department and may make correspondence with the Supreme Government easier; and [it might be opportune] to establish the mail by that route because it is the shortest and surest road to this capital. The continual passage of troops might prevent the entry of hunters and adventurers from North America, who carry on a scandalous robbery of pelts and horses through that section.

It seems to me convenient that, so long as the Government does not place a respectable force in the Department, for the safety of California, the advanced posts of which I have spoken—Altar and that on the Frontier of Lower California—should be kept reinforced, only leaving in the interior of the country the hundred men that are there under arms with their own officers, and in case that it might be judged necessary to create a force, let it be on the Frontier, keeping it there on the pretext of the Indian raids, it being possible to recruit the Diegueños, who have always been most friendly.

The Americans, when traveling light, can go from their establishment on the Columbia River to our port of San Francisco in nine days. The establishment belongs to the British, but the Americans have taken possession of it. The Supreme Government might well make a representation to the British Minister over this and point out to him at the same time the smuggling which the northern adventurers carry on in the beaver trapping, in the hope of stirring the interest of that nation, and by its complaints we might manage to expel from that nearby place the Americans who are now in contact with Texas.

It might also be worthwhile if the Principal Commander, in conjunction with the Civil Governor of Lower California, making free grants of land on the Frontier, should protect the movement of their citizens without showing any favoritism in it, taking care that honest and useful men shall go there for whatever contingency in which the fatherland may need them.

Upper and Lower California should not be governed by one Governor, nor should they have only one Court of Justice, because, being separated by a desert of more than three hundred leagues, the gubernatorial decisions could not be communicated quickly, and the easy and prompt administration of justice would be lacking. There would arise between the two the jealousies born of the small ambitions of the civil command. Neither is there in both Californias anyone who has the capital indicated by law in order to become Governor, Senator, or Deputy. In this matter I believe some allowances should be made.

All the employees who did not embark at the time of the last revolution, as well as the exiled ones, should not return to California, as much for their lack of energy in the handling of the troops as because of the old enmities that have sprung up between them and the country, as well as because some of them tacitly approved the revolution. Those excepted from this are Lieutenant Don José María Cosio, Ensign Don Nicanor Estrada, and Don Juan

Rocha, Captain Juan María Ybarra, and the Director of the National School, Don Mariano Romero.

The twenty-one missions situated on the coast, if they are administered with economy, can well care for the Indians and can yield the Government much revenue, on the condition that an inspector be appointed who will audit the accounts monthly. The national schooner *California,* now the property of the Government, can bring some products of the country from the missions to the ports of the South Sea [Pacific Ocean], carrying back goods necessary to the garrison.

The Reverend Father President of the missions of Lower California, Fr. Félix Caballero, will pledge himself to cover the salary of the company of the Frontier, on the condition that he be given a discount on duties at some one of the ports of our Republic on the Pacific coast for the vessel on which he may send the certified account of said expenditure. The port of San Francisco is fortified and a garrison should be placed there at all cost, since it is one of the largest in the world, and it is the object of all the ambitions of the Americans, who have none on the Pacific Ocean. The one of San Diego needs some repairs, and in the gorge that separates Upper from Lower California I believe a fort necessary because it is a strategic point.

The convicts which the Supreme Government has sent to the Department since the year 1810 are not convicts there, because, not knowing where to get the means to keep them, they have been given the Territory as their prison. Some of them have committed crimes that have remained unpunished due to the distance of the courts in which their cases should be tried. Perhaps it might be remedied if the desert islands of Santa Bárbara were to serve as prisons, obliging those who are condemned to them to cultivate the soil and thus prevent on the other hand some ambitious person from populating them with other people.

Lower California

It is necessary to place a garrison in that territory at Cabo San Lucas; all vessels that sail from the ports of Guaymas, Mazatlán, and San Blas must pass near it, and if the Americans, due to the ambitious aims which they manifest, should seize this point and should fortify it and keep two warships cruising those waters, they would hold a small Gibraltar which would deprive us of the trade of the South Sea, and they could attack our coasts; furthermore, there are fifty or sixty American whaling vessels which alternately go there annually on the pretext of refreshing their stores and carry on a scandalous contraband.

The national schooner *Correo Mercado* should be in the port of La Paz at the orders of the General Commandant so that coast may be looked after and so that it may carry the money for the troops from Mazatlán by a paymaster. There is a naval officer who will take the vessel on his own account, pledging himself to perform the services with that vessel without any expense to the public treasury. In this way one might prevent the money-changing that the merchants and treasury employees carry on at the expense of the garrison, forcing them to take only goods at a very high price, and in order to realize something on them the soldier in most cases has to lose half the value.

Mexico, October 21, 1837
[Signed] Andrés Castillero

1837
Indian Attacks Near San Diego

Juana Machado

In Alta California, secularization proceeded in a slightly different fashion at each mission, but the overall pattern was fairly uniform. The governor appointed a commissioner for each mission. His task was to administer the property and possessions of the mission, including its *ranchos* and agricultural lands, and to supervise the distribution of land to the Indians and the establishment of Indian *pueblos*. But it never worked out quite that way: some of the commissioners were honest and tried to take their responsibilities seriously; many others saw their positions as opportunities to become rich, either by selling mission goods or by helping themselves to generous portions of the mission lands and cattle.

Many Indians left. Those who remembered the traditional ways of life found it impossible to return to them—seventy years of Spanish and Mexican presence had so altered the environment that it was impossible to live as one's great-grandparents had. Cattle and horses had trampled native plants; settled agriculture had fundamentally altered the physical geography; and formerly abundant game had been chased farther and farther to the east. In places like San Juan Capistrano and San Gabriel, Indian groups organized to press their claims to the land they had worked at the missions and on the farther-flung mission *ranchos*. In some places, like San Luis Rey, they actually gained formal title to some of the land.

In a number of places, California Indians retained their community structures and habits, but it was a hard fight. A small number of Indians were granted individual allotments of land, but they found it difficult to prosper in a landscape increasingly dominated by large private *ranchos*. In a society in which wealth was based on land, their subordination was guaranteed. Most of the Indians who stayed within the coastal boundaries of established Mexican California hired themselves out as wage laborers on the *ranchos* or in the *pueblos*.

After becoming governor in the 1830s, Alvarado instituted a liberal land policy for the *Californios*. His generosity in granting large tracts of land to many different people was his very effective way of healing the wounds that the factional divisions of the 1830s had inflicted. But as more land went to the *Californios,* less, inevitably, went to the Indians. As the number of private *ranchos* in Alta California increased, more *Californios* found themselves coming into direct contact with Indians on the eastern frontier. Previously, non-Indian groups had ventured east only intermittently, on exploring expeditions conducted by the army or in pursuit of Indians who had fled the missions or stolen horses. As the frontier spread east, it encountered fierce resistance from native groups determined to halt non-Indian incursions. This was especially the case in the western Colorado River areas of both Californias. Many of the groups in this general vicinity had been trading contraband goods and horses with North American trappers and traders for over a decade. The hostilities in California were part of a larger pattern of increased Indian activity in northern Mexico, as various groups struggled for land and goods in the new world that was being created with trade items from the United States.

In the 1830s, hostilities broke out east of San Diego. Rancho Jamul, the site of the attack described in the following selection, was located about twenty-two miles southeast of Mission San Diego. The Pico family had claimed ownership there since 1829. It bordered Rancho Otay, which the Estudillo family had claimed in the same year.

Juana Machado was a native of San Diego, where her father served as a corporal in the *presidio*. She first married Damiano Alipaz. After his death in 1835, she married Thomas Ridington, a North American sailor who settled in San Diego in 1833 and worked as a shoemaker. Her account demonstrates that the eastern frontier around the border between Baja and Alta California never came fully under Mexican control.

From "Times Gone By in Alta California" by Juana Machado

Early one afternoon, an Indian woman named Cesárea came to where Doña Eustaquia was sitting at the door looking toward the street and, in a loud voice, asked her for salt. The mistress ordered that salt be brought her, but the Indian woman, by sign, gave her to understand that she wished her to give it to her, herself. The mistress got up and the Indian woman followed her. Arriving at a secluded spot, the Indian woman, in a tongue which Doña Eustaquia understood well, told her that the Indians were going to rise, kill the men, and make captives of the women.

Doña Eustaquia, with much prudence, went to the room where her daughters were sewing; she told them to leave their work, take their *rebozos* (all of the women wore *rebozos* at that time), and go for a walk along the edge of the cornfield, saying that she would soon follow them.

With much secrecy she called the majordomo, a relative of hers named Juan Leiva, and told him what Cesárea had revealed to her, saying besides that she herself had for some days noticed things among the Indians which had made her suspicious, although these had not been great.

The majordomo assured her that there was no danger whatever, advising her to calm herself, as he had men and twelve firearms well loaded. Doña Eustaquia again urged him to place her and her family in safety. He, confident of his strength, refused to do what she advised. Then Doña Eustaquia told him to send a *carreta* with oxen along the road to the cornfield. She started on the road to meet her daughters. The *carreta* came along to them, with only one hide in it; in this *carreta* they arrived at Jamacha ranch (belonging to the already mentioned Doña Apolinaria, who had a major-domo in charge there) in the middle of the night; thence after telling the majordomo and his family what was going on, they continued the journey to San Diego and reported to the *Alcalde,* Don José Antonio Estudillo, who at once sent people to protect those at the ranch, but they arrived late.

The Indians did not attack the same night but the following; all of a sudden they fell upon servants at the ranch, who were the majordomo, Juan Leiva, his son José Antonio, a youth name Molina, and another from Lower California named Comancho. They killed all at the cornfield except Juan Leiva, who broke away toward the house to defend his family.

When he went toward the gun room, an Indian cleaning woman of the house who had locked that room and put the key in her pocket mockingly showed him the key, saying that there were no hopes in that direction.

Leiva ran to the kitchen and defended himself with coals of fire for a while; but at the end they killed him and threw his body into the hall of the house. Afterward they overcame his wife, Doña María, a little son named Claro, and his two daughters, Tomasa and Ramona (fifteen and twelve years old, respectively).

The Indians were going to kill Doña María and the boy, when the supplications of Doña Tomasa made them desist. They took off all the woman's clothes and those of the boy, and in spite of the screams and moans of all the family, they carried off the two girls toward the Colorado River. Before starting they removed everything from the ranch, taking with them horses, cattle, and all other things of value, and burned the houses.

Poor Doña María covered her nakedness with grasses and thus reached Mission San Diego, where Fathers Vicente Pasqual Olivas and Fernando Martín were in charge.

All the efforts that were made to recover the lost property and much great effort to ransom the kidnapped girls were useless. To this day, what was the fate of those unhappy creatures is unknown. Sergeant Macedonio Gonzales, celebrated Indian fighter, told us that once he went from Mission San Miguel in Lower California to Jacumba Mountain with a considerable force to see about rescuing these girls, who were his nieces. On reaching the foot of the mountain he saw many men and women Indians above, eating meat of the cattle which they had stolen. When they saw him they began to shout and threaten him, saying that they also had courage, and if he wanted to come up where they were, Tomasa and Ramona were there.

He said that he actually saw these two girls, apparently with white bodies painted and with hair cut in Indian fashion. He saw their bodies because in that time the Indians did not wear clothes, except a covering of rabbit skins, which they called *pajales*, over their privates; he did not dare to fire, fearing that they really were his nieces and the shots might kill them.

Afterwards the Indians left the rock to which they had ascended and disappeared. It was not possible for him to climb with his horses to that height. He spoke kindly to the Indians and made them very generous offers of cattle, horses, etc. as ransom for the girls, but the Indians accepted nothing.

Some years afterwards, when these same Indians were at peace, he again offered them ransom, but all his efforts were in vain.

1838
Secularization in Baja California

Julián Pérez

In Baja California, mission secularization proceeded more gradually than in Alta California. Given the lack of priests to replace the Dominicans, an arrangement was worked out whereby the missions were secularized one by one when the resident missionary retired.

In the late 1830s, Governor Castillo Negrete decided to move more rapidly against one of the leading priests, Fr. Gabriel González of Todos Santos. Fr. González resisted, arguing, as the Franciscans had in Alta California, that the land belonged to the Indians. The ranchers of the peninsula, especially in the south, retorted that there were so few Indians that the mission lands should more properly be regarded as the clergy's private *ranchos* and therefore not worthy of any special status. A bitter controversy broke out between González and the governor. In one episode, the governor led a force to Todos Santos, but González and a band of armed men drove them all the way back to La Paz. The following account is taken from a narrative composed in 1860 by Julián Pérez, who was closely associated with the ranchers of San Antonio.

From a Letter by Julián Pérez
in the Reminiscences of Manuel Clemente Rojo

January 10, 1860

The Civil Governor tried to carry out the law of the Sovereign National Congress for the secularization of the missions. There were no longer any neophyte Indians among whom to distribute the land and livestock of the missions; thus the Fathers were the owners of everything and used everything for their own benefit as though it were their own; there hardly remained, in any of the missions, an occasional old Indian who halfway served in the groves like the rest who used to cling to the missionaries, with no salaries and poorly fed. The primitive race had disappeared with the mixture of the white race and the children of the Indian girls which they had from the soldiers they married; they no longer considered themselves neophytes but *gente de razón,* and thus, little by little, the aborigines were dying out; and around the time we are talking about, the missionary Fathers were alone, and rather than busying themselves in their missions, they went from one place to another to say Mass in the little towns or small congregations…marrying, baptizing, and burying for money and for very high fees, with which they got fat incomes in the midst of the unhappiness and poverty of the citizens. Señor [Castillo] Negrete ordered that, for want of neophyte Indians, the mission lands be distributed among those people who had gathered and settled in the missions. First, he separated the irrigated portion, leaving it for the benefit of the church; second, he separated a piece of land for the benefit of the school; third, he distributed among each of the neophytes one of the best pieces of land and distributed the rest in equal portions among the citizens. This disposition, which seemed fair and suited to the true spirit of the law, so displeased the President of the Missions, Fr. Gabriel González, and his second, Fr. Ramírez, that they immediately began to complain about it, saying that the Law of Secularization did not deal with the missions of Lower California but rather with those of Upper California, which the Deputy Don José Antonio Carrillo had asked for in Congress; because in order to include those of the Peninsula in that measure, it was necessary for the Civil Governor to have waited to receive prior orders from the Government of Mexico before making those distributions, through which the Church was stripped of its rights, which were sacred; and that both the Civil Governor of the Territory, who was distributing the ecclesiastical goods, and those favored with them were committing the sin called canonically "simony"; and that all the simonists were excommunicated by different canons and dispositions of the councils, and most particularly by the Ecumenical Council of Trent. Therefore, no one should expect to be saved if he did not restore to the Church what he was stealing from it in this way, with grave harm to religion and to the propagation of the Faith among the infidels. And he would speak in this tone in homes and in church, as I heard him do many times, as much as he could, in order to hinder and discredit the measure, adding that Señor Negrete was a heretic, and other things like that which I don't even recall anymore.

Señor Negrete said that the [secularization] law ought to be obeyed like the others, without waiting for new orders from the Government to put it into practice; and since he was ordering the secularization of the missions while at the same time regulating the way of doing it, it was useless for the Government to concern itself with doing a second time what Congress already had done. And thus, with very good reasons and a great deal of dignity, he cleared himself of the charges which were being made against him and carried on his measure, topping it off with the founding of public schools in all the centers of population and ordering the local judges to watch persistently both the teachers, so that they would attend their schools punctually, and the heads of families, so that they would not be careless about sending their children to them; because in everything, Sir, it was necessary at that time not only to do things, but also to oblige people to take what was good for them almost by force. There were heads of families who did not want to send their children to school, alleging that they needed them at home to help them work, and they said that in order to save oneself it was not necessary to know how to read or write, and that rather, by learning these things, they would corrupt themselves and do a great deal of evil, writing love letters to seduce virgins and other things like that, which [allegations] would only be excusable on account of the ignorance of those poor people.

1840
Indian Attacks near Guadalupe

José Luciano Espinosa and María Gracia

Indian attacks persisted throughout the last years of Mexican California. The following account was related to Manuel Clemente Rojo by José Luciano Espinosa, a rancher, and María Gracia, an Indian woman living at Mission Guadalupe.

Jatiñil, the leader of a northern Baja California group, had assisted José Manuel Ruiz in a campaign against the Cocopah in 1803 and had developed close ties with Fr. Félix Caballero in the 1820s. But when Caballero insisted that he be baptized in the mid-1830s, Jatiñil refused and withdrew his people farther east, away from Caballero's influence. Even though he assisted Macedonio González's campaigns against the Indians in the late 1830s, he continued to view Caballero as an enemy. In 1840, he launched an attack on Mission Guadalupe, which Caballero had founded forty miles south of Rancho Jamul four years earlier (making it the last California mission to be founded), to replace San Miguel de la Frontera. Mission Guadalupe was closed shortly after the attack. In this same year, Mission Santa Catalina was burned and destroyed by an alliance of Cocopah, Quechán, and other indigenous people. In this area, the mission frontier was in retreat.

From the Account of Don José Luciano Espinosa

At the beginning of February of 1840 I went from my *rancho* of Santo Domingo to Mission Guadalupe, bringing Father Félix Caballero some otter skins which I had treated, as I did every year, because he used to provide me with everything I needed to keep up my fleet of otter hunters, which I had every year on the coast; I had already settled my accounts with the Father and gotten from him new articles and money to be paid back the following year, when at the time I was going to leave, I went into the mission corral to harness my beasts and go; as I was doing these chores I saw that the native chief Jatiñil had arrived with many armed men, but that did not bother me, because it was a tribe which was always peaceful and which, far from bothering the mission establishments or the *ranchos,* used to go out to campaign against the rebellious Indians and assisted the escort in all its expeditions, conducting itself like a true friend of the *gente de razón.* Corporal Orantes was standing up and half leaning on the gate of the mission when the Indians reached it; and hardly was he within reach of the first one who approached when the latter gave him a blow on the head with a club, a blow which Orantes was not expecting because, just like me and all the rest of us, he did not distrust Jatiñil's tribe. As a result of the blow which he received unexpectedly, Orantes fell to the ground, and there several Indians piled on him and finished the job of killing him. When I saw and heard these things, I jumped the wall of the corral where I was— I did not want to go out the gate—so that they might not see me, and I began to run at full speed toward a little plain half a league away, toward the west of the mission, where Lieutenant Garraleta had gone with seventeen soldiers from the escort to drill them; but in spite of my precautions, they still saw me, and several Indians followed me, running after me, shouting at me, and threatening that they were going to kill me; at this point I went into a little forest, and as I was going in, a crow which happened to be around there flew out; and I heard clearly when the Indians said, "Let's not follow him anymore, Espinoza is a wizard and has turned himself into a bird; look at him, there he goes." With this they left me alone, but I was already quite far from the direction in which I was going at first, anxious as I was to see Lieutenant Garraleta. Fatigued, I stayed for a few hours in the shade of some bushes on the southern slope of the Guadalupe gulch, and from there I went to Ensenada de Todos Santos, where I arrived the following day about ten in the morning.

From the Account of María Gracia

We had no idea that such a thing could happen, when we heard the shouts of the Indians who were killing Corporal Orantes and those of others who were calling Father Caballero to kill him. The Father had said Mass and was going to have breakfast when this was happening. I was setting the table at which the Father was going to eat, and I looked out the dining room window, which opened on the patio, and saw everything all full of blood, and Corporal Orantes dead; I saw that the Jatiñils were killing Francisco and José Antonio, neophyte Indians of Mission San Miguel who had come to Guadalupe to plant wheat and barley on the table lands of *El Tigre*. The Jatiñils took their time doing this while the Father and I, seeing what was happening, became filled with fear and went to take refuge in the church; but considering that the gentiles would not respect the main altar, where we thought of taking shelter first, we went up to the choir, because there we were less obvious to those who entered the church; the Father, when he saw that they were shouting at him to kill him and that all their rage was directed towards him, begged me for God's sake not to give him away, promising me that if the Virgin Mary got him out of that conflict he was in, he would give me everything I might need from then on in order to live leisurely and with no need to serve anyone as long as God remembered me. That is what he told me, and he had me sit down on top of him, hiding him with my clothes even from those who might see me. I, frightened to death as I was, and without being at all sure about my own life, felt sorry for Father Félix and did everything that he ordered me to do, knowing that if the Indians came to discover that I was hiding him, then they would inevitably kill me, even though they had no intention of harming me, because that is how they are: they never forgive anyone who hides an enemy or a person upon whom they want to take vengeance for something that person has done to them. I remember all this as though it had just happened right now: I was sitting on top of Father Caballero, having hidden him well with my tunic, when I heard footsteps going up the choir stairs where I was in that position; I felt cold as Jatiñil approached with his bow in one hand and said to me, "How's it going, relative?" I do not even know what I answered, and I began to cry, begging him not to harm me. "Don't be afraid," he told me, "I haven't ordered anyone killed, but the people who have come with me killed Corporal Orantes and also Francisco and José Antonio; the one I am looking for is the Father, because he is forcing baptism on the people of my tribe in order to enslave them in the mission just like you are without enjoying your liberty and living like horses. Where is the Father?" "Why do you ask me," I answered, "when I don't even know how I got here, because I'm so afraid from seeing you so mad?" "Well, I'm going," he said, and went down without saying another word; in a very short time everything was quiet, and recovering my courage, I went down to the patio; all the Indians had left already, and I could only make out the dust that they raised along the north gulch opposite the mission as they moved toward the mountain.

1841
The Arrival of a North American Wagon Train

Mariano Guadalupe Vallejo

A land route between Santa Fe and Alta California was opened in 1829 by trader Antonio Armijo. First used almost exclusively for commerce, the difficult path gradually attracted small numbers of people who wished to emigrate to California. In 1836, Missouri resident John Marsh attached himself to a New Mexico trading party and made the trip to California. Marsh settled on a *rancho* at the foot of Mt. Diablo, east of San Francisco. His enthusiastic letters back to his friends in Missouri about Alta California helped spark the formation there of a small group called the Western Emigration Society.

Small missionary parties began departing Missouri for Oregon in the mid-1830s. In 1841, a larger collection of people was preparing to set out on the Oregon trail. A group interested in California managed to join this larger party, which included six Jesuits under Pierre de Smet who were headed for Oregon. At Soda Springs, Idaho, the California group, led by John Bidwell and John Bartleson, detached themselves from the Oregon group and headed southwest. They followed the Humboldt, Carson, and Walker Rivers and crossed the Sierra Nevada. The group of thirty-one people arrived at Marsh's ranch in November.

Since plans for this westward journey had been widely reported in the Missouri papers, the news reached Mexico even before the group had set out. After its experience in Texas, the Mexican government wanted to stem the westward tide of North Americans. The Ministry of War therefore ordered that all foreign immigrants would need legal passports to remain in the country. When Marsh told the group about this regulation, about half of them decided to go to San José to try to obtain the necessary

Mariano Guadalupe Vallejo. Courtesy of The Bancroft Library, University of California, Berkeley.

papers. They were put under arrest and brought before the commanding general of the northern district of Alta California, Mariano Guadalupe Vallejo, who happened to be at the former Mission San José conferring with José Castro. When Vallejo found out that Marsh's letters had sparked the overland journey, he sent for him and demanded that Marsh post bond for the newcomers. Marsh and John Sutter, a Swiss immigrant who was living in the Sacramento Valley, did so. After some hesitation, Vallejo decided to issue the group temporary passports, telling them to get permanent passports as soon as possible.

Vallejo had been named military commander of the north by Alvarado. He created a kind of personal fiefdom for himself in Sonoma, and he was the wealthiest and most powerful individual north of Monterey. A man of genuine liberal sympathies in many respects, he admired much about the United States. Some even suspected in the 1840s that he secretly wished for American annexation of Alta California. Yet he also took seriously his duties as a Mexican officer, and he was deeply distressed by his country's apparent inability to enforce its own laws and regulations in Alta California. This resulted in a profound and lasting ambivalence on his part about the North Americans who started arriving with increasing frequency in the 1840s. The following selection is a letter he wrote to the Ministry of War after his experience with the Bidwell party.

FROM A LETTER BY MARIANO GUADALUPE VALLEJO

Most Excellent Sir: On the return of Captain Don José Castro to this Department, I had a number of conferences with him; and I had decided that he should return to that capital in company with Captain of Militia and Secretary of the Commandancy General Don Victor Prudón, to place in Your Excellency's hands an exact report of the state in which this country finds itself, a country that is so promising but which can accomplish nothing; for its happiness is conditional, and its misery positive. Its geographic location, the mildness of its climate, the fertility of its soil, the amenity of its fields, the safety of its ports, among which that of San Francisco deserves to rank among the principal ones of the world, its navigable rivers and inlets, etc. guarantee it a state of prosperity which it is not permitted to attain, due to its lack of population. From that lack of population results its lack of defense, and from this, its insecurity. Thus it is that daily, throughout the whole extent of the Department with the exception of this frontier, where I maintain a military force of forty men at my own expense, there are Indian raids which ravish the fields with impunity and destroy the only effective wealth of the country, the cattle and horses. The otter and beaver which abounded in California have been exterminated, the first by the Russians and the latter by the Columbians [trappers from the Columbia River], who still continue to trap them to the point of extinguishing the species, as the Russians have done with the otter. And we have to endure all those ills because we cannot prevent them, since we have not troops. All that we have suffered and shall endure, if we do not avert the tempest which is presaged for us by the thick clouds that darken our political horizon, is derived from one and the same source; it comes from one single cause: all of it we should attribute to the lack of troops.

This has been, Your Excellency, the motive which inspired me with the idea of addressing to you, by the aforementioned Commissioners, the various notes which they shall have the honor to place in Your Excellency's hands, all of them relative to the exigencies of the country, with the hope that Your Excellency's zeal and acknowledged patriotism will be exerted to contribute toward the salvation of this valuable portion of Mexican Territory. The Commissioners will be able to satisfy Your Excellency about all of which you may judge opportune to inform yourself.

On the ninth of November, last, while at Mission San José, during a conference with Don José Castro, I received word of the arrival at the town of San José of a party of thirty-three foreigners from Missouri. I had them appear before me to demand their passports, and I was told that they had none, because they did not deem them necessary, since they did not use them in their country. I took a list of their names and the object of their journey. I asked them to return to their country and to get the required documents, and I gave them provisional papers so that they might travel in safety to Monterey to see the Governor and get the necessary permission from him to travel in the country. I gave the Governor an account of everything but do not know the results. I took what seemed to me the only way to reconcile justice with the present circumstances, since we find ourselves forced to accept them, as we cannot prevent them from entering, and all because we lack troops. This party numbers thirty-three, but it is said that a larger one is on the way.

The total population of California does not exceed six thousand souls, and of these two-thirds must be counted as women and children, leaving scarcely two thousand men. But we cannot count on the fifteen thousand Indians in the towns and missions, because they inspire more fear than confidence. Thus we have this lamentable situation in a country worthy of a better fate. And if the invasion which is taking place from all sides is carried out, all I can guarantee is that the Californians will die; I cannot dare to assure you that California will be saved. This people, loyal to their flag, will follow the same course and fate. They will be replaced by or dominated by another race at least. Those others will probably conserve their great past, raising their flag to wave in the breeze. Thus also the noble people of California will preserve their noble attitude of free men while a drop of blood remains in their veins, and will bite the dust before kissing the enemy's hand.

Have the kindness to excuse this burst of feeling in a soldier who laments not having arms when he sees the treasure being stolen. I regret to bother Your Excellency's patriotic zeal, but I must be a truthful steward when speaking of the national interests. The danger seems closer than the help, and it is urgent, and it is with the hope of getting it that I have the honor of addressing Your Excellency.

1842
Typical Land Grants

Juan Bautista Alvarado

Under Mexico, the Spanish system of making land grants was expanded and put on a more secure footing. Laws passed in 1824 and 1828 established the principles that the lands belonged to the nation and that governors were entitled to grant vacant lands to various classes of persons. Before 1834, only fifty grants were made in Alta California, and a number of these were older grants being brought into conformity with Mexican law. The pace of grants substantially increased after secularization and especially after the cessation of political turmoil in 1838. About half of the almost nine hundred grants claimed during the entire Mexican period were made in the period from 1841 to 1846.

Over the years, a certain order was introduced into the grant process. A person desiring a grant was required to submit a petition to the governor or, after Alvarado organized the political jurisdictions of the territory more rationally, to the prefect of a district. The petitioner had to provide his (or in rare cases, her) name, age, country of birth, occupation, and the amount of land desired. The land had to be described in word and in picture (the picture was called a *diseño*). While the land was sometimes described in terms of specific distances from one boundary to the next, it was very common for man-made or natural monuments to be used to delimit the property. Thus the survey descriptions are studded with mentions of a cactus or a small hill or a bush or a group of rocks or a stream. The lack of precision that stemmed from the use of these changing landmarks was not a significant problem when the territory's population was relatively light—only about eight thousand non-Indians lived there in 1846. But this vagueness placed a terrible burden on Mexican grantees who tried to retain their property during and after the population explosion caused by the gold rush and a transfer of political power to the United States.

Juan Bautista Alvarado. Courtesy of the California History Room, California State Library, Sacramento, California.

After the survey was submitted, the governor or prefect requested local officials to declare whether or not the land was truly vacant and the grant could be made without harm to others. When this was done, the governor or prefect would issue a formal grant, which in turn would have to be approved by the *diputación* or another appropriate body. The local official would then put the grantee into formal possession of the land, once a final measuring was done and boundary markers had been put in place. The process was complex, but it generally worked well during Alta California's Mexican period, where the object of the laws was to engage as many community agencies as possible in order to create and sustain a broad consensus about the nature and use of the land. Later, the complexity would prove to be a curse when American lawyers would demand convincing evidence in the form of specific documents to demonstrate that every step had been followed to the letter.

The following two documents were prepared in connection with land grants. The first is a petition prepared by John Rowland (phonetically spelled "Roland"), a Pennsylvanian who immigrated to California in 1841. The second is a grant given in 1842 by Governor Alvarado to Joaquín Estudillo in the San Francisco Bay area. Both documents are less than precise. Rowland said that he was asking for four leagues "more or less." The Estudillo grant is described by boundaries which could easily change over time because of weather (the *Arroyo San Leandro*) or population movements ("the drainage of the springs now occupied by the Indians who have settled there"). But these sorts of potentially variable boundaries served the communities who drew them quite well in the sociopolitical context in which they were created.

Petition of John Rowland

To His Excellency the Governor
Most Excellent Sir:

I John Roland, a native of the United States and naturalized in the Mexican Nation, married to a Mexican woman and resident of New Mexico by whom I have seven children, four sons and three daughters, desiring the repose of my family and their well-being, which is the chief object of my cares, have come to establish myself in this Department and to attain the same. I need a tract of land on which to put my property and which I can cultivate for the support of my said family, and as there is in the ex-Mission of San Gabriel a vacant place at La Puente in the midst of the land of those persons whom I name in this petition: being on the East bounded by El Chino and San José, and on the West by the River San Gabriel, on the North by the land of Don Luis Arenas, and on the South by the land of the Señores Pérez, of the Señores Nietos and Los Coyotes, wherefore I beseech your Excellency that you will be pleased to grant me in property the land which I solicit—which may be four leagues (land for cattle), a little more or less. I pray Your Excellency to do what I ask, whereby I shall receive favor and justice.

John Roland

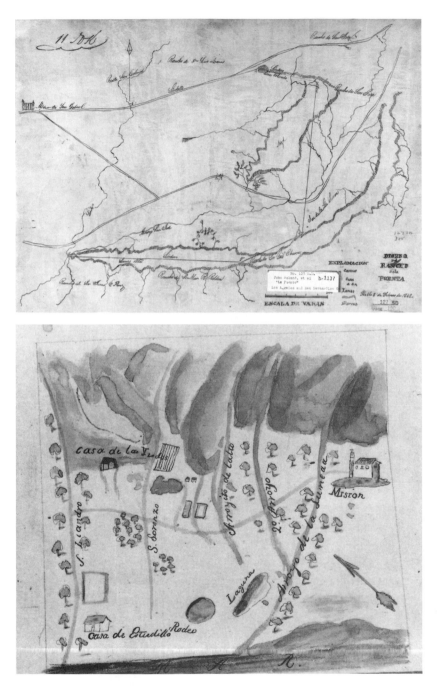

Diseños *for the La Puente and San Leandro ranchos. Courtesy of The Bancroft Library, University of California, Berkeley.*

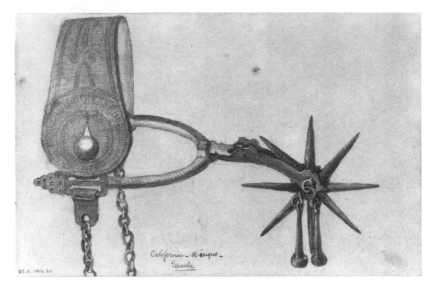

Californio *spurs sketched by Fritz Wikersheim. Courtesy of The Bancroft Library, University of California, Berkeley.*

LAND GRANT TO JOAQUÍN ESTUDILLO

Whereas, the citizen Joaquín Estudillo has petitioned for his personal benefit and that of his family for a part of the land known under the name of San Leandro, the boundary of which being on the North the *Arroyo San Leandro;* on the East the drainage of the springs in the lands occupied by the Indians now settled there; from this point in a straight line south to the *Arroyo de San Lorenzo,* without including the lands cultivated by the Indians already mentioned; and on the West by the bay, having previously taken all the necessary steps and regulations on this subject: In virtue of the powers conferred on me, in the name of the Mexican Nation, I hereby grant him the land mentioned, giving to him the right of possession thereof by these presents, and by the approbation which he has obtained from the Departmental Junta, being subject to the following conditions:

1. He has the power to fence it without interfering with the passages, roads, and other rights. He shall enjoy it freely and exclusively, applying it to any use or culture most agreeable to him, but within a year he shall build a house, and said house must be inhabited.

2. He shall solicit to be placed in lawful possession in virtue of this document, from the competent Judge by whom the boundaries shall be marked out, and on their borders he shall, besides placing landmarks, plant some fruit trees or some forest trees of some utility.

3. The land granted is one square league, a little more or less, as it is shown by the sketch annexed to the folder on this matter. The Judge who shall place him in possession must have the land measured according to law, leaving the remainder for the uses the Nation may decree proper.

4. Should he contravene these conditions he shall lose his right to the land, and it shall be denounced by any other person.

In virtue whereof I order this title, being good and valid, that a copy of it be recorded in the Book of Record, and that it be delivered to the party interested for his security and other ends.

Given in Monterey, October 16, 1842
Juan Bautista Alvarado
Constitutional Governor of the Department of the Californias

1840s
Life on a California Rancho

JOSÉ DEL CARMEN LUGO

The following selection describes the rhythm of life on a Mexican *rancho* in Alta California. The *rancho* was the backbone of the hide and tallow trade, which dominated the local economy in the 1830s and 1840s. The slaughter *(matanza)* of the cattle was one the highlights of *rancho* activity. *Vaqueros,* who were both Indian and Mexican, would drive the cattle from their grazing areas into a central field and kill them by slashing their necks. Other laborers would strip the hides and leave them in the sun to dry. Still others, often women, would carve chunks of fat from the carcasses and place them in large vats, in which they would boil them. When the fat cooled, it would solidify into chunks of tallow or lard. The animal remains would often be left on the ground for other animals to pick clean. The hides would ultimately be carted to Anglo-American ships. They would often end up in New England to be made into leather for the burgeoning shoe industry—raw materials for the first American industrial revolution.

José del Carmen Lugo, the author of this reminiscence, was born in Los Angeles in 1813 and grew up on San Antonio Rancho. He was granted Rancho San Bernardino in 1842.

FROM "THE LIFE OF A RANCHER"

The Californian way of life in my early years was as follows: at eight o'clock in the evening, the entire family was occupied in its prayers. In commending themselves to God, they recited the rosary and other special prayers which each one addressed to the saint of his or her name or devotion. Husband and wife slept in the same room, and nearly always in the same bed. If there were any children, and the dwelling

This drawing of vaqueros *catching cattle in preparation for slaughter appeared in* Forbes's California *in 1839. The scene is familiar to U.S. audiences, for we have seen it in countless movies and rodeos. However, before the Civil War, such scenes would have been very strange to U.S. readers, for whom most of the "West" was still east of the Mississippi River, and who had little to no experience with cattle drives and roundups. Much of what we think of as essential to the American West was imported from Spanish and Mexican frontier life. Courtesy of the California History Room, California State Library, Sacramento, California.*

had conveniences and separate apartments, the boys slept in the galleries outside in the open air, and the girls in an enclosed quarter to which the parents kept the key, if there was a key, a thing that was not very common.

At three o'clock in the morning, the entire family was summoned to their prayers. After this, the women betook themselves to the kitchen and other domestic tasks such as sweeping, cleaning, dusting, and so on. The men went to their labor in the field, some to herd cattle, others to look after the horses. The milking of the cows was done by the men or the Indian servants. Ordinarily some woman had charge of the milking, to see that the milk was clean and strained. The women and the Indian servants under them made the small, hard, flat cheeses, the cheese proper, butter, curds, and a mixture made to use with beans.

The women's labors lasted till seven or eight in the morning. After that they were busy cooking, sewing, or washing. The men passed the day in labor in the fields, according to the location—some preparing the ground for sowing seed, bringing in wood, sowing the seed, and so on. Some

Cattle brands, prepared by Luis María Peralta in 1819. Courtesy of the Honnold-Mudd Library Special Collections, Claremont, California.

planted cotton, some hemp, some planted both. This was done by those who had facilities for it; they planted and harvested the things they needed most for the benefit of their families, such as rice, corn, beans, barley and other grains, squash, watermelons, and cantaloupes.

The lands in the immediate vicinity of Los Angeles were set to fruit trees such as grapes, pears, apples, pomegranates, here and there an olive, cactus fruit in some places, peaches, nectarines, and other minor fruits. The owners of fields could not obtain seeds of oranges, lemon, cider-producing fruits, or others that were found at the missions, because the padres selfishly refused to allow them to grow elsewhere than at their missions.

Fruit trees were not cultivated on the *ranchos,* because very few persons were able to own ranches until very recently; that is, 1836 or 1837 and on.

During the time Spain was in power here, a few *ranchos* were granted, those of the Nietos, Verdugos, Domínguez and Bartolo Tapia. I am not positive, but I have heard it said that the *Rancho de la Bayona* was also granted in the time of the King, to the family of Zúñiga. These are the only *ranchos* that I know as having been granted during the Spanish regime.

Many people occupied *ranchos* provisionally with their stock, and this was allowed because there was not room enough for them in the town or the community corral. In 1822, an order came from the *Alcalde* that the Judge should destroy corrals on the *ranchos,* and the owners of stock should place them in community corrals. At this time my father was in Monterey, and he secured permission to maintain a corral on the little ranch where he lived, the one that the river destroyed in 1825....

Returning to the way of living of the Californians: the type of ordinary life that I have described was more or less followed by people living on *ranchos* as well as by those residing in the towns.

The house on a little ranch was of rough timber roofed with tules. It rarely had more than two rooms. One served as the entry and living room, the other as a sleeping room. If the family was large, the two rooms were divided. Many of these houses had a door faced with sheepskin, cowhide, or horsehide. No door had a lock or key, nor was it necessary to close it on the outside when the whole family left, because there was no one who would enter to steal, and nothing which would be worth taking. If the family was to be absent for several days, they would take with them their one thing of value, namely, the little chest of clothes, and some bedding and a cot.

Some ranchers or other people of the town had beds of cottonwood or poplar lined with leather on which they slept. On this bed there were sheets, blankets, coverlets, pillows, and so on, according to the resources of the owner.

Some slept on great frameworks resembling a hammock with cross-bars on which was thrown a cowhide. The person who had nothing else slept on a cowhide or horsehide. I am speaking, of course, of the first years that I knew. Later some conveniences were introduced when trade with the outside began. The families who were able usually had furniture of the sort most needed, such as a table, a long bench, and a few little stools. Some had seats of whalebones, other little stools, often of reeds, narrow slats, or some other splints. These stools were the most common. Outside the house on each side of the door there were benches of adobe on which people could sit; they were less than a *vara* in height. Some were plastered and whitewashed like the wall of the house. Others, like some of the houses, were not whitewashed, because lime was scarce and hard to obtain without bringing it from a distance.

The kitchen in some places was supplied with a small adobe arrangement on which were placed the cooking pots. In other places there were only stones upon which the pots were placed, the fire being underneath them. The hour for breakfast was very early for the men who had to go to their labors. Others breakfasted later. For this breakfast the wealthy had good Spanish chocolate made with milk or water according to taste, with bread, tortillas, and wheat or corn porridge with butter, and so on. The poor people had their early meal of milk with pinole or toasted corn, or perhaps parched corn. Others breakfasted on beans, while some had a solid meal of roasted or dried meat with chili, onions, tomatoes, and beans, since there would not be another until four or five in the afternoon, according to the time of the year.

During Lent, when fasting was observed, people did not have their first meal until twelve o'clock noon, and the second at eight in the evening. These two meals, at midday and at night, generally consisted of fish, abalone, *colachi* (which was merely squash chopped fine and boiled), and *quelites* (which were native herbs well boiled) mixed with beans half and half. There was no coffee or tea.

Another dish was *lechetole,* which was wheat cooked in milk with plenty of *panocha* (a sort of candy made of brown sugar), or squash cooked with milk and *panocha,* curds, cheese, cottage cheese, and clabber. The supper during Lent was of *colachi, quelite,* and beans, with cornmeal tortillas.

Two rancho scenes drawn by William Rich Hutton in the late 1840s. The first is of the landscape after the slaughter of the cattle; the second portrays ranch hands, many of whom were Indians, preparing tallow. Reproduced by permission of The Huntington Library, San Marino, California.

There was another tortilla which the old women made of corn. It was coarse, and the last that was made, and they called it *niscayote.* They added butter, and to sweeten it sugar, *panocha,* or honey was used. The only difference between the Lenten season and the rest of the year was that in Lent no meat was eaten except by the individual who had permission from the Church because of sickness or other exemption.

Those who had plates, who were few in number, ate on them. Those who did not have them used clay bowls which had the same shape as the ordinary plates. Knives, forks, and spoons such as those used today on the table were possessed by only a few people. With the poorer class, which was the greater part of the population, the general thing was to use forks and spoons of horn. Those who did not have even this made a spoon for every mouthful by loading the meat or beans or whatever they had on a piece of tortilla, and all went together to the stomach. They used their knives for all work.

The food was generally eaten in the kitchen beside the fire. Those who had the conveniences, of course, with tables, ate as is done today, with tablecloths and so on. But the number of these was very limited.

The mode of living was the same in town as in the country. The government exacted compliance with the precepts of the Church from all. All, excepting the sick or crippled, had to attend Mass every Sunday and on other days at the call of the Church. If it was found that anyone failed continuously in this duty without satisfactory reason, the authorities were ordered to hunt him out and reprimand him.

At Eastertime, all without exception had to confess and receive the Holy Sacrament and take part in the catechism; and the Father gave each one a paper saying that he had complied with the precepts of the Church in that year. Nevertheless, when I reached the age for confession, this requisite was not in use, or at least not enforced. We confessed and did penance and took part in the catechism because our parents obliged us to comply with the orders of the Church, but the Government did not mix in these things. I am speaking of the years 1826 or 1827 and on.

There was a very poor old man named Sotelo. When he went, without hat or shoes, and covered only with a blanket, to where the Father was to be examined in the Christian doctrine so that they would give him the paper to present for confession, the Father, as a joke, asked him two or three questions, although the old man could hardly see or speak:

"Tell me, Señor Sotelo, why did our Lord choose death on the Cross?"

"Because my soul needed it."

"Why did God make man?"

"For the women."

This was the doctrine of old Sotelo. After a short dialog of this sort, the Father gave him the paper, and the old man went contented to his confession....

When I was eight or ten years old, that is, from 1821 to 1823, there were great numbers of wild and very troublesome horses. They would come to the very outskirts of the town and eat the pasturage, leaving the gentled horses without food and even often coaxing them away. The Government finally decided, in agreement with the *pueblo,* to have a general killing of these wild horses.

I remember seeing three corrals for this purpose here in Los Angeles. Two were constructed by the town and one by my father. Corrals were also built for this purpose by other persons in the vicinity of the town. Cowboys, on horseback, drove whole herds of wild and tame animals into these enclosures and closed the great gates. There were some small gates through which only one horse could pass at a time. Two or three lancers were stationed at each of these gates to spear the wild horses as they emerged, this being done after the ranchers had indicated the animals they were claiming. The slaughter of wild horses continued until none but the animals that had

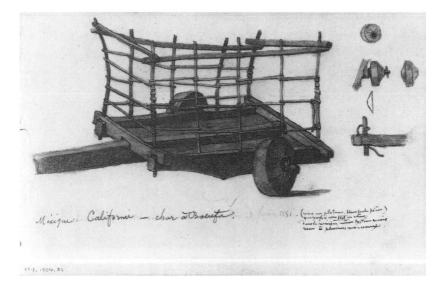

Drawing of a carreta, the basic rancho wagon, by Fritz Wikersheim. Courtesy of The Bancroft Library, University of California, Berkeley.

been claimed were left in the corrals. Many thousands of horses were slaughtered in these times. I saw a corral constructed for this purpose on the *Rancho de los Nietos*.

To make the corral, posts called *estantes* were driven into the ground and the spaces between them were filled with smaller poles tied together with leather thongs. The corrals were round, and in size were as much as a hundred *varas* from one side to the center. A *vara* was less than a yard.

The hides stripped from these horses were staked out to dry, the stretching being done to prevent their shrinking. With no more treatment than this, they were sold or put to other uses as seemed desirable.

The hauling of hides and tallow to San Pedro, which was the only hauling that I saw myself, was in *carretas,* or carts, each of which could carry fifty hides. The *carretas* were made as follows: the two wheels were joined by an axle, which was merely a pole some three *varas* long and six by four inches in thickness, with a hub called a *limón* [lemon] at each end, smoothed and pierced as necessary for the pins or clamps. Midway between the two *limones,* or hubs, was another pole of the same form, smoothed and pierced for receiving pins like those of the *limones.* This pole would have a length of seven *varas* or shorter, and of proportionate thickness, a little stronger than the axle. To this long shaft the yoked oxen were harnessed.

The wheels of the *carreta* were of wood—alder, poplar, oak, or live oak—and round, with openings in the center for the axle. The wheel was bare, that is, it did not have an iron rim. In fact, no iron entered into the making of a *carreta*.

Herbs and Remedies Used by the Indians and Californios

ANDREW GARRIGA

The following selection was written by Fr. Andrew Garriga, a Spaniard who worked in California in the late nineteenth and early twentieth centuries. Garriga worked in King City and Gonzales and also ministered at Mission San Antonio, near King City. There he came across a collection (he does not say in exactly what form it was) compiled by Fr. Doroteo Ambris, who worked at San Antonio from 1846 to 1883. Garriga wrote, "When I administered, as a priest, among the Indians and old Californians, I noticed some wonderful cures effected by these people without the help of a physician, but simply by the derivation or application of herbs or other substances easy to obtain....I thought it would be a pity if, when these people died, their secrets would pass away with them." So, using Ambris's compilation as a base, he collected and organized a number of these treatments. His work affords a singular perspective on the manner in which daily life was lived in Mexican California.

FROM A COMPILATION OF HERBS AND REMEDIES USED BY THE INDIANS AND SPANISH CALIFORNIANS, BY ANDREW GARRIGA

Blindness: They say that the juice of *Jamatai* (soaproot) put on it with a small feather will dissolve them (cataracts).

   Colds: Drink tea of *Palo Santo (lignum vitae)* and *Miel de Abejas* (bees' honey), or tea of mountain pine leaves, or tea of *Yerba de la Hiedra* (poison oak), or tea of blossoms of *Sauco* (elderberry tree), or of the root of wild *Peonia* (peony), or of *Marrubio* (white horehound), or of *Borraja* (borage), or drink powders of the root of wild *Peonia* with some water.

An Indian village, or ranchería, along the Feather River in the late 1840s. Drawn by Fritz Wiker-sheim. Courtesy of The Bancroft Library, University of California, Berkeley.

Earache: Put in the ear oil of Laurel (bay tree).

Deafness: Crush eggs of ants and mix with the juice of raw *Cebolla* (onion) and pour into the ear.

Eyes: Apply a poultice of *Yerba del Ojo.* Steam the leaves a little so as to make them softer, and keep the poultice on the sore eye during the night. Or wash them, from time to time, with balm of *Romero* (rosemary), or with the tea of *Rosa de Castilla* (rose of Castile), or with tea of *Yerba de la Golond-rina* (swallow seed).

Hemorrhage: Drink tea of *Culantrillo* (maidenhair) and eat *Arroz* (rice), cooked plain, with plenty of salt, or do either of the two, or take a spoonful of the juice of apples every five minutes, till relieved. If it repeats, do it again. If it comes from a wound:

1. Put *Hollin* (soot from chimney) with white of eggs;
2. Or catch frogs, roast in a well-covered vessel and, when dry, reduce them to powder and put it on the wound;
3. Or fill the wound with clean cobwebs dipped in wheat flour.

Insanity: When insanity is not from a hopeless cause, this may be tried. It has brought several back to their senses. Anyway, it can do no harm. A poultice of Laurel (bay tree) leaves, some nutmeg, cinnamon, and olive oil cooked together and put on the head. It starts an abundant perspiration. Change poultice when it begins to get cold. Soon the patient will come to, as if he awoke from a sleep.

Rheumatism: Inflammatory. It swells the joints. Drink the pure juice of a lemon every morning half an hour before breakfast, or drink tea of *Yarcas* (tarweed), or take powders of sulfur, niter, *Mostaza* (mustard), *Rubardo* (rhubarb), one ounce each, and of gum of *Guaicaca* (guaicum), one-half ounce. Mix powders well. Take two teaspoons of it with some water the first night and then only one teaspoon every other night. This prescription is very old and famous. It has cured many hard cases. Do not mind the trouble the first dose will give you....

Sciatica: This is rheumatism of the nerves. It does not swell the joints.

> 1. Make tea of the leaves of Eucalyptus (gum tree).* Drink some of it and put a plaster of the leaves (steamed) on the pain every night.
> 2. Change of climate and giving the mind a rest may relieve or even cure it permanently. The same is good for all neuralgias.

Teeth: For numb or too-sensitive teeth: boil *Romero* (rosemary) in vinegar and wash your mouth with it, or boil roots of *Lanten* (plantain) instead of *Romero* in the same way.

For toothache: Chew green *Yerba de la Muela,* or make tea of it and wash your mouth to and fro with it, and spit it out.

---

* The reference to the non-native Eucalyptus tree indicates that these remedies continued to develop after Alta California became part of the United States.

1840s
Life and Customs in Mexican California

Antonio Coronel

Antonio Coronel was born in Mexico City in 1817. In 1834, he came to Alta California with his parents, three sisters, and a brother as members of the Híjar-Padrés colony. The family settled in the Los Angeles area, where the father, Ignacio, was a schoolteacher and storekeeper. Antonio was granted a *rancho* in 1846. He became prominent in the city of Los Angeles, where he lived until his death in 1894. Like those of José del Carmen Lugo, his reminiscences reveal the details of daily life in Mexican California.

From *Tales of Mexican California* by Antonio Coronel

When the Híjar-Padrés colony arrived in California, the total population loosely called white (*gente de razón*) was no more than five thousand, including the garrisons. The education of the inhabitants consisted generally of Catholic doctrine introduced by the Fathers. The same Fathers taught one or two Californians to write, after a fashion. In the *presidios* there were a few Californians with a little more primary education: reading and writing, the rudiments of which formed the principal, or essential branch of instruction. Even this small advance was due to the military officers resident in the *presidios,* who had been educated elsewhere or learned from contact with the old Spanish officers and the merchants and others who came on ships. To this nucleus add the arrival of Mexican families, well-educated and soon scattered throughout the country.

In the interior settlements there were very few people who could be said to write and figure. Even after the arrival of intelligent and educated people, education remained at a low level. The women learned even less, because they had been convinced that book-learning was bad for girls; they

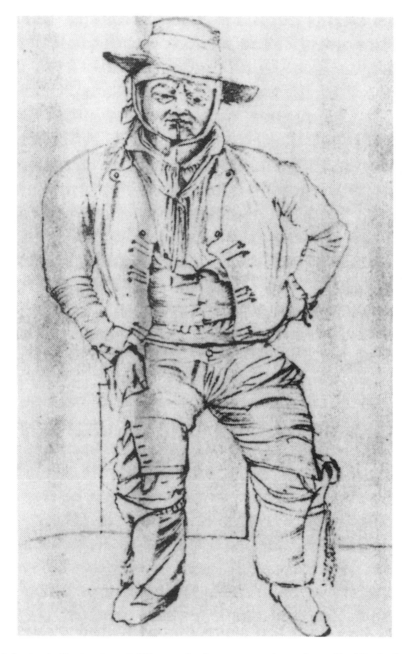

A drawing by Russian visitor I. G. Voznesenskii depicting a rancho *worker outfitted for the demanding labor his occupation required. Mexican California was a tough, harsh frontier land, far removed from the prevalent but inaccurate vision of early California as a blissful and pastoral Eden. Courtesy of Richard A. Pierce, Kingston, Ontario, Canada.*

could barely read, let alone write. But in spite of their lack of education, the ladies were highly moral, diligent, and clean, dedicated to their household duties; some even carried out duties that properly belonged to men. These women were charitable and hospitable; they did not care to sell food but shared among families, one supplying what another might lack.

A traveler could go up to any house in California, confident he could stay however many days he liked and pay nothing for roof, bed, food, and even horses to continue his journey. But the mothers took great care of their daughters, and the traveler often met only the men of the family.

The men busied themselves almost exclusively with livestock, which meant they only worked at certain times, such as the roundup and branding or slaughtering time. The hides and tallow were their income as well as all the coinage there was at that time. The Californians were not much given to farming, because they could buy grain at the missions. A few grew crops for their families only—but as the missions declined, agriculture of necessity became more widespread.

The men who were already full-grown in that epoch kept the character of their Spanish ancestors. They were upright and honorable men, imperious, and their word without documents or witnesses was good for any amount of money. This character also declined rapidly as what was termed "Enlightenment" arose. The most important family value was respect for the head of family—to the point where the parents still governed married sons and daughters, who had to submit humbly to punishment still.

Daughters had very little choice of husbands. The parents arranged marriages for young people before they even met each other. Young married couples lived with one or the other set of parents, just as if they were still minors. They helped with the work, and the parents provided for all. Just what relations were is impossible to calculate. The inhabitants of California were all related to each other, by law and by custom.

Religious education was observed in all homes. Before dawn each morning, a hymn of praise was sung in chorus; at noon, prayers; at about six P.M. and before going to bed, a Rosary and another hymn. I saw this on several occasions at balls or dances when the clock struck eight: the father of the family stopped the music and said the Rosary with all the guests, after which the party continued. I saw the same thing sometimes at roundups, when the old men stopped work to pray at the accustomed hours, joined by all present.

When young people met their godparents anywhere, they were obliged to take off their hats and ask a blessing. The godparents' obligation was to substitute for the parents if they should die, if necessary provide for the godchild's keep and education, and give good advice. The *compadrazgo* was a relationship between the parents and godparents of the child, ties recognized by the Church but not by civil law. At every baptism the priest explained the obligations entailed by the relationship. When two men were united in a friendship superior to the common run, they called each other *valedor*—this term was often used among the ranchers as a term of appreciation and trust.

Women's work was harder, longer, and more important than men's. They were in charge of the kitchen. They made all their clothes, which was a laborious task because the petticoats were edged with lace or embroidered with cutwork in the most exquisite fashion. They were also fond of fine bed linens, and the sheets and pillowcases had to be lace-edged or embroidered too. Since clothing was expensive, they turned and altered used clothing until it was almost new. Most of them ironed the clothes with their hands, patting and stretching the fabric until it was perfectly smooth. They also sewed exquisite clothes for their husbands, fathers, and brothers: broadcloth jackets with worked buttonholes, embroidery on some of them, braid and trapunto [decorative quilting] on others. Vests were generally made of silk or wool, embroidered in colors; the short breeches also. The sleeves on riding jackets, made of wool or corduroy, were trimmed with velvet, corduroy or fringe. The women also had to comb the menfolks' hair every day and tie it up. Many women also baked bread, made candles and ordinary soap, and some I knew brought in the harvest and threshed the grain.

With regard to the clothing I described above, I was referring to families who enjoyed a good economic position. Poor people wore the same kinds of clothes, but made of cheaper material. The clothes worn by well-off ladies of 1834 and 1835 were a short, narrow tunic of silk or organdy, a high, tight bodice trimmed with silk ribbons or flowers according to the caprice of the lady, and red flannel (or another color) underneath according to taste. A shawl, similar to the Spanish *mantilla,* was also worn, and low cloth slippers.

The hair was pulled back smoothly and braided, tied with ribbon and a small ornament or silk flower very prettily. The final touch was a silk handkerchief at the neck, the ends crossed and tied in front. Some women

Antonio Coronel reenacting a traditional dance with Pichona Abadie Harmer. Photograph by Charles Lummis, 1887. Courtesy of the Southwest Museum Braun Research Library, Los Angeles, California.

used a *camorra,* which was a black silk handkerchief tied gracefully around the head.

We have already mentioned that men's work was exclusively on the ranches. Some grew crops, but there was no market except what they might sell to the *presidios.*

Men's clothing consisted of knee breeches slit six inches on the outer side and adorned with ribbon or braid and four to six silver buttons (or other metal, depending on the individual's relative prosperity); the fly front had another such button, almost the size of a *peso.* A long vest of wool, silk, velvet, or corduroy (according to economic circumstances), variously adorned, was worn under a longer jacket of the same material and adorned in the same style.

High-heeled boots were made of a whole tanned deerskin, dyed black or red and tooled or embroidered with silk according to the preference of the individual. The leather had a lace or drawstring to put the foot into; then it was rolled down to a little below the knee, covering the calf and half the instep, and tied with the lace. To go with the boot, shoes were made of what was called *berruchi,* four to six pieces of red and black calfskin or suede with an embroidered vamp. The sole was a single thickness of flexible calfskin to grip the stirrup securely. The toe had a point, turned upward, to keep the *tapaderos* of the stirrups from rubbing the shoe.

The hat was broad-brimmed with a round crown, stoutly made of wool. It was kept on with a chin strap two inches wide, formed into a big rosette under the chin. Almost all the men covered their heads with a black bandanna tied like an Andalusian peasant.

The saddle had a big, rough, wooden tree, strong enough to stand hard use. Underneath, it was padded with calfskin; cowhide thongs secured it to the horsehair cinch. A square of tooled calfskin went over the saddle, and over that a larger hide, more finely carved, embroidered with silk or even silver or gold, nearly covered the horse on both sides. These were called the *corazas*. There was also a matching crupper and saddlebags to carry necessities.

The most important item for any Californian was the lariat. This was made of four or six rawhide strips one-half inch wide, plaited and worked until the lariat was perfectly flexible. When it was not needed, it was tied to the back of the saddle with a special strap; when in use, it hung on the pommel.

The knife was also of first importance. It was carried in a sheath on the outside of the right boot, fastened to the bootlace. Every man had a sword—though the civilians had not much use for it—carried on the left of the saddle under the leg. The *serape* was also indispensable, and much more useful. When not worn, it was rolled and tied behind the saddle with the lariat. In the hazards of ranch work, if it happened a man had to spend the night out, the saddle served for a pillow, the *corazas* and saddlebags for a bed, the *serape* for a blanket.

This same Californian, if he had to go on a campaign to fight Indians, or for military service, added a long, padded leather coat of seven layers, which covered him from neck to knee. This *cuera,* as it was called, provided protection from arrows. A small oval shield, concave on the inside, presenting the convex side to the enemy, could be slipped on the left arm. The usual weapon was an old flintlock shotgun, perhaps a lance, or a pair of pistols. This last was very unusual, and only the leaders carried pistols, but every man had a good Spanish blade from Toledo.

Officers wore the same dress, distinguished only by their insignia of rank. All these customs eventually changed, particularly after the arrival of the colonial families from Mexico. The Californians took up the long pants buttoned from hip to ankle on both sides, low boots, short jacket, and the low-crowned, wide-brimmed, white felt hat and Mexican saddle.

The ladies exchanged their fitted dresses for voluminous ones, took out their braids and piled their hair up elaborately, held with small combs instead of the large one they had used up until then. Women of modest means, and usually the older women of any economic level, wore petticoats of suitable material (instead of the tunic) from the waist down. The blouse had sleeves below the elbow, and the neck and chest were covered with a black silk or cotton kerchief folded diagonally and tied in back; the front was pinned to the waist of the petticoat.

The small-town women continued using the shawl, of linen or cotton, and homemade shoes called *berruchis* because they were pointed like the men's, only smaller, with a point at the heel too. All women usually wore stockings, leaving no part of themselves uncovered but face and hands—any more display was considered immodest.

1842
Rehearsal for Invasion

Thomas ap Catesby Jones and Antonio María Osio

Thomas ap Catesby Jones was commander of the Pacific fleet of the
United States Navy in 1841. He arrived at Callao, Peru, in May 1842, and
by September he was troubled by the moves of the British fleet in the
Pacific. He also picked up rumors that the United States and Mexico were
close to war. Fearing that the British would try to wrest control of California, Jones decided to forestall that possibility by hurrying there himself
and occupying it. He arrived at Monterey on October 19 and was able to
occupy the port on the next day. He soon discovered that there was, in
fact, no war between the United States and Mexico. With great ceremony,
he returned the port to the Mexican authorities, Governor Alvarado and
military Commandant Mariano Silva.

The first of the following selections is the letter Jones wrote to Navy
Secretary A. P. Upshur on October 24, 1842. Jones makes it clear that he
had decided it was better to act in the face of uncertainty than do nothing;
he had decided to occupy the port even though the English captain of a
Mexican ship he met outside of Monterey told him there was no war. No
one fired on him when he entered the harbor, and two Mexican officers
came out to his ship and told him there were no hostilities between the
two countries. Finally, the most prominent American resident of Monterey, Thomas O. Larkin, told him that the most recently arrived newspapers from Mexico made no mention of war. Jones rationalizes in a somewhat convoluted fashion that Mexico was the aggressor for having
declared "conditional war" on the United States.

The second selection is Jones's proclamation to the citizens of Monterey. He insists, against all appearances, that he actually has come to
offer liberty and protection to the people. The third selection is an account of this episode by Antonio María Osio, a Mexican resident of

Monterey at the time. Osio had just completed a five-year stint as chief customs administrator.

From a Letter by Thomas ap Catesby Jones

The Honorable A. P. Upshur
Secretary of the Navy
Washington, D.C.
Sir,

My letter of September 13, No. 2 q (confidential) apprised you of my sudden departure from Callao and the reasons for that movement.

On the same day, the *Dale* parted company, bound to Panama under the annexed order marked "No. 1." From September 13 to October 19, nothing worthy of note transpired, not having seen a single strange sail north of the Equator.

At daylight on the morning of October 19 (the *Cyane* in company) we were close in with Point Pinos, the southern point of this bay. At meridian of the same day, under English colors, I boarded a Mexican bark a few hours from Monterey, the master of which was a foreigner engaged in the coasting trade under the Mexican flag but was utterly ignorant, or professed to be so, of any difficulties between the United States and Mexico. He believed that the latest accounts from the United States were up to January 1, 1842, and from the City of Mexico, the first of May.

At 2:45 p.m. I anchored (under our own proper flag) the two ships as close to what is called the castle of Monterey—a dilapidated work, mounting eleven guns—as the depth of water would allow, with springs on the cables and everything ready for attack or defense, anxiously expecting a visit from some American or neutral resident from whom I might obtain disinterested information, the better to enable me to understand the true relations between the two countries: but no such person came near me. At length, a boat bearing the Mexican flag, conveying two officers, approached the ship. Trepidation was manifest in their deportment, and such was their reserve that nothing satisfactory or even coherent could be extracted from them, except that they had never heard of any difficulties between Mexico and the United States and knew nothing of war, that there was no late news from Mexico or the United States, etc., etc., etc.

U.S. troops taking Monterey in October 1842. Drawn by William H. Myers. Courtesy of The Bancroft Library, University of California, Berkeley.

From the mate of a ship wearing American colors at anchor near me, whom I had called on board, I learned that the ship, the *Fama* of Boston, was recently from the Sandwich Islands, that her departure from Novahoo (it is a curious fact that the latest news from Mexico is often received at Monterey via the Sandwich Islands) had been delayed a week or two in consequence of late letters from Mazatlán reporting war between Mexico and the United States, that they approached the coast cautiously, believing that there was war, but had heard nothing later since their arrival, that there was also a report on the coast that England was to take possession of Upper California and was to guarantee to Mexico the possession of Old, or Lower California, this in a measure corroborating the impressions under which I had left Lima.

The stir on shore was now general, the guns on the castle were manned, and everything seemed prepared for using them. Horsemen were collecting, and messengers appeared to be passing to and fro in every direction—in short, everything that I could see or hear seemed to strengthen the impressions under which I entered the port, and none more so than that no American citizen came on board, although I heard that there were or ought to have been several of my countrymen in Monterey.

The time for action had now arrived—whilst nothing had occurred to shake my belief in the certainty of hostilities with Mexico, the reiterated rumored cession of California to England was strengthened by what I have already related. Hence, no time was to be lost, or another day might bring Admiral Thomas with a superior force to take possession in the name of his sovereign, or General Micheltorena, the new Governor General of California, might appear to defend this capital—within less than three days' march of which he was then said to be. If I took possession of the country and held it by right of conquest in war and there was war with Mexico, all would be right. Then, if the English should come and claim under a treaty of cession, as such treaties do not give title till possession is had, I should have established a legal claim for my country to the conquered territory and at least have placed her upon strong grounds for forcible retention or amicable negotiations as after circumstances might dictate. If Admiral Thomas should afterwards arrive and attempt to supplant our flag on shore, the marines of the squadron to man the guns on the fort without weakening our ships would insure us the victory, and the responsibility would rest on the English commander. On the other hand, if it should turn out that amicable relations had been restored between the United States and Mexico, that Mexico had not parted with the Californias, and that at the time I demanded and took possession of Monterey there was no war, the responsibility of the act at first might seem to rest on me—certainly not upon our government, who gave no orders upon the subject. But if I am right (and of which there can be but little doubt) in assigning to Mexico that attitude of a nation having declared conditional war, then under all the circumstances of the case, Mexico is the aggressor, and as such is responsible for all evils and consequences resulting from the hostile and menacing position in which she placed herself on the fourth of June last.

But I may be wrong in all my deductions and conclusions; if so, I may forfeit my commission and all that I have acquired in seven and thirty years' devotion to my country's service. Terrible as such a consequence would be to me and to my family, it was not sufficient to deter me from doing what I believed to be my duty when a concatenation of unforeseen and unforeseeable events rendered prompt and energetic action necessary for the honor and interest of my country. Come may what will, I have the proved satisfaction of believing that however severely my judgment may be condemned, no one will question the motives which impelled me to action.

Thus arguing, whether right or wrong, I had no means beyond the limits of my squadron for determining. I decided under all circumstances that it was my duty to take possession of the place in the name of the United States and accordingly sent Captain Armstrong on shore, under a flag of truce, to demand a surrender of California to the forces under my command. Not wishing to be unnecessarily precipitate in negotiating with the Governor, I gave him eighteen hours to consider my proposition, which was submitted in Spanish as well as in English at 4:00 P.M. on October 19. (See paper marked 1b. P. 2.)

The Governor (John B. Alvarado, the same who so wantonly seized the American and English settlers in California and sent them in irons to the city of Mexico in April 1840 as alluded to in your letter of December 4, 1841, to the President) unhesitatingly consented to surrender the Department over which he presided, without asking a single question or ever inquiring why we appeared in hostile array against his country; nevertheless the summons was left with him and the terms of capitulation open for discussion until nine o'clock next morning.

At half-past eleven at night, I was aroused from my cot by the call of two Mexican officers (bearing letter c. No. 3), sent as commissioners to treat for the surrender of Monterey.

The interview lasted over two hours, and as the terms first submitted by me underwent various alterations and had to be made in duplicate, both in Spanish and English, half-past nine o'clock next morning was appointed for signing the articles and eleven for changing the flags.

The Mexican commissioners, however, as if impatient to surrender the country, were on board at half-past seven instead of half-past nine o'clock and signed the articles before duplicates could be made, and at eleven o'clock the Town and Department of Monterey was surrendered to the arms of the United States, according to the terms expressed in paper (d. No. 4), and for particulars of what subsequently happened I beg leave to refer you to the accompanying papers marked and numbered e. No 5, f. No 6, H. No 8, I No. 9, K no. 10, l, No 11.

(It is here I prefer for you to state [in your report] that at the close of the nocturnal interview, after the terms of capitulation had all been arranged, Mr. Larkin, an American merchant long residing at Monterey who accompanied the Mexican commissioners as their interpreter but had not before been on board, inquired which side had declared the war. When he was informed that the declaration was conditional and on the part of Mexico, he

Manuel Micheltorena, the last Mexican-appointed governor of Alta California. Courtesy of the California History Room, California State Library, Sacramento, California.

said that there were very late-dated press from Mexico on shore which made no mention of any difficulties whatever between the two countries. I requested him to send me all the information he could obtain on shore, public or private, that was later than June 4. Next morning, he, Mr. Larkin, came off at an early hour, without bringing letter or paper of any kind—still affirming, however, that there were late Mexican papers on shore but that he had not been able to obtain them. This circumstance, so far from rendering a change of purpose, was well calculated to increase suspicion and to render prompt action more necessary than ever, especially when taken in connection with what I had before learned, viz. that General Micheltorena, a fast friend of General Santa Anna, had recently arrived from Mexico with six hundred troops, accompanied by additional officers, for the purpose of raising a local regiment, and was then within a few leagues of Monterey on his march to that port, and that a vessel was hourly expected with military stores, cannon, etc., etc. for the defense of Monterey.)

The party [Jones's party] that landed was composed of seamen and marines from both ships, amounting to one hundred and fifty rank and file....Captain James Armstrong of this ship, who acted as commissioner to treat with the Mexican authorities, was also with the party on shore and had a general supervision over all persons and things on shore, and it affords me the highest satisfaction to be able to assure you that everything was conducted in the most orderly manner and that to this day no word of complaint has been uttered against any man of the part debarked.

The afternoon and night of October 20 passed in perfect quietness, and the next day I visited the town and fortifications over which our national flag was now flying. Again I was told that there was very late and pacific news from Mexico in Monterey...in the office of the Mexican commissary, one of the commissioners who had negotiated the articles of capitulation, several bundles of Mexican papers as late as August 4 were found without the envelopes having been broken. The general tone of the articles relating to the United States in those papers was pacific, and the certainty that Mexico had not commenced hostilities against the United States up to August 22 was established by private commercial letters from Mazatlán. This information induced me to suppose that the crisis in our controversy with Mexico had terminated favorably, or at any rate that war had not yet commenced.

I also came to the conclusion that the reported cession of the Californias to England could not be true, from the efforts Mexico is making to strengthen herself in this quarter; the Mexican newspapers likewise contradict the rumors of cession with warmth and even advert to Mr. Monroe's declaration as regards the establishment of new colonies in the American continent by European powers as an insurmountable obstacle to a cession were Mexico even so much disposed to part with those valuable possessions, of which, however, she has not the least idea.

This change in the aspect of international affairs called for prompt action on my part. The motives and only justifiable grounds for demanding a surrender of the territory were thus suddenly removed, or at least rendered so doubtful as to make it my duty to restore things as I had found them, with the least possible delay. I held a short conference with Captain

Armstrong and Commander Stribling, the result of which was the tender of retrocession marked (g. No. 7), which being promptly accepted by the Mexican authorities, was carried into effect at the hour named, with all the honors and ceremony customary or due on such occasions. Subsequently, the usual official visits were reciprocated by the respective representatives and officers of the two Republics, and it is most gratifying to be able to say that notwithstanding what has happened since our arrival here, no incident has occurred to interrupt for a single moment the most friendly intercourse between the inhabitants of the town and the officers of the squadron.

As this affair may possibly be the subject of strict scrutiny and severe criticism, both at home and abroad, I beg leave most respectfully to refer you to the accompanying papers (A and D) upon which I risk my own and, so far as devolves on me, my country's justification.

I have the honor to be,

very respectfully your obedient servant,

Tho. ap. C. Jones
Commander Pacific Squadron

Proclamation of Thomas ap Catesby Jones to the People of the Californias

To the inhabitants of the two Californias:

Although I come in arms, as the representative of a powerful nation upon whom the central government of Mexico has waged war, I come not to spread desolation among California's peaceful inhabitants.

It is against the armed enemies of my country, banded and swayed under the flag of Mexico, that war and its dread consequences will be enforced.

Inhabitants of California! You have only to remain at your homes in pursuit of peaceful vocation to ensure security of life, persons, and property from the consequences of an unjust war into which Mexico has suddenly and rashly plunged you.

Those Stars and Stripes, infallible emblems of civil Liberty—of Liberty of speech, freedom of the press, and above all, the freedom of conscience, with constitutional rights and lawful security, to worship the Great Deity in the way most congenial to each one's sense of duty to his Creator, now float triumphantly before you and henceforth and forever will give protection and security to you, to your children, and to unborn countless thousands.

All the rights and privileges which you now enjoy, together with the privilege of choosing your own magistrates and other officers for the administration of justice among yourselves, will be secured to all who remain peaceably at their homes and offer no resistance to the forces of the United States.

Each of the inhabitants of California, whether natives or foreigners, as may not be disposed to accept the high privilege of citizenship and to live peaceably under the Free Government of the United States will be allowed time to dispose of their property and to remove out of the country without any other restriction, while they remain in it, than the observance of strict neutrality, total abstinence from taking part directly or indirectly in the war against the United States or holding any intercourse whatever with any civil or military officer, agent, or other person employed by the Mexican Government.

All provisions and supplies of every kind furnished by the inhabitants of California for the use of the United States, their ships, and their soldiers will be paid for at fair rates.

No private property will be taken for public use without just compensation.

Thomas ap C. Jones
Commander in Chief of the United States Naval Forces on the
Pacific Station and of the Naval and Military Expedition
for the occupation of Old and New California.
Flag ship United States. Monterey Bay, October 19, 1842

FROM *The History of Alta California*
BY ANTONIO MARÍA OSIO

...A few days later, the frigate *United States* and the sloop *Cyane,* commanded by Commodore Jones, anchored in Monterey. Jones then sent a message to Señor Alvarado informing him that he would take possession of Monterey, since war had been declared between Mexico and the United States. He advised Alvarado not to expose his people to the horrors of war, because he did not have sufficient soldiers to oppose Jones's troops. He also stated that he expected Alvarado to comply with his demands by eleven o'clock the following day. The message was delivered by the Commodore's secretary and Don Juan Armstrong, the commander of the frigate. Señor Alvarado was in shock as he read the note, which was written in Spanish. After a period of silence, his face suddenly became pale and then immediately turned red, as if blood were about to burst from his eyes. In a voice choked with emotion, he told the Commodore's secretary, who was a Spaniard, that if he had only half the number of men in the Commodore's force he would consider their forces equal. Then he would not have needed to try to frighten him with threats. It would bring him pleasure as well as honor to fight him in defense of his country. However, since he could not do this, he would comply.

It was almost sunset when the Commodore's representatives left Señor Alvarado's house. That night Alvarado sent a communiqué posthaste to General Micheltorena informing him of the unexpected arrival of the American warships under the command of Commodore Jones. Alvarado attached a copy of Jones's demand, and the reply he would give the Commodore the following day. It stated that he was compelled to surrender, because his force was not large enough to oppose Jones, and because he and his men wanted to protect his people from bombardment. Jones could accordingly take possession of Monterey at the appointed hour or before. Alvarado also informed Jones that he had sent an urgent communiqué, dated that day, to the Commander General of the Territory to advise him of the situation.

Flying flags of truce, yet with their guns aimed at the town, the ships maintained their positions as they waited for the appointed hour to arrive. At ten o'clock on that ill-fated day, all the small boats were lowered into the water to transport the soldiers, who were commanded by Captain Armstrong. Once ashore, Armstrong headed for the Governor's home. There, the true *Californios,* people who loved their country and were proud of their nationality, were forced to witness a painful ceremony for the very first time. The national flag of the three guarantees was lowered from its native flagpole so that it could be replaced by the stars and stripes. This flag was alleged to be the symbol of liberty, but that was actually a lie. It belonged to an oppressor who displayed arrogance against the weak. As he was inspecting the papers in the government archives, the Commodore found some recent newspapers that completely convinced him that Mexico and the United States were not at war. Therefore, since he had acted wrongly, he promised that he would evacuate the town at four in the afternoon, and as soon as the Mexican flag had been raised, he would honor it by firing his cannons in salute.

Antonio María Osio. Courtesy of the California History Room, California State Library, Sacramento, California.

Retrospective: An Indian in California

Julio César

The political stability that marked Alvarado's governorship began to unravel in the early 1840s. More foreigners moved into the territory, especially into the sparsely settled areas north of Monterey. The newer arrivals were different from previous immigrants. Many from the United States brought with them a cluster of beliefs asserting that the United States was destined, by providence, geography, and cultural and racial superiority, to extend its rule west to the Pacific: Manifest Destiny. The true believers who arrived in California with this vision were much less willing to respect Spanish culture and assimilate into Mexican society than the merchant arrivals of the 1820s and early 1830s had been.

In April 1840, in response to rumors that foreigners were planning a revolt against his government, Alvarado rounded up about a hundred British and American residents and jailed them in Monterey. He soon released the more genteel members of the group, but forty-seven of them, including trappers, distillers, and a set of marginal characters under the loose leadership of Kentucky native Isaac Graham, were expelled and sent to San Blas. There, the British and American consuls intervened, and the Mexican government, already in debt to Britain and unwilling to antagonize either that nation or the United States, ordered the group's release. Some, including Graham, were compensated and allowed to return to Alta California. This increased the sense of some *Californios* that Mexican officials did not have Alta California's best interests at heart.

The presence of so many foreigners also deepened a rift within Alta California's elite. In particular, the relationship between Alvarado and Vallejo cooled dramatically. They quarreled, ostensibly over who had the power to make appointments in the north. The real issue, however, was the governor's fear that Vallejo was more interested in creating a semifeudal fiefdom for himself in the north and in currying favor with the new arrivals there than in contributing to the common defense of the territory. Alvarado and Vallejo both sent emissaries to Mexico City to plead their cases. When the envoys arrived, they discovered that Manuel Micheltorena, an army officer, had been appointed governor of Alta California in place of Alvarado.

Micheltorena arrived in California in 1842. On his march north, he received Thomas ap Catesby Jones in Los Angeles, where the American officer apologized for his occupation of Monterey. The new governor took up residence in Monterey in 1843. The fragmented *Californios* quickly became unified in opposition to this outsider. They professed to be appalled at the behavior of the Mexican troops Micheltorena had brought with him, but they were more upset at the preliminary steps the governor took to arrest the process of secularization. He stated, for instance, that any mission lands that had not been distributed to private parties should be restored to the control of the Church. By 1844, the territory was in open revolt against the governor, and he was driven out in February 1845.

As they had done in the 1830s, the *Californios* decided to split the political and military commands. Pío Pico became the political leader of Alta California and José Castro assumed the position of military chief. The two men quickly became estranged. Castro argued that the territory needed to strengthen its military defenses against further U.S. hostilities. Pico countered that the most effective defense of Alta California would be to commit residents to its future by making them landowners. He quickly began to distribute and sell off the remaining mission lands, focusing more on speed than on technical formalities, with the goal of secularizing the missions so completely that no future Micheltorena could ever undo the process. Accordingly, many of Pico's 1845 and 1846 grants rested on flimsy legal foundations.

Pico and Castro were never able to agree on how to govern Alta California jointly. By the beginning of 1846, the post-Micheltorena politics of the territory replicated the post-Victoria politics of the early 1830s. Alta California effectively had two governors, with Pico dominant in the south and Castro holding sway in the north. But this time, neither Mexico nor Baja California would be able to send an official to unify the factions, for events far away were undermining the very existence of Mexican Alta California.

In Washington, D.C., in 1845, President John Tyler signed a bill annexing Texas to the United States. Mexico did not accept the legitimacy of this action. It also disputed the claim of the United States and Texas that the southern and western boundaries of Texas extended to the Río Grande. Mexico correctly insisted that Texas's boundary had always been

A rough shelter in the vicinity of Arroyo de los Alamitos, *near San José, as sketched by Fritz Wikersheim. Structures like these provided temporary shelter for ranch hands like César. Courtesy of The Bancroft Library, University of California, Berkeley.*

at the Nueces River, one hundred and fifty miles to the north. In 1846, President Polk ordered General Zachary Taylor to occupy the disputed land between the two rivers. As Polk expected, Mexican troops fired on Taylor's force. This allowed Polk to declare to Congress that American blood had been shed on American soil, and Congress responded by enthusiastically declaring war on Mexico in May 1846.

In California, John C. Frémont, in command of what was alleged to be a surveying expedition, had already stirred things up. In March 1846, he camped at Gavilán Peak outside Monterey, and Castro ordered him out of the territory. Frémont, in a calculated insult, raised the American flag before departing. He headed toward Oregon but soon returned south and set up his headquarters about forty miles north of Sutter's Fort. On June 12, he moved his camp further south, about twenty miles closer to Sutter's Fort. Two days later, a group of thirty-three armed foreigners from the Sacramento Valley went to Sonoma and arrested Vallejo in the name of the Republic of California, an entity which existed only in their minds. They soon stitched together a flag, which featured a star and a bear and thus gave their movement the name—Bear Flag—by which it would be known. The *Californio* ranchers of the area soon organized a resistance against the rebels, and one *Californio* was killed in a skirmish at Olompali (near present-day Novato). A few days after that, Kit Carson, scouting for Frémont, captured and executed three *Californios*. On July 7, Commodore

John Sloat took Monterey, and Alta California learned that the United States had declared war on Mexico. The Bear Flaggers were then formally integrated into Frémont's battalion.

When Robert Stockton, Sloat's successor, learned that Castro had gone south in an attempt to join forces with Pico, he and Frémont headed out in pursuit. Frémont traveled by land, bypassed Los Angeles, and went to San Diego, which he captured in late July. Stockton arrived at the port of San Pedro on August 6. With these two forces closing in on them, Pico and Castro decided to flee, Castro to Sonora and Pico to Baja California. Stockton and Frémont then placed U.S. Marine officer Archibald Gillespie in charge of Los Angeles, and both returned north. Stockton sent a ship, the *Cyane,* to Baja California and Mazatlán under Samuel du Pont. Du Pont entered La Paz, where Baja California Governor Francisco Palacios Miranda pledged not to take any action against the invasion of Baja California.

But the *Californios* were not so easily defeated. Under the leadership of José María Flores, an officer who had come to Alta California with Micheltorena, they regrouped and drove Gillespie from Los Angeles by the end of September. Soon they controlled all of Alta California south of San Luis Obispo. In response, Frémont marched south with a force of about four hundred. At Natividad, near San Juan Bautista, the *Californios* inflicted heavier losses on his men than they suffered themselves. Meanwhile, Stockton sailed south with about seven hundred men and retook San Diego. From the east, General Stephen Watts Kearney headed for Los Angeles from New Mexico. As he approached San Diego, the *Californios* defeated him at San Pasqual, a short distance north and inland, on December 6. However, on January 8, Stockton's troops defeated the *Californios* at the San Gabriel River, just north of Los Angeles. Flores turned the command over to Andrés Pico, who surrendered to Frémont at Cahuenga (now North Hollywood) on January 12, 1847. By the terms of the capitulation, the *Californios* agreed to cease hostilities and return to their homes. In return, Frémont agreed that their lives and property would be protected.

In Baja California, the *diputación* refused to countenance Governor Miranda's acceptance of the North American invasion and named Mauricio Castro, one of its members, as civil governor in February 1847. In the spring, another U.S. ship, the *Portsmouth,* forced San José and La Paz to formally surrender, but resistance was building in the countryside. The central government appointed Manuel Pineda as military commander. He arrived in Mulegé in September and began to organize the town. When the U.S. ship *Dale* appeared at the beginning of October and attempted to take the city, the invaders were beaten back. Assisted by militia from a number of the southern towns, notably Comondú, Pineda organized an attack on La Paz. But the arrival of two U.S. vessels in December forced him to break it off. An attack on San José also had to be suspended when two U.S. ships arrived with reinforcements. The Baja California forces withdrew to San Antonio, about sixty miles south of La Paz, and continued to harass U.S. troops effectively in the countryside for the remainder of the conflict. The U.S. conquest was not complete until Pineda, Castro, and over one hundred soldiers were captured in a series of engagements around San Antonio, Todos Santos, and Bahía Magdalena in March and April 1848, before word that a peace treaty had been signed reached Baja California.

The Treaty of Guadalupe Hidalgo was negotiated for the United States by State Department official Nicholas Trist. During an armistice in August and September 1847, Trist presented Mexican peace commissioners with a draft in which the United States would receive both Californias, in addition to New Mexico. However, Trist's private instructions from President Polk and Secretary of State James Buchanan were that the United States's rock-bottom demands were Alta California, New Mexico, and the Río Grande border of Texas. In a meeting with the Mexican negotiators on September 2, Trist dropped the U.S. demand for Baja California. The successful Baja California defense of Mulegé, the attacks on San José and La Paz, and the continuing resistance in the countryside all helped to keep Baja California off of the negotiating table during the final bargaining sessions. It remained part of Mexico, while Alta California went to the United States.

Julio César was a witness to these events. A Luiseño, he had joined the community around the secularized Mission San Luis Rey when Fr. Francisco González de Ibarra was the priest at the church and Pío Pico was the administrator of the mission property. César's description of life at the former mission clearly indicates how secularization in Alta California failed to benefit the indigenous population, for whom it was supposedly designed. Like many other native Californians, César worked desperately to find a place in the new cash economy.

César's account also illustrates that the tensions between settlers and Indians in southern Alta California and northern Baja California which we have already seen continued during the North American invasion of the Californias. He narrates how eleven *Californios* were killed by Indians shortly after the battle of San Pasqual. This episode was most likely in retaliation for the earlier killing of a group of Indians by some *Californios.* César insists that the Indians involved were Cahuillas, but they were more likely Luiseños. To avenge this killing, José María Flores sent José del Carmen Lugo after the Indians. Lugo and his men killed thirty-eight Luiseños and Cupeños at the Luiseño *ranchería* of Aguanga, northeast of San Diego. These tensions continued after the Americans took control of the region. In 1851, Cupeño chief Antonio Garra (called Juan Garras by César) organized a revolt against the newcomers in which several Americans were killed. Garra was captured by the Cahuilla chief Juan Antonio (called Antonio Berras by César) and handed over to the authorities in San Diego, where he was executed. César himself eventually became a laborer near San Juan Bautista. By 1860, there were slightly over thirty thousand Indians in Alta California—their population had declined ninety percent in one hundred years.

FROM THE REMINISCENCES OF JULIO CÉSAR

Julio César, a full-blooded Indian born at San Luis Rey, around the year 1824—Fr. Ventura was the priest there, according to information I was given. I was about fourteen years old when I went to serve at the mission, and at that time the minister was Fr. Francisco. I do not remember his last name. Among the Indians he was called *"Teguedeumia,"* an Indian word that meant that the Father was very well known and admired by the Indians. And, in fact, he was a very loving and good priest.

When I first entered the mission to serve, they had me sing in the choir at the sung Masses. Don Pío Pico was the administrator of the mission. Very soon after I entered he left, so I never served Señor Pico. Don José Antonio Estudillo then became the administrator, followed by Don José Joaquín Ortega, who was followed by Don Juan María Marrón.

When I began to serve, there still was a large Indian population and the mission was very rich. At that time it had the following *ranchos:* San Mateo—*ganado mayor.* Las Flores—*ganado mayor.* There was a type of small Indian town here with a chapel where the priest said Mass for the Indians every eight days. Santa Margarita—it was a large cultivated area with immense plantings of wheat, corn, and other grains. There also was *ganado mayor.* Pala—a large cultivated area like Santa Margarita which also had a corner plot of land for planting beans and corn. There was a large Indian population at this *rancho.* They had their own chapel and the priest would come to officiate there every eight days. Temécula—cultivated lands of wheat, beans, corn, etc. There also was *ganado mayor.* It also had a large Indian population and its own chapel. The priest would come once a month. San Jacinto—*ganado mayor.* San Marcos—*ganado menor.* Pamuza—*ganado menor.* Pauma—*ganado menor.* Potrero—this is the present-day Indian *pueblo.* That is where the non-Christian Indians lived. Even though the *rancho* belonged to the mission, it was not used. Agua Hedionda–sheep ranch. Buenavista–sheep ranch.

When Don Pío Pico left his position as administrator of San Luis Rey, he bought the Santa Margarita *rancho,* including the cattle that belonged to the mission. I think he gave five hundred head of cattle in exchange for the *rancho.* After he bought Santa Margarita, he took two more *ranchos,* which were San Mateo and Las Flores.

When Don José Antonio Estudillo stopped being administrator he took a *rancho*–San Jacinto, livestock and all. No one ever found out if it really belonged to the Indians.

Don José Joaquín Ortega, during his administration, took possession of nearly everything that belonged to the mission, but he did not take any of its land. It was said that Señor Ortega left the mission stripped bare, taking everything, including the dishes and cups. I was not at the mission when Señor Marrón took over as administrator, but I learned that he found hardly anything left in the house, and there was nothing at all in the storehouses.

When Señor Ortega was administrator I already was a good-sized boy and was working in the fields. Since I was the boy who helped him with his stirrups, I went everywhere with him. However, when there was a sung Mass, I had to sing. For my services I received no other pay than my food and clothing. At the mission there was an Indian teacher named Domingo, and he taught me music.

The system that the priests had followed was continued by Señor Pico during his administration. There was a nunnery [dormitory] for single girls. A matron named Bernardina was in charge of it. There were separate quarters for unmarried men, and I was there during Pico's administration.

The same way of life continued under Estudillo and Ortega. During the administration of Marrón, the Indians were already living outside the mission.

When I was a boy, the way the Indians were treated was not good at all. They didn't pay us anything. They only gave us food, a loincloth, and a blanket which they replaced each year. They did, however, give us plenty of whippings for any wrongdoing, however slight. We were at the mercy of the administrator, who ordered that we be whipped as many times and whenever he felt like it. Pío Pico, as well as those who followed him, were despots. Señor Pico required us to carry our hat in our hand as long as we were within his range of vision, even if we were at a distance from him.

In answer to the question you asked me about whether we were taught to read and write—we were only taught to pray and sing Mass from memory. They did not teach me to read church music. There were singers and musicians, but everything was done from memory. I never saw a sheet of music placed in front of anyone.

I recall hearing it said that there was a school at Alisal where Indian children were taught to read and write. Two Indian children from each mission would be taken there. However, this was before I was born. It was no longer done during my time.

When Fr. Peyri left California, he took two boys from San Luis Rey to Rome. One of them was named Diego. He returned to California, and I saw him at the *pueblo* of San José, where he died. The other, whose name I do not remember, eventually reached the point of singing the Mass. I heard it said that after he was ordained he went to Mexico and died there.*

During the time of the missions, neophytes were prohibited from riding horseback. Only the *alcaldes, caporales,* and *vaqueros* were allowed to do so. [Interviewer: He is not sure if this is true or not.]

At the time of Fr. Francisco's sudden death, I was in San Diego, working at the old building where they stored hides. I worked at loading hides on one of Don José Antonio Aguirre's ships. Señor Estudillo sent a drove of perhaps more than one hundred mules to the Mexican mainland on that very same ship. Many sheep that I had brought from San Luis Rey were loaded on that ship as well.

When I returned to that mission, Fr. Francisco already had been buried and Fr. José María Zalvidea was the minister. He already had spent some time with Fr. Francisco, having come here from San Juan Capistrano.

When Señor Marrón took charge of the mission, almost all of the goods had already disappeared. Indians no longer served at the mission, even though some Indians remained there. Later, in the time of the Americans, the goods that were left at the mission were divided up among the Indians

---

* César is referring to Pablo Tac and Agapito Amamix. Both of them died in Rome while they were studying for the priesthood.

at Pala. I did not get anything, because in 1849 I had gone to the placer gold mines in the north and I never returned to San Luis Rey.

I knew Fr. Zalvidea very well and I served him as a singer. He was a very good man, but he was already very sick. He had mental disorders. He battled continuously with the devil, whom he accused of threatening to conquer him. He gave himself many beatings using *silicios* [pieces of flint]. He drove nails into his feet. In short, he tortured himself in many of the cruelest possible ways.

Fr. Zalvidea died in 1846 at San Luis. Fr. Oliva and other people came to take him back to San Juan Capistrano. Among them was Doña Apolinaria Lorenzana, *la beata*.* He [Fr. Zalvidea] did not want to be moved from San Luis. Nevertheless, they made preparations to take him back on a certain morning, but during the night he died. Nobody, not even Benito, the page and sacristan, knew when the poor priest gave up his soul to the Creator. At that time I was not at San Luis but at Santa María.

In 1846, I was in the *pueblo* of Los Angeles when Commander General Don José Castro arrived with Governor Pico and their respective troops. There had been much talk before this of quarrels and disagreements between the two of them, and that they were going to fight to see who would govern. It turned out, however, that the Americans took Monterey and San Francisco. The Governor and General Castro then met at the Santa Margarita *rancho* in San Luis Obispo and made peace. They promised each other that they would work together like good friends to defend the country from the invaders, but it did not result in what is called "heavenly music." For when they found out in Los Angeles that the Americans were closing in on them from San Pedro and San Diego and that they could no longer find a way to defend the country, Señor Castro headed off for Sonora with some companions and Governor Pico headed south to the border of Baja California.

When the American forces entered Los Angeles under the command of Commodore Stockton, they found only women, children, and Indians. The men who belonged with the Governor or the army had scattered. The forces entered in sections—one by way of the *rancho,* or rather the orchard

---

* Apolinaria Lorenzana was one of a group of twenty orphans and foundlings who were sent to Alta California from Mexico in 1800. She lived at the *presidios* of Santa Bárbara and San Diego and then at Mission San Diego, where she served as nurse and housekeeper. Frequently asked to stand as godmother at baptisms, she was called *la beata,* the devout one. She also received two land grants, which she lost after the U.S. invasion. She died in poverty.

of Don Eulogio Celis, another across the mesa, and the third from above or the *pueblito*. They brought three excellent bands of musicians with them.

The Commodore and the main body of his troops departed very quickly to San Pedro, leaving behind a small force or squad under the command of Captain Gillespie and other officers. They hired me to carry water for the troop that was stationed in the middle of the *pueblo*.

A few days later, there was an uprising of the *Californios* led by Servilo Varela and his brother Hilario. The revolution gained momentum, and Captain Don José María Flores was the leader. The insurgents laid siege to the American squad. Although they were prepared to defend themselves from the barricade they had set up on the hill, after a few days had passed and seeing that no aid was arriving from any direction, Commander Gillespie accepted the conditions of surrender imposed upon him by Flores. The Americans were to march to San Pedro and board ship. Gillespie and his men left with beating drums and flag unfurled and headed for San Pedro, where, according to what I heard, they set sail only to reappear later in Los Angeles.

Los Angeles remained in the possession of the *Californios,* who continued to prepare their defense, because they expected that the Americans would return with forces to regain control of the plaza.

I learned of the defeats suffered by the Americans at Los Cuervos,* which is near the Domínguez *rancho* on the road to San Pedro, and another at San Pasqual, but since I was not an eyewitness, I cannot give an account of them.

In January 1847, the American forces returned, under the command of Commodore Stockton and General Kearney. They engaged in battle on January 8 and 9 at the *Paso de Bartolo* and at the mesa and battered down the *Californios,* who then scattered. Stockton and his troops triumphantly entered Los Angeles. The few *Californios* there were wandering about aimlessly because they did not know what they should do, since there was no one there to give them orders. They finally came together under orders from Battalion Commander Andrés Pico, and they surrendered to Colonel Frémont in Cahuenga. After that time I saw Señor Frémont a number of times in Los Angeles. His troops stayed at San Fernando. He entered into negotiations with Don Andrés Pico.

---

* The *Californio* forces expelled Gillespie from Los Angeles on September 30, 1846. On October 6, Captain William Mervine arrived at San Pedro on the *Savannah*. He decided to attempt to retake the *pueblo*. On October 8, his force of about three hundred men was turned back by the *Californios* at Los Cuervos and he had to withdraw.

After the Mormons came, that is, the Mormon battalion* which entered by way of San Bernardino, they hired me to tame young mares, because they had purchased a large number of wild horses.

I am going to tell about something sad that happened to me during the war against the Americans. First, two citizens from San Diego were traveling through Los Angeles on the way to their *pueblo*. As they were passing through San Luis Rey, they were captured and shot by the *Californios* who were camped at that place, because it was believed that they were spying for the gringos.

When the Indians from San Luis saw this, all of them abandoned the mission. Then some *Californio* named Mariano Domínguez decided to force the Indians who had fled to the Potrero [the Indian *pueblo*] to come back down to the mission. He wanted to use force to make them come back, but by now the Indians had stopped obeying orders, unlike during the old days. Sergeant Francisco Basualdo went with Domínguez. When they arrived at the Potrero (I was there with the rest of the Indians), the Indians grabbed them and tied them up in a room. Later they learned that there were a number of *Californios* at Pauma and it was decided that they should be taken prisoner, which was done. I did not go with the others.

Santiago Osuna, José López, José María Alvarado, Manuel Serrano, Ramón Aguilar, Santos Alipaz (who had a little boy with him), Juan de la Cruz (from Baja California), Eustaquio Ruiz, and three others were captured by the Indians. The total number was thirteen, including Domínguez and Basualdo. One of them was a Cahuilla Indian.

They brought them first to the Potrero, where they stayed one day. From there they took them to Agua Caliente and the Cahuillas took possession of the prisoners. Their chief was named Antonio Berras.

The chief of the Indians at Mission San Luis Rey was Gerónimo Padre. These mission Indians did not want them to harm the prisoners. They had sent those people there for greater security, so as to have them as hostages, because they did not know if the California authorities would insist on forcing those from the mission to go down to there.

Antonio Berras and his Cahuillas, who were instigated by Juan Garras (Cahuilla), Segundo Mandon, and by a white man named Bill Marshall, shot all the prisoners except for the one Indian.

---

* A group of about five hundred Mormons was recruited into the Army in Iowa in the summer of 1846. They reached Los Angeles in January 1847. After the war, they established a settlement at San Bernardino.

The *Californios* concocted a plan with the Cahuillas from San Bernardino to see if they could capture the mission Indians, because it was believed that these Indians had been the ones who killed those prisoners. The Cahuillas tricked the *Californios* by keeping silent the fact that they themselves were the assassins. They attacked the mission Indians at the placed called Aguanga, and they killed thirty-three of them—all young people. In order to accomplish this, the Cahuillas had allied themselves with those from the mission. When the *Californios* were ready, they went and attacked the mission Indians. They encountered no resistance, because they already had been disarmed by the Cahuillas.

If it had not been for Don Manuelito's able assistance, all of the mission Indians would have died. He put up a good defense after seeing them attacked. That is why he is now the chief of the Indians from the Potrero. From what I have been told, he is a rich man.

When the placer gold mines were discovered, Don José Raymundo Alanis of Los Angeles hired me, and I went to Los Mclones. We were there nine months and took out a lot of gold. Altogether there were fourteen of us men. My pay was two and a half *reales* a day. The other workers earned the same. The gold was all embedded in rocks because it was a mine. When we would leave work, the guard would search everything we were carrying to make sure that no one was taking away the smallest bit of gold for himself.

At the end of the nine months I decided to work on *ranchos* and in *pueblos*, at any kind of job that came my way. I was in Baja California once, about six years ago, at the *Real de San Rafael,* working and traveling most of the time during the seven months I was employed by that boss. We went there to mine for gold, but nothing was done, for lack of water.

Now I find myself as poor as always, in this place called Tres Pinos. I am never lacking food or drink, because I am always willing to work. The people are very fond of me and they help me by giving me work so I can earn a few *reales.*

I was married in Los Angeles. I have a son, and here in Tres Pinos a grandson and two granddaughters.

Tres Pinos (San Benito County)
May 25, 1878
Julio César
His mark

Appendix A: Chronology

1479	The Treaty of Alcácovas, between Portugal and Spain, recognizes Spanish sovereignty over the Canary Islands; a Spanish war of conquest against the indigenous Guanches begins in 1483 and continues until 1496
1492	Final defeat of the Moors and successful conclusion to the Spanish *reconquista* First voyage of Columbus across the Atlantic
1510	Publication of *The Labors of the Very Brave Knight Espandián* by Garci Rodríguez de Montalvo; "California" appears for the first time in Europe, as a mythical island "on the right-hand side of the Indies"
1514	Composition of the *Requerimiento*
1521	Conquest of Tenochtitlán by Cortés
1522	First Spanish outpost on the Pacific coast of Mexico, at Zacatula
1531	Founding of Guadalajara, which will become the financial center of the expansion of New Spain into the north and west
1533	First landing in California, by Fortún Jiménez
1535	First Spanish colony in California established by Cortés; it lasts a year
1539	Journey of Francisco de Ulloa to the California coast
1540	Sea journey of Hernando de Alarcón to the mouth of the Colorado River
1540–1542	Overland exploration journey of Francisco Vásquez de Coronado
1542	Voyage of Juan Rodríguez Cabrillo and Bartolomé Ferrer up the California coast
1552	Publication in Spain of *A Brief Account of the Devastation of the Indies* by Bartolomé de las Casas
1564–1571	Spanish conquest of the Philippine Islands and establishment of Manila gives Spain a location and harbor as a hub for its trade with Asia
1565	First permanent Spanish settlement on the North American mainland founded at San Agustín, Florida
1579	Francis Drake in the Pacific Ocean
1587	Pedro de Unamuno reconnoiters the Alta California coast on his return voyage from Manila
1588	Defeat of the Armada by English vessels signals beginning of a long and gradual decline in Spain's power
1595	Sebastián Rodríguez Cermeño explores the Alta California coast on his return from Manila
1602–1603	Voyage of Sebastián Vizcaíno up the California coast
1607	First permanent British establishment, Jamestown, on the eastern North American coast in the area between French Canada and Spanish Florida
1610	First permanent Spanish settlement in the present-day U.S. Southwest founded at Santa Fe

1615	Nicolás de Cardona unsuccessfully attempts to establish an outpost in Baja California
1632	Francisco de Ortega unsuccessfully attempts to establish an outpost in Baja California
1683	Settlement in Baja California by Admiral Isidro de Atondo y Antillón; the outpost lasts only two years
1697	First permanent Spanish settlement in the Californias at Loreto: founding of the Royal Presidio of Loreto and of Mission Nuestra Señora de Loreto Conchó
	Indigenous population of Baja California exceeds 50,000
1699	Founding of Mission San Francisco Javier Viggé Biaundó
1700	Death of Carlos II, the last Hapsburg ruler of Spain, and accession of Felipe V, the first Bourbon ruler of Spain; under Bourbon rule, French and Enlightenment influence increases in Spain
1705	Founding of Mission San Juan Bautista de Ligüí and Mission Santa Rosalía de Mulegé
1708	Founding of Mission San José de Comondú
1719	Founding of Mission La Purísima Concepción de Cadegomó
1720	Founding of Mission Nuestra Señora de Guadalupe de Huasinapí and Mission Nuestra Señora del Pilar de la Paz Airapí
1721	Founding of Mission Nuestra Señora de los Dolores Apaté
1724	Founding of Mission Santiago el Apóstol Aiñiní
1725	Founding of Mission Nuestro Señor San Ignacio de Kadakaamán
1728	Danish explorer Vitus Bering, sailing for Russia, discovers the strait separating Siberia in Asia from Alaska in North America
1730	Founding of Mission San José del Cabo Añuití
	Indigenous population of Baja California is approximately 30,000; population of Spaniards and others, approximately 200
1732	Chartering of the colony of Georgia expands the British mainland colonies south to the border of Florida
1733	Founding of Mission Todos Santos
1734	Pericú revolt in southern Baja California results in the destruction of four missions—La Paz, Santiago, Todos Santos, and San José—and the deaths of two priests, Lorenzo Carranco and Nicolás Tamaral
1737	*Presidio* established at San José del Cabo
	Founding of Mission San Luis Gonzaga Chiriyaqui
1740	Indigenous population of Baja California is approximately 20,000; Spaniards and others, approximately 330
1741	Russian expedition guided by Bering reaches North America
1744	Approximately 4,500 indigenous people live at the Baja California missions
1751	Founding of Mission Santa Gertrudis de Cadacamán
1759	Accession of Carlos III to the Spanish throne
1760	Indigenous population of Baja California is approximately 19,000, approximately 6,000 of them live at the missions
1762	Founding of Mission San Francisco de Borja Adac

1763	Treaty of Paris ends the Seven Years' War; France loses its mainland North American possessions and Spanish and English colonies now border each other at the Mississippi River
1765	José de Gálvez appointed visitor-general of New Spain
1767	Founding of Mission Santa María Cabujakaamung
	Approximately 7,000 indigenous people live at the Baja California missions. Expulsion of the Jesuits from Spain and its possessions, including Baja California
	Gaspar de Portolá appointed first governor of the Californias
1768	Franciscans from the College of San Fernando, led by Fr. Junípero Serra, arrive in Baja California
	Meeting presided over by Gálvez at San Blas decides on the colonization of Alta California
1769	Indigenous population of Alta California exceeds 300,000
	Combined land and sea expedition from Baja California to San Diego
	Founding of Mission San Fernando de Velicatá
	Founding of presidio at San Diego and Mission San Diego de Alcalá
	Land journey from San Diego north to San Francisco Bay, led by Portolá, fails to recognize Monterey Bay
	First attack on Mission San Diego by Kumeyaay
1770	New land and sea expedition recognizes Monterey; founding of presidio at Monterey and Mission San Carlos Borromeo
1771	Founding of Mission San Antonio de Padua
	Mission San Carlos moved from Monterey to Carmel
	Founding of Mission San Gabriel Arcángel
1772	Founding of Mission San Luis Obispo de Tolosa
	Franciscan and Dominican agreement to divide the California missions results in the first boundary between Baja and Alta California
1773	Approximately 440 indigenous people live at the Alta California missions. Junípero Serra's trip to Mexico City results in the removal of Pedro Fages from his post as commander of Alta California
1774	Founding of Mission El Rosario
	Approximately 4,300 indigenous people live at Baja California missions
	First overland expedition from Sonora to Alta California, led by Juan Bautista de Anza and guided by Baja California Indian Sebastián Taraval, demonstrates that the journey is possible with careful planning
1775	Founding of Mission San Juan Capistrano and Mission Santo Domingo
	Kumeyaay attack on San Diego results in the destruction of the mission and the death of Fr. Luis Jayme
1775–1776	Second overland expedition from Sonora to Alta California led by Anza brings over 200 men, women, and children to Alta California
1776	Founding of the presidio of San Francisco and Mission San Francisco de Asís
1777	Founding of Mission Santa Clara de Asís
	Founding of the pueblo of San José
	The capital of the Californias is moved from Loreto to Monterey
1780	Founding of Mission San Vicente Ferrer

1781	Quechán rebellion in the Colorado River area closes the land route between Sonora and Alta California
	Founding of the *pueblo* of Los Angeles
1782	Approximately 3,000 indigenous people live at Baja California missions; approximately 3,600 live at Alta California missions
	Founding of Mission San Buenaventura
	Founding of the *presidio* of Santa Barbara
1783	Treaty of Paris recognizes the independence of the United States of America; the western boundary of the new nation borders Spanish possessions along the Mississippi River
1784	Death of Junípero Serra
	First permanent, year-round Russian settlement in Alaska founded on Kodiak Island
	Publication of Captain James Cook's *A Voyage to the Pacific Ocean* increases European interest in the northern Pacific
1785	Fermín Francisco de Lasuén becomes president of the Alta California missions
1786	Founding of Mission Santa Bárbara and Mission San Miguel de la Frontera
1790	Approximately 3,000 indigenous people live at Baja California missions; total indigenous population of Baja California is approximately 7,500; *mestizos,* Spaniards and others, approximately 1,000
	Approximately 7,700 indigenous people live at Alta California missions; approximately 1,000 *mestizos,* Spaniards live in Alta California
1791	Founding of Mission Santa Cruz, Mission Nuestra Señora de la Soledad, and Mission Santo Tomás
	Visit of Alejandro Malaspina to Monterey
1794	Founding of Mission San Pedro Martír
1797	Founding of Villa de Branciforte
	Founding of Mission San José, Mission San Juan Bautista, Mission San Miguel Arcángel, Mission San Fernando Rey de España, and Mission Santa Catarina
1798	Founding of Mission San Luis Rey de Francia
1799	Founding of New Archangel (Sitka) by the Russians. The outpost was destroyed by the Tlingits in 1802, but was rebuilt and became the capital of Russian America
1800	Approximately 3,100 indigenous people live at Baja California missions; total indigenous population of Baja California is approximately 5,000; *mestizos,* Spaniards, and others, approximately 1,400
	Approximately 13,600 indigenous people live at Alta California missions; approximately 1,800 *mestizos,* Spaniards, and others live in Alta California. Spain cedes Louisiana Territory to France
1803	France sells Louisiana Territory to the United States
1804	Founding of Mission Santa Ynés

1806	Approximately 2,300 indigenous people live at the Baja California missions; approximately 2,000 *mestizos,* Spaniards, and others live in Baja California
1810	Founding of Mission El Descanso
	Approximately 19,000 indigenous peoples live at the Alta California missions; approximately 2,100 *mestizos,* Spaniards, and others live in Alta California
	United States annexes the territory of West Florida, also claimed by Spain, which becomes the state of Louisiana in 1812
	Fr. Miguel Hidalgo begins Mexican armed movement for independence
1812	The Russian American Company founds Fort Ross
1813	Liberal Spanish parliament calls for the secularization of the missions in America
1817	Founding of Mission San Rafael Arcángel
1818	Privateer Hipólito Bouchard destroys the *presidio* of Monterey in his attack on the Alta California coast
1819	Spain cedes East Florida to the United States and renounces its claim to West Florida in terms of Adams-Onis treaty
1820	Indigenous population of Baja California is approximately 3,000; population of *mestizos,* Spaniards, and others is also approximately 3,000
	Approximately 21,000 indigenous peoples live at the Alta California missions; approximately 3,200 *mestizos,* Spaniards, and others live in Alta California
1821	Juan O'Donojú, the last Spanish viceroy of New Spain, signs the Treaty of Córdoba, which grants independence to Mexico
1822	Agustín de Iturbide becomes emperor of Mexico
1823	Founding of Mission San Francisco Solano
	Iturbide abdicates his throne
1824	Chumash Revolt
	Constitution of the United Mexican States declares Mexico a republic. Guadalupe Victoria elected president
1825	Approximately 20,000 indigenous people live at the Alta California missions
1828	Vicente Guerrero becomes president of Mexico
1829	Revolt of Estanislao
1830	Approximately 600 indigenous people live at the Baja California missions
	Approximately 18,300 indigenous people live at the Alta California missions; approximately 4,200 Mexicans and others live in Alta California. Anastasio Bustamante becomes president of Mexico
1831	Divided government in Baja California, with members of the *diputación* rotating terms as governor
	Battle of Cahuenga in December pits forces loyal to Alta California governor Manuel Victoria against forces loyal to the territorial *diputación;* Victoria leaves Alta California in January 1832

1832   Divided government in Alta California, with Agustín Zamorano ruling in the north and Pío Pico and José María de Echeandía in the south

     Approximately 16,800 indigenous people live at Alta California missions

1833   Antonio López de Santa Anna elected president of Mexico; he subsequently retires to his estate and leaves vice-president Valentín Gómez Farías in power

     Secularization law passes Mexican congress

     Arrival of José Figueroa ends regionally divided government in Alta California

1834   Founding of Mission Guadalupe del Norte

     Gómez Farías organizes an effort to colonize Alta California by dispatching the Híjar-Padrés expedition

     Secularization begins in Alta California

1836   Texans rebel, defeating Santa Anna at San Jacinto

     Arrival and departure of Governor Mariano Chico; revolt in Alta California against his successor, Nicolás Gutiérrez

     Appointments of Luis Castillo Negrete and José Caballero restore stability to Baja California

1837   Caballero dispatches Andrés Castillero to Alta California; he negotiates an end to factional disputes in Alta California and Juan Bautista Alvarado is eventually accepted as governor

1840   Approximately 8,000 non-Indians live in Alta California, including 1,000 foreigners

     Governor Alvarado arrests and deports a number of Anglo-American foreigners. The Mexican government allows a number of them to return to Alta California

1841   Bidwell-Bartleson party becomes the first wagon train to enter northern Alta California from the United States

1842   Thomas ap Catesby Jones seizes Monterey

1845   United States annexes Texas

     Californios expel Governor Manuel Micheltorena after military maneuvering near Cahuenga

     Divided rule in Alta California, with José Castro ascendant in the north and Pío Pico in the south

1846   United States declares war on Mexico and invades Alta California

1847   Hostilities generally cease in Alta California

     Resistance to the U.S. invasion of Baja California

1848   Treaty of Guadalupe Hidalgo gives the United States approximately one-half of the territory of Mexico, including Alta California

Appendix B: Governors of the Californias

The Californias were governed as one entity from 1769 to 1804. Governors in those years are shown in bold type in the center of the following table, and also in the column for the province (Alta or Baja California) where they were resident. Similarly, José María Echeandía was governor of both Californias from 1825 to 1829, and his years of office are indicated in the same way. Governors during other years are shown in bold type. Officials whose names do not appear in bold type were the senior officers in either Baja or Alta California. Although their titles varied considerably, they functioned as the Californias' lieutenant governors and as governors of the part of the Californias in which they lived.

Baja California	Alta California
Gaspar de Portolá (1767–1769)	
Gaspar de Portolá (1767–1769)	
Juan Gutiérrez de la Cueva (1769)	Gaspar de Portolá (1769–1770)
Antonio López de Toledo (1769–1770)	
Matías de Armona (1769–1770)	
Matías de Armona (1769–1770)	Gaspar de Portolá (1769–1770)
Bernardo Moreno y Castro (1770–1771)	Pedro Fages (1770–1774)
Felipe de Barri (1771–1775)	
Felipe de Barri (1771–1775)	Pedro Fages (1770–1774)
	Fernando de Rivera y Moncada (1774–1775)
Felipe de Neve (1775–1782)	
Felipe de Neve (1775–1776)	Fernando de Rivera y Moncada (1775–1777)
Joaquín Cañete (1776–1777)	
Fernando de Rivera y Moncada (1777–1781)	**Felipe de Neve (1777–1782)**
José María Estrada (1781–1783)	
Pedro Fages (1782–1791)	
José María Estrada (1781–1783)	**Pedro Fages (1782–1791)**
José Joaquín de Arrillaga (1783–1791)	
José Antonio Roméu (1791–1792)	
José Joaquín de Arrillaga (1791–1792)	**José Antonio Roméu (1791–1792)**

José Joaquín de Arrillaga (1792–1794)

José Francisco de Ortega (1792–1794)   **José Joaquín de Arrillaga (1792–1794)**

Diego de Borica (1794–1800)

José Joaquín de Arrillaga (1794–1800)   **Diego de Borica (1794–1800)**

José Joaquín de Arrillaga (1800–1814)

José Joaquín de Arrillaga (1800–1804)   Pedro de Alberni (1800–1802)

José Joaquín de Arrillaga (1802–1804)

Felipe de Goycoechea (1805–1814)   **José Joaquín de Arrillaga (1804–1814)**

Fernando de la Toba (1814–1815)   **José Darío Argüello (1814–1815)**
José Darío Argüello (1815–1821)   **Pablo Vicente de Solá (1815–1821)**
Fernando de la Toba (1822)
José Manuel Ruiz (1822–1825)   **Luis Antonio Argüello (1822–1825)**

José María de Echeandía (1825–1829)

José María Padrés (1825–1826)   **José María de Echeandía (1825–1829)**

Miguel Mesa (1826–1829)

Manuel Victoria (1829–1830)   **José María de Echeandía (1829–1831)**

Mariano Monterde (1830–1831)   **Manuel Victoria (1831)**
Diputación Territorial, by rotation (1831–1833)   **José María de Echeandía, in the south (1831–1833)**

Agustín Zamorano, in the north (1831–1833)
Pío Pico, in the south (1832)

Mariano Monterde (1833–1834)   **José Figueroa (1833–1835)**
Diputación Territorial, by rotation (1834–1835)
Miguel Martínez (1835)   **José Castro (1835–1836)**
Miguel Conseco (1836)   **Nicolás Gutiérrez (1836)**

Mariano Chico (1836)
Nicolás Gutiérrez (1836)
Juan Bautista Alvarado (1836–1842)

Fernando de la Toba (1837)
Luis del Castillo Negrete (1837–1842)
Francisco Padilla (1842–1844)   **Manuel Micheltorena (1842–1845)**
Francisco Palacio Miranda (1844–1846)   **Pío Pico (1845–1846)**

Alabado A Latin hymn which the missionaries taught the Indians as part of morning prayer

alcalde A local magistrate, usually a member of the municipal council; the chief executive officer of a pueblo. He possessed a combination of executive and judicial authority. The term was also used to refer to the chief indigenous official in the mission communities

alférez An ensign; the lowest-ranked military officer, approximately equal to today's rank of second lieutenant

almud A dry measure of weight, the equivalent of about .13 bushels. Also a land measurement, *almud de tierra,* equivalent to about half an acre

amole Soapweed, also called soaproot

armas (defensas) Weapons, defense. Also the leather apron worn by the soldiers and fastened to the pommel of the saddle

arroba A bulk measurement equal to 25.36 pounds

arroyo A creek or stream

atole A cooked mixture of water and ground, dried grains; a staple mission food

audiencia A judicial and legislative council administering royal affairs over a substantial geographic area in the New World. Judicially, it was subordinated to the Council of the Indies. In a legislative role, it acted as an advisory council to the viceroy

ayuntamiento A municipal corporation in charge of administering and governing a town; a town council

baidarka A portable boat made of skins stretched over wood frames, widely used by Alaskan coastal natives and Aleuts

cacique Traditional chief of an Indian town or tribe

Californio Regional name for a non-Indian inhabitant of California. All *gente de razón* reared, or later, born and reared in California were *Californios.* The term was used in Antigua California since 1700 and came into popular use in Alta California by the 1820s, with the growth of the first generation of California-born Mexicans

cañada A gully or ravine

carreta A two-wheeled cart

castillo A fortress or coastal defense battery

caudillo A leader

cayuco A small boat used for fishing

chalupa A narrow canoe or small boat that has a cover and two masts for sails

chaparral A dense thicket of entangled thorny shrubs and dwarf trees. In English, "chaparral" also refers to the ecological community of shrubby plants adapted to dry summers that is common in the Californias

cholo A derogatory term for a *mestizo* or person of mixed European and Indian heritage

comisario The officer in charge of the warehouse

comisionado Noncommissioned soldier (usually a sergeant or corporal) appointed by the commander of the *presidio* to serve as a liaison between the *presidio* and the towns or missions. Duties included supervising the *alcalde* and exercising military and judicial authority. With secularization the *comisionado* also became the temporary supervisor of former missions

compadrazgo A kinship or relationship through one's godparents

compadre Godfather, protector or benefactor, friend

compañero A companion

congregación Compact settlement of indigenous people administered by a missionary

corazas Protective breastplate

Corpus Christi A feast day celebrated in honor of the Eucharist

criollo A person born in the New World of peninsular Spanish ancestry

cuera From the word *cuero,* which means "hide" or "leather." A heavy, knee-length, usually sleeveless jacket made of up to seven layers of buckskin or cowhide and bound at the edges with a strong seam

días de fiesta Feast days or holidays

diputación An elected assembly; a consultative body to the governor of the territory

diseño A sketch of the boundaries of a land grant

encomienda Indians and land granted to a *conquistador* or nobleman with the understanding that he would provide for the welfare and civilization of the Indians and their instruction in Christianity in return for their labor

fanega A dry measure of weight, the equivalent of about 1.6 bushels. Also a land measurement, *fanega de sembradura,* equivalent to 8.8 acres

farallón Steep rocks, cliffs, or headlands

ganado Livestock. *Ganado mayor* refers to cattle and *ganado menor* refers to sheep, goats, or pigs

gente de razón Literally, "people with the capacity to reason"; any non-Indian people

gentile A non-Christian Indian

hacienda As a unit of measurement, it was equivalent to five square leagues, or 21,690 acres. Also, very large estates were generally called *haciendas.* Variable factors defining *haciendas* included capital, labor, land, markets, technology, and social recognition

hijo del país Native son

jacal Hut or crude dwelling

jara Dart or arrow

jefe Leader, head, or superior. Followed by adjectives such as *militar, político, principal,* and *superior*

jeme The distance between the extended thumb and the forefinger

legua A standard Spanish measure of distance (a league), approximately 2.6 miles

matanza A slaughter of herd animals

mayordomo A foreman or supervisor of a mission under the priest, or of a ranch under the owner; majordomo

memoria A requisition

mestizo A person of mixed European and Indian heritage

mezquite Mesquite, a tree commonly found in the plains of the Gulf and Pacific deserts.

neophyte Term used to describe the Christian mission Indians

paisano Fellow countryman

panocha Cakes of crude brown sugar made by boiling down cane pressings; the staple sweet of the frontiersmen and the poor of New Spain

paseo A short trip

Pater Noster The Christian prayer "Our Father," the Lord's Prayer

peso The monetary unit of Spanish America; eight *reales* equaled one *peso*. In the first half of the nineteenth century, a *peso* was roughly equivalent to one U.S. dollar and two Russian rubles

pica A measure of length, equivalent to about thirteen feet

pinole Parched corn, ground and mixed with sugar and water for a drink (also refers to the ground seeds of other plants)

poblador A settler

pozole A thick soup of cornmeal, beans, hominy, marrowbones, and scraps of meat

Propaganda fide Latin for the Propagation of the faith. The name of a Vatican congregation under whose auspices the Franciscan missionary colleges were founded

ramada A simple structure made by setting forked posts in the ground as corners and laying other posts across them as superstructure, roofed with thatch

ranchería An Indian village or settlement. The Spanish usually used it to refer to non-Christian Indians. It is now a common term in English for small communities of Alta California Indians

real A monetary unit: eight *reales* equaled one *peso*

rebozo A shawl or wrap

reducción A mission, or the process of missionization; the state of affairs resulting from the indigenous peoples' being grouped together closely at and around the missions

regidor A member of the *ayuntamiento*

repartimiento A medieval system of dividing land and Indians implemented by the Spanish in the colonization of the Indies, beginning in the early 1500s

Salve Regina A prayer to the Virgin Mary

serape Also spelled "sarape," a narrow blanket worn by men or thrown over the saddle

síndico A public attorney or advocate/representative of a mission

solares Plots of land for houses

span The equivalent of a quarter of a *vara*, about eight inches

suerte Land separated from surrounding lands by bounds or landmarks. Arable land for agriculture

Te Deum Laudamus A traditional Latin hymn of praise to God

temescal A sweat lodge

testimonio Personal reminiscence

tule Any of several grassy or reedlike plants growing in the marshy lowlands of the western United States. The Spanish word derived from Náhuatl *tullin*

valedor A protector or defender

vaquero A cowboy. In Mexican California they were generally indigenous people, frequently from Baja California, who tended the large stock herds under the direction of a *mayordomo*

vara A measure of length, approximately 33 inches

villa A royally chartered settlement with certain rights to self-government

zacate Grass, hay, forage

Suggestions for Further Reading

Part I: Exploration

Blackburn, Thomas C., and Kat Anderson, eds. *Before the Wilderness: Environmental Management by Native Californians*. Menlo Park, Calif.: Ballena Press, 1993.

Bouvier, Virginia M. *Women and the Conquest of California, 1542–1840: Codes of Silence*. Tucson: University of Arizona Press, 2001.

Fernández-Armesto, Felipe. *Columbus*. Oxford and New York: Oxford University Press, 1991.

Fontana, Bernard L. *Entrada: The Legacy of Spain and Mexico in the United States*. Tucson: University of New Mexico Press and Southwest Parks and Monuments Association, 1994.

Gutiérrez, Gustavo. *Las Casas: In Search of the Poor of Jesus Christ*. Translated by Robert R. Barr. Maryknoll, N.Y.: Paulist Press, 1993.

Gutiérrez, Ramón A., and Richard J. Orsi, eds. *Contested Eden: California Before the Gold Rush*. Berkeley: Published for the California Historical Society by the University of California Press, 1997.

Kelsey, Harry. *Juan Rodríguez Cabrillo*. San Marino: Huntington Library, 1986.

Mathes, W. Michael. *Vizcaíno and the Spanish Expansion in the Pacific Ocean, 1580–1630*. San Francisco: California Historical Society, 1968.

Rawls, James. *Indians of California: The Changing Image*. Norman: University of Oklahoma Press, 1984.

Seed, Patricia. *Ceremonies of Possession: Europe's Conquest of the New World, 1492–1640*. Cambridge: Cambridge University Press, 1995.

Thomas, David Hurst, ed. *Columbian Consequences*. Vol. I, *Archaeological and Historical Perspectives on the Spanish Borderlands West*. Washington and London: Smithsonian Institution Press, 1989.

Thomas, Hugh. *Conquest: Montezuma, Cortés, and the Fall of Old Mexico*. New York: Simon and Schuster, 1993.

Weber, David J. *The Spanish Frontier in North America*. New Haven and London: Yale University Press, 1992.

Part II: Colonization

Alonso, Ana María. *Thread of Blood: Colonialism, Revolution, and Gender on Mexico's Northern Frontier*. Tucson: University of Arizona Press, 1995.

Bolton, Herbert Eugene. *Rim of Christendom: A Biography of Eusebio Francisco Kino*. New York: Macmillan Co., 1936.

Crosby, Harry W. *Antigua California: Mission and Colony on the Peninsular Frontier, 1697–1768*. Albuquerque: University of New Mexico Press, 1994.

————. *The Cave Paintings of Baja California*. 1975. Reprint, San Diego: Sunbelt Publications, 1997.

Dunne, S.J., Peter Masten. *Black Robes in Lower California*. Berkeley and Los Angeles: University of California Press, 1952.

Jackson, Robert H. *Indian Population Decline:The Missions of Northwestern New Spain, 1687–1840*. Albuquerque: University of New Mexico Press, 1995.

Jones, Jr., Oakah. *Los Paisanos: Spanish Settlers on the Northern Frontier of New Spain*. Norman: University of Oklahoma Press, 1979.

Martínez, S.J., John J. *Not Counting the Cost: Jesuit Missionaries in Colonial Mexico, A Story of Struggle, Commitment, and Sacrifice*. Chicago: Jesuit Way, 2001.

McCawley, William. *The First Angelinos:The Gabrielino Indians of Los Angeles*. Menlo Park, Calif.: Ballena Press, 1996.

Moorhead, Max L. *The Presidio: Bastion of the Spanish Borderlands*. Norman: University of Oklahoma Press, 1975.

Polzer, S.J., Charles W. *Kino, a Legacy: His Life, His Works, His Missions, His Monuments*. Tucson: Jesuit Fathers of Southern Arizona, 1998.

Polzer, S.J., Charles W., and Thomas Sheridan, eds. *The Presidio and Militia on the Northern Frontier of New Spain: A Documentary History*. Vol. 2, Pt. 1, *The Californias and Sinaloa-Sonora, 1700–1765*. Tucson: The University of Arizona Press, 1997.

Radding Murrieta, Cynthia. *Wandering Peoples: Colonialism, Ethnic Spaces, and Ecological Frontiers in Northwestern Mexico, 1700–1850*. Durham: Duke University Press, 1997.

Williams, Jack S. *Los Presidios: Guardians of California's Mission Frontier* (forthcoming).

Part III: Settlement

Beilharz, Edwin A. *Felipe de Neve: First Governor of California*. San Francisco: California Historical Society, 1971.

Cutter, Donald C. *Malaspina in California*. San Francisco: John Howell, 1960.

Engstrand, Iris H. W. *Spanish Scientists in the New World:The Eighteenth Century Expeditions*. Seattle and London: University of Washington Press, 1981.

Geiger, O.F.M., Maynard. *The Life and Times of Junípero Serra, O.F.M.* 2 vols. Washington, D.C.: Academy of American Franciscan History, 1959.

Guest, O.F.M., Francis F. *Fermín Francisco de Lasuén (1736–1803): A Biography*. Washington, D.C.: Academy of American Franciscan History, 1973.

————. *Hispanic California Revisited*. Edited and with an introduction by Doyce B. Nunis, Jr. Santa Barbara: Santa Barbara Mission Archive Library, 1996.

Jackson, Robert H., and Edward Castillo. *Indians, Franciscans, and Spanish Colonization:The Impact of the Mission System on California Indians*. Albuquerque: University of New Mexico Press, 1995.

Mason, William M. *The Census of 1790: A Demographic History of Colonial California*. Menlo Park, Calif.: Ballena Press, 1998.

Milliken, Randall. *A Time of Little Choice:The Disintegration of Tribal Culture in the San Francisco Bay Area, 1769–1810*. Menlo Park, Calif.: Ballena Press, 1995.

Paddison, Joshua, ed. *A World Transformed: Firsthand Accounts of California Before the Gold Rush*. Berkeley: Heyday Books, 1999.

Phillips, George Harwood. *Indians and Intruders in Central California, 1769–1849*. Norman: University of Oklahoma Press, 1993.

Uhrowczik, Peter. *The Burning of Monterey: The 1818 Attack on California by the Privateer Bouchard*. Los Gatos, Calif.: CYRIL Books, 2001.

Whitehead, Richard S. *Citadel on the Channel: The Royal Presidio of Santa Barbara, Its Founding and Construction, 1782–1798*. Edited with an epilogue by Donald C. Cutter. Spokane: The Santa Barbara Trust for Historical Preservation and The Arthur C. Clark Co., 1996.

Part IV: Mexican California

Haas, Lisbeth. *Conquests and Historical Identities in California, 1769–1936*. Berkeley, Los Angeles, and London: University of California Press, 1995.

Hague, Harlan. *Thomas O. Larkin: A Life of Patriotism and Profit in Old California*. Norman: University of Oklahoma Press, 1990.

Harding, George L. *Don Agustín Zamorano: Statesman, Soldier, Craftsman, and California's First Printer*. Los Angeles: The Zamorano Club, 1934.

Harlow, Neal. *California Conquered: The Annexation of a Mexican Province*. Berkeley: University of California Press, 1989.

Hurtado, Albert. *Indian Survival on the California Frontier*. New Haven: Yale University Press, 1988.

———. *Intimate Frontiers: Sex, Gender, and Culture in Old California*. Albuquerque: University of New Mexico Press, 1999.

Hutchinson, C. Alan. *Frontier Settlement in Mexican California: The Híjar-Padrés Colony and Its Origins, 1769–1835*. New Haven and London: Yale University Press, 1969.

Miller, Robert Ryal. *Juan Alvarado: Governor of California, 1836–1842*. Norman: University of Oklahoma Press, 1998.

Monroy, Douglas. *Thrown Among Strangers: The Making of Mexican Cultures in Frontier California*. Berkeley, Los Angeles, and London: University of California Press, 1990.

Padilla, Genaro M. *My History, Not Yours: The Formation of Mexican American Autobiography*. Madison: University of Wisconsin Press, 1993.

Ríos-Bustamante, Antonio. *Mexican Los Angeles: A Narrative and Pictorial History*. Encino, Calif.: Floricanto Press, 1992.

Rosenus, Alan. *General Vallejo and the Advent of the American*. Berkeley: Heyday Books in conjunction with Urion Press, 1995.

Sánchez, Rosaura. *Telling Identities: The Californio Testimonios*. Minneapolis and London: University of Minnesota Press, 1995.

Weber, David J. *The Mexican Frontier, 1821–1846: The American Southwest Under Mexico*. Albuquerque: University of New Mexico Press, 1982.

PERMISSIONS

Part I: Exploration

The Log of Christopher Columbus. Translated by Robert H. Fuson. Camden, Me.: International Marine Publishing, 1992. 75-77.

Garci Rodríguez de Montalvo. *The Labors of theVery Brave Knight Esplandián.* Translated by William Thomas Little. Binghamton, New York: Center for Medieval and Early Renaissance Studies, 1992. 456-459. Reprinted with the permission of the Center for Medieval and Early Renaissance Studies.

Bartolomé de las Casas. *The Devastation of the Indies: A Brief Account.* Translated by Herma Briffault, introduction by Bill M. Donovan. Baltimore and London: The Johns Hopkins University Press, 1992. 43-46.

Lewis Hanke. "The Requerimiento and Its Interpreters." *Revista de Historia de América* 1 (1938): 26-28. Reprinted with the permission of the *Revista de Historia de América.*

Bernal Díaz del Castillo. *The Conquest of New Spain.* Translated by J. M. Cohen. London: Penguin Books, 1963. 232-235. Reprinted with the permission of Penguin Books, Ltd.

Aztec Poems: *The Broken Spears: The Aztec Account of the Conquest of Mexico.* Edited with an introduction by Miguel León-Portilla. Boston: Beacon Press, 1969. Expanded and updated edition © 1992 by Miguel León-Portilla. 137-138, 146-149. Reprinted with the permission of Beacon Press, Boston.

The Conquistador in California: 1535, The Voyage of Fernando Cortés to Baja California in Chronicles and Documents. Translated and edited by W. Michael Mathes. Baja California Travels Series, 31. Los Angeles: Dawson's Book Shop, 1973. 104. Reprinted with the permission of Dawson's Book Shop.

Rodríguez Cabrillo: translated by Rose Marie Beebe from *Colección de diarios y relaciones para la historia de los viajes y descubrimientos,* 5 vols. Madrid, 1943–1947. 1:32-34.

Vizcaíno: diary translated by Rose Marie Beebe from *Colección de diarios y relaciones para la historia de los viajes y descubrimientos,* 5 vols. Madrid, 1943–1947. 4:62-64. Letter translated by Rose Marie Beebe from *Californiana I: Documentos para la historia de la demarcación comercial de California, 1583–1632.* Edited by W. Michael Mathes. Colección Chimalistac de libros y documentos acerca de la Nueva España, 22. Madrid: Ediciones José Porrúa Turanzas, 1965. 370-372.

Ascención: translated by Rose Marie Beebe from *Colección de documentos inéditos relativos al descubrimiento, conquista, y organización de las antiguas posesiones españolas de América y Oceanía.* Edited by Luis Torres de Mendoza. Madrid, 1867 8:560 570.

Part II: Colonization

Juan María de Salvatierra, S.J. Selected Letters About Lower California. Translated and annotated by Ernest J. Burrus, S.J. Baja California Travels Series, 25. Los Angeles: Dawson's Book Shop, 1971. 104-113. Reprinted with the permission of Dawson's Book Shop.

Piccolo: *Jesuit Relations, Baja California, 1716–1762*. Translated and edited by Ernest J. Burrus, S.J. Baja California Travels Series, 47. Los Angeles: Dawson's Book Shop, 1984. 79-83. Reprinted with the permission of Dawson's Book Shop.

Sigismundo Taraval. *The Indian Uprising in Lower California, 1734–1737*. Translated with introduction and notes by Marguerite Ayer Wilbur. Los Angeles: The Quivira Society, 1931. 82-97.

Balthasar: *Jesuit Relations, Baja California, 1716–1762*. Translated and edited by Ernest J. Burrus, S.J. Baja California Travels Series, 47. Los Angeles: Dawson's Book Shop, 1984. 229-231. Reprinted with the permission of Dawson's Book Shop.

Sistiaga: *Jesuit Relations, Baja California, 1716–1762*. Translated and edited by Ernest J. Burrus, S.J. Baja California Travels Series, 47. Los Angeles: Dawson's Book Shop, 1984. 115-117. Reprinted with the permission of Dawson's Book Shop.

Miguel del Barco. *The Natural History of Baja California*. Translated by Froylan Tiscareño, with introduction by Miguel León-Portilla. Baja California Travels Series, 43. Los Angeles: Dawson's Book Shop, 1980. 43-44, 49-51, 103-105, 121, 156-159, 180-181, 249-250.

Miguel del Barco. *Ethnology and Linguistics of Baja California*. Translated by Froylan Tiscareño, with introduction by Miguel León-Portilla. Baja California Travels Series, 44. Los Angeles: Dawson's Book Shop, 1981. 41-42, 71-72, 83-84. Reprinted with the permission of Dawson's Book Shop.

Gálvez: *The Spanish Occupation of California*. Translated by Douglas S. Watson and Thomas Workman Temple II. San Francisco: Grabhorn Press, 1934. 19-23.

Costansó: *The Spanish Occupation of California*. Translated by Frederick J. Teggart. San Francisco: Grabhorn Press, 1934. 44-47.

Crespí: translated by Rose Marie Beebe from *Francisco Palóu, Noticias de la Nueva California*. Edited by Vicente García Torres. Documentos para la historia de México, cuarta serie. México: 1857. 6:313-323.

Portolá: ranslated by Rose Marie Beebe from *Fernando Boneu Companys, Documentos secretos de la expedición de Portolá a California: juntas de guerra*. Lérida: Instituto de Estudios Ilerdenses de la Excma. Diputación Provincial de Lérida, 1973. 55-64.

Writings of Junípero Serra. Edited by Antonine Tibesar, O.F.M. 4 vols. Washington, D.C.: Academy of American Franciscan History, 1955–1965. 1:167-171. Reprinted with the permission of the Academy of American Franciscan History.

Francisco Palóu. *Palóu's Life of Fray Junípero Serra*. Translated with introduction by Maynard Geiger, O.F.M. Washington, D.C.: Academy of American Franciscan History, 1955. 118-120. Reprinted with the permission of the Academy of American Franciscan History.

Francisco Palóu. *Historical Memoirs of New California*. Edited by Herbert Eugene Bolton. 4 vols. Berkeley: University of California Press, 1926. 1:236-239, 300-302. Reprinted with the permission of the University of California Press.

Part III: Settlement

Letter of Luis Jayme, O.F.M., San Diego, October 17, 1772. Translated and edited by Maynard Geiger, O.F.M. Baja California Travels Series, 22. Published for the San Diego Public Library by Dawson's Book Shop, Los Angeles, 1970. 38-49. Reprinted with the permission of Dawson's Book Shop.

Fages: Maynard Geiger, trans., ed. "A Description of California's Principal Presidio, Monterey, in 1773." *Historical Society of Southern California Quarterly* 69.3 (September 1967):327-336. Reprinted with the permission of the Historical Society of Southern California.

Writings of Junípero Serra. Edited by Antonine Tibesar, O.F.M. 4 vols. Washington, D.C.: Academy of American Franciscan History, 1955–1965. 1:295, 299-307, 311. Reprinted with the permission of the Academy of American Franciscan History.

Santa María: *The First Spanish Entry in San Francisco Bay, 1775.* Edited by John Galvin. San Francisco: John Howell Books, 1971. 37-45, 55-71.

Fuster: *Writings of Junípero Serra.* Edited by Antonine Tibesar, O.F.M. 4 vols. Washington, D.C.: Academy of American Franciscan History, 1955–1965. 2:449-454. Reprinted with the permission of the Academy of American Franciscan History.

Font: *Anza's California Expeditions.* Translated and edited by Herbert Eugene Bolton. 5 vols. Berkeley: University of California Press, 1930. 4:349-369. Reprinted with the permission of the University of California Press.

Francisco Palóu. *Historical Memoirs of New California.* Edited by Herbert Eugene Bolton. 4 vols. Berkeley: University of California Press, 1926. 4:125-126, 133-138. Reprinted with the permission of the University of California Press.

Neve: *Regulations for Governing the Province of the Californias.* Translated by John Everett Johnson. San Francisco: Grabhorn Press, 1929. 41-52.

Writings of Junípero Serra. Edited by Antonine Tibesar, O.F.M. 4 vols. Washington, D.C.: Academy of American Franciscan History, 1955-1965. 3:293-297. Reprinted with the permission of the Academy of American Franciscan History.

Neve: Edwin A. Beilharz. *Felipe de Neve: First Governor of California.* San Francisco: California Historical Society, 1971. 165-166. Reprinted with the permission of the California Historical Society.

Francisco Palóu. *Palóu's Life of Fray Junípero Serra.* Translated with introduction by Maynard Geiger, O.F.M. Washington, D.C.: Academy of American Franciscan History, 1955. 243-248. Reprinted with the permission of the Academy of American Franciscan History.

The Callis letter was translated by Rose Marie Beebe from documents in the Archivo General de la Nación (Mexico City), Provincias Internas 120, expediente 4 (consulted microfilm copy at The Bancroft Library, Berkeley). The Soler letters were translated by Rose Marie Beebe from the Archive of California at The Bancroft Library (CA 3:254-255).

Ronald L. Ives. *José Velásquez: Saga of a Borderland Soldier.* Tucson: Southwestern Mission Research Center, 1984. 181-182, 188-198. Reprinted with the permission of the Southwestern Mission Research Center.

Toypurina: translated by Rose Marie Beebe from documents in the Archivo General de la Nación (Mexico City), Provincias Internas 120, expediente 2 (consulted microfilm copy at The Bancroft Library, Berkeley).

Silberio and Rosa: translated by Marie Duggan and Rose Marie Beebe from documents in the Archivo General de la Nación (Mexico City), Californias 65, expediente 6.

Fernández: translated by Rose Marie Beebe from the California Mission Documents, Santa Barbara Mission Archive-Library, Old Mission, Santa Barbara. The Fernández letters are grouped with document no. 330. Reprinted with the permission of the Santa Barbara Mission Archive Library.

Argüello: Randall Milliken. *A Time of Little Choice: The Disintegration of Tribal Culture in the San Francisco Bay Area, 1769–1810*. Menlo Park, Calif.: Ballena Press, 1995. 299-303. Reprinted with the permission of Ballena Press.

Concepción Horra: translated by Rose Marie Beebe from documents in the Archivo General de la Nación (Mexico City), Provincias Internas 216, expediente 14.

Writings of Fermín Francisco de Lasuén. Translated and edited by Finbar Kenneally, O.F.M. 2 vols. Washington, D.C.: Academy of American Franciscan History, 1965. 2:201-205. Reprinted with the permission of the Academy of American Franciscan History.

Arrillaga and Estudillo: Diane Lambert, Naomi Reinhart, Ludivina Russell, Gregory von Herzen. *A Year in the Life of a Spanish Pueblo: San José de Guadalupe in 1809*, Official Correspondence. Research Manuscript Series on the Cultural and Natural History of Santa Clara, No. 9 Santa Clara: Department of Anthropology and Sociology, Santa Clara University, 1998. 8-9, 18-19, 23-24, 26. Reprinted with the permission of Santa Clara University.

Edward D. Castillo, trans., ed., introduction. "The Assassination of Padre Andrés Quintana by the Indians of Mission Santa Cruz in 1812: The Narrative of Lorenzo Asisara." *California History* 68.3 (Fall 1989), 120-124. Reprinted with the permission of the California Historical Society.

Vassili Petrovitch Tarakanoff. *Statement of My Captivity Among the Californians*. Translated by Ivan Petroff, with notes by Arthur Woodward. Los Angeles: Glen Dawson, 1953. 9-16. Reprinted with the permission of Dawson's Book Shop.

Solá: translated by Peter Uhrowczik from a special edition of the *Gaceta del Gobierno de México,* vol. X, no. 37, March 24, 1819. Reprinted with the permission of Peter Uhrowczik.

Juan Bautista Alvarado. *Vignettes of Early California: Childhood Reminiscences of Juan Bautista Alvarado*. Translated by John H. R. Polt, with introduction and notes by W. Michael Mathes. San Francisco: Book Club of California, 1982. 6-7, 12-13, 17-21, 30. Reprinted with the permission of the Book Club of California.

Part IV: Mexican California

Zakahar Tchitchinoff. *Adventures in California of Zakahar Tchitchinoff, 1818–1828*. Introduction by Arthur Woodward. Los Angeles: Glen Dawson, 1956. 12-21. Reprinted with the permission of Dawson's Book Shop.

Antonio María Osio. *The History of Alta California*. Edited with introduction and annotations by Rose Marie Beebe and Robert M. Senkewicz. Madison: University of Wisconsin Press, 1996. 40-42. Reprinted with the permission of The University of Wisconsin Press.

Rafael González. *A Spanish Soldier in the Royal Presidio of Santa Barbara*. Edited by Richard S. Whitehead and translated by Jarrel C. Jackman. Santa Barbara: Bellerophon Books, 1987. 14-17. Reprinted with the permission of Bellerophon Books.

Minna and Gordon Hewes, eds., trans. "Indian Life and Customs at Mission San Luis Rey: A Record of California Mission Life Written by Pablo Tac, an Indian Neophyte [Rome, ca. 1835]." *The Americas* 9.1 (July, 1952):92-106. Reprinted with the permission of the Academy of American Franciscan History.

Manuel Clemente Rojo. *Historical Notes on Lower California.* Translated and edited by Philip O. Gericke. Baja California Travels Series, 26. Los Angeles: Dawson's Book Shop. 1972. 54-55. Reprinted with the permission of Dawson's Book Shop.

Angustias de la Guerra Ord. *Occurrences in Hispanic California.* Translated and edited by Francis Price and William H. Ellison. Washington, D.C.: Academy of American Franciscan History, 1956. 25. Reprinted with the permission of the Academy of American Franciscan History.

Pío Pico. *Don Pío Pico's Historical Narrative.* Translated by Arthur P. Botello, edited with an introduction by Martin Cole and Henry Welcome. Glendale, Calif.: Arthur H. Clark Co., 1973. 31-34. Reprinted with the permission of The Arthur H. Clark Company, Spokane, Washington.

Virmond: translated by Rose Marie Beebe from a document in the Archivo General de la Nación (Mexico City), Documentos para la historia de México, Segunda Serie, Tomo 4, No. 20.

Argüello: *The Californios versus Jedediah Smith, 1826–1827: A New Cache of Documents.* Edited with an introduction by David J. Weber. Spokane, Wash.: Arthur. H. Clark Co., 1990. 51-55. Reprinted with the permission of The Arthur H. Clark Company, Spokane, Washington.

Alfred Robinson. *Life in California During a Residence of Several Years in that Territory.* New York: Wiley and Putnam, 1846. 27-34.

Sánchez: Sherburne F. Cook. *Expeditions to the Interior of California: Central Valley, 1820–1840.* University of California Publications, Anthropological Records, vol. 20, no. 5. Berkeley: University of California Press, 1962. 174-175. Reprinted with the permission of the University of California Press.

Piña: Sherburne F. Cook. *Expeditions to the Interior of California: Central Valley, 1820–1840.* University of California Publications, Anthropological Records, vol. 20, no. 5. Berkeley: University of California Press, 1962. 178-179. Reprinted with the permission of the University of California Press.

Bandini: translated by Rose Marie Beebe from a document in the Archivo General de la Nación (Mexico City), Documentos para la historia de México, Segunda Serie, Tomo 4, No. 21.

Carrillo: *The Coming of Justice to California: Three Documents.* Edited by John Galvin and translated by Adelaide Smithers. San Francisco: John Howell Books, 1963. 50-52.

Estudillo et al.: Lucy Killea. "The Political History of a Mexican Pueblo." *The Journal of San Diego History* 12.4 (October 1966):37-39. Reprinted with the permission of the San Diego Historical Society.

Anzar and Castro: Zephyrin Engelhardt, O.F.M. *Mission San Juan Bautista: A School of Church Music.* Santa Barbara: Mission Santa Barbara, 1931. 53-56, 61-62. Reprinted with the permission of the Santa Barbara Mission Archive Library.

Victor Eugene August Janssens. *The Life and Adventures in California of Don Agustín Janssens, 1834–1856.* Edited by William H. Ellison and Francis Price and translated by Francis

Price. San Marino, Calif., Huntington Library, 1953. 30-34. Reprinted with the permission of the Henry E. Huntington Library.

George Tays. "Captain Andrés Castillero, Diplomat." *California Historical Society Quarterly* 14.3 (September, 1935):255-258. Reprinted with the permission of the California Historical Society.

Doña Juana Machado Alipaz de Ridington. "Times Gone By in Alta California." Translated and annotated by Raymond S. Brandes, *Historical Society of Southern California Quarterly* 41.3 (September 1959):203-205. Reprinted with the permission of the Historical Society of Southern California.

Pérez: Manuel Clemente Rojo. *Historical Notes on Lower California.* Translated and edited by Philip O. Gericke. Baja California Travels Series, 26. Los Angeles:Dawson's Book Shop. 1972. 109-111. Reprinted with the permission of Dawson's Book Shop.

Espinosa and Gracia: Manuel Clemente Rojo. *Historical Notes on Lower California.* Translated and edited by Philip O. Gericke. Baja California Travels Series, 26. Los Angeles: Dawson's Book Shop. 1972. 41-43. Reprinted with the permission of Dawson's Book Shop.

George Tays. "Mariano Guadalupe Vallejo and Sonoma: A Biography and a History." *California Historical Society Quarterly* 17.1 (March, 1938), 56-58. Reprinted with the permission of the Historical Society of Southern California.

Robert Ryal Miller. *Juan Alvarado, Governor of California, 1836–1842.* Norman: University of Oklahoma Press, 1998. 179-180. Reprinted with the permission of the University of Oklahoma Press.

Donald E. Rowland. *John Rowland and William Workman: Southern California Pioneers of 1841.* Spokane, Wash.: Arthur H. Clark Co.; Los Angeles: Historical Society of Southern California, 1999. 187-188. Reprinted with the permission of the Historical Society of Southern California and The Arthur H. Clark Company.

José del Carmen Lugo. "Life of a Rancher." *Historical Society of Southern California Quarterly* 32.3 (September, 1950):215-219, 231-232. Reprinted with the permission of the Historical Society of Southern California.

Andrew Garriga's Compilation of Herbs and Remedies Used by the Indians and Spanish Californians. Edited by Francis J. Weber. Los Angeles: Archdiocese of Los Angeles, 1978. 17-44. Reprinted with the permission of Monsignor Francis J. Weber.

Antonio Coronel. *Tales of Mexican California.* Edited by Doyce B. Nunis, Jr., and translated by Diane de Avalle-Arce. Santa Barbara: Bellerophon Books, 1994. 78-81. Reprinted with the permission of Bellerophon Books.

Jones: United States National Archives. Naval Records Collection of the Office of Naval Records and Library. Record Group 45. Letters from Officers Commanding Squadrons: 1841–1846, Pacific Squadron: 1841–1846.

Antonio María Osio. *The History of Alta California.* Edited with introduction and annotations by Rose Marie Beebe and Robert M. Senkewicz. Madison: University of Wisconsin Press, 1996. 208-209. Reprinted with the permission of University of Wisconsin Press.

César: translated by Rose Marie Beebe from Julio César's testimonio, "Cosas de indios de California." 1878. MS. C-D 109. Berkeley: The Bancroft Library. Reprinted with the permission of The Bancroft Library.

INDEX

About the Editors

Photograph by Steven Taddei

Rose Marie Beebe is professor of Spanish at Santa Clara University. She is, with Robert Senkewicz, translator, editor, and annotator of *The History of Alta California by Antonio María Osio* (1996), which received the Norman Neuerburg Award from the Historical Society of Southern California. They also jointly edited *Guide to the Manuscripts Concerning Baja California in the Collections of The Bancroft Library* (2002). She served as president of the California Mission Studies Association during 2001–2005.

Robert M. Senkewicz is professor of history at Santa Clara University. He is the author of *Vigilantes in Gold Rush San Francisco* (1985).

Beebe and Senkewicz are co-editors of the *Boletín: The Journal of the California Mission Studies Association*. They are currently working on a translation and annotation of the nineteenth-century California women's testimonios at The Bancroft Library.